Language in Late Capitalis

Routledge Critical Studies in Multilingualism

Language in Late Capitalism
Pride and Profit

**Edited by Alexandre Duchêne
and Monica Heller**

Routledge
Taylor & Francis Group
NEW YORK   LONDON

First published 2012
by Routledge
711 Third Avenue, New York, NY 10017

Simultaneously published in the UK
by Routledge
2 Park Square, Milton Park, Abingdon, Oxon OX14 4RN

*Routledge is an imprint of the Taylor & Francis Group,
an informa business*

Typeset in Sabon by IBT Global.

Library of Congress Cataloging-in-Publication Data
A catalog record has been requested for this book.

ISBN13: 978-0-415-88859-2 (hbk)
ISBN13: 978-0-203-15586-8 (ebk)

Contents

Figures and Tables

FIGURES

TABLES

Acknowledgments

This volume emerged out of a series of conversations we were privileged to have on both sides of the Atlantic. It began as an invited session at the 106th Annual Meeting of the American Anthropological Association in 2007, in Washington, D.C. It continued, with a slightly larger set of participants, at the Sociolinguistics Symposium 17 in 2008 in Amsterdam. Finally, in 2009, with the support of the Swiss National Science Foundation, we were able to hold a workshop at the Institute of Multilingualism in Fribourg. We are grateful for these opportunities, and for the many conversations in and out of the meeting rooms that they inspired.

We would also like to acknowledge the research support of the Swiss National Science Foundation and the Social Sciences and Humanities Research Council of Canada, which led us to ask the questions underlying this volume in the first place.

The actual preparation of the volume could not have been done without the support of Kyoko Motobayashi, who read many of the manuscripts carefully more than once, and who helped shape them in many ways.

Our workplaces, the Institute of Multilingualism (Université/HEP de Fribourg) and the Centre de recherches en éducation franco-ontarienne (University of Toronto), provided excellent conditions for our work on this book, whether helping us manage transatlantic coordination or hosting the visiting partner. We are particularly grateful to our research assistants and administrative staff.

1 Pride and Profit

Changing Discourses of Language, Capital and Nation-State

Monica Heller and Alexandre Duchêne

THE EMERGENCE OF THE ECONOMIC

In the mid-1990s Monica was part of a team of researchers working in a semirural region of central Ontario, Canada's largest province. We were looking at the role of local institutions in the construction of ideas about being and speaking French. Most of what we heard was what you would have expected at that time: an insistence on the importance of government funding of things like day camps, childcare centers or literacy programs for maintaining French as a minority language in English-dominated Ontario. Local militants worked hard to encourage people to participate in such activities, arguing that they should be proud to be francophone, not ashamed of their minority identity.

And then one day we picked up the latest issue of the local French-language newspaper, in which, among the usual lists of birthdays and marriages, news of the region's French-language schools and community associations, and commentary on provincial- or national-level events and their impact on Canada's francophone minority, we found an article on a new community economic development organization. This organization introduced itself to the community as an organization devoted to the "development of innovative goods and services and creation of businesses and jobs that demonstrate the added value of the francophones and bilinguals of [the region], reflecting their considerable impact on the region's vitality."[1] For the first time, we were hearing something new: the discourse of rights, identity, cultural and linguistic preservation, and pride was no longer completely hegemonic. Talk of "added value" and "economic development" became increasingly common.

It is this shift that is at the center of this book. Indeed, we have noticed it popping up in all kinds of sites around the world. Let us give two more examples, as a way of indicating the range of phenomena involved on different continents.

In 2009, Alexandre participated in a meeting in the city of Fribourg, in Switzerland. The meeting was organized by a community association lobbying for greater support for French–German bilingualism in the canton of Fribourg, which, while officially bilingual, is often felt to be dominated by French. The goal of the meeting was to bring together a wide variety of social actors (mainly politicians, academics and educators) to debate a cantonal policy document on regional bilingualism. At one point, the representative of the local Portuguese heritage language school took the floor. While the meeting was meant to focus on French and German, she had come to argue for even greater linguistic diversity.

In Switzerland, throughout most of the postwar period, labor imported from southern Europe was understood to be temporarily residing in the country as "guest workers," and therefore not requiring investment in the development of their linguistic repertoire. Most countries of origin in fact established heritage language programs, which were tolerated by the state as a means to facilitate children's eventual reintegration upon their return "home," and supported by the Swiss left as a matter of children's right as residents of Switzerland to learn their native tongue and to learn about their country of origin, in order to foster healthy identity development and ethnic pride. This discourse was strengthened as "guest workers" attempted to recast themselves as "immigrants."

While this last discursive element was indeed present in this representative's contribution, she also introduced some different terms. First, she criticized the document by insisting on the importance of looking at the question of linguistic diversity not only in terms of French–German bilingualism (or trilingualism with English), but in terms of multilingualism. "The world," she said, "will be multilingual, or it will not be." Second, she started and finished her talk by stating, "multilingualism is an added value," linking it to the importance of Portuguese (and other languages) in the national and global market.

And a last example. In 2009, Monica was travelling in Yunnan, a province of southwestern Chinese province with the highest concentration of ethnolinguistic minority citizens in the country (China officially recognizes fifty-five ethnic minority groups, which are understood to each have distinct languages). While Yunnan's revenue is mainly based on tobacco (and there is a lively commercial sector based on cross-border trade with Myanmar (Burma), Thailand, Laos and Vietnam), tourism has become increasingly important. A major component of this tourism includes paid visits to "ethnic villages," cleaned up or reconstructed "folk" villages whose layout and architecture are presented as typical of a particular minority. Guides, almost always young women, must be officially recognized members of the minority group in question. They wear brightly colored versions of "typical dress" provided by the tourism company and are assigned tourists (usually groups of Han majority men) to take through the village, where other group members sing in the minority language, dance and serve "typical" food and drink. At the end, there is often the opportunity to buy souvenirs.

As it happens, we were atypical tourists, in that we were a lone couple (not a large group) and Western, although Monica's partner has lived in China and speaks fluent Mandarin. Tour guides loved having us as their assignment, since it meant they didn't have to shout into a megaphone, or keep a large group together. Finding out that they didn't have to try out their memorized English script was also a huge relief. So we had time to kill while other guides struggled with their unruly groups, and this gave us the opportunity to interrupt the tour guides' script, and engage in conversation. We often used it to ask about how the guides got their jobs, and what those jobs were like. As Westerners with neocolonial guilt complexes, we feared participating in the commodification of minority identity, as well as its gendering and sexualization. But as one young woman explained, this was her first access to the cash economy, and likely the only way to have access to the cash economy without having to leave home as a migrant worker. It gave her much more control over her life than she had had before as a peasant, enabling her to better support her ill grandmother and to travel occasionally to the nearest large town to shop.

We use these three examples to show that during the 1990s and into the twenty-first century, we are witnessing the widespread emergence of discursive elements that treat language and culture primarily in economic terms. This discourse does not abruptly or entirely interrupt or replace older discourses which treat language as political and cultural, associating it with the formation of the nation-state; rather, the two are intertwined in complex ways. Nonetheless, we will argue here, something new is happening, something that shifts the terms on which social difference is made and on which relations of power are constructed. This book is an attempt to describe what that is, as well as to develop hypotheses as to what explains it, by looking at the relationship between the characteristics of late capitalism and the ideologies and practices of language which help to organize and legitimize them. Finally, we will look at what this shift means for the field of sociolinguistics: for how we understand our goals, our approaches, and our ways of making sense.

In this introduction we will provide an account of this shift. We argue that the dominant discourse and ideology of language as whole, bounded system inextricably tied to identity and territory is central to the legitimization of the nation-state as a particular historical mode of regulation of capital. But capitalism has as one of its fundamental characteristics the continual expansion and serial saturation of markets. Following Giddens (1984), Appadurai (1996) and Harvey (2006), and others, we argue that we find ourselves now at a particular moment in this process that we can call late capitalism, and that stretches the system of national regulation of markets to and possibly beyond its limits. The resulting tensions in the nation-state regime give rise to new discursive tropes in which language plays a particularly central role not only because of its place in regulation and legitimization of political economic spaces but also because of the emergence of the tertiary sector as a defining element of the globalized new economy.

We structure our discussion around the intertwined tropes of "pride" and "profit," the key terms used to justify the importance of linguistic varieties and to convince people to speak them, learn them, support them, or pay to hear them spoken. They also index debates about the nature of language itself, as the idea of language as whole, bounded system cedes ground to the idea of language as a set of circulating, complex communicative resources. Following McElhinny, we take up the notion of "keywords" (Williams 1989 [1983]), as a "site at which the meaning of social experience is negotiated and contested" (McElhinny 2007, 7). Admittedly "pride" and "profit" are not keywords in exactly the way in which Williams used them, insofar as they only partly cover the terrain of terms contested in public discourse concerning language and identity (others include "community," "value," "economic development" and "practice"; see Heller and Bell, and McElhinny, this volume). Nonetheless, looking in that way at "pride" and "profit" as the terms connect to the role of language in late capitalism allows us access to the dynamic, and often contradictory, cultural assemblages of our time.

PRIDE, A PRODUCT OF THE MODERN NATION-STATE

We take as our starting point the position, most forcefully argued by Eric Hobsbawm, that the modern nation-state can be understood as a means of constructing and regulating a market of a size and capacity amenable to industrial capitalism (Hobsbawm 1990). The central idea is that for industrial capitalism to function, the emerging bourgeoisie required access to material resources and to labor in ways both manageable and legitimate, through an articulation of political and economic control. The construction of a national market depended on the reorganization of populations and boundaries, and their inscription into a common process despite obvious internal differences (most notably differences related to positions of power). A central contradiction of the nation-state pits the division of labor against equal opportunity.

Many authors have argued that language plays a central role in the neutralization of this contradiction, in two ways (Bourdieu and Passeron 1977; Higonnet 1980; Outram 1987). First, it has been used as a major means of simultaneously constructing homogeneity and boundaries, bringing some people into citizenship through language learning, and excluding others. These others are both internal (groups which get constructed as "indigenous" and "minority") and external (racialized colonial subjects). Second, it strengthens liberal democracy's ability to mystify and justify social stratification, by setting up linguistic value hierarchies that are in principle democratically accessible. However, these hierarchies are constructed through mechanisms of social selection, legitimized by discourses which locate failure at mastery in the moral fiber or physical characteristics of the excluded, rather than in the desire of the powerful to remain so.

Bauman and Briggs (2003) have pointed out that the white male bourgeoisie developed discursive rationales for the use of the labor of others by constructing those others (women, children, nonwhites, the working class and colonial subjects) as incapable of the rationality on which depended, they were able to claim, the exercise of full rights of citizenship. If you don't speak the language of the nation, and speak it properly, you show that you lack the ability to reason and the strength to prevail that citizenship requires; you therefore can't claim access to political and economic power. If you haven't learned it, it is because you lack the competence to do so, for either moral or physical reasons (underdeveloped brains, weakness, emotionality, inability to concentrate, or stupidity). If you have, you still need to constantly prove yourself against the measures developed by the dominant group, who use the agencies of the state (schools, bureaucracies, language academies, the media) to describe what counts as linguistic competence and the means to identify it.

Securing control over defining what counts as legitimate language thus became an important means for securing access to, and maintaining, positions of power within modern nation-states. Equally important, of course, as both Gramsci and Bourdieu argued forcefully, has been the ability of liberal democracies to saturate everybody's consciousness, that is, to convince the powerful that they deserve their power, and the marginalized that it makes sense to be at the margins (Bourdieu 1982; Gramsci 1971). Inscription in the common cause of the nation-state is a key element of that process, through the mobilization of feelings of pride of membership. Being a proud citizen of a country, or member of a nation, and treating its symbols (flag, language, literature, map) with respect, are essential dimensions of inhabiting nation-state versions of what Bourdieu referred to as "habitus" (Bourdieu 1972). "Pride" calls you into being as a citizen, not as a woman or a member of an ethnicized or racialized minority or a religious group, not as a worker, not as someone who likes to sing or who loves the color yellow. It helps you go to school, vote, enter the military and pay your taxes. It helps you watch your spelling and decide which beer to drink. It also becomes available, of course, as a means to contest centralizing nation-state regimes. Anticolonial movements of resistance (whether mobilized in the context of imperialism or internal colonialism) have generally simply taken up the discourse of national pride to mobilize populations in favor of creating new nation-states, rather than contesting the logic of the nation-state as a political economic model (Duchêne 2008; Heller 2011; McDonald 1989; Schnepel 2004; Stroud 2007; Weidman 2006).

"Pride," then, helps to build the modern nation-state's signature structure of feeling. It orients us to the reproduction of the national market and of the institutions, legitimizing discourses and forms of expression (such as "languages") that sustain it. It helps us focus on the political means of democratically gaining access to power that veil the modes of social selection underlying the reproduction of economic inequality. It allows for the legitimization not only of the production of profit, but also of its unequal distribution. At the same time, it also becomes available for contesting the specific places of groups in a system of relations of power, as well as, occasionally, a means for imagining alternative forms of belonging (like "citizen of the world") that would likely require other modes of social organization.

However, as we now will show, its force also depends on the maintenance of the political economic conditions that constructed it. The logic of expansion of capital has outstripped the ability of nation-states to adequately regulate markets, resources and populations, while not disrupting them entirely. The neoliberalization of state institutions, policies and discourses is one manifestation of contemporary adjustments; the emergence of the trope of "profit" as legitimizing in and of itself is part of that process. In the next section we will discuss this move into late capitalism (or high modernity), and in particular the role of language in the emergence of this new mode of legitimization of relations of capital.

PROFIT, OR LANGUAGE AS CAPITAL

We can illustrate the shift into late capital with the figure of a single person. Bernard Desrosiers, as we will call him, captures it in his own life trajectory, and in the way he tells his story. Bernard is from the same region of central Ontario with which we opened the chapter. He says that in the early part of his life, in the 1960s, he thought the best thing for Canada was for state services, and as many individual people as possible, to be bilingual in French and English. His own bilingualism was a source of pride, and a sign of his embodiment of good Canadian citizenship. Indeed, his position was an internalization of the discourse developed by the Canadian state in reaction to the Québécois (modern, nationalist "pride"-trope) independentist movements of the 1960s; those movements called into question the ability of the Canadian state to adequately represent francophones. In order to preserve its own legitimacy, Canada had to shift its legitimization discourse from one based on ties to the colonial legacy of the (in any case rapidly crumbling) British Empire, to one focused on the distinctiveness of Canada as a place for speakers of both French and English (as well, eventually, as having to recognize the linguistic and cultural rights of immigrants and indigenous groups). This included such symbolic moves as the invention of a new flag and anthem (Breton 1984), as well as the 1969 adoption of an Official Languages Act. While this act actually focused mainly on state services and on the bilingualization of the public service, it quickly got linked to state support for the development of second official language education, of official language minority groups (anglophones in Québec, francophones everywhere else), and of the discursive construction of individual French–English bilingualism as the hallmark of good Canadian citizenship. It was, then, this discourse, which Bernard had absorbed and made his own (along with most other Canadians, who either adopted or resisted it, and do to this day).

But then, in the 1970s, he became influenced by an emerging discourse of francophone nationalism, in which the thing to be proud of was being a Franco-Ontarian, and of speaking French as much as humanly possible. He eventually became a key figure in struggles for French-language minority schooling, and in setting up and running the regional francophone cultural centre *cum* community association, an activity which kept him occupied from the late 1970s through to the mid-1990s.

In this capacity, Bernard learned to keep the center running by applying for government grants for cultural and linguistic maintenance activities. By 1998, he was having difficulty keeping the system going. It was difficult to attract participants; as Bernard told us, the people who showed up as board members or at assemblies or at the day camp were "TLMs" (= toujours les mêmes—always the same ones). The TLMs were getting older, moving away or simply no longer as compelled by the center's activities as they had once been. The earlier struggles had in many ways had their effect, that is, they eased open the door to social and economic mobility for previously marginalized minority francophones.

In addition, the various levels of government the community institutions depended on had radically revamped their minority language funding programs; many of them were cut and the ones that remained, or which were newly set up, focused on "employability" and "economic development" (Silva and Heller 2009). This shift was partly a response to the difficulty of justifying expenditures that were in some ways aimed at a population no longer as possible to call into existence, but more broadly needs to be understood as just one element in the widespread neoliberalization of states at that time (we will discuss this process further below).

The center's board realized that tactics had to change; Bernard did not see things that way. After a yearlong struggle, the board ousted Bernard, revised its mission statement and hired a new director better able to function under the new conditions, with a closer relationship to the community economic development agency which saw the light of day in the same period (Heller 2001a, 2011). The center embarked on a new set of projects: building a residence for retired community members, running a summer festival, raising money for a village museum, developing a project in eco-tourism and organic farming, and so on. The notion of pride in francophone identity remained a central theme, but found itself reinscribed in a new discursive frame.

We can understand the Swiss example in similar ways. The heritage language schools were no longer able to attract the kind of "Portuguese immigrant" child they were set up for, not because people were not having children, but because those children were no longer understood as necessarily destined for a "return home." They are therefore no longer interested in forms of national education that would facilitate that return. The schools therefore encountered a problem of legitimacy. The example shows a new strategy: the recasting of heritage language education as value-added. The "profit" discourse of "multilingualism" saves the market under conditions that would otherwise see such programs disappear.

This shift is, therefore, not discursive in a simple sense: it is related to structural changes in political economic conditions, and it materially concerns people's livelihoods, orients their activities and frames how they make sense out of and feel about things (hence the previous reference to "habitus"). Bernard alone ran through a whole set of emotions during the year of struggle, from frustration to determination to anger to sadness to bewilderment; the board members talked on the phone, met for long evening discussions, drew up draft after draft of the new mission statement.

For the Chinese, the complicated problem of minorities becomes more manageable if their exoticness becomes a commodity; the commodity, of course, makes no sense without Chinese reorientation to capitalism in recent years. Similarly, it is that marketization that makes selling their authenticity attractive (or at least tolerable) to minorities: it provides their surest mode of access to the market because it inscribes identity in it.

We want to emphasize that the local events in these specific places are not understandable without some form of historicization. Earlier, we traced how the trope of "pride" was substantively connected to specific interests in the construction of national markets. Here, we will first trace how that trope gets taken up, intertwined and reconfigured under late capitalist conditions with a new trope of "profit," and then turn to ways in which the idea of language as "profit" moves away altogether from modern ideologies of language, culture and identity, to treat language instead as a technical skill. While we can provide an account of the political economic changes involved, we also emphasize that the contemporary historical period destabilizes habitus, leaving us searching for ways to handle tensions between older conventionalized frames and an emergent sense of restructuring which we cannot yet quite name. The discourse of "profit" is probably best captured in terms of what Raymond Williams called "structures of feeling" (Williams 1973), a sense of historical shift that is not yet amenable to crystallization, institutionalization and conventionalization. This book aims at working away at the tension involved in that indeterminacy.

Language and the Expansion of Capital

Five interconnected processes characterize the shift we are discussing. The first is the *saturation of markets*. Industrially produced goods and services, even those with a short shelf life, eventually reach all possible consumers. Just having a comb like everyone else's is not terribly interesting; it needs to be cheaper, more distinctive or just for you.

Expansion is therefore the second connected process, although it takes two forms. The first form is the hunt for new markets, that is, to start the process all over again with a new set of consumers. The opening of China to market capitalism created the major such opportunity of the late twentieth century. Sometimes these markets need to be developed; certainly they always need to be reached. The second form is the search for cheaper sources of goods and labor; here China also plays an important role. Both require moving beyond familiar territory, and, as we discovered in the 1980s, also test the limits of nation-state regulatory modes. And the planet being, in the end, finite, it becomes increasingly difficult to find ways to simply expand (Harvey 2006).

Distinction (or *added value*) is the third. Value can be added in a number of ways, including a focus on what makes a set of consumers distinctive (that is, developing niche markets), and adding material or symbolic value to products (Appadurai 1996). Among the ways in which these two goals can be achieved is by harnessing identity symbols (or "pride") to define symbolically distinctive goods and niche markets. Yunnanese ethnic minority villages provide a good example of the former; an example of the latter might be the European backpackers who are drawn to the Yunnan–Tibet border to live with minority families and trek through the mountains. A third kind is the production and export of authentic Yunnanese products, although that has only begun to happen around one product (*pu-erh* tea); we see that process more developed in other areas, from the circulation of "French-Canadian" artisanal soap on French Christmas markets (Budach et al. 2007) to the marketing of Filipina nannies (see Lorente, this volume).

The fourth process is *tertiarization*, that is, the development of the economic sector that, unlike the primary sector's focus on extraction of primary resources (food, metals, wood, etc.), or the secondary sector's concentration on their industrial transformation, is instead centered on information, services and symbolic goods. The tertiary sector owes its growth to the necessity of managing global networks of production and consumption, and to the increasing market for symbolic goods or symbolic modes of adding value to products or forms of distinction to consumers. Tertiarization is strongest in precisely those parts of the world that have relinquished control over primary- and secondary-sector production in the expansion process, as well as in those parts of where even tertiarization has been outsourced (as in the iconic example of call centers).

The final, related process is *flexibilization* (Gee et al. 1996). As markets grow and are increasingly integrated, and as it becomes more difficult and more important to find new ways to source cheap goods or labor, niche markets, or sources of distinction, it becomes more important to be able to change any of these modes quickly. Companies and their work sites open and close, or move from one part of the planet to another. At the individual level, workers are constructed as equally flexible, able to shift sites and modes of work, requiring new forms of education in Foucauldian self-discipline (Urciuoli 2008).

Taken together (they are, in any case, not extricable one from the other), these processes destabilize the nation-state's ability to regulate markets, that is, to regulate the production and circulation of goods, services (including information) and producers and consumers (Castells 2000). They also destabilize therefore its ability to control the production and circulation of legitimizing discourses.

There are several consequences of this destabilization that are relevant to our concerns. The first is the state's attempts to retain a measure of control, by adapting to the new conditions. We know these attempts as "neoliber-alization," that is, the state's agreement to pull back from the regulation of the private sector and to facilitate (in specific ways) global expansion and circulation. "Pride" no longer works as well as the sole trope of nation-state legitimization; rather, the state's ability to facilitate the growth of the new economy depends on its ability to legitimize the discourse of "profit." Second, this opens up the possibility of creating new sites of discursive production outside of or indirectly related to state control, whether supranational agencies, NGOs, the private sector or religion, the arts and culture. Third, the role of language and communication become increasingly important, while at the same time being reconfigured in new ways under these new conditions.

Language and the Discourse of Profit

Language is involved in two major ways in the globalized new economy: as a source of symbolic added value, and as a mode of management of global networks. As the first, it is tied to the commodification of national identities, in the form of the marketing of authenticity; on this terrain, the trope of "profit" appropriates the trope of "pride," in ways that are often rife with tension. To the extent those identities are mobilized in such processes as the construction of niche markets or the selling of labor pools (among other elements of the globalized networks we are concerned with), global management also links "pride" to "profit." However, global management, in its search for taylorist modes of regulation carried through from modern economic activities, often also looks for ways to technicize and standard-ize linguistic regulation techniques. These efforts construct language as a technical skill, decoupled from authenticity.

We carry through with us today the idea that things (including people and places) are valuable because of a privileged link to nature; the Romantic idea that nature confers authenticity, whether on things that come from it or on people who live close to it, retains its power to convince. The link made by nationalism between nature and nations allows for national, as well as regional or local, identities to serve as authenticating symbols when places, goods or people are put onto the market. Those identities can be semiotically constructed and conveyed in a number of ways; some of the most common include using a flag, national colors or iconic features of the built or natural landscape (such as the Eiffel Tower, the Statue of Liberty or Uluru).

But language is also often corralled into the branding effort: we find, for example, use of characteristic scripts (Cyrillic for Russian, for example);

of iconic names of people, places or things; or even (bounded or cropped) pieces of text. It can also serve in this way as a (sometimes partial) language of service, as when a vendor of soaps at a French Christmas market says customers ask first to hear her speak with her Canadian accent before they turn their attention to what she is selling.

This leaks into other aspects of language of service and information, as producers and consumers link national-type identities (or categories derived from modernist nationalism, including ethnicity, race and class) with their supposed cultural characteristics, mustering the whole discursive complex of modernity and colonialism in the organization of economic relations in the globalized new economy. So efficient Germans sell good cars, while trips to Brazil are fun because of all the dancing (Kelly-Holmes 2000; Piller 2001); similarly, national or regional identities can be used to construct niche markets, which must be reached in certain languages and certain communicative styles, and prefer some kinds of products over others (for example, many people claim that Québécois like their soft drinks sweeter, their cheese less pasteurized and their produce fresher than other North Americans, and they like to be addressed in French, albeit less formally than other francophones). Linguistic variability localizes and flexibilizes, as long as it indexes something recognizable as a place or a social category.

We get the full force of pride in the service of profit with the "produit du terroir," the rare comestible produced only on limited territories without much human intervention. In Québec, the artisanal cheese industry has taken off, aided by government relaxation of milk-production quotas and pasteurization rules initially designed for the regulation of industrialized dairy farming; cheeses are given authentifying names linked to rural places or historical figures, wrappings bear their pictures, and text in French and English. (In response, a major industrial cheese producer initiated an "artisanal" line of cheeses, named after a French colonial settler.) The cheeses evoke idyllic rural francophone settlements of the eighteenth and nineteenth centuries, the same heartland evoked by Québécois nationalism as its authenticating core. They are "francophone Québec" products made and sold by "francophones."

Cheese sales, however, are somewhat easier to handle linguistically than the provision of services or information or language-based entertainments; the putative linguistic homogeneity of the authenticating heartland can be evoked, it does not necessarily have to be performed. Cheeses can have bilingual wrappings without risking too much of their authenticity; performances have to have an audience speaking the same language (or at least, wanting to hear only that language) in order to maintain the full force of linguistic authentification. But that audience also has to be interested in acting as a set of consumers.

The linguistic inscription of "pride" into "profit" opens up a discursive gap between "communities," on the one hand, and "producers" and "consumers," on the other. People who have up until now constructed themselves as members of the same community (or different ones) have used that frame to orient their rights and obligations, that is, to understand how they should be treated, how they should treat others, what activities it makes sense to undertake and what goals to set. Understood in national terms, you should share the natural resources that are part of national heritage. Commodification of that heritage raises a number of questions: how do you construct a product as unadulterated and naturally national if you drive a wedge of difference between producers and consumers into the undifferentiated mass of citizens, thereby staking a claim to be more suitable owners of identity than those to whom you wish to sell? How do you maintain its integrity if you sell it to others, in ways which inevitably require different kinds of performances, that is, an adulteration of the product? How do you justify the choice of certain products over others? This can lead to tensions over who controls the newly marketable resources, how value is assigned to them, and how profits from them are distributed.

At the same time, the idea of authenticity as a source of value, and as one means of making both distinction and flexibility, has competition from taylorism, the management technique that became standard for industrial production and seeks to maximize efficiency by breaking production down into a standardized sequence of steps. Standardized regulation of activity (including linguistic activity) is also available as a means of coordinating global relations, since it facilitates both coordination and circulation. It also serves as a means to guarantee a different form of quality, making a double promise: (1) we guarantee that you will never get a product of lesser value, even if in order to do so we can also never give you a product of greater quality; (2) whatever this product evokes in the way of associations for you, including the ones we would like you to cathect, be assured that you will always find it, in this form, wherever you may find yourself (flexible and mobile person that you are). It plays familiarity off exoticism, stability off mobility, and centralization off fragmentation.

Linguistic taylorism in the new economy takes a number of forms and raises a number of issues related to the difficulty of applying a mode of regulation invented for physical and mechanical labor to linguistic and cultural work. This difficulty is compounded by the attempt to simultaneously attend to standardization and variability, as service and information providers attempt to speak to niche markets, and to flexibly provide a range of services (Duchêne and Heller in press).

As is by now widely known, the main strategy for dealing with these conditions is to provide workers with standardized scripts which mimic socially conventionalized interactions (Cameron 2001), or to use those scripts for the provision of automated services, removing the human element altogether. This strategy requires making a series of script form choices regarding which linguistic elements to include, from conversational sequencing and the pragmatics of utterances to specification of relevant linguistic dimensions (prosody, phonology, lexicon, syntax, morphology, phonology). To the extent to which variability is understood to be important to attend to, taylorism requires the multiplication of standard scripts. It also requires standardizing speakers, whether producers or receivers of services (thus, for example, in most Canadian call centers, a code appears on the screen of designated bilingual workers indicating whether service is to be provided in French or English—both is not an option, either for caller or responder).

Taylorizing talk (or writing) also moves language away from being understood as the natural possession of the "native" (natural-born) speaker to being understood as a skill that we don't even need a human to be able to produce. It allows us to think of language as something measurable, so that standardized benchmarks can be used in teaching and in the evaluation of communicative competence. We see such forms of measurement used in the standardized tests used for employee recruitment or assessment of job performance, or for immigration gatekeeping. If taken to an extreme, these practices would entirely decouple language from identity, and open the door to a radical reinvention of legitimizing discourses for social organization.

However, they exist side by side with nativist ones, so that questions are constantly raised about the bases on which to decide what counts as a benchmark, what are reasonable items to put on a standardized test, and who is best placed to decide, not to mention whether such modes of regulation make more sense than simply having a "native speaker" make all the decisions (assuming who counts as a native speaker and what counts as his or her language is evident). We slide around somewhere between the prototypical poles of the organic native speaker arising from the earth, and the robot able to automatically not only produce any utterance imaginable, but also to translate it into any language of the world.

As a result, in addition to the increasing importance of language in the globalized, tertiarized new economy, issues surrounding its regulation create even more tertiary language-related sectors. We see increased activity in many areas where language is central not just as the process but as the product of work (Boutet 2008; Duchêne 2009; Heller and Boutet 2006): translation, language teaching, voice recognition, as well as language-based arts, marketing and information. These "language industries" are among the hallmarks of late capitalism.

They too, of course, are shot through with the same tensions between "pride" and "profit" that the rest of late capitalist activities produce. Those tensions arise from the limits of the ability of heretofore dominant (if not hegemonic) discursive formations to orient and legitimize ways of making sense and forms of social action in the globalized new economy, their modification within emerging discursive frames, and the difficulty of firmly establishing new frames. We suggest that this difficulty is due in part to the contradiction with old ones that they represent (interaction is in fact difficult to regulate), but also to their partial dependence on those older frames.

As a result, the terrain of language actually presents a privileged window into the workings of late capitalism, and a terrain on which we can see its tensions being worked out.

SOCIAL ACTORS, DISCURSIVE STRUGGLES AND SOCIOLINGUISTICS

In order to do this, however, we need to take a close look in a variety of places. For a number of years now, sociolinguistics has recognized that its traditional attention to fixed places and moments, or to fixed groups, no longer provides the tools to investigate the kinds of questions we are now asking (Coupland 2003; Heller 2002; Jaffe 2009), although it is precisely its ability to examine the unfolding of social interaction, and the edges of its indeterminacy, that makes it useful for our present purposes. In that sense, sociolinguistics continues to provide useful ways of grasping the articulation between agency and structure, or to put it in Giddensian terms, of discovering and describing how the process of social structuration actually works (Giddens 1984). Late capitalism moves us toward finding ways of discovering and describing the complex articulations and processes constraining contemporary social markets and the life trajectories of social actors. It is hard to do this if you can only look at single moments in single sites.

Anthropologists such as Appadurai, Marcus and Hannerz (Appadurai 1996; Hannerz 1996, 2003; Marcus 1995) have suggested that one way to move forward is to focus on either flows (the circulation of objects, people and ideas) or on sites differentially situated with respect to connecting processes (what Marcus terms doing a "multisited ethnography"). Sheller and Urry (2006) propose a "new mobilities paradigm" in which mobility and not fixity is a central object of analysis. Giddens (1984) proposes searching for linkages by following up the consequences (intended or not) of moments of (only partly constrained) social action, across both time and space. Cognitive sociologists such as Cicourel (2002) argued that it is possible to track down distributed knowledge across institutional spaces and social networks; Lemke (2000) suggested conceptualizing this distribution in terms of "scales" in order to capture relative duration, diffusion and institutionalization (and this has been quite widely taken up in sociolinguistics in recent years; Blommaert 2010).

Here we take an approach informed most by Marcus, Appadurai and Giddens, in order to respect the fundamental notion that so-called "macro" processes are not ontologically or epistemologically distinct from so-called "micro" processes (Heller 2001b). Our position is that social processes must of necessity be observable, and that structuration (perseverance over time and space through institutionalization and its accompanying conventionalization of behavior, development of legitimizing and sense-making discourses and saturation of consciousness) happens in the kinds of linkages Giddens describes.

We also seek to use the idea of linkages to understand contemporary phenomena as elements of historical, political economic processes. Our goal here is to use sociolinguistic modes of analysis to discover something about the processes of social change in which we are inscribed, and their consequences for the possibilities and obstacles for life trajectories, the production and circulation of resources, and for the construction of legitimacy.

By assembling studies of different kinds of phenomena, involving different kinds of social actors with different positions with respect to the conditions on the ground of late capitalist markets, we aim to make some contribution toward a kind of Marcusian multisite ethnography (loosely speaking, of course, since we did not set out together at the same time with the same questions; rather we are trying here to understand our data in similar terms). We need to emphasize that the collection of situations presented here is not meant to be exhaustive, and is indeed skewed toward Europe and Canada, with only one contribution from Asia, and none at all from vast stretches of the rest of the world. There are of course many reasons for this, starting with the structure of the field of sociolinguistics itself. To mention only one aspect of the unevenness of this conversation, many contributors to this volume began their careers with an interest in linguistic minorities and language contact, a question that became a "question" in the heady days of post–World War II decolonization (internal and otherwise). Nonetheless, Europe in particular has long been the key site for the development of capitalism and its relationship to nationalism, and Canada has been an important arena for working out the problems of noncanonically heterogeneous states. This is therefore an attempt to raise questions, rather than to claim exhaustivity, and indeed we raise them as part of what we need to consider here, as part of the field of "language in late capitalism."

Each author approaches a specific set of phenomena as a complex and unfolding process, examining the negotiation and contestation of social experience among certain sets of actors. They do this through descriptive and analytic techniques which foreground temporality and spatiality. Techniques that foreground temporality are understood in the forms of genealogy (the linkages among discourses across time, or how discursive elements are taken up, circulated, reframed and resemiotized) and history (accounts of the political economic, situated, material development of practices), often in combination. Spatial techniques examine the links among practices co-occurring in different sites, the consequences some can have for others, or the circulation of resources, discourses and people across sites.

The chapters assembled here allow us to think through the implications of being situated in different ways in the shifts of late capitalism, that is, with respect to the five processes we evoked earlier (saturation of markets, expansion, making of distinction, tertiarization and flexibilization). Our premise is that the landscape is uneven, unbounded and fluid, and that social actors occupy different (and differentially advantageous) positions with respect to access to the resources that circulate across it. We therefore seek multiple points of entry, while attempting to gain some perspective on where those points of entry are located with respect to each other.

The chapters in this volume, then, treat a variety of discursive spaces, of categories of social actors, and of material and symbolic resources involved in diverse trajectories in the globalized new economy. They may be in the heart of tertiarization or else, rather, in areas where industrial production is cheap; they may be close to or far from spaces of decision making regarding what counts as linguistic competence; they may be constructed as producers or consumers; they may be involved in markets where "pride" remains central, where it lies in uneasy coexistence with "profit," or where "profit" takes over completely.

In all the cases studied, language is shown to play an increasingly important role under the conditions of late capitalism, and in particular they reveal a heightened focus on linguistic variability (sometimes thought of in nationalist terms as problems of "dialect" or as problems of "multilingualism"). Some of the cases involve the management of communication over widespread networks, for example, in the ways English becomes a lingua franca in globalized international activities or markets; some involve the deployment of varieties marked as local in positioning around the marketization of authenticity; some involve the amassing of multiple forms of linguistic capital in navigating access to multiple market.

The chapters in this volume all cover much the same terrain, focusing in each case on different elements of the processes we have sketched out here. Some speak to the changing role of the state, some to new conditions of work; some focus on the appropriation of authenticity in the marketization of resources that become commodities, others on the strategies of social actors as they navigate new market conditions. All insist on the ways in which "pride" and "profit" are co-constitutive discursive tropes.

This co-constitution is visible in the tensions and struggles each chapter recounts. The shift to late capitalism changes market conditions, and therefore repositions social actors with respect to their access to capital. Gal points to the ways in which these actors are both institutional (indeed, also state and supranational, in the case of the European Union, which is her focus) and individual, and to how their fates are inextricably intertwined. She argues that the pride and profit tropes of modernist capitalism find themselves recast in late capitalism onto new spaces, on ways that open up opportunities for some, while marginalizing others. Change is uneven, but its form is familiar.

At the same time, differentially located actors navigate the new waters in a variety of ways. Sometimes actors positioned favorably on modernist markets attempt to maintain the value of their capital by resisting its appropriation by other actors' attempts at commercialization; this is clearly the case of the Swiss football fans discussed by Del Percio and Duchêne who radicalize their "pride" position and practices in the face of investors' and other fans' interest in turning them into sources of profit (in the strict monetary sense as well as a symbolic sense). In others, actors try to appropriate the "profit" trope in the interests of maintaining their position in new market conditions; this is the case of Basque and Catalan linguistic minorities in Spain, francophones in Canada or Welsh speakers in Great Britain, who try to import management or economic development techniques into linguistic revitalization (see chapters by Urla, and by Heller and Bell), or who commodify authenticity as a tourist product (see chapter on Catalan literature by Pujolar and Jones).

We see similar tensions between "pride" and "profit" in other institutions traditionally legitimized by the one, now traversed by the other. Sport, politics and literature are not the only institutional spaces affected; Blackledge and Creese show how heritage language education in Britain is torn between older discourses focusing on linguistic and cultural reproduction, and newer ones seeing it as a source of capital of distinction, notably on the British postsecondary education market, or of capital necessary for access to globalized networks. Daveluy discusses the ways in which the Canadian military's legitimacy depends on its recruitment of both francophones and anglophones, constructing bilingualism as capital of distinction in processes of recruitment to military jobs, while at the same time military management renders that capital useless on the job.

Heller and Bell show how these complex interconnections work themselves out in the ways in which late capitalism positions francophone Canadian workers. Understood as a labor category, "francophones" have long engaged in gendered job-related mobility that sustains the fictively fixed communities at the center of nationalist ideologies, and that themselves become labor markets requiring mobility. Authenticity becomes a source of capital for some, while marginalizing others whose authenticity legitimizes and sustains those who define them (and to whom they are often related). New conditions stretch this symbiosis to its limits, pushing some francophones to reimagine themselves as "citizens of the world" no longer bound by the ethnolinguistic organization of the Canadian political economy.

We also see the positioning of institutional actors seeking to mobilize the authenticity resources legitimately "owned" by others as a way to increase profit. Del Percio and Duchêne already allude to such actors in their discussion of the commercialization of the football industry; Lorente shows how capital's traditional partner, the nation-state, redefines its economic policies in ways which facilitate the production of Filipino transnational workers, and constructs them both as an export product and as a source of national pride.

Lorente also points to a further important development on the markets of late capitalism, namely, the transmutation of authenticity into commodifiable skills, in particular linguistic ones. Here authenticity is recast by the state: it is no longer a matter of local rootedness and monolingualism, but rather of flexibility and multilingualism. Being a Filipina "supermaid" does not mean being able to teach the children under your care Tagalog, or to cook them Filipino food (although it might sometimes be that, too); it is rather a matter of being able to speak the language of the employer.

Boutet focuses on the ways in which such language skills have emerged as central to the tertiary sector; separate from the Romantic notions of authenticity that still underlie evaluations of linguistic competence even in the globalized new economy. Taking a historical perspective, she shows how language has moved from being understood as an obstacle to industrial production, to being not only a process but also a product of work in the new economy (Duchêne 2009; Heller 2010). This raises a number of questions about how to define what counts as linguistic proficiency, and about who counts as a legitimate speaker. At the same time, both the industrial and the tertiary sectors regulate language heavily, employing much the same disciplinary techniques. What is less clear is how effective taylorist practices are in the regulation of communication (rather than manual or mechanical labor), or what effect the new centrality of linguistic form and practice in economic production has on our ideas about language.

Because of course we need to think about what we mean by "our" ideas. McElhinny insists that sociolinguistics is but one conversational space in which these processes unfold, and that sociolinguists are but one set of stakeholders in the questions raised by these papers. Taking the notion of "community of practice" as a key window into the exploration of the circulation of ideas in neoliberal spheres, she shows that its popularity in feminist sociolinguistics and in business sectors has to be understood in the same terms. It allows both to foreground agency over reproduction, in ways that can be both liberatory and oppressive, often (but not always) unintentionally and perversely.

We want to build on this to use the papers assembled here to raise the question of what kind of job sociolinguistics might be doing in late capitalism, given that our conditions of work are as affected as anyone else's, and that we are stakeholders too. McElhinny suggests that one approach we can take is to track the circulation of discourses and practices, taking perhaps better care than we have in the past to situate ourselves in the chains of production and consumption and to see what the consequences are of the workings of those chains for the distribution of resources and for the attribution of value to them, even for the conditions of the markets that we are involved in themselves. Gal suggests a somewhat different approach, one that emphasizes the importance of showing exactly how linguistic ideologies and practices are tied to political economic processes. The other papers here, less explicitly perhaps, adopt elements of both these approaches, asking, for example, what it means for management techniques to be imported into linguistic revitalization (Urla), for measurements of "vitality" to be inserted into linguistic minority politics (Heller and Bell), for ethnolinguistic "authenticity" to be marketized (Del

Percio and Duchêne, Pujolar and Jones), or for "linguistic duality" to be erased by hierarchical management (Daveluy).

What all these chapters show us is that the new centrality of language in late capitalism, while apparently empirically supported (and not say "just" a discourse), is not either simply a matter of celebration. It may well make sociolinguistics a sexier discipline than it might have appeared to be in the past, but, as Boutet reminds us, the regulation of language is the regulation of language, whether the idea is to produce silence or regimented talk. Both require disciplining linguistic action, and produce resistances and conformities, disengagements and investments, and uneven material and symbolic profit.

There may well be more continuity than rupture than we have thought in the globalized new economy. Nonetheless, we seem to be nearing the limits of linguistic national (or national linguistic) regimes to organize our lives, finding systems breaking up into circulating flows, local agentivity poking holes into institutional reproduction and the boundary between authenticity and artifice breaking down. The papers all point to tensions connected to the difficulty we are having in keeping the old regime going, although it is far from clear what else we might get up to. Language in late capitalism remains a fraught terrain, with high stakes for increasing numbers of players.

NOTES

1. " . . . développement de biens et de services novateurs et de création d'entreprises et d'emplois qui montrent la valeur ajoutée des francophones et des bilingues de [la région] où l'on reflète leur impact considérable sur la vitalité de la région." We have replaced the region's name in order to ensure participants' anonymity. Canadian data cited here comes principally from a series of research projects funded by the Social Sciences and Humanities Research Council of Canada. Swiss data come mainly from research funded by the Swiss National Science Foundation (Switzerland). We gratefully acknowledge their support, as well as the contributions of our many co-investigators, research assistants and project participants.

REFERENCES

Appadurai, Arjun. 1996. *Modernity at Large: Cultural Dimensions of Globalization*. Minneapolis: University of Minnesota Press.
Bauman, Richard, and Charles Briggs. 2003. *Voices of Modernity: Language Ideologies and the Politics of Inequality*. Cambridge: Cambridge University Press.
Blommaert, Jan. 2010. *The Sociolinguistics of Globalization*. Cambridge: Cambridge University Press.
Bourdieu, Pierre. 1972. *Esquisse d'une théorie de la pratique*. Genève: Droz.
Bourdieu, Pierre. 1982. *Ce que parler veut dire*. Paris: Fayard.

Bourdieu, Pierre, and Jean-Claude Passeron. 1977. *Reproduction in Education, Society and Culture.* London: Sage.

Boutet, Josiane. 2008. *La vie verbale au travail. Des manufactures aux centres d'appels.* Toulouse: Octares.

Breton, Raymond. 1984. "The Production and Allocation of Symbolic Resources: An Analysis of the Linguistic and Ethnocultural Fields in Canada." *Canadian Journal of Sociology and Anthropology* 21(2): 123–144.

Budach, Gabriele, Claudine Moïse, Alexandre Duchêne, and Mary Richards. 2007. "Bison, feuille d'érable et fleur de lys au Canada: les stéréotypes existent-ils toujours?" In *Stéréotypage, stéréotypes, fonctionnements ordinaires et mises en scène,* edited by Henri Boyer, 29–45. Paris: L'Harmattan.

Cameron, Deborah. 2001. *Good to Talk?* London: Sage.

Castells, Manuel. 2000. *The Information Age: Economy, Society and Culture* (3 vols.). Oxford: Blackwell.

Cicourel, Aaron. 2002. *Le raisonnement médical: une approche socio-cognitive.* Paris: Liber.

Coupland, Nik, ed. 2003. "Sociolinguistics and Globalisation. Special Issue." *Journal of Sociolinguistics* 7(4): 465–623.

Duchêne, Alexandre. 2008. *Ideologies Across Nations: The Construction of Linguistic Minorities at the United Nations.* Berlin: Mouton de Gruyter.

Duchêne, Alexandre. 2009. "Marketing, Management and Performance: Multilingualism as a Commodity in a Tourism Call Center." *Language Policy* 8(1): 27–50.

Duchêne, Alexandre, and Monica Heller. in press. "Multilingualism and the New Economy." In *The Routledge Handbook of Multilingualism,* edited by Marilyn Martin-Jones, Adrian Blackledge and Angela Creese. London: Routledge.

Gee, James, Glynda Hull, and Colin Lankshear. 1996. *The New Work Order: Behind the Language of the New Capitalism.* Boulder, CO: Westview Press.

Giddens, Anthony. 1984. *The Constitution of Society.* Berkeley: University of California Press.

Gramsci, Antonio. 1971. *Selections from the Prison Notebooks of Antonio Gramsci.* New York: International Publishers.

Hannerz, Ulf. 1996. *Transnational Connections: Culture, People, Places.* London: Routledge.

Hannerz, Ulf. 2003. "On Being There . . . and There . . . and There! Reflections on Multi-site Ethnography." *Ethnography* 4(2): 201–216.

Harvey, David. 2006. *Limits of Capital.* New York: Verso.

Heller, Monica. 2001a. "Critique and Sociolinguistic Analysis of Discourse." *Critique of Anthropology* 21(2): 117–141.

Heller, Monica. 2001b. "Undoing the Macro-Micro Dichotomy: Ideology and Categorisation in a Linguistic Minority School." In *Sociolinguistics and Social Theory,* edited by Nik Coupland, Srikant Sarangi and Christopher Candlin, 212–234. London: Longman.

Heller, Monica. 2002. *Éléments d'une sociolinguistique critique.* Paris: Didier.

Heller, Monica. 2010. "Language as Resource in the Globalized New Economy." In *Handbook of Language and Globalization,* edited by Nik Coupland, 250–265. Oxford: Blackwell.

Heller, Monica. 2011. *Paths to Post-Nationalism.* Oxford: Oxford University Press.

Heller, Monica, and Josiane Boutet. 2006. "Vers de nouvelles formes de pouvoir langagier? Langue(s) et économie dans la nouvelle économie." *Langage et société* 118: 5–16.

Higonnet, Pierre. 1980. "The Politics of Linguistic Terrorism and Grammatical Hegemony during the French Revolution." *Social Theory* 5: 41–69.

Hobsbawm, Eric. 1990. *Nations and Nationalism Since 1760*. Cambridge: Cambridge University Press.

Jaffe, Alexandra, ed. 2009. *The Sociolinguistics of Stance*. Oxford: Oxford University Press.

Kelly-Holmes, Helen. 2000. "Bier, Parfum, Kaas: Language Fetish in European Advertising." *Cultural Studies* 3(1): 67–82.

Lemke, Jay. 2000. "Across the Scales of Time." *Mind, Culture and Activity* 7: 273–290.

McDonald, Marion. 1989. *We Are Not French*. London: Routledge

Marcus, George. 1995. "Ethnography in/of the World System: The Emergence of Multi-sited Ethnography." *Annual Review of Anthropology* 24: 95–117.

McElhinny, Bonnie. 2007. "Language, Gender and Economies in Global Transitions: Provocative and Provoking Questions about How Gender is Articulated." In *Words, Worlds and Material Girls: Language, Gender, Globalization*, edited by Bonnie McElhinny, 1–40. Berlin: Mouton de Gruyter.

Outram, Dorinda. 1987. "Le langage mâle de la vertu: Women and the Discourse of the French Revolution." In *The Social History of Language*, edited by Peter Burke and Roy Porter, 120–135. Cambridge: Cambridge University Press.

Piller, Ingrid. 2001. "Identity Constructions in Multilingual Advertising." *Language in Society* 30: 153–186.

Schnepel, Ellen. 2004. *In Search of a National Identity: Creole and Politics in Guadeloupe*. Hambourg: Buske.

Sheller, Mimi, and John Urry. 2006. "The New Mobilities Paradigm." *Environment and Planning A* 38: 207–226.

Silva, Emanuel da, and Monica Heller. 2009. "From Protector to Producer: The Role of the State in the Discursive Shift from Minority Rights to Economic Development." *Language Policy* 8: 95–116.

Stroud, Christopher. 2007. "Bilingualism: Colonialism and Postcolonialism." In *Bilingualism: A Social Approach*, edited by Monica Heller, 27–49. New York: Palgrave.

Urciuoli, Bonnie. 2008. "Skills and Selves in the New Workplace." *American Ethnologist* 35(2): 211–228.

Weidman, Amanda. 2006. *Singing the Classical, Voicing the Modern: The Postcolonial Politics of Music in South India*. Durham, NC: Duke University Press.

Williams, Raymond. 1973. *The Country and the City*. London: Chatto and Windus.

Williams, Raymond. 1989 [1983]. *Keywords: A Vocabulary of Culture and Society*. Glasgow: Fontana Press.

2 Sociolinguistic Regimes and the Management of "Diversity"

Susan Gal

INTRODUCTION

For the European Union (hereafter EU), language diversity constitutes a key contradiction. On the one hand, the EU supports linguistic diversity in its own workings and among member states that rely on linguistic distinctions for their legitimacy. On the other hand, territorially organized linguistic diversity is an obstacle to another EU commitment: maximum mobility of labor, production and commodities across the continent to achieve advantages in global markets. The EU is a new kind of economic and increasingly a political organization. Its expansion is in part a response to the recent intensification of global capitalism. Yet, despite its much-remarked novelty as an organizational form, the language ideologies the EU is promulgating—in which tropes of "pride" and "profit" play a central role—are strikingly similar to those developed by European nation-states over the last century and a half.

Such continuity within a new organizational structure and in novel economic circumstances would be surprising if processes of late capitalism *directly* impacted linguistic practices and policies. But they do not. Rather, the tropes and frames—the language ideologies—discussed in this volume mediate between political economy and linguistic practices. Furthermore, the present chapter argues that ideologies of language have a semiotic organization and a history of their own that do not simply reproduce the logic and history of capital. They must be examined as a distinct order of phenomena, with their own dynamic, so that we can understand their mediating role. Accordingly, the goal of this chapter is to explicate the semiotic organization of "pride" and "profit" as terms in an *axis of differentiation* that allocates contrasting values to linguistic forms. With that understanding, we can return to examine EU policies and see why they seem so familiar and how to interpret the forms of change that become apparent.

Today, in European discourses of "pride," language is framed as a cultural treasure, exemplary of tradition, usually a national tradition. In discourses of "profit," the value of language is framed in narrower economic terms, as a means to material gain. This particular contrast is historically specific. But a comparative look at sociolinguistic arrangements in the world shows that the linkage of language to contrasting values is very widespread.

For example, in precolonial Java, *alus* and *kasar*—translatable as "smooth" and "rough"—were values that distinguished and ranked linguistic forms and forms of personhood (Errington 1988; Geertz 1960). These too constituted an *axis of differentiation*. In the Wolof villages of Senegal, the major axis of differentiation was perhaps best termed "restraint" vs. "volatility" (Irvine 1990), with nobles seen as more restrained than griots. It is among such distinctions that we should place "pride"/"profit."[1] As Heller and Duchêne (this volume) note, a discourse of profit does not replace or simply interrupt discourses of pride, rather "the two are intertwined in complex ways." I argue that for this pair—as for the others—a specific semiotic process defines *how* they are intertwined, thereby significantly shaping the ways speakers, social movements and political economic forces mobilize these contrasts, appropriate them for their own purposes or contest and try to undermine them.

To be sure, the contrast here summarized as "pride"/"profit" differs from others not only in the qualities and values picked out as poles of differentiation, but also in that it arose in the context of commercial markets and has been swept up in the history of capitalism. But the similarities are equally important: those living in a capitalist political economy come to presuppose and naturalize "profit" and "pride" and to see these as self-evidently contrasting values, with linguistic entailments, just as those in, say, a Javanese settlement assumed that human essences were composed of certain contrasting qualities. In both we should attend to the following kinds of semiotic properties.

As elements in an ideology of differentiation, "pride" and "profit" are co-constituted: they define each other. Like other axes of differentiation, this one also includes many strands of parallel contrasts. Each pole of the axis is *indexed by* linguistic forms that are also understood to contrast. The linguistic forms that index the values (and associated person types or situation types) are discursively constituted as *iconic* of them. For example, Wolof speakers whose speech is heard by coparticipants as ebullient are understood to *be* expressive, not simply to be speaking that way. Most importantly for my purposes, there is a characteristic form of change imagined in such ideologies: *fractal recursion*. An opposition, salient at some level of relationship, can be projected onto other levels. "Thus the dichotomizing and partitioning process that was involved in some understood opposition . . . recurs at other levels, creating either subcategories on each side of a contrast or supercategories that include both sides but oppose them to something else" (Irvine and Gal 2000, 38; see also Gal and Irvine 1995). When one opposition is institutionalized or otherwise fixed, previous iterations are often *erased* or forgotten. In this way, ideologies of differentiation construct partial and perspectival visions of sociolinguistic worlds, highlighting some values and denying others (Woolard 1998).

This semiotic process has made the "pride"/"profit" distinction available as a means of differentiating linguistic practices. The contrasts thus created have, in turn, been harnessed to formulate, motivate, justify or explain emerging struggles in social relations. Elite writers as much as ordinary speakers have relied on this multipart process to mediate between capitalist political economic arrangements and linguistic practices. The process itself both provides routes for change and enables the possibility of veiling change in the cloth of familiar continuity.

The chapter has three sections. The first emphasizes the long-standing existence of "pride"/"profit" as an axis of differentiation by examining its early construction and the elements out of which it was assembled. By the eighteenth century, literary men in Europe had created contrasting genres of writing, each associated with one of these two values, in an attempt to understand an emerging market society and rank their own positions within it. I offer illustrations of the semiotics of differentiation over several centuries. The ideas of "profit" and market rationality were linked to notions of self-interest and an impersonal, timeless, placeless, universal realm. Juxtaposed to this were concepts of particularity and emplacement of selves, passion and tradition. The valences attached to these ideas changed repeatedly over the centuries. In addition, contrasts were fractally reiterated and their codependence was repeatedly erased, then recuperated, as they were used to argue for diverse political and economic goals.

The second section jumps to the nineteenth and twentieth centuries to show that strands of the same contrasting values were central to the process of *monolingual* standardization. The evidence comes from elite discourses about the ranking of speech forms and the enactment of those hierarchies in social institutions. The same values that earlier organized genres of writing were extended to differentiate linguistic registers (often recasting regional dialects). As the values were hierarchically arranged, so were the registers and people types that were indexically associated with them. The formation and legitimation of European nation-states depended in part on monolingual standardization, a sociolinguistic regime. That familiar story needs no repetition here. Rather, I point illustratively to the role played by ideologies of differentiation in that project.

That monolingual regime was hegemonic in Europe for over a century. Evidence from a selection of EU documents suggests that a second phase of standardization is now underway to make *multilingualism* the dominant ideal, an attempt to conceptually arrange and thereby manage the EU's increasing linguistic "diversity." [2] The EU's existing contradictions as a suprastate organization in late capitalism are exacerbated by eastern expansion, the revitalization of regional languages, the presence of migrants' languages from all over the globe and the increasing use of English and other languages of worldwide distribution. Yet, the move to valorize multilingualism is not a grand change of sociolinguistic regime. It is rather the redeployment of the same value distinction—in a fractal recursion—now indexed not by linguistic registers but by multiple standardized languages. This, I argue, is how the current regime seems familiar, despite change.

Finally, a third section stays in the twentieth century but moves from elite discourses to the linguistic activities of speakers as described in ethnographic reports. I show that, even when reacting against EU policies, speakers are mobilizing the *same* axis of differentiation and the semiotic process outlined here. My examples include evidence from the eastern European members of the EU, for whom the current standardization of multilingualism, though billed as inclusive, has effects similar to the standardizations of the eighteenth and nineteenth centuries, contributing to a restratification of the population along lines of linguistic skill and the reproduction on these new grounds of western advantage.

HISTORIES OF CATEGORY DIFFERENTIATION

The historical sketches in this section show that conceptual categories display dynamics separate from the political economic processes in which they participate. These quick histories also give a glimpse of how the current contrasts forming the axis of differentiation summarized as "pride" and "profit" were put together, over a long stretch of time, out of heterogeneous conceptual elements.

Scholars are currently reexamining the set of conceptual frames labeled European "modernity." This includes the broad configuration in which "pride" and "profit" are embedded, and out which they emerged in the eighteenth to twentieth centuries. These re-readings are inflected by disciplinary differences. Given disparate points of departure, it is noteworthy that many scholars—over several decades—have retold the histories of the foundational concepts in ways that recall the complex semiotic process of differentiation outlined in the previous section. They show how concepts/terms and the values associated with them emerged together; one category was defined as what the other was not. Yet, practices relegated to one category were invariably—if less visibly—crucial in the other. In short, these categories were co-constitutive. There is also a focus on the linguistic practices that indexed the contrasting values. Most importantly, cultural and intellectual histories illustrate the way the opposed concepts/terms were iterated in recursions—reapplications of the co-constitutive contrast—thereby creating more differentiations or unifying concepts into larger oppositions. Four works and the processes of conceptual development they describe will give a sense of these patterns in the emergence of the multi-stranded "pride"/"profit" contrast.

Agnew's (1986) intellectual history chronicles social relations in seventeenth- and eighteenth-century English theaters and markets, two institutions that in an earlier period shared spaces and personae. He describes the way theaters and markets came to be separated and contrasted as counterbalanced forms of expression, exchange and interaction. As market transactions were understood to involve the abstract roles of buyer and seller that united widely disparate moments in time and great spatial distances, so nonmarket, by contrast, social relations were simultaneously identified as specifically located or emplaced and tied to the particularities of individual selves. Agnew draws a parallel between this cultural conception and the claim, made by Wordsworth and Coleridge at the start of the nineteenth century, that literary art, and especially poetry, constituted a different sort of value than the (monetary) value found in markets: more a matter of individual genius, craft and sentiment. With this argument, poets attempted to elevate their own social position. Calling poetry "priceless" was a claim to set its value apart and higher than money, to be sure, but also higher than other kinds of writing.

We see in Agnew's descriptions a process of creating separate realms each with its own characteristic forms of expression (theater and market), and the fractal reiteration of that distinction many decades later *within* the realm of written production, so that poetry is made to seem even more distinct from market forms of expression than are other written works. Ironically, of course, books and plays were commodities and in that role not at all separate from markets. They were dependent on markets for their materiality (paper, printing) and distribution. In addition, they were sold and thus had market value. Strikingly, we see the erasure of the original co-constitution of market and theater, and the erasure of what we (if not contemporaries) can see as the market principles at play in the expressive world supposedly farthest from market value.

Dealing with different materials, Poovey (2008) makes a parallel argument in literary history. She traces the emergent divisions among forms of writing that were all considered fairly similar in seventeenth-century Britain, but vastly different by the end of the eighteenth century. Economic and literary genres came to be seen as instantiating different values, as in Agnew's story. Economic writing was seen as mathematically regular, abstract and therefore rational, with universal claims. Literary writing, by contrast, relied on individual craft, originality, feeling and aesthetics. By the nineteenth century, the two sorts of writers, especially in London, began to see their works as directly opposed—novels vs. financial commentary, romances vs. political economic explanations. They also saw themselves as similarly contrasted. Economic writers seemed more numerate and rational than the others, in what we would now call an iconic relation to their written products. Poovey argues these contrasts came to be "two models of value, models that seem to have almost nothing in common" (2008, 417). This result rests on significant erasures: forgetting their joint origins and their codefinition, but also the fact that they used many of the same rhetorical methods (see McCloskey 1985) and dealt with much the same subject matter: life in capitalism.

An account of western European political theory echoes the distinctions of value chronicled by Agnew and Poovey, yet adds to our understanding of this multistranded contrast by showing how human motivation was imagined to be arrayed along what in this volume we are calling the "pride"/"profit" axis. Hirschman's (1977) classic essay draws on writings in French, English, Italian and German, analyzing the "political arguments for capitalism before its triumph." He tracks how "passion" and "interest"— in today's terms, emotions and economic instrumentalities—came to be contrasted and opposed in European scholarly debates. By attending to the changing semantics of words in the most influential political and economic writing of the seventeenth to the nineteenth centuries, he also shows how passion came to be seen as particular and interest as universal.

Reason had long been contrasted to the passions, but the passions— avarice, pride, lust, ambition for glory—were thought to be more negative and more powerful. Scholars applied the distinction between passion and reason to subdivide the passions. Among the passions, avarice was redefined as a quiet, reasonable passion. It gained the label "interest." As Hirschman shows, this allowed thinkers in the eighteenth century to posit that "interest," having been derived from avarice, but tamed by reason, would be strong enough to control the more destructive passions in a way reason could not (1977, 43). Passions varied by time and individual whim, but "interest," the "desire for gain," came to be considered "a universal . . . which operates at all times, in all places and in all persons" (Hume, cited in Hirschman 1977, 54). The origin of the "interest" category was erased, as interest was seen as diametrically opposed to passions/emotions in subsequent centuries. There were many political economic considerations in the invention of the concept of "interest" in the eighteenth century, and writers differed in their use of it. But the semiotic logic of intellectual debate played a crucial part.

My final example is an intellectual history about European philosophies of language. Read along with the others, Bauman and Briggs's work (2003) shows how a timeline stretching from an imagined tradition to modernity became part of the axis of differentiation we have been tracking, modernity aligned with supposedly universal time, place and interest, and tradition aligned with the particularities of emotion/passion, creativity and specificity in time and place. Philosophies about what language is, and how it *should* operate, framed and thus underwrote this multistranded differentiation of value and allocated to the contrasted poles not only linguistic genres, but also features of language in general.

Bauman and Briggs use Locke and Herder as figureheads to represent two approaches to language that they show were developed in tandem— in our terms co-constituted—in the seventeenth and eighteenth centuries. Lockean approaches saw denotation as the key function of language, arguing that ambiguity, the "cheat and abuse of words," was like the clipping of precious metal from English coinage that threatened profit and hence political stability (Appelby 1992). Fixing the meanings of words would reduce political and economic deception. To stabilize meaning, language should be made maximally transparent in denotation. Similarly, the credibility of texts should not depend on their relation to earlier texts—as in medieval appeals to precedential authority—but only on how faithfully words and texts, seen as autonomous from society, represent the observable world.

More than a century later, Herder rejected this separation of language from culture and society. Instead, he saw language, and especially poetic form, as the key to tradition: a sedimentation of the sociocultural past in the present. While Locke posited language as a universal human faculty, Herder looked for the "differences that make [men] what they are, make them themselves, it is in these that the individual genius of men and cultures is expressed" (Berlin 1997 [1960], 15). We see here the conjunction of several strands in the distinctions already discussed. Herder's appreciation of other cultures and his demand for pride in the German language (vis-à-vis French and Latin) were sources for the later study of cultural particularity, the construction of the concept of tradition as an object of reflection and the revalorization of "passion" as a positive value. Bauman and Briggs go on to provide examples of what one can call recursions in which the contrasts between broadly Lockean views and Herderian views were reproduced within a Herderian framework. For instance, the Grimm brothers used the tools of a positivist science to investigate poetic traditions that could be constituted as objects of study only within a Herderian approach.[3]

Elites ranked the values and linguistic practices they formulated, creating hierarchies among people types via their typical linguistic practices. Most people were not credited with rational, accurately representational speech, so Lockean assessments justified hierarchy: rural people, lower classes and women could not exercise reason. Herderian conceptions also justified hierarchy: tradition had its source in the *Volk*, who were middle class or landed peasants, not women and lower classes (2003, 184–185). Yet the two approaches were unified in creating yet another level of hierarchy—a recursion "up"—a more encompassing distinction: only those with reason and reflexivity could judge linguistic accuracy on the one hand, and safeguard authentic tradition on the other (2003, 193). Although they created distinct philosophies about language's role in political reform, both approaches identified a stratum of the educated, who were to be the arbiters of modernity in the realm of language; both posited an ideal uniformity in language as the foundation of politics, though one ideal rested on individual reason, the other on group culture. In time, both strands were harnessed to formulate and justify the conceptual underpinnings of nation-states.

DIVERSITY AND ITS STANDARDIZATION[4]

My discussion so far has relied on intellectual and cultural histories to trace the long-term emergence of discourses that defined the axis of differentiation summarized here as "pride" and "profit." The project of monolingual language standardization that swept Europe in the nineteenth century was a key site for *enactment* of these distinctions. It allocated these contrasting values to specific speech forms that had not yet been regimented in this way. Notwithstanding the nineteenth century's "sentimentalization" of "mother tongues" (Ahlzweg 1994) and the connotation of uniformity in a term like "standard," recent scholarship sees standardization as an ideological project of differentiation and hierarchization.

Early studies were more focused on the technology of standardization, in policy and implementation. The process seemed to be (a) selection or invention of a linguistic variety as a source of norms; (b) codification of the norms; (c) elaboration of norms, especially in literature but also in signage, schooling and government; (d) building prestige for the norms; and (e) acceptance of the norms by a significant portion of a community for a significant portion of daily activities. Classic sociological works linked this standardization to nationalism and the political project of building nation-states. They suggested that print markets, the demands of industrialization and general education have been motor forces behind both nation-states and language standardization (e.g., Anderson 1991 [1983]; Gellner 1983).

More recent work has emphasized that standardization became politically potent because it was an ideological project that naturalized the differentiation and hierarchical ordering of linguistic forms making them the justification for differential ranking of speakers, often those who were otherwise united by a shared and supposedly emotional connection to a mother tongue. Linguistic difference became the naturalized sign connecting political and economic changes to lived understandings of those changes (Bourdieu 1991; Inoue 2006; Silverstein 1996). The specific differences signaled through standardization in Europe—and later more broadly—were the ones arrayed on the multistranded axis we have been examining.

To be sure, sociolinguistic literature has long recognized that linguistic forms index these contrasts: speakers consider one variant to be intimately authentic, the other economically useful; one "emotional" the other "instrumental"; one used at home, the other at work. The newer studies insist, however, that these values are not mere reflexes of the uses to which speakers put their repertoires. Speakers' valuations are evidence, not explanation. The co-constitution and contrast of values, and the indexical link between linguistic forms and values, are discursive formulations and institutional achievements. Actual usage does not adhere to such schemes. It relies on them as models, as speaker types to be voiced or mobilized for particular purposes in specific contexts.

The innovation introduced by standardization was the extension of an old schema that categorized genres to conceptualize and organize linguistic registers. As a sociolinguistic regime, standardization lends value and meaning to one register (the standard) by making it the index of the universal/"profit" pole of this axis of differentiation, while other registers are demoted with reference to the first, but gain a different kind of value as indexes of particular places, times or identities. Not just anyone can speak these; they are often ethnic emblems. The standard register, in contrast, is supposedly independent of place, time or speaker identity; it is "for everyone," a "voice from nowhere." Boasting wide communicative reach, the standard register indexes economic interests. It promises "profit" in the form of upward mobility via widespread contacts or in the labor market (Gal and Woolard 2001; Woolard 2008). Particularity is often overridden by the universal; this is the characteristic form of value hierarchy that standardization creates.

In enactments of co-constitutive values, the perspective of the observer is crucial, setting the parameter of comparison. This is because reiterations—fractal recursions—can proliferate at many levels of contrast. A focus on the "pride" pole can re-create the "profit"/"pride" contrast inside the "pride" category. When compared to national standards, regional languages index particular places and traditions; they signal "pride." Creating a standard register in a regional language recreates the particular/universal distinction within the category of the particular, making *some* regional linguistic forms doubly particular. The nonstandard regional forms sound like the local forms of an already particular language. More hierarchies are created within what was thought to be a unified regional form. Gaining universal values for a regional language requires downplaying the palpable authenticity pole, at least within the region (Woolard 2008).

Viewed in a different comparative context, the national standards seem to *combine* the opposed values. By invoking an international world of many standard languages, the universal/particular contrast can be projected to a wider realm: each standard comes to signal a particular location and national past in that wider world (Gal 2006). Standards are a universal form from the narrower state perspective, yet indexical of place, authenticity and tradition from a more encompassing one. Focusing on one view or perspective tends to erase the other. Yet, as we will see , a suprastate institution creates the social site that more firmly anchors an overarching perspective.

A Europe of (New) Standards

It is within the history of regimented registers that the responses to increasing linguistic diversity by the EU must be analyzed. They seem very familiar, yet not quite the same. The semiotic process of differentiation I have been outlining provides one route into understanding this continuity-in-change—revealing what has changed, what has been reproduced and with what repercussions.

Over the years, repeated statements from various organs of the EU—the Council, the Parliament, other EU bodies, some member states—have declared support for "linguistic diversity," despite the norm of monolingualism. An NGO to address such issues—the Bureau for Lesser Used Languages—was financed as early as 1982. Yet, the EU does not make binding language policy. The founding principle of "subsidiarity" stipulates that primary responsibility for the maintenance and support of national, regional and minority languages legally resides at member state or regional levels. Nevertheless, there has been EU support for such programs, mostly as part of community development efforts (Grin and Moring 2002, 2–3). Thus, the EU is committed to linguistic diversity, but, as we will see, the meaning of this term is in motion.

The evidence analyzed here derives from a series of reports about language issues financed and prepared by order of the European Commission at roughly ten-year intervals—1986, 1996, 2008—with a focus on the most recent one. Scholars from relevant disciplines prepared the reports; they combine historical, demographic and archival research with surveys and interviews; they end with analyses and recommendations. The European Commission is the EU's executive body, responsible for proposing legislation, developing plans and strategies, and executing these, including the deployment of funds. This makes it a powerful office. In contrast to the European Council that represents governments, and the European Parliament that is an elected body representing citizens, only the Commission is said to have a mandate to "think European," that is, to plan and execute EU-wide goals. The reports I analyze do not set policy, nor do they represent the opinion of the Commission. They are merely high points, spaced over two decades, in an ocean of writing about language within and around the EU. Yet, as informational documents requested by and prepared for the influential Commission, they both shape and reflect discourses in an elite context of scholars and administrators.

Reading the reports as instances of language ideology, I draw attention to two points: the first is the changing object of study; the second is the changing way moral and financial support for various "kinds" of languages has been formulated and justified. What are the principles and values that implicitly authorize claims? What model of future speakers is implied or recommended in these reports? How are these linked to differentiation and ranking?

Tellingly, the first report (Simone et al. 1986) concerns the definition of "linguistic minority." Legal, economic, political, cultural, demographic and historical definitions are all found to be inadequate. The authors stress the political delicacy of the issue. They adopt as their model and guide the terms of international agreements that closed the First and Second World Wars and the subsequent argumentation by the United Nations (see Duchêne 2008). The second report (Nelde et al. 1996), less concerned with legalities, provides new evidence about speakers, their usage, age structure, literary and mass media efforts, and defines its object as "those autochthonous communities whose languages are not the official languages of their respective states." (Nelde et al. 1996, i). These authors also point to a historical process: "[M]inoritization of languages . . . the concept of minority by reference to language groups does not refer to empirical measures, but rather, to issues of power" (Nelde et al. 1996: 1; see also Williams 2005: 1–21). Subsequent reports write less about "linguistic minorities" than "regional and minority *languages*" (Grin and Moring 2002, 2, 51, 53, my emphasis). This is a shift in focus that makes fewer assumptions about speakers, their multilingualism, compact geographic location, origins, autochthony, cohesion, community, and relations to nation-states.

The 2008 "Final Report of the High-Level Group on Multilingualism" diverges strikingly from the previous two documents. It does not deal with minorities or even languages but with "multilingualism." To be sure, that label fits most speakers of "regional and minority languages." But it also includes migrants entering the EU, adults and students traveling within the EU for work and education, the enlargements of 2004 and 2007, global tourism, and the globalization of many jobs, especially in IT (cited in Moore 2010, 1–2). The 2008 report identifies some new linguistic objects of anxiety unimagined in the earlier reports: national standards are perceived to be threatened by the use of English as a *lingua franca* and by what is seen as an overabundance of immigrant languages, some standardized, others not. As Duchêne (2008) has noted, this change in focus decisively separates the current European concern with multilingualism from earlier United Nations discourses on minority languages, and indeed from the problems of minorities in other parts of the world. The EU's situation is certainly novel in this way.[5]

This shift in object is matched by dramatic transitions in the claims these reports make about language. The first follows United Nations documents recognizing "the right of every child to use his or her own mother tongue and the right of communities to develop their own language and culture" (Simone et al. 1986, 32). To this discourse of "rights" is added the rhetoric of languages as "cultural wealth," or "heritage." The second report makes a further distinction, noting its "profound shift in discursive position" (1996, ii):

> [P]revious suggestions have conceived of minority language groups in emotive terms associated with the 'traditional' activities which are the emotional converse of rational "modernity," concerned with the poetic, the literary or the musical, but never [before] with the economic . . . our argument involves the need to develop action [that promotes minority languages] not for the benefit of the various language groups as a European heritage, but for the economic advantage of the entire [European] Community. (Nelde et al. 1996, 60, my ellipsis)

The ideological axis of differentiation we have been discussing is clearly invoked here. Aligning themselves with what they call the neoliberal discourse of "human capital" that triumphed in the 1990s, Nelde et al. emphasize, "Given what is claimed concerning the importance of diversity as one of the advantages which Europe has over competing regions of the world economy . . . [there is a need to] promote minority language groups as sources of diversity that derives from language and culture" (Nelde et al. 1996, 60).

These text segments locate minority languages on the traditional ("pride") pole of an axis of differentiation, implicitly in contrast to national standards at the universal/"profit" pole. Nelde and his colleagues then reapply this contrast *within* the category of the traditional, subdividing the "traditional" into two components, one that is more traditional, the other more "profit" oriented. Linguistic forms are then distributed over this new subdivision. Some aspects of minority languages (as in poetry, literature, music) belong at the traditional pole, but there are other aspects, heretofore unnoticed, that are more economic, more profit oriented. This seems a good example of the discursive shift that Heller and Duchêne (this volume) have described, showing convincingly that it has been evident worldwide in recent decades and precipitated by changes in late capitalism. In a complementary argument, I suggest the form and logic of the shift—as instanced at least in European materials—is the outcome of a somewhat separate semiotic process of differentiation.

The 2008 report seems to take quite a different tack, identifying different objects that seem to threaten a united Europe and that must therefore be managed, in this case through categorization. The 2008 report proposes what seems like an entirely new sociolinguistic regime: multilingualism. As we saw, multilingualism was earlier considered a problem of minorities; it would be solved by their assimilation or by "normativizing" the minority language and extending its use (Nelde et al. 1996, 44). By contrast, multilingualism in the 2008 report is proposed as a sign of Europeanness itself, at the core of the "European idea." In fact, trilingualism is constituted as Europe-in-essence: the ideal is for each speaker to control a *lingua franca*, a mother tongue, plus a freely chosen language of affinity. According to the much repeated and amusing phrase, "Europeans should speak their mother tongue plus two other languages, one for business and one for pleasure."

The goal of generalized multilingualism is novel. Yet, the values assigned to the languages of the ideal multilingual speaker in the slogan are very familiar. They sound a lot like "pride" and "profit." A language of wide communication is placed on the "profit" end of the axis, and contrasted with the emotional weight and particularity of mother tongue. The third language, "for pleasure," is elsewhere in the report called a "personal adoptive language" or a "second mother tongue." Like the mother tongue, it too is supposed to be particular and personal:

> By drawing a clear distinction, when the choice is made, between a language of international communication and a personal adoptive language, [we separate two decisions] one dictated by the needs of the broadest possible communication, and the other guided by a host of personal reasons . . . individual or family background, emotional

ties . . . cultural preferences. . . . open choice. (Final Report p. 11, cited in Moore 2010, 19)

As Moore (2010) observes in his analysis of this report, the ideological underpinnings remain the same as those of monolingual standardization in the nineteenth and twentieth centuries, but the values are differently distributed among linguistic forms. The axis of differentiation that earlier constituted monolingual standards, is now adopted by EU experts to envision and authorize a specific pattern of continent-wide multilingualism. The familiar contrast in values is not viewed within the parameter of the nation-state; it is not signaled by registers of a national standard. The sphere of comparison is Europe-wide: a world of standards in which each is an index of authenticity (as discussed earlier). Such an "upward recursion" of this axis of differentiation invites a category of instrumental, universal, apersonal placelessness to contrast with the authenticity and emplacedness signaled (at this level of contrast) by standard languages. A *lingua franca* points to such a category of value, purportedly only for instrumental business, a language of nowhere and no one in particular. Moore calls this ideological configuration a "standardization of diversity." Hence, we get a sense of both familiarity and newness in the sociolinguistic regime envisioned by the 2008 report.

It is important to emphasize, as Moore (2010) does, that the three types of language and their uses, as outlined in the report, are not descriptions of practices or of functions. Like the intellectuals of earlier centuries, EU experts, under the veil of description, and perhaps unintentionally, are extending and reconstructing an ideological image. Like all ideologies of differentiation, this one produces recursions, as we have seen. It also produces erasures. Thus, English (the most common *lingua franca*) obviously has a plethora of important uses unmentioned in the report—from pick-up bars, to foreign vacations. It indexes not only activities (e.g., business) but also aspects of the speaker's identity (what kind of English? What kind of persons know English? Where have they been and where are they headed socially?). Mother tongues are similarly wide in their uses and the social relations they index. Some groups demand business be done in their mother tongue; commodities labeled in a "personal adoptive language" are likely to be more, not less, profitable. The ideological framework we have been analyzing is not a description of use but operates as a vision or model that highlights some and erases other aspects of sociolinguistic situations. Speakers do not simply replicate them, but rely on them to create novel and situated indexical meanings.

Multilingualism itself is an iconic sign. In the old dispensation it was an image of wavering; it provoked doubts about the speaker's national loyalty. In the new framework it is iconic of flexibility and the "cosmopolitan," comfortable in more than one place:

> Speaking different languages means having both roots and wings, being at home in several cultures at once, being able to see oneself from the outside . . . reveling in linguistic polygamy. . . . Cosmopolitan Europeanization . . . means not just speaking a common language (English) but loving many European national languages. . . . monolingualism by contrast means blinkered vision. (Beck and Grande 2007, 100, my ellipses)

Just as the monolingual standard was ideologically understood as unifying opposed values in the context of the nation-state—via Locke as well as Herder—so noted sociologist Ulrich Beck tries to frame multilingualism as a sign that unifies the particular and the universal: he uses organic metaphors (roots and wings), familial, even passionately sexualized images, that are, however, rationally based in reflexivity and vision, to imagine a utopian relationship among people in a unified Europe.

Yet, if this multilingual sociolinguistic regime is also a form of standardization, then we may ask, what hierarchies are reproduced or created?[6] If the semiotic process of differentiation contributes to making a new ideal type of speaker in Europe, then how does this actually happen, in specific historical cases? How are languages, linguistic varieties and even accents reframed in practice, so they take on different indexical values? I turn to these questions, with the help of ethnographic materials.

ETHNOGRAPHIES OF LINGUISTIC "EUROPEANIZATION"

My evidence so far has come from written texts about language in the rarified realms of pan-European elites. But the "pride"/"profit" axis is very broadly distributed. It has been inculcated as the standard in schooling and in labor markets. Evidence of such language ideologies among people who do not write treatises comes from interviews and casual comments. More subtly, ethnographic observers have described speakers' situated reactions to the linguistic forms they hear and use, inferring from such reactions the values speakers associate with the linguistic differences they recognize. In what follows, I rely on both kinds of evidence in three case studies that show how the valorization of multilingualism that is championed by the EU, under the pressure of late capitalist processes, is experienced, reiterated and resignified. Each of the cases—from Italy, Austria and Hungary—has its own historically specific dynamic, but each displays some aspect of the perspectival, differentiating process I have described.

The first example illustrates how linguistic signs come to index opposition to the EU and its perceived support of global markets. In her recent ethnography, Cavanaugh (2009) describes Bergamasco, the dialect/language of the northern Italian city of Bergamo. Although no longer ubiquitous, it is nevertheless still actively spoken, invariably paired with the Italian national standard. In a familiar pattern, the use of Bergamasco indexed and evoked "sentimental ties to local place and cultural authenticity" (2009, 63). Use of Italian signaled the speaker's education and engagement with the national Italian economy. Cavanaugh notes the range of variation in use: "Italian words with a Bergamasco accent, Bergamasco sentences with Italian words in them, Italian utterances structured around Bergamasco syntax . . . [many] utterances draw on both languages" (Cavanaugh 2009, 29).

By deploying this range of possibilities, self-described Bergamaschi—who distinguished themselves from mere Italians—made further distinctions among themselves, using the same contrast. That is, the category of Bergamaschi could be notionally subdivided—in a fractal move—into subcategories that were themselves distinguished from each other by the Bergamaschi/Italian contrast, if only momentarily. Speakers could adopt the really authentic (but no longer existent) Bergamasco peasant voice; or sound like modern Italians. The range of linguistic variation signaled these contrasts in actual situations, where the relative Italianness of speakers with respect to each other is what shaped the interpretation. National politics had little to do with these contrasts. Individuals and situations were *not* permanently classified this way.

A further iteration ("upward") becomes evident if we consider Bergamasco accents as heard from the perspective of Italy as a whole. The Northern League was active in Bergamo during Cavanaugh's fieldwork. Such right wing associations have been made more effective in part by the political platform offered by the EU. Nevertheless, their anti-EU messages decry global trade, regulation from afar, immigration. Invariably, and predictably, this anti-"profit" message comes wrapped in local "pride" (see Holmes 2000). Most of the champions of Bergamasco in Bergamo did not sympathize with the Northern League. But if the parameter of comparison was a national television show, then a mere whiff of the Bergamo accent, which would hardly count as local in Bergamo, was enough to evoke for Italian listeners from other regions the conviction that the speaker took a right-wing political stance. Within a national frame, the modernity/tradition contrast took on a Europe-wide significance and thus political connotations, extending and partially erasing the older sense of tradition (voice of the peasant) linked to Bergamasco (Cavanaugh 2009, Chapter 6).

The Austrian case is an example of a different kind of resignification, also based on changed perspective and recursions. Many students from the valleys of Carinthia are bilingual speakers of Slovenian and the national standard, Austrian German. Their parents struggled hard to establish bilingual schools, and to gain legal recognition for Slovenian under the monolingual norms of the 1970s. Nevertheless, the children who attended these schools were reluctant to take up the rural, unsophisticated and backward voice that Slovenian continued to signal within Carinthia, further stigmatized by Carinthia's anti-immigrant, anti-minority politics.

When these students went to Vienna to attend university, they felt "freedom" and "openness." In addition to the rich cultural offerings, they faced striking linguistic heterogeneity. Many languages were routinely heard on the street. More importantly, a novel parameter of comparison became available, especially after Slovenia was admitted to the EU and Slovenian was no longer heard only as the language of minorities. Many of their kin who had stayed in Carinthia were still denying their knowledge of Slovene in attempts to assure upward mobility there. But the young people in Vienna could view themselves through a new ideology, one in which Slovenian—even the mountain dialect—no longer indexed backwoods tradition, but instead became the language (often their third after German and the obligatory school English) that made them trilingual and thus truly "cosmopolitan Europeans," as in Beck's utopian vision (Weichselbraun 2011).

My third example considers how the ideal of a trilingual Europe, while ostensibly inclusive and unifying, in practice has stratifying effects, reproducing long-standing east/west disparities. Unlike the erasure and stigmatization of immigrant languages, stateless languages and nonstandard forms, this phenomenon has not been extensively explored. I discuss the circumstances of elite speakers in Hungary in order to show the fine grain of stratification. The speakers I consider are in the highly educated, professional strata of Hungary, those who had hopes of "joining Europe" in 1989. Yet this position seems always just out of reach. When the Hungarian educated elite finally achieved competence in a second language—usually English—and attained the ability to reproduce this skill for their children, two languages were no longer sufficient to "join Europe" in an elite capacity.

A glimpse at the recent past shows why, for aspiring Hungarian elites, the ideal of trilingualism as icon of Europe appears to be a case of raising the bar. In Hungary, the overall population became *more* monolingual in the years of the Cold War than they had been in the nineteenth century and the interwar period. At the start of the twentieth century, as new states emerged from the multilingual Habsburg Empire, they aimed to modernize by reaching for the monolingual norm of the time. They destroyed the social institutions that had maintained multilingualism in previous centuries. In the decades after the Second World War, the western states increasingly taught foreign languages; in the state-socialist east, access to foreign travel, foreign mass media and education were restricted. In Hungary, foreign languages—except Russian—were viewed with official suspicion. Multilingualism was not linked to political power or cultural influence. Economic advantage depended on party connections. Domestic journals and university hierarchies often rejected scholars who published in Western languages. For these, as well as other reasons, the "profit"/"pride" configuration of language ideology was not reproduced in Hungary and much of the east as it was in the west, until the final years of the cold war.

Given this history, it is small wonder that in a recent Eurostat Newsrelease (2009), when speakers aged twenty-five to sixty-four were asked to judge their own language skills, only 29% of Germans said they were monolingual, 35% of Britons, 38% of Italians and 75% of Hungarians. These numbers, of course, both reflect the past and, by their very public presence, re-create the image of Western advantage.

Since the end of the cold war, the "profit"/"pride" distinction has been recuperated in Hungary with enthusiasm, along with capitalist social relations. Two examples of elite Hungarian women—educated before 1989—and their children can suggest how socioeconomic stratification since the cold war has been shaped by requirements of linguistic skill and the recursions of value they index on the "profit"/"pride" axis, in ways not experienced in earlier decades.

Anna is aged forty-five, with a doctorate in chemistry. She now works as regional coordinator for an American pharmaceutical company in Budapest, overseeing drug trials in Hungary and also in other parts of the world. She communicates electronically in English all day, staying in touch with company branches on five continents. She has a ten-year-old son and is planning a temporary transfer to the corporation's main office in the United States, largely for the sake of the child. Consulting with me, she asked when would be the best time for her son to learn English quickly and painlessly. I said even at twelve to fourteen, children learn easily, if with a slight accent. Oh no, she said. She would not deprive the child of a good accent.

Julia is a fifty-year-old sociologist, working for a consulting firm in Budapest, and also for a research institute of the Academy of Sciences. In the firm, she writes applications on behalf of municipalities that seek government funds for development. Her work is entirely in Hungarian. She occasionally writes for English-language journals and sometimes goes to international conferences. On her advice, Julia's twenty-something daughter studied French and English in college, but did not do well on the national language exams. As a last resort, the mother sent her daughter to academic acquaintances in Scotland for more exposure to English.

Because I have been in close contact with Anna and Julia for over twenty years, I know their knowledge of English was hard won. Having studied only Russian in school, they both struggled and paid considerable sums to learn English as adults, in the kind of language schools that now dot the inner cities of most eastern European capitals. Anna's daily usage since then has made her into a fluent if not entirely confident speaker, especially in her firm's corporate style. Yet, she knows she is not eligible for the truly high-paying and prestigious jobs that have opened up in the last two decades in her sphere of work. Despite her skills and experience she has hit a glass ceiling: she cannot aspire to the next rank of European manager in her firm. The most desirable positions go to those with the same professional training, but with a third language. Both women are determined to gain entrée to just such positions for their children.

Despite this similarity, the women are quite differently situated within the domestic economy. Anna was less well placed in the socialist hierarchy in the 1990s, and was willing to take what seemed like a risky step at the time: to work in the distinctly separate world of Western firms starting to operate in eastern Europe. Julia, on the other hand, followed her parents' socialist-era path into academic life. Like academics under socialism, she is employed by the state, and holds two jobs to make ends meet. By contrast, Hungarian salaries in firms such as Anna's, though not as high as in the western branches, are calculated (if not paid) in Euros. In this bifurcated economy, Anna—but not Julia—is part of a stratum that, largely through differential linguistic skills, can consume and travel in ways unimaginable for others in the same country whose responsibilities are otherwise quite similar.

Anna and Julia often characterized their bilingual repertoires in "profit"/"pride" terms. As mother tongue, the special flavor and literary beauty of Hungarian have never been in doubt. There is also a centuries-old adage that Hungarian is not a "world language" (*világnyelv*); "one cannot go far with it." English is the language believed to serve the "broadest possible communication," confirming the common-sense view that it is an instrumental "necessity" for getting a good job. In juxtaposition, the two languages also carry the other contrasts on this axis of differentiation.

Yet Julia and Anna never judged English in exclusively instrumental terms. Rather, the value category that English represents was minutely subdivided: degrees of speakers' modernity, rationality and professional expertise that English indexes in interaction depended on the supposed "quality" of the English spoken. This is reminiscent of "misrecognitions" in monolingual standardization and has been described for other postsocialist contexts (Prendergast 2008). Julia and Anna recursively applied the "pride"/"profit" contrast within the category of the "profit" language. They made very fine distinctions among their acquaintances, judging "accent" especially. This is reflected in their considerable efforts to assure for their children what the mothers imagine to be native English competence. Anna, however fluent, felt humiliated in interactions with her international contacts, painfully attending to the differences between her own English and that of those non-native speakers who had had English instruction in childhood. Each such interaction re-created a hierarchy between speakers with different skills, one that, like the differences between monolingualism, bilingualism and trilingualism—but at a narrower category—all too often reproduced on newly linguistic terms a long-standing hierarchy of west over east.

CONCLUSION

This chapter started with an empirical puzzle about the apparent familiarity of language ideologies promulgated by the EU, despite the great changes in political economy to which the EU is a response and in which it is an active participant. In order to solve that conundrum, this chapter took a detour into the history of "pride"/"profit," as an axis of differentiation that creates contrasting values and posits linguistic forms that index them. The EU's language ideology turned out to consist of reiterations, at a broader compass, of the same value contrasts that had guided the creation of standard languages in nineteenth- and twentieth-century nation-states. A single axis of differentiation underpins both, but the contrasting values are attached to different linguistic practices.

The same mode of analysis proved revealing in understanding ethnographic materials from three European sites. The "pride/profit" axis and its correlates—for example, modernity/tradition, reason/passion—are not limited to the documents and institutions of governments and suprastate organizations. They are part of an old and widespread ideology of differentiation in Europe that has been harnessed to capitalist processes for centuries. It continues to be used politically to proliferate categories of value and forms of personhood linked to linguistic practice. The categories create or reproduce what are understood by speakers to be self-evident hierarchies, as in standardization.

These empirical conclusions lead to a conceptual one. The current phase of capital has important, specific effects. Indeed, the changing and expanding logic of capitalism and its encounters with political forms like nation-states transform all aspects of the social world, including linguistic practices. But these effects are not direct. They are always mediated by language ideologies that formulate and interpret political economic changes in ways that make them relevant to language, or mobilize arguments about language that justify political and economic action. As this volume argues, language ideologies have a logic of their own that requires analytical attention. This chapter further suggests that one kind of language ideology constructs difference and consists of a semiotic process—indexical, iconic and fractal, with erasures—that creates, frames and reiterates cultural contrasts of value. The dramatic and historically specific changes wrought by late capitalism in production, consumption, and management incite and exploit such differentiations and result in their partial transmutations.

NOTES

1. This is not the only axis of differentiation of importance in Europe; other contrasts have been similarly significant and often cross cut the conceptual distinctions discussed here. For instance, the famous perceived opposition between individual and society would certainly complicate the processes discussed here. Other patterns of contrasts not only cross cut but have been in outright conflict with the one examined here in the course of the last two centuries. In the Austro-Hungarian Monarchy, for instance, there were struggles against the instrumental/authentic distinction among elites and the general population in the middle of the nineteenth century (Gal 2011).
2. The quotation marks around "diversity" signal that EU discourses usually use this term to refer to linguistic difference that is officially recognized and

positively valued, such as national standards; other terms are used when the proliferation of linguistic forms is seen as threatening to European unity. Moreover, even when diversity is recognized, nonstandard forms are rarely taken into consideration (see Gal 2006).

3. It is worth remarking that, like Bauman and Briggs, all of the writers I have discussed were not only noticing but also (re)constructing the contrasts and iterations they describe, just as I too am engaging in the same kind of intertextual project.

4. My thanks to Robert Moore for suggesting this felicitous phrase.

5. My thanks to Alexandre Duchêne for clarifying discussion of this issue.

6. As many observers have noted, not all multilingualisms are alike. What Beck and others have in mind carries great prestige; a minority language paired with an eastern European state language or with a stateless, migrant or nonstandardized language does not. This is another form of hierarchization that I have discussed elsewhere (Gal 2006).

REFERENCES

Agnew, Jean-Christophe. 1986. *Worlds Apart: The Market and the Theater in Anglo-American Thought 1550–1750*. New York: Cambridge University Press.

Ahlzweg, Claus. 1994. *Muttersprache-Vaterland: Die deutsche Nation und ihre Sprache*. Opladen: Westdeutscher Verlag.

Anderson, Benedict. 1991 [1983]. *Imagined Communities: Reflections on the Origin and Spread of Nationalism*. London: Verso.

Appleby, Joyce. 1992. *Liberalism and Republicanism in the Historical Imagination*. Cambridge, MA: Harvard University Press.

Bauman, Richard and Charles Briggs. 2003. *Voices of Modernity*. New York: Cambridge University Press.

Beck, Ulrich, and Edgar Grande. 2007. *Cosmopolitan Europe*. Cambridge: Polity.

Berlin, Isaiah. 1997. *Three Critics of the Enlightenment*. Princeton, NJ: Princeton University Press.

Bourdieu, Pierre. 1991. *Language and Symbolic Power*. Cambridge, MA: Harvard University Press.

Cavanaugh, Jillian. 2009. *Living Memory: The Social Aesthetics of Language in a Northern Italian Town*. Chichester, UK: Wiley Blackwell.

Duchêne, Alexandre. 2008. *Ideologies across Nations: The Construction of Linguistic Minorities at the United Nations*. Berlin: Mouton de Gruyter.

Errington, J. Joseph. 1988. *Structure and Style in Javanese*. Philadelphia: Pennsylvania University Press.

Eurostat Newsrelase. 2009. "Among Adult Population 28% Speak at Least Two Foreign Languages." European Language Day of Languages, 24 September 2009. Accessed January 2010. http://ec.europa.eu/eurostat.

Gal, Susan. 2006. "Contradictions of Standard Language in Europe: Implications for the Study of Practices and Publics." *Social Anthropology* 14(2): 163–181.

Gal, Susan. 2011. "Polyglot Nationalism: Alternative Conceptions of Language in 19th Century Hungary." *Langage et Société* 136: 31–53.

Gal, Susan, and Judith T. Irvine. 1995. "The Boundaries of Languages and Disciplines: How Ideologies Construct Difference." *Social Research* 62(4): 966–1001.

Gal, Susan, and Kathryn Woolard. 2001."Introduction." In *Language and Publics: The Making of Authority*, edited by Susan Gal and Kathryn Woolard, 1–12. Manchester: St. Jerome's.

Geertz, Clifford. 1960. *The Religion of Java*. Chicago: Chicago University Press.

Gellner, Ernest. 1983. *Nations and Nationalism*. Ithaca, NY: Cornell University Press.

Grin, François, and Tom Moring. 2002 *Final Report: Support for Minority Languages in Europe*. European Bureau of Lesser Used Languages.

Hirschman, Albert O. 1977. *The Passions and the Interests: Political Arguments for Capitalism Before its Triumph*. Princeton, NJ: Princeton University Press.

Holmes, Douglas. 2000. *Integral Europe: Fast Capitalism, Multiculturalism, Neofascism*. Princeton, NJ: Princeton University Press.

Inoue, Miyako. 2006 "Standardization." In *International Encyclopedia of Languages and Linguistics*, edited by Keith Brown, 121–127. Amsterdam: Elsevier.

Irvine, Judith T. 1990. "Registering Affect: Heteroglossia in the Linguistic Expression of Emotion." In *Language and the Politics of Emotion*, edited by Catherine Lutz and Leila Abu-Lughod, 126–161. Cambridge: Cambridge University Press.

Irvine, Judith T., and Susan Gal. 2000. "Language Ideology and Linguistic Differentiation." In *Regimes of Language*, edited by Paul Kroskrity, 35–84. Santa Fe, NM: School of American Research Press.

McCloskey, Deirdre. 1985. *The Rhetoric of Economics*. Madison: Wisconsin University Press.

Moore, Robert. 2010. "Standardizing Diversity: A Guided Tour of Recent Multilingualism Policy in the European Commission." Unpublished.

Nelde, Peter. 1996. *Euromosaic: The Production and Reproduction of the Minority Language Groups of the EU*. Luxembourg: Office of Official Publications of the European Communities.

Poovey, Mary. 2008. *Genres of the Credit Economy: Mediating Value in 18th and 19th Century Britain*. Chicago: Chicago University Press.

Prendergast, Carole. 2008. *Buying Into English: Language and Investment in the New Capitalist World*. Pittsburgh, PA: University of Pittsburgh Press.

Silverstein, Michael. 1996. "Monoglot Standard in America: Standardization and Metaphors of Linguistic Hegemony." In *The Matrix of Language*, edited by Donald Brenneis and Ronald Macaulay, 284–306. Boulder, CO.: Westview.

Simone, Raffaele, Serena Ambroso, Patrizia Malgarini, and Paola de Sangro. 1986. *Linguistic Minorities in Countries Belonging to the European Community*. Luxembourg: Commission of the European Communities.

Weichselbraun, Anna. 2011. "'People here speak five languages!': The Reindexicalization of Linguistic Minorityhood in Vienna, Austria." Unpublished master's thesis, University of Chicago.

Williams, Glyn. 2005. *Sustaining Language Diversity in Europe: Evidence from the Euromosaic Project*. New York: Palgrave Macmillan.

Woolard, Kathryn. 1998. "Introduction: Language Ideology as a Field of Inquiry." In *Language Ideologies: Theory and Practice*, edited by Bambi Schieffelin, Kathryn Woolard and Paul Kroskrity, 3–50. New York: Oxford University Press.

Woolard, Kathryn. 2008. "Language Identity and Choice in Catalonia: The Interplay of Contrasting Ideologies of Linguistic Authority." In *Lengua, nación e identidad. La regulación del plurilingüismo en Espana y América Latina*, edited by Kirsten Suselbeck, Ulrike Mühlschlegel and Peter Masson, 302–324. Berlin: Ibero-Amerikanisches Institut.

3 Commodification of Pride and Resistance to Profit

Language Practices as Terrain of Struggle in a Swiss Football Stadium

Alfonso Del Percio
and Alexandre Duchêne

INTRODUCTION

In the winter of 2010, Football Club Basel (henceforth FCB), a major football[1] team located in the northern part of German-speaking Switzerland, launched a promotional DVD. This widely distributed film, titled *FCB: Der Film* (FCB: The Movie), is available in major supermarkets, in bookstores and in FCB's stadium shop. It aims to provide FCB fans with insight into what goes on behind the scenes in one of Switzerland's most successful football teams. It is, in reality, an unambiguous marketing product dedicated to a club considered to incarnate—as the DVD proclaims—both a cult and a cultural good ("Der charismatische Verein ist heute Kult und Kulturgut in einem" / The charismatic association is today both cult and cultural good).

The opening section of the DVD displays pictures of local buildings (the Basel Trade Fair Tower, the cathedral, the town hall, a historic bridge), the local surroundings with the river Rhine, as well as local and international personalities. The DVD depicts everyone speaking in their own language and thereby presents the viewers with a wide range of linguistic varieties—from the local dialect to English or Spanish—and confers both a touch of local authenticity and a mark of internationalism on the club. These pictures alternate with images of the St. Jakob-Park, FCB's stadium, the *Muttenzerkurve* (the most prominent stand in the stadium), the fans with their flags and banners, and the team, particularly the most prominent and charismatic players. The soundtrack is composed of songs, testimonies and authentic ambient sounds at the stadium. The main melody of the DVD is a recording of a typical chant ("Fuessball das isch unser Läbe"/ Football is our life), which fans at St. Jakob-Park always sing toward the end of a match and which documents football's as well as fan culture's potential to construct cohesion, community and identity. Testimonies from a former and the current coach, the team captain and a local player are also recorded on the soundtrack. These key spokespersons talk about passion, spirituality and emotions. They talk about ambition, victory and progress, and explain how the FCB has developed into a club that matters in the international world of football. Finally, the soundtrack documents supporters' chants, shouts and slogans, thereby demonstrating what constitutes the stadium's "unique" atmosphere.

This DVD is interesting for a number of reasons. First, its manner of portraying the club's glory involves not only football players in the film, but also local personalities, local hallmarks and local fans. Pride in the football team merges with pride in one's people and place. Second, the inclusion of original songs, local dialect and fan practices conveys a sense of authenticity and uniqueness. Third, although speaking different languages, the actors—fans, organizers, the club, the owner of the stadium—are depicted as a harmonious whole, united under the banner of pride and investment in the players' success. They are constructed as sharing the same interests, as investing in and producing the same discourse, as wholeheartedly subscribing to a collective undertaking. Furthermore, the fans are constructed as a homogeneous group. They are portrayed as a unified community with shared customs, and as an integral and valued part of the sporting event with equal weight to any of the other stakeholders. Finally, the history of the club is described in the DVD as taking the form of linear progress toward internationalization and global recognition, constructed as an advantage for all involved. Overall, this DVD, as one of many other examples highlighted in this chapter, capitalizes on notions such as authenticity, community, progress and shared interests in order to create a commodifiable image that viewers are supposed to be proud of.

Indeed, the DVD offers an idyllic construct of the current football industry and its practices. However, what we observe on the ground is far more complex than the picture it conveys. Tension and strife are present, constantly challenging what constitutes pride and profit, and leading to the central questions approached in this chapter: Who owns pride? Who profits from it? Who decides what pride is made of and for what purposes pride is cultivated? What becomes commodified and why? How is commodification challenged and by whom? Like many other contributors to this book, we argue that language plays a key role in these struggles. It is a marker of local authenticity and expressed by the songs chanted or the slogans shouted by fans during a match. Language is also an object to be commodified by the investors via the appropriation of songs by advertisers. Finally, language practices during a match are an object of regulation by both the organizers, who aim to conform to global commercial standards, and the supporters, who use language as a means to define belonging and exclusion. Language is a terrain that enables struggles over ownership, resources and legitimacy to become visible.

In order to analyze these processes, we focus on a particular setting: the St. Jakob-Park football stadium shown in the DVD. As elsewhere in Europe, the organization of the St. Jakob-Park stadium underwent major changes in the last decade in terms of professionalization, commercialization and internationalization. Due to the club's success in national and international competition, football matches in Basel shifted from being local, anonymous events to translocal and transnational affairs with major economic interests at stake. As demonstrated in this chapter, investors have become principal agents in the football industry, and broadcasting, advertising and investment are today an inherent part of the game. The commercialization of football has also attracted new clients (i.e., new spectators) who attend football matches because of a club's national or international prestige. At the same time, football as an event is still tied to local identity, local place and local history as well as local customs. It is also (sometimes unofficially) related to organizations like fan clubs that act as the guardians of tradition and pride. It is this complex dialectic between a globalized supralocal commercial logic, a newly emerging clientele, and the presence of an old fan base with strong loyalty to local identities and practices that we explore, examining why and how *pride* and *profit* co-occur, intersect and clash, and what particular role language plays in these processes.

The chapter starts with a discussion of the intersection between sociolinguistics and the sociology of sport, followed by a description of the history of the St. Jakob-Park stadium, its organization and management, and the fan organizations. We then analyze three major areas of tension in the FCB and the stadium. We first examine the ways language is regimented by economic actors and, in particular, by Basel United AG, the company in charge of the stadium's management, and we explore how these measures of regimentation are contested and subverted by the local fans. Second, we provide an analysis of how fans appropriate local songs and transform them into soccer chants, while investors attempt to capitalize on these practices. Finally, we highlight the way tension between discourses of pride and manifestations of profit results in struggles over legitimate fan culture.

LANGUAGE, SPORTS AND FOOTBALL IN A CHANGING WORLD

Social scientists (Appadurai 1996; Bröckling, Krasmann and Lemke 2010; Harvey 2005; Lemke 2007) have made us aware that key political, economic and social transformations in late capitalism (such as the liberalization of national markets, the globalization of space, the shift from primary and secondary sectors to a service industry, the increased circulation of people, goods and information, the emergence of new technologies) have intensely challenged fundamental ideologies inherited from modernity, albeit without erasing them. Fixity, standardization and identity coexist nowadays with flexibility, variability and hybridity. The nation-state as a regulating actor coexists with international organizations and within a global economy. These concurrent phenomena rely on a complex dialectic between pride and profit (see Heller and Duchêne, this volume).

These processes have been analyzed in the literature in relation to a number of terrains and forms of identity. Here, we focus in particular on language and sport. In the past decade, sociolinguists have given particular attention to the impact social and economic transformation has on language ideologies and language practices in various terrains. One set of research focuses on the roles language plays in the new globalized economy. Far from being prohibited or seen as an obstacle to the productivity, as was typical of the "old" economy (Boutet 2001), it is the primary working tool and the primary material of business (Boutet 2008; Cameron 2001; Duchêne and Heller in press b; Gee, Hull and Lankshear 1996; Heller 2003, 2010; Heller and Boutet 2006). Communication skills as well as multilingualism become important as management strategies for accessing specific markets. The global market is, in fact, a multilingual market. Transnational networks in which, it turns out, localization (i.e., adaptation of global strategies to local market conditions) is central for successful globalization, cannot function without some form of linguistic diversity. Similarly, in terms of both local and international varieties, language is a marketing strategy and a selling argument in advertising (Kelly-Holmes 2006; Piller 2001). It can lend either an international touch to a product by, for instance, using the lingua franca of English, or a local air by employing regional linguistic varieties. Niche marketing capitalizes on local linguistic features in order to create distinction and authenticity for consumers of cultural goods who seek the unique and exotic (Coupland, Garrett and Bishop 2005). In sum, language becomes both an instrument for internationalization and a product in itself that can be commodified.

Sociolinguists have also explored how practices that construct identity deal with new forms of circulation and regulation of goods, people and discourses. If nation-states have historically been associated with legitimizing discourses that link language, culture, identity and citizenship (Bauman and Briggs 2003), the current forms used to globally expand these markets, and the neoliberal forms of (de-)regulation that characterize them, call the discursive regime of nationalism into question. From a strict marker of national identity and community, language is increasingly evaluated in regard to global interests and new market conditions, thereby revealing tensions about speaker legitimacy and linguistic legacies (Heller 2011) for the nation-state and for its linguistic minorities (Urla, this volume).

These social and economic transformations of language and speakers have obliged sociolinguistics to venture—in addition to more classical sites like schools, bureaucratic institutions and courtrooms—into a different, less-explored terrain where the commodification of language and the new forms of regulating language operate. Tourism (Duchêne and Piller 2011; Heller 2011; Jaworski and Pritchard 2005; Pujolar and Jones, this volume), the globalized new economy workplace (Cameron 2000; Dubois, LeBlanc and Beaudin 2006; Duchêne 2009, 2011; Duchêne and Heller in press a; Gee, Hull and Lankshear 1996; Heller 2003; 2010; Roy

2003), pop culture (Pennycook 2009), artistic productions (McLaughlin 2010), and many others have become fruitful venues for capturing the complex changes we are experiencing.

Interestingly enough, despite the diversity of settings in which those processes have been explored, little to no work has been done on the sport industry in general or football in particular. The following passages highlight some of the reasons why we believe this setting constitutes an interesting and relevant addition to critical work done in the field of sociolinguistics.

The world of sports can be considered as the predominant venue for national and local identity to be formed and enacted (Bairner 2001). As Kellas states, "[T]he most popular forms of nationalist behaviour in many countries is in sport, where masses of people become highly emotional in support of their national team" (1991, 21). This is particularly true for football, which has been historically constructed as the national sport of most European countries. It is a sport that is also closely connected to local identity; players and supporters of different local teams compete with each other within a national territory under the banner of a city or a region. National and local successes are major components of pride. Football as an event provides a distinct opportunity for passionate expression of national and local identity (Bairner 2001; Henry, Amara and Al Tauqi 2003).

Fans and fan organizations play a key role in this process by establishing pronounced cultural, yet locally variable practices that make the fans part of the actual game and a constitutive element of the uniqueness and authentic experience of a football match. The songs, slogans, banners and other practices also present the fans as locally and territorially anchored members of a community that is characterized by a strong commitment to, and engagement and pride in a national or local team—as well as in fandom itself.

Sports teams, however, have increasingly developed from local and national organizational structures to regional, supra-regional and global forms of governance. International organizations, created initially to unite national sport federations under one umbrella (Holt 2009), have become progressively predominant in the processes of internationalization, professionalization and commercialization of sports, and have emerged as the sport industry's most authoritative actors. In the football industry, UEFA (European Union Football Association) as well as FIFA (Fédération internationale de Football Association) became central actors not only on the international level but also on a local and national one (King 2003). They have set global standards that each member of the organization and each club must respect, and they have decreed common and universal values for football to uphold (Holt 2009).

This globally focused governance has been instrumental in the commercialization of sports and has thus given rise to a managerial approach within an enterprise culture (Conn 1997). The growing importance of the football industry's brainchildren, the European and World Championships, has indeed attracted massive economic investors of all kinds, who in due course have become key players in the structuration of the football industry and the international organizations (Holt 2009). Capitalist logic has in many ways supplanted the power of nations within those organizations, as Sudgen (2002) emphasizes with regard to FIFA: "[The] nation-state is being overridden by a network of international financial interests enmeshed through global communication networks." Indeed, sports events and athletes have become the backbone for advertising campaigns wherever marketers see an opportunity to promote a particular brand (Chanavat and Bodet 2009; Couvelaere and Richelieu 2005). The increased commercialization of sport in general and its heavy mediatization mainly through TV—which has taken on an international character due to satellites and digital technology (Holt 2009)—construct sports as a form of entertainment and a product that is destined to be sold. As Slack (1998) states,

> Athletes in the major spectators sports are marketable commodities, sport teams are traded on the stock market, sponsorship rights at major events can cost millions of dollars, network television stations pay large fees to broadcast games, and the merchandising and licensing of sporting goods is a major multinational business.

In fact, sports, along with many other cultural activities nowadays, have become a good, a commodity, conditioned by an economic market that defines its value both in symbolic and material terms. This market-driven commodification of sports does not simply transform the game of football as an international sport; it also affects the way local clubs react in the face of imposed global governance and standards, and in terms of competition—and not only competition on the field, but also competition in the economy. Furthermore, as Howe (1999) argues, the commercialization and professionalization of sports have had an impact on the ways in which players are trained, treated and traded (for specific discussion of football players as commodities in a global football market, see Campbell 2011; Poli 2010), and on the relationship between football clubs and fan organizations (Morrow 2003). O'Brien and Slack (1999) go in a similar direction by showing that supporters, instead of being spectators who participate in the game, are evolving into consumers of a product; in return, they expect the players, the club and, more generally, the football industry to deliver what they, supporters as consumers, expect.

As we have seen, sports in general and football in particular are a major locus for national and local pride to be expressed and enacted. At the same time, these industries have dramatically changed, becoming global, professional and profit oriented. But pride and profit do not operate separately; they are intertwined in a complex dialectic. The commercialization of sports also includes the commodification of what constitutes the particularity of a football team. Local songs, T-shirts or other souvenirs, and symbols of a local or a national team are aggressively promoted far beyond the boundaries of a region or a nation, often with the support of international brands (Hare 1999). As such, pride in nation and place is not only the property of an area or its legitimate inhabitants; it can also be consumed as a product on a global scale.

Furthermore, the existence of global actors, international regulations and economic transnational investment does not imply a strict homogenization of practices that can be seen all over the globe and shared by all sports, all supporters and all players. To the contrary, the football industry also capitalizes on variability, on what differentiates one team from another, one football stadium from another—in sum, what makes them unique and notable.

Nonetheless, even if pride can be transformed into profit, commercialization is not simply accepted by the masses. Of course, local supporters react differently depending on local conditions (Dubal 2010), but commercialization and international regulations do not go unnoticed or remain uncontested. Fans often consider the local practices they create to be their own property, and those who regard themselves as the legitimate proprietors of authentic pride and as a major feature of what defines their "community" generally interpret the commodification of pride as a serious corruption of their customs. Similarly, the regulations imposed on supporters' behavior by global governance (Brown 1998; Dubal 2010; Nash 2010; Scalia 2009), as well as the fans' strong national identification and emotional investment in a team, set the stage for a long-term struggle between commodifiable discourses and practices in football that construct the sport as a setting for global friendship, security, fraternity, universalism and the (re)production of national feelings and locally-shared fan culture (Batuman 2011; Lee and Maguire 2010; Segrave 2000).

As much as sociolinguists have somewhat ignored sport as a setting for research, sociologists of sport have also rarely drawn particular attention to language as a constitutive manifestation of local identity or as an object of commodification in the football industry. We believe, however, that language plays a central role in creating a football club as a product, and in their supporters' identification with that local-national product. The importance of language as a marker of authenticity renders it particularly salient as a commodifiable resource. Finally, we believe that language plays a central role in regimenting the practices and behavior of viewers at a match in order to ensure international conformity and to realize commercial aims. In sum, we hold that particular attention to language within the football industry, and more precisely within a football stadium, should engender a more detailed understanding of the complex ways in which social and economic changes occur, are regimented and resisted.

Similarly, we also believe that sports in general and football in particular constitute a fruitful terrain for sociolinguists. As an industry that is both closely linked to local-national histories and political concerns and clearly oriented toward internationalization and commercialization, football and other sports offer an alternative setting in which to examine how language continues to operate as an instrument of distinction and community in late capitalism. It also engenders further questions as to the ownership of language, the legitimacy of speakers and the role of language in resistance to unequal relations of power. More generally, it is a terrain where we can question how pride is constructed through discursive practices that are simultaneously utilized as commodities to generate profit.

We address these issues by focusing on traditions and practices that can be observed in a football stadium. A stadium as a place of business is established on neoliberal managerial logic and created for commercial purposes; it relies on economic investors and adopts international standards for its business model. A stadium is also a space dedicated to pride. The building, the location and the structure of football stadiums bear witness to the value placed on the heroes (the players, the team) and the location (a city or a region). Furthermore, a stadium encompasses a variety of actors (owners, investors, politicians, players, football clubs, fan associations, supporters) who have both common and diverging interests. A stadium is, moreover, made for "the people," for those who have an emotional share in the success and failure of the thing that conveys the identity of the place. Finally, it is a place where authenticity is produced, belonging is expressed and where local ideologies intersect with international commercial interests.

Our analysis is based on an ethnography, conducted between 2007 and 2011, of Switzerland's largest stadium, St. Jakob-Park (locally called *Joggeli*), located on the periphery of Basel. Our data include observations of the main fan section, including fans' practices and location in the stadium; recordings of chants; forum postings; informal discussions with fans, security officials and stadium employees; institutional documents (reports, regimentations and rules, advertisements); websites of the main actors; and fan magazines and newspaper articles. Through a careful examination of practices and discourses observed in and on the topic of a stadium, we aim to better understand the ways in which pride and profit intersect at a particular place at a particular time, and how the convergence of disparate interests are constructed by particular actors for particular reasons.

THE FOOTBALL STADIUM:
HISTORY, STRUCTURE AND ACTORS

At the end of the 1990s, FIFA enacted security and infrastructure norms and regulations for stadiums that host international matches. The old *Joggeli*'s suitability to host international competitions was questioned, and more and more fans and investors began insisting that the building required modernization. A first estimate showed that renovating the old building would be extremely expensive, and several local actors opted to invest in a new football stadium. In 1997, the project obtained its building license, and the investors scored a coup by contracting Basel's star architects, Herzog & de Meuron, to design the stadium. In 1999, when construction officially started, the cooperative that managed the old *Joggeli* stadium was dissolved, and an incorporated company, Basel United AG, was founded to manage the new stadium. The investors and Basel United AG actively involved the local population and authorities during the entire planning and construction phase, and were thereby successful in creating an atmosphere of loyalty, enthusiasm and pride in the new stadium. In 2001, the first match was played to a sold-out crowd.

The building was envisaged as a temple of commerce and consumption, with sporting events being only one part of the stadium's economic activity. The stadium also comprises a shopping center with fifty shops, office spaces, apartments, exhibition rooms, several restaurants, a gym, a nursing home, and other business establishments. The whole complex is managed by the service provider Basel United AG, which manages not only the stadium and its functional spaces such as the shopping center at St. Jakob-Park, but also the local ice hockey arena (St. Jakob-Arena), the local vintage car museum (Pantheon Basel) as well as Basel's hippodrome (Reitsport-Areal Schänzli). Basel United AG is also responsible for security inside and around the building, and is consequently the first point of contact for local authorities and other actors for questions concerning public safety and related needs. The enterprise also negotiates with economic actors who want to invest in the stadium's space: Basel United AG rents the spaces, closes advertising and sponsoring contracts, and organizes the stadium's catering. They also create the Stadium Rules and regulate the sporting events via the stadium public address-announcer, security services and various visual and audio aids.

Although the stadium hosts other events such as concerts, musicals and other performances alongside football matches, it was built in conformity to interests, norms and standards imposed by actors from the football industry. Its foremost objective was to give the most prestigious local club of the city, FCB, a new home stadium.

FCB is, however, only the main tenant of the stadium, and bears no responsibility for the stadium's organization and management. Thus, they also have no rights to Basel United AG's profits. Nevertheless, the relations between Basel United AG and FCB are far more complex than a simple tenant–landlord relationship. Despite the fact that the club is not directly involved in the marketing of the stadium spaces, it is its visibility as the top Swiss football team and a regular participant in European competitions that attracts investors. And while the club may not be responsible for security within the stadium, it shares with Basel United AG accountability for damage caused by its fans in and around the St. Jakob-Park stadium. As a consequence, both enterprises—Basel United AG and its main tenant, FCB—are so closely linked and codependent that the public often confuses them, believing them to be the same organization instead of two completely separate organizations with different investors.

The stadium is divided into five spectator sections; officially, these are designated by the letters A, B, C, D, G (see Figure 3.1). However, fans decline to use these letters, regarding them as too anonymous, and they choose to retain the more traditional and authentic names (A = Tribüni; B = Gellert; C = Bahndamm; D = Muttenzerkurve; G = Gallerie), which are all holdovers from the old *Joggeli*.

In this chapter, we have decided to focus on the *Muttenzerkurve* (section D) for two reasons. First, it is THE place for fans to go. This section seats 4,000 fans who are generally organized according to fan organizations. FCB counts several fan clubs that compete with each other and constantly fight for dominance over the *Muttenzerkurve*. Every organization represents a specific type of fan culture, that is, every group stands for a version of the ideal role that fans in this particular part of the stadium should play, how they should act, sing and support the players, what language they should use, and whose direction they should follow. The second reason for the *Muttenzerkurve*'s particular relevance for our study is that it underwent key transformations in the last few years. The move to the new stadium in 2001 and a power vacuum caused by the aging of former leaders in local

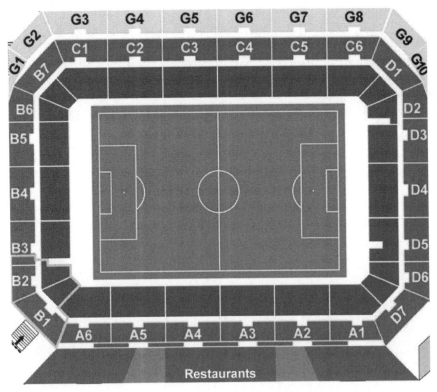

Figure 3.1 Map of the St. Jakob Park stadium. Source: http://www.baselunited.ch/images/pdf/stadionschema.pdf (Accessed March 3, 2011).

fan culture resulted in a shift in dominance over the stand and, as a consequence, a shift in fan culture. The following excerpt of an interview of a supporter published in *Muttenzerkurve*'s fan magazine, *Schreyhals* (which means "yeller" in English), depicts this shift.

Original Text (German)
Wir Alten trafen uns meistens gleich beim Bierstand, während die Jungen sich in der Kurve breit machten und sich dort zu entwickeln begangen. Ich denke, am Anfang ist das uns kaum noch aufgefallen. Das kam dann erst mit dem Umzug ins neue Joggeli. Die Doppelhalter und das Megafon mussten bei uns Alten einen harten Kampf austragen. Ich persönlich hatte eigentlich nichts gegen die neue „Ultra-Generation". Ich war und bin immer noch relativ deutschlandorientert, dass man jetzt plötzlich nach Italien blickte war für mich einfach ein neuer Trend. Doch Viele hatten daran nicht sonderlich Freude. Bei einigen Alten holten sich die Jungen aber dennoch Pluspunkte: Einerseits brachten sie die Pyromanie wieder zurück und andererseits durch die Choreographien: Damit können die Leute an etwas teilhaben, was einfach geil aussah. Die Jungen mussten für ihre Sache kämpfen und heute kann man sagen, dass sie sich durchgesetzt haben. (Schreyhals 15, 2008)

Translation
Us older fans, we usually met at the beer stand, while the younger ones took possession of the *Muttenzerkurve* and started to evolve. I think, at the beginning, these changes hardly caught our attention. We only realized what happened after the move to the new *Joggeli* [the new stadium.] Their banners and megaphone had to put up a tough fight. I for one, I had nothing against this new «*ultra*-generation.» I did and still do look to Germany for inspiration; that people turned to Italy was simply a new trend to me. But lots of people didn't like these changes. Nevertheless, the younger ones managed to win the respect of some older fans. On the one hand, they brought back flares, and, on the other, the choreographies. This gave people the chance to participate in something that was just plain cool. The younger fans fought hard for their cause, and today you have to say they won.

As this supporter explains, the major power shift was caused by ideology and how well fans were organized. Fan organizations differentiate themselves in terms of ideology or culture, which is usually characterized in national terms: German fan culture, Italian fan culture, English fan culture. These categories refer originally to the nations in which these practices were first introduced, but the typical characteristics have since been taken up in various part of Europe; Slovenian fans can, for instance, have an Italian fan culture. More importantly, however, the categories refer to clear differences in the way supporters feel they should behave at a match. In Basel, the German fan tradition had long been predominant due to

Germany's geographic proximity and the fact that television broadcasting (an important aspect of socialization and initiation into fan culture) in this region traditionally showed German football games. The German tradition is characterized by spontaneous, unorganized, and individual rather than collective fan practices. At the start of the new millennium, however, a new generation of young men from Italian migrant families introduced an Italian fan culture as an alternative to the old one. Also called *ultra*, meaning extreme, this fan culture is characterized by its explicit call for an extremely passionate, emotional, authentic and committed relationship to the supported team. In order to establish this degree of dedication, the *ultra* culture cannot rely on spontaneity; instead, it is rigorously planned, organized and regimented by fan associations.

As in Italian cities with major fan organizations such as Naples, Rome, Milan or Turin, the *Infernos*, the FCB fan organization that has adopted an *ultra* culture, argue that songs must be chanted in the local dialect, must pay tribute to symbols and places in Basel, and must glorify local players or heroes. ("German" fan culture has no explicit discourse about linguistic form, and, not surprisingly, it tends to use standard German.) Concretely, the *Infernos* advocate well-organized acoustic support (songs, drums, megaphones) and visual accoutrements (flags, confetti, flares, choreography) as well as the upholding of a pure and authentic fan culture that draws on the economically uncorrupted and total devotion of fan to football team and its locally anchored traditions and history. Furthermore, in contrast to the German fan culture, which is more spontaneous and does not imply collective behavior, the *ultra* fan culture involves collective chants and other oral practices orchestrated by a few actors called *capos*[2] who conduct and control the whole *Muttenzerkurve* with megaphones. In the *Muttenzerkurve*, there are three *capos* delegated by the fan group in power, currently the *Infernos*. From the bottom of the stand, the *capos* also coordinate visual effects such as flying flags, Bengal lights, and the choreographies. They also invent, write and develop songs and chants to be sung or shouted during the match. The *Infernos* have been in power since the late 1990s, when they successfully imposed their fan practices in the *Muttenzerkurve* and are now the legitimate representatives of the fans for FCB, for Basel United AG, as well as for the press and the local authorities.

In the next three sections, we highlight the ways in which specific practices are linked to economic transformations emerging within the football industry. More precisely, we explore the impact of the football industry's commercialization by analyzing (1) the forms taken by control over practices when a football match is constructed as a commercial event, as well as the forms taken by fan resistance to this regimentation; (2) the commodification of authentic linguistic practices (i.e., songs) and the reaction of fans to this commercial instrumentalization of their products; and (3) the struggle to define the legitimate fan.

REGIMENTED PRACTICES AND CONTESTED
PRACTICES: COMMERCIAL CORRECTNESS
AND CELEBRATION OF AUTHENTICITY

In May 2006, on the last day of the season for the "Super League" (Swiss football's top league), and after the final whistle of the match between FCB and FC Zurich, several hundred fans from the *Muttenzerkurve* stormed the field at St. Jakob-Park and attacked the visiting club's players. These riots resulted in property damage and were considered to be the worst hooligan riots in Switzerland ("schlimmsten Hooligan Krawalle der Schweiz" / the most terrible hooligan riots of Switzerland) by the national and international press (http://www.swissinfo.ch).

The considerable amount of damage to infrastructure and people caused by the incident, along with worries over the deterioration of Swiss football's reputation and fears on the part of commercial investors led the local authorities to set up a task force composed of members of the local government, the police, representatives of FCB, Basel United AG and the Swiss Football League. The explicit aim of this task force was to propose measures to prevent a repetition of violence of this kind and to transform the local fan culture into a safe and positive one ("Massnahmenkatalog für sichere Fussballspiele 2006" / Catalogue of measures for secure football games 2006).

For the local authorities (police and local government), the principal interest in these measures was to create conditions to ensure public safety and to minimize public security costs. The concerns on the part of FCB, Basel United AG and the Swiss Football League were also related to commercial aspects, but with entirely different motivations. The violence endangered the image of the club and the entire Swiss football industry and it was feared that potential investors would withdraw their economic support. Other economic actors, such as catering firms and betting companies, the sports equipment industry and the financial industry, who all used the stadium as a commercial and a marketing platform, were hesitant to be associated with an event that received negative media attention. So, whereas the representatives of the local government held that the football matches and, particularly, the fans and their culture had to be regulated in order to reduce security costs and ensure safety, the football industry saw regulations as necessary for generating profit and laying the groundwork for successful commercial events.

The task force came up with measures for safe football games and a constructive fan culture in *Joggeli* ("Massnahmenkatalog für sichere Fussballspiele und eine positive Fankultur im Joggeli"/ Catalogue of measures for secure football games 2006). This document envisages a series of regulatory measures and, among other things, led to the adaption of the *Stadium Rules of St. Jakob-Park*. The following passages demonstrate how this document regulates practices within the stadium and how it creates the conditions for a commercially profitable event.

The Stadium Rules are available in electronic form in four languages (German, French, Italian and English) on the websites of FCB and Basel United AG, and they are posted on the walls of the stadium. In its heading, the text features both the logos of Basel United AG and St. Jakob-Park. It is signed by the head of Basel United AG as well as by a representative of the stadium's owner. The document is divided into ten sections (1. General, 2. Application Area, 3. Authorized Group of Person, 4. Access check, 5. Behavior in the stadium, 6. Prohibited items and behavior, 7. Flags, 8. Punishment of violations, 9. Sound and image recordings, and 10. Final provisions; their translation). Observing these rules is compulsory for every fan, as the "general terms and conditions" of Basel United AG equate buying a ticket for a match with tacit acceptance of the Stadium Rules.

1. General
The basis and right to enforcement of the Stadium Rules of St. Jakob-Park Basel are founded in the domiciliary right and in private as well as public law regulations. The Rules are also based on the guidelines and provisions of the SFL and follow FIFA, UEFA and SFV regulations.

Article 1 contextualizes the Stadium Rules in a national and international legal and football industry discourse. Furthermore, the explicit reference to legal texts and the mention of the directives and clauses of associations representing the football industry—the Swiss Football League (SFL), the Union of European Football Associations (UEFA) and the Fédération Internationale de Football Association (FIFA)—effectively relieves Basel United AG from the undesirable role of author of the regulations. After all, the restrictions on personal freedom and the degree of responsibility laid out by the Stadium Rules are the same ones prescribed by the prevailing legal texts and institutions. On the other hand, the explicit reference to these institutions of power lends the Stadium Rules augmented authority and legitimacy. Finally, although the legal texts aim to ensure common welfare and safety independent of any commercial goal, the directives and clauses of the SFL, UEFA and FIFA are in fact imposed by the football industry.[3] In other words, while the document ensures safety within the stadium, it simultaneously allows the service provider Basel United AG to create the conditions necessary for football matches to be successful commercial events.

Articles 6 and 7 are particularly interesting for our purpose because they list prohibited items and behavior. In this respect, language which is "racist, anti-foreigner, radical, sexist or political paroles and emblems," as well as its medium ("megaphones and banners etc. with slogans which are damaging to personality and large-sized banners or propaganda banners, as well as larger quantities of paper"), are construed to be potentially dangerous. They are compared to objects like "weapons or items resembling weapons (guns, knives, knuckle dusters, baseball bats etc.)" or "gas spray cans, pepper spray, caustic or colouring substances, pressure containers with health damaging gases." Consequently, and in order to transform language into a safe element, Basel United AG must maintain control over the flags, banners, flyers, and so on, as well as the texts printed on these media; it determines what can or cannot be said (and done) at St. Jakob-Park. The same holds for the megaphone, which plays a central role in *ultra* fan culture.

These regimentations demonstrate how the Stadium Rules collectively target football fans and index their behavior. Even if the rules officially apply equally to all people attending an event at the stadium, be it for a concert, musical or a football match, the actual object of regulation is clearly the *Muttenzerkurve* in St. Jakob-Park. Therefore, the text can be considered as an instrument to maintain, protect and, above all, control football fan behavior, make it safe and hygienic (in Cameron's sense 1995), and create the conditions for politically and economically acceptable commercial events.

From the perspective of the fan organizations (in particular the *Infernos*), these measures represent an interference in a domain—the management of discursive practices within the *Muttenzerkurve*—that fans normally command and that should be kept clear of the stadium organizers' influence. Consequently, the Stadium Rules, and more specifically the police and the private security officials enforcing the document, are perceived as a challenge to the existing status quo and a danger to the actors who currently wield power. To demonstrate this attitude, members of the *Infernos* or other organized fan groups regularly cover the Stadium Rules posted on the columns and walls of the *Muttenzerkurve* with flyers, stickers, tags or posters. Many examples of fans' contesting the rules and their intended effect through songs and chants can be observed during the matches. The following song from the *Muttenzerkurve* provides a good example:

Capo (leader):
[turning his back to the field, he uses his megaphone to instruct the fans standing in front of him]:
He, hütte hetts sicher e huffe funktionäre / (hey, there are many officials here today)
[pointing at section A (Tribüni) where VIPs and officials usually sit]
die miend das vrstoh, schluss mit kommärz und scheiss restriktione, die loose zwar worschienlich jetzt nid zue, aber trotzdäm, alli zämme / (they have to understand, no more commercialization and damned restrictions, they are probably not listening to us right now, but anyway, all together)
[putting his hand forward]
Fahne, fackle / (flags, Bengal lights)

Capo assistants
[strewn all over the stand and mustering the entire Muttenzerkurve's attention to the capo's (leader) invocations]
Muttenzerkurve fans
[the fans raising their arms]:

> fahne fackle und no meh / (flags, Bengal lights and much more)
> das wän mir im stadion gseh / (are what we want to see in the stadium)
> schluss mit buesse und vrbot / (no more fines or bans)
> das versaut nur unsere sport / (that messes up our sport)
> wäg vo kommerz und repressione / (no more commerce and repression)
> das wo zellt sind emotione / (emotions are what counts)

This song (which rhymes in Basel German) contrasts opposing conceptions of fan culture: one kind is based on "fahne fackle und no meh" (flags, Bengal lights and much more) as well as on "emotione" (emotions), representing the Infernos' understanding of fan culture; the other draws on "kommerz, repressione, buesse" (commerce, repression, fines) and "vrbot" (interdictions), referring to the Stadium Rules. The fans accuse the officials of being responsible for both the introduction of the Stadium Rules and the commercialization of fan cultures in Europe and all over the world. Moreover, in this passage, the *capo* (leader) benefits from their presence in the stadium to better contrast the corrupted representatives of commercialization of football to traditional and authentic fan culture. This example shows how songs are employed to contest regimentation, but also reveals the economic discourses represented by the officials, which are believed to be one of the interests underlying the regimentation itself.

THE APPROPRIATION OF TRADITIONAL SONGS: PRIDE IN BELONGING AND CAPITALIZING ON AUTHENTICITY

If songs (like other semiotic practices) are the object of regimentation and if, conversely, they can be used to contest authority, they also have a central function within a fan organization itself. As mentioned in the introductory section, songs are distinct practices closely associated with local identity and a particular fan organization; indeed, they are an expression of devotion to the supported football club. The fans actually sing uninterruptedly for ninety minutes, the entire duration of a game. An ideology of language as a medium for motivation and power emerges from behind this practice. Through their chants, fans want to propel their team to victory. Numerous chants evoke the figure of the "zwölfti maa," the twelfth man. For the fans, chanting and supporting the team transforms them into the twelfth man on the field (in football, every team has eleven players). Thus, the voice of every fan contributes to an FCB victory, and, as a matter of pride, every good fan should be hoarse after a match. In addition, contrary to approaches in other fan cultures, the *Infernos* construct their songs as a way to enact authenticity. They argue for a distinct repertoire of songs that does not draw on an ensemble of chants common to fans all over the world and sung in all stadiums. Authenticity here means that the songs must be in *Baseldütsch*, that they are written by the *Infernos* themselves, and that they draw on local myths and histories. Sometimes the melodies are adopted from another local song; sometimes they are composed by the fans.

If songs are so important within the fan organizations, they also become an object of commercial interest for local brands that recognize the economic potential of this traditional emblematic semiotic feature. The following section highlights the tension between the ways in which fans appropriate and adapt local songs within their fan culture, and the ensuing appropriation and capitalization of these chants by businesses. In doing so, we focus on a specific song that has evolved into an object of discord: the club's anthem, a song that was initially adapted by FCB supporters and progressively appropriated by the stadium's organizers and commercial investors.

According to *Inferno* lore, at the beginning of the new millennium, three fans decided to appropriate the song that is considered to be the city of Basel's traditional anthem, and to transform it into an FCB hymn with the following text:

> *Original song (Swiss German—Baseldütsch)*
> z basel am mym ryy
> jo dert mecht y syy
> wäit nit d luft so mild und lau
> und der himmel isch so blau
> z basel, z basel
> z basel am mym ryy
> z basel, z basel
> z basel am mym ryy
>
> rotblau isch hütt d farb
> spiile uff ganz stargg
> renne züri d'buude-n-y
> schiesse d gool zum näggschte siig
> rotblau, rotblau,
> rotblau isch hüt d farb
> rotblau, rotblau,
> rotblau isch hüt d farb
>
> dr gegner isch grad gschoggt
> wenn's ganze joggeli roggt

s'wärde d'bei ganz lahm und schwer
dr FCB gwünnt eimol mehr

super basel, super FCB
super basel,super FCB

Translation
Basel on my Rhine,
yes it is the place I want to be
isn't the air mild and warm
and the sky so blue
in Basel in Basel
in Basel on my Rhine
in Basel in Basel
in Basel on my Rhine

red-blue are today's colors
let's play great
let's charge into Zurich's goal
let's score another victory
red-blue red-blue
red-blue are today's colors
red-blue red-blue
red-blue are today's colors

the opponent is instantly shocked
when the whole joggeli rocks
their legs become heavy and lame
FCB wins another game

super Basel, super FCB
super Basel, super FCB

This song is a reformulation and adaptation of the original text,[4] written by a local poet, Johann Peter Hebel (1819–1885). It was conceived as a regional anthem to be sung during local official and military festivities, and every schoolchild in Basel can sing it. Whereas the *Infernos'* adaptation exactly repeats the first verse praising the city's landmarks, the Rhine, the mild climate and the blue sky, the second and third verses are completely rewritten. Only the melody, the meter, the rhymes and the structure of the text (with the repetition of the last verse) remain as in the original. Furthermore, in the *Infernos'* adaptation, there is a tendency to formulate the text in an archaic variety of the local dialect, Baseldütsch. The high number of "y's" as well as the use of "gg" mirrors the variety of Baseldütsch traditionally spoken by the local bourgeoisie. The original text, however, wasn't written in Baseldütsch, but in Alemannisch, a German dialect, and has another orthography than the one used by the *Infernos*. Thus, the *Infernos* interpret the original text as more local than it effectively is, and construct the hymn as an embodiment of local authenticity.

As happened with the chant "You never walk alone" for Arsenal London, or "Forza Napoli" for the Calcio Napoli, over the course of the past decade, *s'Basler Lied* (Basel's song) became a distinctive mark of the FCB. At the beginning of every FCB match, fans in the *Muttenzerkurve* (and some other stands as well) sing their anthem as a ritual or a collective performance. The stadium management and Basel United AG quickly grasped the importance of the song for the fans as well as its commercial potential.

One day, in summer 2007, before the opening whistle of a match, and while the fans prepared to sing *s'Basler Lied* by raising their FCB scarves in the air, the song began to play over the loud speakers. For the first time, *s'Basler Lied* became an object of debate. The fans in the *Muttenzerkurve* resented the fact that actors from outside the stadium had commandeered their anthem, thereby imposing a foreign quality on their property.

A few months later, the dispute escalated. In autumn 2007, a local producer of cookies (*Läckerlihuus* or House of Läckerli) decided to invest in the football industry, and sponsored *s'Basler Lied*. This local enterprise produces a variety of cookies, the *Läckerlis*, which are promoted as an integral part of the region and Basel's culinary tradition. The enterprise paid a significant amount of money to Basel United AG in order to have its logo displayed on the two big flat screens in the stadium while the anthem was played. Briefly put, the performance of *s'Basler Lied*, originally conceived by members of the *Infernos* as a song "vo de Fans für d'Fans" (from fans, for fans), was appropriated and subsequently commercialized by the sports industry.

The appropriation of the *s'Basler Lied* by actors from outside the world of fans and, particularly, by Basel United AG, reached its apex when Basel United AG decided to upload the text and melody of the song onto its website, as well as to put the copyright symbol on the document, thereby designating their rights to the song. This resulted in an emblematic dispute within the *Muttenzerkurve* on the importance of sponsors for the existence of FCB and, in particular, on the appropriateness of singing a song sponsored by a business.

To illustrate these quarrels, we discuss two postings that appeared in the FCB Forum, an online platform where FCB fans discuss football in general and FCB matters in particular. While the majority of the forum's users watch the games from the *Muttenzerkurve*, a significant minority sits in other sectors. This heterogeneity, the fact that the forum allows users to remain anonymous and, finally, the impossibility for the *Infernos* to maintain control over the discussion using the homogenizing techniques and strategies adopted within the *Muttenzerkurve*, all enabled critical voices to emerge and interact with the dominant positions. The event concerning the commodification of *s'Basler Lied* was discussed quite intensely within the forum as the following excerpt shows.

Original post (German and Swiss German)
[Fan 1]: Ich war schockiert, entsetzt und enttäuscht. Ein weiterer Schritt vorwärts, das Lied und die Stimmung im Stadion zu dämpfen. Nach der Absetztung von «You'll never walk alone» . . . übertreffen sich die Verantwortlichen hiermit vollkommen. Die Läggerli im Hintergrund gingen noch, wäre das Logo vom Läggerlihuus nicht auch noch drauf. Dies hat mit Kommerz zutun und es sollte bekannt sein, dass wir uns seit Jahren dagegen wehren.
[Fan 2]: Und usserdäm müm do inne emol e paar lüt begriffe, dass dr FCB e Unternähme isch und wirtschaftlich funktioniere muess!! Im hütigi Fuessball spielt s›finanzielle e zentrali Bedütig. Jede Verein muess für sich sälber entscheide, was für ihn s›beschti isch. Dr FCB will Erfolg ha und das brucht Gäld aber au Glück! Ansunschte müm mr uns ufem Niveau vomene FC Aarau z›friede gäh! (http://www.FCBforum.ch/forum/archive/index.php/t-26110.html [21.02.2011])

English translation
[Fan 1]: I was shocked, outraged and disappointed. A further step to bringing down the song and the atmosphere in the stadium. After the cancellation of "You'll never walk alone" . . . the people responsible outdid themselves completely: The Läggerli in the background would have been okay, if the logo of the Läggerlihuus hadn't been there, too. This is commercial and it should be known that we've been fighting against this for years.
[Fan 2]: And, some people here need to understand that FCB is an enterprise and has to run economically!! In football today finances play a prominent role. Each club has to decide what is best for them. FCB wants to be successful and for that they need money as well as luck! Otherwise, we would have to live with playing on the same level as FC Aarau!

These two postings show the heterogeneity of the *Muttenzerkurve* as both Fan 1 and Fan 2 are members of the stand. Fan 1 very deliberately displays an emotional involvement in his intervention ("I was shocked, outraged and disappointed"), criticizes the commercialization of the song and gives vent to his feelings of disillusionment and loss. An emotional discourse enmeshed with a critique of the commercialization of fan culture is very typical of the discourse produced by partisans of an authentic ("ultra," "Italian") fan culture. On the other hand, Fan 2 produces a very sober and quite elaborate argumentation that places Swiss football and FCB within a discourse in the global sports industry, an industry where money plays a prominent role, and where only those able and willing to invest capital will be successful.

The dispute between representatives of an emotional and traditionalist conception of fan culture and those who advocate (or tolerate) the involvement of actors coming from the world of business in order to secure the club's financial stability and enable continued success dominated the FCB Forum as well as the discussions within the *Muttenzerkurve* for weeks. The longer these discussions went on, the more they shifted from a debate on the legitimacy of football governed by economic actors to a dispute over the right these actors have to manipulate a song created by fans for fans. In other words, the dialogue revolved around whether or not it was legitimate for an outside economic actor to interfere in a domain clearly perceived to be under the authority of the *Muttenzerkurve* and its leaders, the *Infernos*. The *Infernos* perceived these events as trespassing on their territory and, consequently, as a challenge to their uncontested supremacy over fan practices within the *Muttenzerkurve*.

After several weeks, the leaders of the *Infernos* (and with them, of course, the whole stand) decided to put an end to these discussions and to boycott the song or started singing it later in the match. This resulted in some rather ludicrous situations when the song was announced by the stadium speaker, the advertisement of the *Läckerlihuus* appeared on the two big flat screens, the background music started, the text was displayed—but nobody sang. By boycotting *s'Basler Lied*, the *Infernos* managed to reestablish the power structures concerning the rules governing discursive practices within the *Muttenzerkurve*. After a few months, Basel United AG was obliged to abrogate the contract granting the rights to *s'Basler Lied* to the *Läckerlihuus*.

As we have demonstrated, songs are appropriated, transformed and reappropriated, and discourses of pride and profit become an object of dispute. What at first appeared to be tension between interests is in effect much more complex. Authenticity is appropriated by all sides: the *Infernos*, Basel United AG and the *Läckerlihuus*; however, whereas the Infernos construe their chants as a form of authenticity that indexes their belonging to a certain place, namely, Basel, the football industry and businesses recognize authenticity as a resource which can be commodified and capitalized on.

THE (IL)LEGITIMATE SUPPORTER: LANGUAGE PRACTICES AS A MEANS OF DISTINCTION

The tension between fans as legitimate holders of authenticity and the emergence of a football industry appropriating this authenticity and capitalizing on it results in struggles that redefine the characteristics not only of legitimate fan culture but also of the legitimate fan. This debate has become particularly evident with the emergence of the ultras' categorization of *Modefans*—which can be translated as fair-weather fans. A *Modefan* is a type of spectator, as well as a term that has materialized (only) in the discourse of traditional fans within the *Muttenzerkurve* over the last ten years. (People characterized as *Modefans* by the ultras have no corresponding sense of themselves as a group, and indeed have no idea that the ultras categorize them in this way.)

Since 2001, when Basel began to assert its dominance in the Swiss football league (in the 1980s and 1990s, the team lived through two unsuccessful decades), and particularly since the FCB qualified for the UEFA Champions League in 2002, going to the stadium and especially watching the game from the *Muttenzerkurve* became fashionable. The team's success also initiated a major mediatization of its matches. Because the media constructed the matches as international events, the games began to involve journalists and broadcasting companies from all over the world. In addition, the appeal of the opposing teams rose, with some of Europe's most important and prestigious European football teams—FC Barcelona, Manchester United, FC Bayern München, FC Juventus Torino—coming to Basel. These aspects, combined with the special aura created by the relative novelty of a small Swiss team hosting major international sport events, transformed the matches into historical happenings.

These mediatized events attracted and still attract new spectators. Some of the new supporters come from neighboring regions—for example, Baden Württemberg, the area of Germany bordering on Basel, or from Alsace, the French region adjacent to Basel. These viewers take advantage of the opportunity to attend an international football event in what has become the most prestigious stadium in the region. There are, however, also many inhabitants of Basel amongst the newcomers who are interested in European football, and who look forward to seeing major European football stars, or who want to participate in a local cultural event that is internationally broadcasted. Migrants from Basel are also part of the new crowd. Their motivation for coming to the stadium is generally to see a compatriot playing for a prestigious European football team.

Although these new spectators come to the stadium for diverse reasons, they have several things in common. First, most of them are attracted to the *Muttenzerkurve*, either due to its reputation as the place to be for a firsthand experience of the game's authentic spirit, or because of the cheap tickets (the *Muttenzerkurve* is standing room only). Second, the new crowd generally only goes to the stadium to see international matches, and are therefore regarded as occasional supporters. Third, the *Modefans* see the match as a form of entertainment, meaning they do not see themselves as part of a culture or part of an organization. They buy a ticket to an FCB match much in the manner they would buy a ticket to the theater. Interestingly enough, these spectators do not consider themselves to be members of the *Infernos*, but they do understand fan culture as an intrinsic and valuable part of the sporting event. They do not share the faith or dedication that characterize the fans in the *Muttenzerkurve*, but they try, often inadequately, to imitate fans' behavior or songs, and regard these activities as a source of entertainment and as a constitutive element of the *Muttenzerkurve*'s attraction.

For the "real" supporters, however, the presence of fair-weather fans in the *Muttenzerkurve* is highly problematic. "Real" supporters are fans who do not come only when the club is successful, but who are present for every match. They do not only show up for international games: they are partisans who are unconditionally dedicated to the club. The fact that the *Infernos* introduced a new term to describe and distinguish these fair-weather supporters clearly indicates that *Modefans* are neither part of the shared culture of the *Infernos* nor are they accepted by the true fan base.

In a *Schreyhals* interview, a respected leader of the dominant fan organization in the 1980s characterized the *Modefans* as follows:

Original text (German)
Schlimm in der heutigen Zeit finde ich, dass sich das Verhältnis der wahren Fans zu den Konsumenten massiv verschoben hat. Man pfeift schneller und ist rasch unzufrieden. Was für mich gar nicht geht, ist die eigenen Spieler auspfeifen, das gab es früher nicht. (Schreyhals 12, 2007)

Translation
The bad thing about today's game is that the ratio between real and commercial fans has shifted massively. People tend to boo more quickly and to be unhappy easily. To me, it is absolutely inacceptable to boo our own players off the field. We didn't do that in the past.

The interviewee, who is regarded by the *Infernos* as a sort of living legend (as are all former leaders), views the new fans as consumers and imposters; he categorically denies them the status of fan. In a more traditional understanding of fan culture, these new supporters do not fit the definition of true fans. The final line of an FCB song goes "FCB fan kasch nid wärde, FCB fan das muesch si" (you can't become an FCB fan, you have to be [born as] an FCB fan), revealing the conviction that becoming a fan is an impossible undertaking. *Modefans* cannot be real fans because they neither grew up surrounded by local traditions, nor have they followed FCB since their childhood; they do not love the team or dedicate their entire leisure time to it. FCB matches are simply an entertaining event for *Modefans* who reproduce behavior learned by watching TV or during the occasional attendance of a match while on vacation. Consequently, they are held to be consumers corrupted by the logic of capitalism.

By not embracing the *Infernos* and their fan culture in the stands (as well as outside the stadium, but life outside the stadium lies beyond the scope of this paper), *Modefans* have challenged and continue to challenge the balance of power in the stadium. As a reaction, and in order to prevent these new fans from gaining access to the production of knowledge and acquiring ways of making their voice heard within the stand, the *Infernos* adopted a series of strategies. On the one hand, authentic and true fans used very explicit language to communicate to *Modefans* that their presence was neither desirable nor requested. For instance, sitting during a football match, particularly in the *Muttenzerkurve*, is viewed as typical and thus unwanted *Modefan* behavior; real fans stand during an entire match. Consequently, the song "Wär sitzt isch e hueresohn" (whoever sits is a son of a bitch) became increasingly part of the habitual song repertoire during a football game. Furthermore, the lyric "gang doch ins A" (go to [Section] A) addresses fans who do not participate in the chants or who are unfamiliar with the words of the songs (Section A being conceived as the VIP sector and the place where people only consume the match and do not live it). At the same time, the *Infernos* decided to introduce a policy prescribing *Baseldütsch*, the local dialect, as the official language for all texts printed on flags, choreographies, as well as for all songs sung in the *Muttenzerkurve*. Furthermore, they composed new songs treating and glorifying FCB and its legendary players or the *Muttenzerkurve* and its members themselves. The aim of these changes was not to exclude all non-Baseldütsch speakers. Rather, the point was to combat the tendency of detaching the international and, particularly, German-speaking canon of football songs from any authentic and genuine value and tradition, and, by consequence, to circumvent the centripetal forces of homogenization—caused by the globalization and commercialization of football—which are believed to have corrupted fan practices. The purification of fan culture, the reinvention of the chant repertoire and the adoption of the *Baseldütsch* as sole legitimate language enabled the *Infernos* to exclude all people ignorant of local rules and songs, thereby forcing them to adhere to the practices imposed by the *Infernos*.

To sum up, while the UEFA Champions League as the major European football organization and the economically most important actor in the sport brings a great deal of prestige and glory to FCB, it also attracts new *Modefans* who neither share the *Infernos'* values nor the very local history and the identification with the team, but instead practice fan activities that the *Infernos* categorize as illegitimate. By returning to their perceived roots and to very local values, traditions and language, the *Infernos* attempted to exclude the Modefans from "their" stand. But, paradoxically, instead of purifying fan culture from the corrupted influences of the *Modefans*, and reinventing authenticity and the aura emanating from it, the *Infernos'* strategies have increasingly attracted fair-weather fans to the stadium. In the past few years, this phenomenon has resulted in a radicalization of the *Infernos* and has compounded the tension and lack of understanding between the parties.

CONCLUSION

The various forms of dispute reported here have allowed us to pinpoint the ways in which specific linguistic practices are intertwined in the construction of both pride and profit. Instead of a linear shift from language as an expression of community and belonging to language as a commodifiable product, we have observed a complex coexistence and interrelationship of both manifestations. Discourses and practices of pride are not just substituted by discourses and practices of profit. On the contrary, *pride* remains a very central element in the construction of legitimacy, authenticity and local belonging. It is still a clear resource when categorizing and indexing groups. Pride remains a powerful instrument for the structuration of social relations, allowing the creation of homogeneity and unity as well as (re) producing power struggles. What also remains is the role of language as a key element in the construction of a group, as a backdrop for regimentation and as an instrument of social selection.

If pride is not new, the social and economic transformation we are experiencing in late capitalism confers a rather new significance on the notion of *profit*. In fact, in many places where pride was a constitutive element of identity and community, new social actors have emerged with new interests, mostly economic ones. Spaces, events, locations and other venues are considered in light of their commercial potential and as loci of consumption. Local interests are articulated to address national and transnational ones, involving a change from amateurism to professionalism and from local *bricolage* to entrepreneurial management, in ways that obey investors' goals and the dictates of international standards. Thus, a profit logic is acutely dependant on forms of regulation resulting in conditions that make a particular event, place or practice commercially appealing. In this setting, the regimentation of practices takes on greater salience. Controlling what is said and done at a match ensures the safety of a stadium, and adopting standard norms and complying with the requirements of outside economic actors leads to profitable events.

The regimentation of practice motivated by pride or driven by profit sometimes obeys a similar logic in terms of norms and regimentation, although the underlying objectives are not the same. Despite the differences in ideology, pride and profit intersect in various areas, as several of our analyses have shown. The convergence of the two trends can take a variety of forms.

Local stadiums and local clubs are increasingly part of a transnational industry that views traditions and authenticity as part of the spectacle that football matches offer. If regulations tend to define what counts as acceptable practices, and thereby homogenize certain behaviors, a football match as an event also relies on the specificity of its culture, which necessarily includes the fans. Besides what happens on the pitch, it is what transpires at the stadium at large that confers a feeling of uniqueness to every match.

As a consequence, a football club and a football stadium can be marketed on the basis of a specific character or unique atmosphere that spectators experience in this place alone. Authentic practices such as chanting songs created by authentic fans are appropriated by the football industry or other companies. Local, authentic and unique practices are then transformed into commercial resources.

This marketization, alongside the growing media presence and the tendency to brand a football club in international competition, is linked to prestige, international visibility and economic recognition; it also induces strong feelings of identification with and pride in a team, which, in return, attracts new consumers. Going to a match does not imply being an authentic supporter; it connotes consuming an authentic fan culture and profiting from the exaltation of pride. The commercialization of pride induces a consumption of pride that consequently validates the transformation of pride into profit.

The intersection of pride and profit engenders marked resistance in the camp of those who hold themselves to be producers and proprietors of authentic and pure fan culture. Commercialization and consumption of this culture is regarded as spoliation of their product and their ownership, as a denaturing of authenticity, and as an invasion by the ignorant outsider into fan territory. The commodification of language and culture in fact challenges the dominant groups' (here, the *Infernos'*) monopoly over what can be said and done. As a reaction to these new economic forces, the *Infernos* strive to reinforce their position of power by going back to a presumed authenticity and purity of the local fan culture. They invent songs that explicitly address the issues of commercialization, they intentionally and exclusively use a dialect that is unfamiliar to fans who are not from the Basel area, and by consequence render their participation in *Muttenzerkurve* activities impossible. In other words, to combat the commercialization and consumption of pride, the producers of pride have opted for a radicalization of pride against profit.

The radicalization of the *Infernos'* discourse and practices, however, does not preclude the continuing industrialization and commercialization of football or vice versa. On the contrary, discourses of pride and manifestations of profit are symbiotic phenomena that tend to imply and even derive from each other. Whereas the radicalization of the *Infernos'* discourse is a consequence of the appropriation of their linguistic practices by economic actors, their return to their perceived roots and their ambition to produce pure authenticity discourages neither the *Modefans* nor the football industry from appropriating their behavior. On the contrary, it is precisely this aura of authenticity that augments their team's allure and its commercial potential, thereby attracting even more unwanted fans and investors. The consequence of the *Infernos'* reaction is not the intended de-escalation of the conflict, but the production of endless struggles between the commodification of pride and resistance to profit.

NOTES

1. Football is the European term for soccer.
2. *Capo* is translated here to mean leader. It is, however, not clear whether the etymology of the term *capo* derives from the Italian term *capo* standing for head or chief, or if the term *capo* has to be understood as an allusion to the *Kapos* in the Nazi regime. Both interpretations seem pertinent and possible because the *capos* are effectively the leaders of the stand, and they exercise a military-like control over the practices therein. On the other hand, the degree of organization and aestheticization of the masses achieved by the *Infernos* is highly reminiscent of the practices conducted by the Nazis.
3. In the 2007/2008 season, UEFA's total revenue amounted to 1,925 Million EUR, and FIFA's to 957 Million USD (UEFA Financial Report2008/2009, FIFA Financial Report 2009.)
4. Z'Basel an mym Rhii,
   jo, dört möcht i sii!
   Wäiht nit d'Luft so mild und lau,
   und der Himmel isch so blau,
   an mym liebe,
   an mym liebe Rhii.

   In der Münschterschuel
   uf mym herte Stuehl
   mag i zwor jetzt nüt meh ha;
   d'Tööpli stöhn mer nümmen a
   in der Basler,
   in der Basler Schuel.

   Aber uf der Pfalz
   alle Lüte gfallt's.
   O, wie wechsle Berg un Tal,
   Land un Wasser überal,
   vor der Basler,
   vor der Basler Pfalz!

REFERENCES

Appadurai, Arjun. 1996. *Modernity at Large: Cultural Dimensions of Globalization*. Minneapolis: University of Minnesota Press.

Bairner, Alan. 2001. *Sport, Nationalism, and Globalization. European and North American Perspectives*. Albany: State University of New York Press.

Batuman, Elif. 2011. "The View from the Stands. Life among Istanbul's Soccer Fanatics." *The New Yorker*, March 7.

Bauman, Richard, and Charles Briggs. 2003. *Voices of Modernity: Language Ideologies and the Politics of Modernity*. Cambridge: Cambridge University Press.

Boutet, Josiane. 2001. "Le travail devient-il intellectuel?" *Travailler* 6: 55–70.

Boutet, Josiane. 2008. *La vie verbale au travail. Des manufactures aux centres d'appels*. Toulouse: Octares.

Bröckling, Ullrich, Krasmann Susanne, and Thomas Lemke, eds. 2010. *Governamentality. Current Issues and Future Challenges*. London: Routledge.

Brown, Adam. 1998. "United We Stand: Some Problems with Fan Democracy." In *Fanatics! Power, Identity, and Fandom in Football*, edited by Adam Brown, 50–69. London: Routledge.

Cameron, Deborah. 1995. *Verbal Hygiene?* London: Routledge.

Cameron, Deborah. 2000. "Styling the Worker. Gender and the Commodification of Language in the Globalized Service Economy." *Journal of Sociolinguistics* 4(3): 323–347.

Cameron, Deborah. 2001. *Good to Talk?* London: Sage.

Campbell, Rook. 2011. "Staging Globalization for National Projects: Global Sport Markets and Elite Athletic Transnational Labour in Qatar." *International Review for the Sociology* 46(1): 45–60.

Chanavat, Nicolas, and Guillaume Bodet. 2009. "Sport Branding Strategy and Internationalisation: A French Oerception of the 'Big Four' Brands." *Qualitative Market Research: An International Journal* 12(4): 460–481.

Conn, David. 1997. *The Football Business*. Edinburgh: Mainstream.

Coupland, Nik, Peter Garrett, and Hywel Bishop. 2005. "Wales Underground: Discursive Frames and Authenticities in Welsh Mining Heritage Tourism Events." In *Discourse, Communication and Tourism*, edited by Adam Jaworski and Annette Pritchard, 199–222. Clevedon, UK: Channel View Publications.

Couvelaere, Vincent, and André Richelieu. 2005. "Brand Strategy in Professional Sports: The Case of French Soccer Teams." *European Sport Management Quarterly* 5(1): 23–46.

Dubal, Sam. 2010. "The Neoliberalization of Football: Rethinking Neoliberalism Through the commercialization of the beautiful game." *International Review for the Sociology of Sport* 45(2): 123–146.

Dubois, Lise, Mélanie LeBlanc, and Maurice Beaudin. 2006. "La langue comme ressource productive et les rapports de pouvoir entre communautés linguistiques." *Langage et Société* 118: 17–42.

Duchêne, Alexandre. 2009. "Marketing, Management and Performance: Multilingualism as Commodity in a Tourism Call Centre." *Language Policy* 8: 27–50.

Duchêne, Alexandre. 2011. "Néolibéralisme, inégalités sociales et plurilinguisme: l'exploitation des ressources langagières et des locuteurs." *Langage et Société* 136: 81–106.

Duchêne, Alexandre, and Monica Heller. in press a. "Multilingualism and the New Economy." In *Handbook of Multilingualism*, edited by Marilyn Martin-Jones, Adrian Blackledge and Angela Creese. New York: Routledge.

Duchêne, Alexandre, and Monica Heller. in press b. "Language Policy in the Workplace." In *Cambridge Handbook of Language Policy*, edited by Bernard Spolsky. Cambridge: Cambridge University Press.

Duchêne, Alexandre, and Ingrid Piller. 2011. "Mehrsprachigkeit als Wirtschaftsgut: sprachliche Ideologien und Praktiken in der Tourismusindustrie." In *Babylon Europe. Zur europäischen Sprachlandschaft*, edited by Georg Kreis, 135–157. Basel: Schwabe Verlag.

Gee, James Paul, Glynda Hull, and Colin Lankshear. 1996. *The New Work Order: Behind the Language of the New Capitalism*. Boulder, CO: Westview Press.

Hare, Geoff. 1999. "Buying and Selling the World Cup." In *France and the 1998 World Cup: The National Impact of a World Sporting*, edited by Huge Dauncey, and Geoff Hare, 121–144. London: Frank Cass.

Harvey, David. 2005. *A Brief History of Neoliberalism*. New York: Oxford University Press.

Heller, Monica. 2003. "Globalization, the New Economy, and the Commodification of Language and Identity." *Journal of Sociolinguistics* 7(4): 473–492.

Heller, Monica. 2010. "Language as Resource in the Globalized New Economy." In *Handbook of Language and Globalisation*, edited by Nik Coupland, 350–365. Oxford: Blackwell.

Heller, Monica. 2011. *Paths to Post-Nationalism*. Oxford: Oxford University Press.

Heller, Monica, and Josiane Boutet. 2006. «Vers des nouvelles formes de pouvoir langagier? Langage(s) et économie dans la nouvelle économie.» *Langage et Société* 118: 5–16.

Henry, Ian, Mahfoud Amara, and Mansour Al Tauqi. 2003. «Sport, Arab Nationalism and the Pan-Arab Games." *International Review for the Sociology of Sport* 38(3): 295–310.

Holt, Matthew. 2009. "UEFA, Governance, and the Control of Club Competition in European Football." Report: *Birbeck Sport Business Centre 2*.

Howe, David. 1999. "Professionalism, Commercialism and the Rugby Club: The Case of Pontypridd RFC." In *Making the Rugby World*, edited by Timothy Chandler and John Nauright, 165–181. London: Frank Cass.

Jaworski, Adam, and Annette Pritchard. 2005. *Discourse, Communication, and Tourism*. Clevedon, UK: Channel View Publications.

Kellas, James. 1991. *The Politics of Nationalism and Ethnicity*. Basingstoke, UK: Palgrave Macmillan.

Kelly-Holmes, Helen. 2006. "Multilingualism and Commercial Language Practices on the Internet." *Journal of Sociolinguistics* 10(4): 507–519.

King, Anthony. 2003. *The European Ritual: Football in the New Europe*. Aldershot, UK: Ashgate.

Lee, Jung Woo, and Joseph Maguire. 2010. "Global Festivals through a National Prism: The Global—National Nexus in South Korean Media Coverage of the 2004 Athens Olympic Games." *International Review for the Sociology of Sport* 44(1): 5–24.

Lemke, Thomas. 2007. *Gouvernementalität und Biopolitik*. Wiesbaden: Verlag für Sozialwissenschaften.

McLaughlin, Mireille. 2010. "L'acadie post-nationale producing franco-canadien identity in the global economy." PhD Diss., University of Toronto.

Morrow, Stephen. 2003. *The People's Game? Football, Finance, and Society*. Basingstoke, UK: Palgrave Macmillan.

Nash, Rex. 2010. "Contestation in Modern English Professional Football." *International Review for the Sociology of Sport* 35(4): 465–486.

O'Brien, Danny, and Trevor Slack. 1999. "Deinstitutionalizing the Amateur Ethic: An Empirical Examination of Change in a Rugby Union Football Club." *Sport Management Review* 2(1): 24–42.

Pennycook, Alistair. 2009. *Global Linguistic Flows: Hip Hop Cultures, Youth Identities and the Politics of Language*. New York: Routledge.

Piller, Ingrid. 2001. "Identity Constructions in Multilingual Advertising." *Language in Society* 30: 153–186.

Poli, Raffaele. 2010. "Understanding Globalization through Football: The New International Division of Labour, Migratory Channels and Transnational Trade Circuits." *International Review for the Sociology of Sport* 45(4): 491–506.

Roy, Sylvie. 2003. "Bilingualism and Standardization in a Canadian Call Center: Challenges for a Linguistic Minority Community." In *Language Socialization in Multilingual Societies*, edited by Robert Bayley and Sandra Schecter, 269–287. Clevedon: Multilingual Matters.

Scalia, Vincenzo. 2009. "Just a Few Rogues? Football Ultras, Clubs and Politics in Contemporary Italy." *International Review for the Sociology of Sport* 44(1): 41–53.

Segrave, Jeffrey. 2000. "The (Neo)Modern Olympic Games: The Revolutions in Europe and the Resurgence of Universalism." *International Review for the Sociology of Sport* 35(3): 268–281.

Slack, Trevor. 1998. "Studying the Commercialization of Sport: The Need for Critical Analysis." *Sociology of Sport* 1(1). Accessed May 8, 2011. http://physed.otago.ac.nz/sosol/v1i1/v1i1a6.htm.

Sudgen, John. 2002. "Network Football." In *Power Games: a Critical Sociology of Sport*, edited by John Sudgen and Alan Tomlinson, 61–80. New York: Routledge.

4 "Total Quality Language Revival"

Jacqueline Urla

As the First World War came to a close in the early part of the twentieth century, the renowned comparative linguist Antoine Meillet published *Les Langues dans l'Europe Nouvelle*. The second edition of his book began with the following short meditation:

> One of the new features of the modern world is that rationality tends to replace irrationality. Undoubtedly languages do not lend themselves to "taylorization" as easily as do industrial enterprises. But the local "patois" are dying just as surely as the small artisans are disappearing in the face of assembly-line mass production. As they become aware of their power over language, the citizens of this new world . . . will know how to reshape the current linguistic anarchy toward the discipline which tomorrow's universal civilization will begin to impose (Meillet [1918] 1928, 4).

Peace, modernity, and progress in the New Europe, suggests Meillet, would require the taming of linguistic diversity. His statement points to the widespread assumption in contemporary Western language ideology that linguistic diversity in a single political community is dangerous (Dorian 1998). The writings of liberal political scientists throughout the twentieth century have variously identified multilingualism as an obstacle to democracy, an impediment to the formation of cohesive political solidarities, and as a drag on economic modernization (May 2001, 2003). As Europeans were embarking on a new future, Meillet hoped that his fellow citizens would see for themselves the necessity of abandoning "regional" languages and the identities to which they are attached.

As we know, such a scenario did not come to pass. In the course of the twentieth century, processes of industrialization, standardization and modernization undoubtedly created crises for the survival of minority or lesser-used languages, but they did not spell an abrupt end to them. The situation that we encounter a century later is at once more contradictory and complex than Meillet could have imagined. The diversity of languages is being simultaneously eroded, decried, defended and exploited as a commodity in the global capitalist marketplace. Attachments to minority languages have not vanished nor have movements advocating for their protection; indeed, in some respects they enjoy more legitimacy than ever before. But the terms and forms in which that advocacy is taking place have shifted.

In this chapter, I am interested in precisely this latter issue: shifts taking place in discourse and the practice of language advocacy today. More specifically, I wish to explore how it is that minority language planning advocates are aligning themselves with the values and practices of cutting-edge business management. In this regard, I found myself returning to Meillet's text to reconsider the reference he makes to "taylorization," the scientific management techniques developed by Frederick Taylor that were instrumental in the rise of mass assembly line production (Nelson 1980). Taylor's revolutionary innovation was to conceive of the factory worker's laboring body and movements as something that could be systematically studied, measured and standardized for greater efficiency. Meillet's reference to taylorism takes the form of a lament—oh, that we might be able to "taylorize" language as we do the workplace. When I first came across this statement, I read it as an example of the modernist view of language as a social fact and hence amenable to planning (Urla 1989). Interesting to me now, however, is not simply the affirmation that language can be planned, *but that it should be labor management techniques in particular that come to signify an ideal form of rational planning.* In what follows we will see that the conjoining of business management with language planning presaged—or more accurately fantasized about—by this scholar a century ago has now become a reality.

For this I draw upon my ethnographic research on the Basque language revival movement in Spain in the past decade and, in particular, on an extended interview with one of the pioneers in adapting Total Quality Management (TQM) methods into language planning efforts. TQM, sometimes referred to simply as "Quality," is a managerial strategy that seeks to increase an organization's competitiveness (Swift, Ross and Omachonu 1998). It first emerged in the 1980s and is based on the premise that workers are more productive when they are "empowered" to take responsibility for the quality and quantity of their output. They are assisted in this by a trademark system of competitive goal setting, team work, awards, and an elaborated program of periodic assessment. Like its ancestor taylorism, to which it is sometimes compared, TQM revolutionized the modern workplace, and its assumptions and methods have spread widely.

In what follows, I will be exploring what exactly made TQM an appealing resource to Basque language advocates at this particular historical juncture in Spain. Rather than view the turn to managerial methods as simply an example of the inevitable colonization of the field of language politics by neoliberal rationalities, I believe case studies such as this one can help us to understand the particular circumstances that engage social actors as strategically motivated and active participants in the reconfiguration of language revival discourse. TQM, I argue, offered many things at once. It played a legitimating role, serving to detach language planning from the conflict-ual realm of Basque nationalist politics and link it with highly legitimate practice of entrepreneurialism. But its value was not just discursive. At a practical level, advocates saw the TQM emphasis on dispersed responsi-bility, recurring and systematic assessment, and its premise of continual improvement to be tools with which to overcome chronic problems that face language revitalization efforts. I conclude with some reflections on how the managerial framework of TQM reconfigures how speakers are asked to think about their language habits, what language is, or what the revival movement is about.

TRAVELING DISCOURSES

Circulation is one of the master tropes used in describing the current econ-omy shaped by globalization and advanced neoliberal political ideologies. People move, goods move, information and media all circulate at an accel-erated pace across large territories. So do discourses. As many scholars have noted, one of the distinctive cultural characteristics of neoliberalism is precisely the application of the concepts, values and practices of entre-preneurial management to an increasing number of arenas of social life (Harvey 2005). The logics of markets and entrepreneurialism are increas-ingly treated as fully transferable frameworks for understanding all man-ner of social-cultural practices. Often the first sign we have of the arrival of such logics is the proliferation of what Shore and Wright (2000) call "semantic clusters," the distinctive terminology of managerial science: best practices, benchmarking, quality, strategic planning, to name a few. But it is important to recognize that this is not just a change of vocabulary. With these terms come practical consequences, new routines of evaluation and measurement, new norms, consultancies and experts that are certified to design and train workers in new management schemas.

Shore and Wright call this phenomenon the "new managerialism," while others use the label "neoliberalism." Much of the analysis to date has looked at the deployment and varied responses to the practices, values and forms of managerial expertise in the workplace (Inoue, n.d., Kasmir 2005) and the public sector (Hyatt 2001; Maskovsky 2001; Strathern 2000). Schol-ars of social movements have noted parallel developments, often discussed under the rubric of professionalization or "ngo-ization." Language politics and language policies have not remained immune. As Williams and Morris (2000) have noted, frameworks and justifications for governmental minor-ity language protection and planning are shifting. In Europe today, they argue, language planning

can no longer be conceived of in terms of the modernist conception of state benevolence, acting on behalf of the language group within a general framework of democracy and rights . . . In common with other forms of planning it is far more likely to be seen in terms of the strategic planning of the business enterprise, with a focus upon forward planning, prioritizing, evaluating strengths, weaknesses, opportunities and threats" (Williams and Morris 2000, 180).[1]

The last two decades of Basque language revitalization provide us with a case in point. The Basque language, spoken in territories located in the Western Pyrenees of France and Spain, has been the object of revitalization efforts since the mid-nineteenth century. In the past century its largest base of supporters is found in Spain, where we also find an equally significant base of support for Basque nationalism. Stigmatized and severely repressed under the Franco regime, both language revitalization and Basque nationalist political aspirations grew substantially after the dictatorship ended in the mid-1970s and part of the Basque-speaking region achieved its own regional government in 1979. At this point, language revival ceased to be exclusively an underground social movement and began also to be an activity with governmental actors and public funding. Basque language promotion in the Autonomous Community today has two parallel tracks: one orchestrated by the regional government's Department of Language Policy, and another composed of a very active assemblage of independent language professional and civic associations. Their collective goal, broadly speaking, has been to reverse the process of language shift that had accelerated in the twentieth century, to combat the social and political marginalization of the Basque language and ultimately to make possible a bilingual society in which Basque can be used, along with Spanish, as an everyday language in all domains of life.

The analysis I offer here is part of a larger project tracing the intersecting ideologies and practices of nationalism and governmentality that inform language revitalization over a longer period of history (Urla forthcoming). Nationalist conceptualizations of language are typically rooted in the "pride" discourse—that is, valuing language as a symbol and element of cultural identity—described by Heller and Duchêne in this volume. Governmentality, on the other hand, refers to discourses and practices aimed at the systematic regulation and management of the behavior of individuals and the life of the population (Foucault 1991). Described by Foucault as the "conduct of conduct," governmentality entails approaching aspects of social life as problems to be mapped and managed. While governmentality is not identical with the discourse of profit, it is the case that governance strategies today have adopted many of the discursive features of neoliberal entrepreneurialism and self-regulation (Rose 1999). Under neoliberalism, the logics and discourse for managing social life, on the one hand, and the logics and discourse of the market, on the other, have fused.

Let us turn, then, to see how this unfolded in the Basque case. What follows is a description of a relatively recent alignment between Basque language advocacy and neoliberal managerial techniques. While this alliance is being observed for other cases as well—Wales, Scotland and the European Union[2]—in the Basque context, the advocates of what I call 'Total Quality language revival' do not just come from government agencies, as we might have predicted. Rather the earliest proponents emerged from the autonomous quasi-leftist language advocacy organizations concerned with increasing the efficacy of their projects. I begin by sketching out the historical/political context in which this turn to quality management methods occurred and describe why, in this context, some of its early advocates saw it to be useful. I then discuss the way Total Quality language planning was then embraced and promoted to the public by the Department of Language Policy.

This particular case can, I think, make at least two contributions. First, it furthers our larger goal of understanding how language diversity and language advocacy is being reconfigured under late capitalism. Second, the turn to such management strategies sheds light on some of the obstacles to changing entrenched and unequal language relations at the same time that it helps us gain a more complex view of the new managerialism as potentially, though not unproblematically, available for hijacking by advocates and speakers of small languages.

TOTAL QUALITY REVIVAL

The first sign I had of interest in entrepreneurial-like tactics and discourse in language revival came in the1990s when I was conducting research on community-based Basque language media. After a decade fighting for Basque language rights and schooling, advocacy had turned to looking for ways of promoting Basque language use via local media projects, mostly bimonthly community magazines, and some local television and radio. The idea behind the initiative was to promote reading and writing in Basque in an accessible and appealing format—local news, lots of photos, free of charge. A coalition of these local media projects known as Topagunea had sought out an "internal improvement grant" from the provincial government to find ways to help the volunteers working in these projects become better at marketing their magazines. The name and purpose of the grant itself was already a sign of how management strategies were entering into the scene of subsidized language activism. Topagunea used the grant to hire a business consultant to run a series of workshops aimed at teaching young language advocates the methods of "competitive strength assessment." I attended these workshops and observed how he walked us through the steps of identifying organizational strengths, weaknesses, opportunities and threats: SWOT analysis.[3] He emphasized the necessity for each group to make an annual strategic plan. Concretize your goals, he advised, and identify the factors that directly determine your ability to meet them.

While the consultant was clearly familiar with and seemingly sympathetic to the political affinities that many language advocates had with the radical Basque nationalist left, he nevertheless told them they had to embrace new ways of thinking about their activism. You have to think differently, he advised, about what you do and your relationship to your audience. Think of your readers, he said, not as your political allies or even as Basques, but as *customers*. Identify your market, and try to provide them with a unique and appealing product.

The workshops were textbook-like lessons in quality management techniques only in this case, the lessons were not for wage workers and managers from the corporate world, but for volunteers in this community-based sector of the language movement. I have to confess I was more than a little surprised at the linking up of what struck me as antithetical worlds. Language revival, particularly in these kinds of community-based initiatives, had for so long been ideologically tied to left-leaning oppositional politics, premised on presumably noncommodifiable values of identity and culture that were seemingly outside of—if not directly endangered by—market place logics. A proponent of the workshops and, at the time, director of Topagunea, Fernando Muniozguren, saw the situation through a more pragmatic lens. If magazines in Basque were to survive, he explained to me, they would have to become self-financing. Language advocacy projects, in his view, were vulnerable as long as they relied exclusively on government subsidies.

> When you begin a magazine there is a sentimental factor. That factor plays a role when you go to a store and they say, sure, we will put an ad in the magazine. But after about 8 months or so, that sentimental factor diminishes and you now have to be more professional; you have to enter the parameters of the market. You have to change your discourse. You have to have quality; you have to show you can sell, that you are useful. Because the market only understands profit and money. So the sentimental factor always exists, but the role it plays declines . . . What we have seen very clearly is that you cannot survive only on militancy and determination. This requires professionalism and constant dedication.[4]

Fernando, a seasoned language advocate, had come of age in grassroots anti-Francoist activism. He exemplified the ways in which the movement was increasingly coming to see the logics of the marketplace as the inexorable context in which the preservation of language, identity and heritage must operate. Professionalism and economic survival were the rubrics under which concepts and methods of entrepreneurialism were making their way into the tactics of language advocacy. The nexus between language and national identity was not gone, but it was no longer felt to be enough.

This shift was not restricted to the world of community magazines. The tactics of the social movement would start to change dramatically at the end of the 1980s as language advocacy groups faced what many saw to be a paralysis in the grassroots movement. After the end of the Franco regime and the formation of the Basque Autonomous Community, Basque language promotion gained public backing from the newly created regional government, which created its own Department of Language Policy, public school system, adult language academies and media network. Language revitalization bifurcated into governmental organized efforts and a heterogeneous nongovernmental sector. In the latter, one could find a variety of organizations from the prestigious Basque Language Academy, the Basque Federation of Ikastolas (Basque immersion schools), to research and advocacy groups of leftist leanings who for varying reasons did not want to come under the control of the regional government and the centrist Basque Nationalist Party that had majority power in it. Relations between governmental and autonomous language advocacy groups were often strained; there was a fair amount of mutual suspicion and duplication of effort between these sectors for much of the eighties. This division in the world of language revival mirrored the rancorous division that had formed at the time of the 1979 Statute of Autonomy between centrist and radical Basque nationalists. Nongovernmental language advocates pointed to the polarization between nationalist sectors as a serious roadblock to sustaining broad-based popular involvement in the language movement. Although they were not a homogenous group, many that I interviewed said they felt a sense of frustration at being pigeonholed as affiliates of the radical left nationalist part, Herri Batasuna. They complained that their initiatives were blocked or treated warily by both Spanish and Basque governments. This situation became even more severe in the 1990s, as Spanish right-wing attacks on Basque nationalism and language normalization increased. Basque language immersion schools were being accused of discriminating against Spanish while at the same time the radical nationalist left, and anyone perceived to be sympathetic to it came under intensified judicial scrutiny as agents of terrorism.

These suspicions worsened the climate for nongovernmental language advocacy, creating a widespread sense of paralysis for many nongovernmental actors in the language normalization movement. Many advocates I interviewed were emphatic about the necessity of sustaining a populist language movement. To be successful, they argued, language revitalization required a wide base of popular participation and strong civic engagement, and this, they were coming to see, was blocked by a polarized political arena. The future of Basque revival, many began to argue, lay with disentangling it from party politics. Greater emphasis began to be placed on fostering local community-based language associations founded on political neutrality.[5]

Basque language activists began to change their focus and methods to confront this impasse. Organizations that had been at the forefront of grassroots language advocacy folded or stepped back, and, after much debate and reflection, in 1997 a new language advocacy coalition of nongovernmental groups was formed: *Kontseilua*, "The Council of Social Organizations." This group adopted a decidedly more European nongovernmental identity that has become the new face of extra-governmental language advocacy. From the modernist design of their offices in an industrial park, to their affinity for strategic planning, language achievement awards and international networking, *Kontseilua* has worked to visually, rhetorically and practically separate the revival of the Basque language from the symbolic universe of either traditionalism or radical politics. Under their leadership, nongovernmental language revival was increasingly shown to be an expertise-based serious project reliant on well-conceived plans and compatible with the logics of entrepreneurialism and state-of-the-art managerial practice.

The aforementioned dynamics of political polarization was one factor motivating the search for new methods of advocacy. A second factor was the increased interest in bringing language planning to the private sector. In 1982, the Law of Basque Language Normalization had permitted significant achievements in increasing the public presence of Basque in schooling and public administration, and the formation of a regional Basque radio and television network, EITB, that put Basque onto the airwaves. But with rare exceptions, Spanish continued to be overwhelmingly the language of work. Language advocates in and outside the government had started to publish position papers identifying the workplace as an emerging and urgent priority.[6] Professional language planning consultancies began to appear to offer these services and various pilot projects were launched in companies wanting to engage in language normalization.[7]

This effort to gain traction for language revival in the private sector coincided with the Total Quality transformation of the world of business. The ideas and methods of some of TQM's main architects, Walter Edwards Deming and Malcolm Baldridge, began in the mid-1980s to transform U.S. and Japanese business practice; TQM went quickly to Europe where, in 1988, the European Foundation for Quality Management (EFQM) was founded as a vehicle for the dissemination of "quality management" concepts and methods within the EU. Basque private industry and the well-known industrial cooperatives of Mondragon/Arrasate were very receptive to these innovations in management. In Spain, Basque industry led the nation in winning European prizes for excellence in "Quality." In 1992, the Basque Autonomous Government created its own equivalent organization, *Euskalit*, the Basque Foundation for the Advancement of Quality, to further consolidate, as its web page (www.euskalit.net) announced, the reputation of the Basque Autonomous Community as a premiere locus for "excellent and globally minded" enterprise.

It was in this context that Inazio Marko, a member of Kontseilua, thought to use TQM methods in a language normalization plan he had been hired to design for LAB, the Basque leftist trade union. Marko's genius was to link the growing focus on language planning for the workplace with the highly prized and well-regarded methods of quality management. An extended interview with him in May 2006 helped me to understand his reasoning for this move and deepen my understanding of how entrepreneurialism was gaining the interest of language advocates.

Efforts to introduce more Basque language use into the workplace actually had a long trajectory; the Basque savings banks, for example, had been working to promote bilingualism in the workplace for many years. But for the most part, language planning in the workplace had consisted almost exclusively of translating documents into Basque and giving workers release time to take language courses. The result was often that Spanish continued to be the dominant language of interaction underneath a veneer of tokenistic Basque. Marko believed that the world of business management had tools that could help them get beyond this. Furthermore, he said, TQM concepts of organizing work in terms of self-monitoring quality circles, its emphasis on teamwork, leadership and mechanisms of assessment and continuous improvement, he said, enjoyed familiarity and legitimacy from their association with "excellence" in the progressive globally competitive workplace. If the process of language normalization, he explained, could be organized in a way consistent with already existing ways of working that made sense, and appeared rational and technically sound, so much the better.

Marko did not, however, turn to TQM simply as a means of garnering acceptance for language revival. Its legitimacy was a good thing, but he believed that TQM principles of organizing work could help resolve some of the perennial problems that plagued Basque language normalization projects. In our conversation he stressed two: (1) inertia when it comes to changing individual language habits and (2) the difficulty of measuring progress in language normalization. Basque language preservation has widespread popular support, he explained. But in practice, it is tough to bring about, even when people ideologically support it. The tendency for campaigns to remain stuck at the level of tokenistic usage of Basque was a complaint frequently made by advocates. We have learned, he said, that changing the entrenched habits of language use in an organization—the taken-for-granted patterns of interacting, verbal and written repertoires, documents, forms—requires a self conscious effort that must be collective and continuously monitored. An organization wanting to participate in language revival had typically gone about this by appointing someone to be the language officer, commonly called the *técnico*, to organize language courses, run awareness campaigns and generally serve as the expert in translating or other language issues. It was not working very well, he said. Intentional language shift is not something that can be delegated to a single person, a language "officer," or even a committee. He stressed that normalization cannot be successful if imposed from above. Everyone must be personally implicated in achieving the goals; everyone must have a stake in a language normalization process for it to work. Equally important, he felt, there had to be some means to systematically measure and compare the efficacy of normalization efforts.[8]

TQM had methods that could address this and other deficits in prior language revival efforts. As noted earlier, TQM promotes workers taking responsibility for quality and quantity of their work. It blurs the classic hierarchical division between management and wageworkers, and exemplifies what Mitchell Dean (1999) has identified as the distinctive features of neoliberal forms of governmentality. These are the simultaneous deployment of technologies of *agency*, oriented to enhancing worker participation and sense of responsibility, and technologies oriented to *performance*, aimed at making results visible and measurable via standardized quantitative indicators (Dean 1999, 164–171). Standards for performance are not to be imposed by top-level managers. Rather, in a TQM workplace, workers are participants in goal setting and self-evaluation, such that they are encouraged to see themselves as having an investment in whether and how well goals are met. In TQM the worker is envisioned not as a separate class to be disciplined, but rather hailed as a responsible, self-monitoring, team player whose interests are fused with those of management. The redesign of production processes into production teams and quality circles, the emphasis on leadership and award structures all work to cultivate a particular kind of worker subjectivity.

In addition to responsibility, a second key concept of TQM is the notion of "continuous improvement" and, alongside it, continuous assessment. TQM is characterized by elaborated and systematic mechanisms for gathering data and providing feedback and assessment with which to identify problems and to measure the degree to which target goals are being met (Swift, Ross and Omachonu 1998). For this, it relies on various diagramming methods, such as the "Program Decision Process Chart," for visually displaying production and feedback processes (Persico 1992, 165). Assessment is not something done at the end of a production process or fiscal cycle, but rather incorporated throughout the work process. Charts such as these are one of the tools by which that process of feedback is organized. The idea that all processes can be improved is thus intimately linked to the practice of perpetual audit and standardized measures or "benchmarks" of achievement.

All of these premises—dispersed responsibility, diagramming methods, systematic and standard measures of achievement—in Marko's view were translatable and beneficial in designing language normalization plans for the workplace. As he talked, he showed me some of the organizational flow charts—indicating pathways of decision making and explicit calendars of assessment—he had devised for the language plan he had developed for the labor union.

Declaring support for Basque, creating bilingual letterhead, even time off for learning Basque, would never be sufficient to the task. Language planners had to learn from the world of business and insert language normalization into an organization's habits of structured assessment and planning. In this way, he underscored, intentional language shift became not a form of politics, but rather *a labor process*. In short, it was useful to conceive of language normalization as a kind of work that could be managed via the same kind of principles of teamwork, leadership circles and assessment regimes now being used for the production of widgets or customer service. The work of our own research institutes and nongovernmental language advocacy organizations, he affirmed, could also benefit from new management methods. TQM had techniques that he believed could bring seriousness, accountability and systematicity to language revival. It could help to overcome the frustrating gap between widespread professed support for Basque revival and a reality of habitual and hegemonic Spanish language use. We are still experimenting with this, he said, but this is helping us to organize our efforts, to be more systematic in our interventions and to document and see more clearly the effects of our labor.

Marko drew attention to the fact that the turn to TQM had originated with nongovernmental language advocates, but it would soon become embraced as the new face of governmental language advocacy as it sought to engage Basque industry in the project of language normalization. This kind of mirroring of nongovernmental projects was in fact quite common in Basque language advocacy. The same year as my interview with Marko in 2006, the Basque Government launched *LanHitz*, a governmental program to promote language normalization in the private sector. This was followed in 2007 by the signing of a new partnership between the Department of Language Policy and the Basque Foundation for the Advancement of Quality. Soon thereafter the *LanHitz* project announced the creation of *Bikain*, the Certificate of Quality in Language Management.

With this, the press release declared, companies and other enterprises would have a competitive award that recognized and rewarded their achievements in the use, presence and management of Basque. Although Inazio Marko had emphasized the practical value of TQM methods, the press releases, websites and newspaper reports that appeared at the time of the launch of *LanHitz* and the *Bikain* Certificate were indicative of an important refashioning of the image of Basque revival that these projects entailed. The Basque Minister of Culture Miren Azkarate's declarations at the presentation of the Bikain Certificate melded past invocations of Basque revival as a question of rights with capitalist business values. In contrast to the negative associations of Basque with political conflict or exclusionary attitudes found in the broader Spanish media, she presented language revival efforts as a positive element in a progressive, cohesive and healthy society and marketplace.

Within fifteen years the majority of the children who will be leading our society and our businesses will be bilingual. We have to show these young people, these future adults, that Basque is a useful language for all spheres of life. And not only on the basis of rights, identity or sentiments, but also on the basis of productivity and competitiveness. Basque, Spanish, bilingualism and multilingualism, in addition to being an agent for social cohesion, is also intimately linked to the creation of wealth and added value for money. Language management is increasingly a strategic element of management for businesses of the 21st century.[9]

In a separate press release announcing the partnership with Euskalit, Patxi Baztarrika, the head of the Department of Language Policy at the time, described the Certificate to be a fundamental and "decisive" step in normalizing Basque in the private sector, assuring that this will be a process based on "parameters of quality and innovation." Increasing the presence of Basque in the workplace, he declared, is a difficult and complex project that requires "serious, competent and professional work." He and Azkarate sought to establish the legitimacy and normality of attending to language management. Azkarate's statements assured the assembled business associations and labor unions at the press conference that the measuring and monitoring of language in the workplace should be seen as normal and legitimate as the monitoring of "any other economic activity." Political leaders thus used their public forum to depoliticize language issues and in effect make them technical issues of workplace processes. Even further, they suggested in no uncertain terms that attending to and cultivating multi- or bilingualism is distinctive of "cutting edge" businesses. Organizations that incorporate Basque into their practice are assured of reaping multiple kinds of rewards from cultivating better relations with workers, becoming more integrated into Basque society, to demonstrating their capacity for innovation, while at the same time projecting a company's sense of social responsibility and unique identity in the marketplace. The government press releases show us new ways in which pride and profitability discourses are being recast and intertwined. Reference to a Basque nationality is still present, but arguments for language planning are not based primarily on sentiments of patriotism. Bilingual workplace practices are instead presented as contributing to social cohesion (a much less directly political concept), while also serving a company's need for distinctive branding.[10]

The following excerpt from the Department of Language Policy's press release for Bikain is worth quoting at length for the way in which in one brief statement it reverses the long-standing association of minority languages and language diversity with backwardness and the antithesis of innovation.

The present and future of our society, and that of the businesses of our country, is plurilingual. Monolingualism is a thing of the past, it is archaic: the dynamic and innovative businesses will be those that are capable of adapting to their environment, linguistically as well as in other ways. For that reason in a society that is increasingly bilingual and multilingual it is difficult to offer a quality service when one is turning one's back on thousands and thousands of citizens who opt to speak Basque and to live in that language.

In a society increasingly bilingual like our own, business that have the will to be cutting edge and break away from the pack, businesses that aim to be innovative and dynamic, businesses that aim to be recognized as leaders and representatives of modernity, necessarily have to progressively integrate Basque as a language of service and work so that they can also function in Basque. The integration of Basque will be a way of strengthening the enterprise itself.[11]

GOVERNMENTALITY FROM BELOW

The rise of TQM-inspired language planning in the Basque Autonomous Community is exemplary of the spread of the practices, norms and values of the marketplace—responsibility, initiative, competitiveness, awards—to an ever-wider array of social spheres that scholars have identified as characteristic of advanced liberal forms of governance engendering along the way epochal shifts in the ways in which we conceptualize social issues and their solutions (Rose 1999; Strathern 2000). Alternately characterized as the spread of "enterprise culture" or the "new managerialism," this phenomenon has received mixed responses to say the least.

TQM has received high praise from business management professionals as the most important innovation for increasing productivity since the invention of scientific management by Fredrick Taylor (e.g., Swift, Ross and Omachonu 1998, xiii). At the same time, its neo-Taylorian ideas and audit practices have been heavily criticized as an invidious form of worker exploitation, initiating speedup, eroding trust and collegiality, and masking inequalities within the language of "empowerment" (Inoue n.d; Shore and Wright 2000). What does looking at TQM from the perspective of this movement for linguistic equality have to add to this debate? And conversely, what are the implications of TQM for how language revival and language itself is conceptualized?

The Basque case exemplifies what Foucault called the tactical polyvalence of discourses (Foucault 1980). In contrast to the deployment of neoliberal forms of governmentality over the poor (Maskovsky 2001), these shifts to managerial methods originated from below, among nongovernmental advocates aligned with progressive, quasi-leftist sectors powerfully shaped, to be sure, by specific historical and political circumstances that forced them to look for new strategies of action. The contingent alliance of neoliberal modes of management with Basque language revival in this context occurs out of a conviction, as we have seen, that the world of entrepreneur-ial management had practical tools and a certain prestige that could serve the project of minority language revival. This is not inconsequential given the mounting criticism which minority language revival was facing from the Spanish right (Neff van Aerstaeler 2006). Rather than a fateful coopta-tion of activists unwittingly falling into the grip of neoliberal ideologies, in this case, the move toward Total Quality language revival is better thought of as a strategic—though not uncomplicated—response to particular politi-cal and practical challenges. Neither exploitative nor progressive in any simple or straightforward way, the appropriation of TQM techniques is symptomatic of the enormous legitimacy managerial discourses and tactics currently enjoy.

Might these methods, with their emphasis on continuous improvement and continuous monitoring, create an increased sense of pressure on work-ers to be accountable for how they speak? Possibly so.[12] It is also possible that their efficacy and seriousness could bring a sense of accomplishment and satisfaction for people who have wanted to be able to use Basque at work and yet seen proposals flounder and evaporate in practice. As Shore and Wright have argued with respect to audit technologies, "[A]lthough their name and form seem to be everywhere the same, each time these technologies enter a new context, their impact varies, often in unpredict-able ways" (Shore and Wright 2000, 58). Management is not practiced in identical ways, and we need specific ethnographic work, not just surveys or interviews like my own, if we want to answer some of these questions.[13]

However, while we may not want to classify managerial techniques as inherently beneficial or repressive, they are not neutral. They engen-der effects at multiple levels, bringing into being new practices, modes of expertise, priorities and subjectivity as workers are asked to moni-tor and view themselves and their work in new ways (Shore and Wright 2000, 57). As anthropologist Sharryn Kasmir has noted, identity is in fact at the heart of these new management styles, not in opposition to them (Kasmir 2005). The kind of self-monitoring, self-actualizing, con-tinuously self-improving dispositions that quality work circles demand are not simply there to be tapped into. Though they may be described as natural traits of all workers, such dispositions like class consciousness itself, are hailed into being (more or less successfully) through ideological and practical structures. The same can be said of the attitudes, beliefs and identifications people have about language. This linguistic consciousness is shaped by, among other forces, language advocacy. Advocacy does not simply protect and encourage speakers' use of a language; it does so in part by reshaping how language and language use is understood. In the case examined here, new institutions like *Lanhitz, Euskalit*, new subsi-dies, consultancies, resources and rewards like Certificates of Quality are transforming the values and significance of Basque. They describe it as value-added, not just a national symbol or cultural heritage. Workers are drawn by these methods into a more sociological understanding of their linguistic habits, pledging to become self-aware and self-managing about their language habits. This, of course, is not entirely new. Advocates have been encouraging a sociological perception of language for some time, but it is now linked to much more rigorous modes of measurement and to a more intentionally depoliticized understanding of language relations. Lest we see this process as a form of ideological domination imposed from outside, it is worth noting that advocates are also implementing TQM in their own organizations as well, and thereby asking them to plan and evaluate their activities more methodically. It also, as we have seen, asked language advocates to think about their own work differently. The marketing seminars in SWOT analysis, for example, were coaching community magazine producers into thinking of the Basque reading public they were trying to create not as a nation but as a market or a set of consumers. At the same time, they were implicitly asked to think of themselves, the community language group, as a quasi-enterprise. TQM tutors these minority media advocates in thinking about themselves less as citizens building a Basque nation or attempting to carve out a public sphere in Basque, than as entrepreneurs competing for a market share.

TQM shifts the way speakers are asked to think about their language habits, about what language is, or what the movement for revival is about. What, in the long run, might this mean for how struggles around minority languages are conceptualized and carried out? Here we find no consensus but some causes for concern. Williams and Morris (2000), for example, are highly skeptical. Their close study of the Welsh Language Board describes an increasingly neoliberal approach to language planning in which the objectives of strategic planning, strength and weakness analysis, and measurement seem to effectively sideline the general framework of democracy and rights within which the state had until then conceptualized protection for minority language speakers.[14] In her study of Scottish Gaelic language policies, McEwan-Fujita (2005) further suggests that the maze of record keeping and formulas for remits instituted by neoliberal policy approaches present obstacles, not avenues, that ironically work against the use of Gaelic for speakers unaccustomed to carrying out these kinds of bureaucratic tasks in their language. Nevertheless other scholars are more optimistic. In his assessment of the European Charter for Minority or Regional Languages, long-time policy consultant François Grin (2003a, 2003b) praises the Charter precisely because it does not argue for language promotion in terms of "rights" but rather opts for a "diversity management" approach. He argues that a less conflictual scenario is created when language diversity is approached as a field of management, similar to health care or education. Grin sees this as a positive step for minority language preservation helping to defuse political antagonisms. This kind of argument has been gaining ground throughout the European Union as a way of handling cultural diversity as a whole.

There have been compelling critiques of such approaches to multiculturalism for the way in which they turn cultural policies into the province of technical experts, thereby suspending a substantive discussion of the structural inequalities and power differences that are constitutive of cultural diversity (Brown 2006). These critiques are very relevant to the transformation we are seeing in the field of language policy. Grin may be right that the shift toward a management approach can make minority language protection more acceptable, but it cannot replace the political analysis and debates societies must inevitably have about how multilingualism fits into citizenship. At the same time, managerialism does not just come from Eurocrats; it can also come from below, deployed for different reasons and in different ways. In this case study, I have tried to show why it is that management methods could hold appeal for minority language activists wanting to normalize not only the use of Basque, but also have minority language promotion subjected to greater rigor and accountability. While, as we saw, many grassroots language advocates seemed to be sharing Grin's call for depoliticizing minority language promotion, it would be wrong to interpret these activists' calls for disentangling language revival from politics as meaning the same thing. They had not abandoned a political understanding of language. Rather what they wanted and needed was to get out from under the machinations of party politics and to approach language revival as a political project in its own right, armed with state-of-the-art science and methods. We must be careful about surface level resemblances in the rhetorics deployed. Our analyses cannot afford to ignore the different kinds of stakes that actors have in managerial methods. Nor can we ignore the climate of hostility toward minority language speakers and activism that makes legitimation so critical. Rather than co-optation, the alignment of Basque revival with the discursive logics of wealth production, efficient and competitive management facilitated its entry into the symbolic universe of private industry; this is in many ways an ingenious retort by a language movement beset by recurring accusations of its utter impracticality, on the one hand, and charges of political radicalism, on the other. In sum, if our discussions as scholars are to intersect with those of activists, we need to consider the varying investments and *Realpolitik* circumstances in which minority language advocates necessarily work, rather than dismiss their actions as misguided or naïve.

That being said, the effects of managerial discourse and methods are not neutral and need to be explored. One of the conversations scholars and language advocates need to have should be about the ways in which management discourse shapes—and I believe narrows—the priorities of language research and the ways in which we come to understand language as a whole. We have seen, for example, that TQM-inspired language planning summons into being a particular kind of linguistic consciousness and identification between a speaker and his or her linguistic behavior. It also continues the process initiated by language surveys—another tool of language advocacy—of bringing language practices into an ever more precise and standardized grid of visibility and regime of calculus. These schemas contribute to the commodification of language. Language tends increasingly to be thing-ified, treated as a discrete, measurable and bounded entity, on this grid of discrete countable units. But, we may ask, what aspects of language get measured and what difficult-to-quantify ways of using Basque fall off the radar of quantifying techniques? Language planning schemas, by their very nature, display a seeming inexorable tendency to reduce linguistic practice to language choice—Basque, Spanish, English, French—with a resulting impoverished understanding of language dynamics and eclipsing of syncretic or translanguage phenomena. Under the strong pressure to plan and measure results, there is little incentive for research exploring the nuanced and complex nature of linguistic interaction or performative uses of linguistic registers. Indeed, this kind of qualitative scholarship is vastly dwarfed by statistical measures of the linguistic landscape and demographic counts.

In a managerial framework, audit can take over. As Shore and Wright (2000) have argued convincingly, audit is surreptitiously coercive. It is incredibly difficult to say no to auditing practices (and the competitive ethos that accompanies them) because they "present themselves as rational, objective and neutral, based on sound principles of efficient management—as 'unopposable as virtue itself'" (Christopher Pollitt quoted in Shore and Wright 2000, 61). In a sea of political sloganeering about language, Marko thought audit could be useful. He sought out assessment to be able to see through ideology, to measure how much Basque was actually used, and as a means of concretizing target goals for language plans. Without denying the political and practical utility measures can provide in a contested political arena, we must also consider how the prominence of these strategies narrow the understanding of language to these presumed discrete entities we call languages, rather than promoting a speaker-centered idea of language as a symbolic practice, a set of resources, through which social reality is fashioned. Standardized measures of language choice and demographic analyses of the linguistic population may be useful for some purposes, but they cannot be a substitute for deeper ethnographic studies of the symbolic meanings of a changing linguistic field. It is only through the latter that we might be able to understand when and why a worker, or anyone else for that matter, chooses to speak one "language" or another.

NOTES

1. Bernard Spolsky's book on language policy, titled *Language Management* (2009) is a recent example of this discursive shift.
2. McEwan-Fujita (2005); Mac Giolla Chríost (2005); Williams and Morris (2000).
3. For a description of these and other strategic management techniques see Thompson and Strickland (1984).

4. Interview with author March 1998. These and all other translations are my own.
5. This is described in greater detail in Urla (2008).
6. The 1999 General Plan for the Promotion of the Use of Basque issued by the Basque Government of the Autonomous Community specifically identified language policy for private enterprise as a priority.
7. The evolution of governmental policies and initiatives to promote language normalization in the workplace is described in Consejo Asesor del Euskara (2005). This report notes the importance of consultations with Quebec language planners in designing language normalization plans for the private sector (27).
8. To do this work, Marko said that he had drawn upon such management strategies as "the balanced score card" (Kaplan and Norton 1996).
9. Azkarate (2007).
10. The argument for use of Basque in business is presented at greater length in a special issue of *BAT: Soziolinguistika Aldizkaria* 57 (2005).
11. The original text in Spanish reads, *El presente y futuro de nuestra sociedad, y el de las empresas de nuestro país, es un presente y futuro plurilingüe. El monolingüísmo es cosa del pasado, es arcaico: las empresas innovadoras y dinámicas serán aquéllas que sean capaces de adecuarse a su entorno, también en lo lingüístico. Por eso, en una sociedad cada vez más bilinge y plurilingüe, es difícil ofrecer un servicio de calidad dando la espalda a los miles y miles de ciudadanos que optan por utilizar el euskera y vivir en dicha lengua. En una sociedad cada vez más bilingüe, como es la nuestra, las empresas que tengan vocación de ser punteras y de alejarse de los puesto de cola, las empresas que pretendan ser innovadoras y dinámicas, las empresas que pretenden que sean reconocidas como líderes y estandartes de la modernidad, necesariamente deberán ir integrando progresivamente el euskera como lengua de servicio y de trabajo, para que funcionen también en euskera. La integración del euskera será una vía para fortalecer la propia empresa.* Oct. 2, 2006. Patxi Baztarrika, President of the Vice Council on Language Policy. Available at http://www.euskara.euskadi.net.
12. Published studies of language planning in workplaces so far do not seem to show resentment probably because to date language normalization plans in private industry have come about voluntarily in predominantly Basque speaking zones at the initiative of workers who want to participate in language revival (BAT 2005; Consejo Asesor del Euskera 2005). There is a strong emphasis on preliminary discussion and consensus building, in order for normalization plans to reflect the desires and capabilities of the participants.
13. See Hyatt (2001) for a demonstration of the value of in-depth ethnography for showing how neoliberal empowerment schemes can fail as they come into conflict with preexisting social norms of neighborhood life.
14. See Williams and Morris (2000), especially Chapters 8 and 9, for an analysis of neoliberal language planning by the Welsh Language Board.

REFERENCES

Azkarate, Miren. 2007. *Euskararen Kalitate Ziurtagiria.* Press Release. 17 Dec. 2007. http://www.euskara.euskadi.net.
BAT: Sociolinguistika Aldizkaria. 2005. Special issue. "Euskararen Erabilera Enpresetan" [Basque language use in the workplace]. No. 57.

Brown, Wendy. 2006. *Regulating Aversion: Tolerance in the Age of Identity and Empire*. Princeton, NJ: Princeton University Press.

Consejo Asesor del Euskera. 2005. *Criterios y estrategias para la promoción del uso del euskera en el ámbito socioeconómico y para un acercamiento más sistemático y eficaz a la normalización lingüística.* A publication of the Department of Culture, Basque Government. Vitoria-Gasteiz: Servicio Central de Publicaciones del Gobierno Vasco.

Dean, Mitchell. 1999. *Governmentality: Power and Rule in Modern Society*. London: Sage Publications.

Dorian, Nancy. 1998. "Western Language Ideologies and Small-Language Prospects." In *Endangered Languages*, edited by Lenore Grenoble and Lindsay J. Whaley, 3–21. Cambridge: Cambridge University Press.

Euskalit, the Basque Foundation for the Advancement of Quality. www.euskalit. net

Foucault, Michel. 1980. *The History of Sexuality. Volume 1: An Introduction.* Translated by Robert Hurley. New York: Vintage Books.

Foucault, Michel. 1991. "Governmentality." In *The Foucault Effect: Studies in Governmentality*, edited by Graham Burchell, Colin Gordon and Peter Miller, 87–104. Chicago: University of Chicago Press.

Grin, François. 2003a. "Diversity as Paradigm, Analytical Device and Policy Goal." In *Language Rights and Political Theory*, edited by Will Kymlicka and Alan Patten, 169–188. Oxford: Oxford University Press.

Grin, Francois, 2003b. *Language Policy Evaluation and the European Charter for Regional or Minority Languages*. Hampshire, UK: Palgrave Macmillan.

Harvey, David. 2005. *A Brief History of Neoliberalism*. Oxford: Oxford University Press.

Hyatt, Susan. 2001. "From Citizen to Volunteer: Neoliberal Governance and the Erasure of Poverty." In *The New Poverty Studies: The Ethnography of Power, Politics, and Impoverished People in the United States*, edited by Judith Goode and Jeff Maskovsky, 201–235. New York: New York University Press.

Inoue, Miyako. n.d. "What Do Women Want? Gender Equity and the Ethics and Aesthetics of the Self in Neoliberal Japan." Unpublished manuscript.

Kaplan, Robert S., and David Norton. 1996. *The Balanced Scorecard: Translating Strategy into Action*. Boston: Harvard Business School Press.

Kasmir, Sharryn. 2005. "Activism and Class Identity: The Saturn Auto Factory." In *Social Movements: An Anthropological Reader*, edited by June Nash, 78–95. Oxford: Blackwell.

Marko Juanikorena, J. Inazio. 2004. Euskara bultzatzeko erantzukizuna eta enpresak. http://www.erabili.com/aer_berri/muinetik/1084208726

Maskovsky, Jeff. 2001. "The Other War at Home: The Geopolitics of Urban Poverty." *Urban Anthropology* 30(2–3): 215–238.

Mac Giolla Chríost, Diarmait. 2005. "Prestige Planning and the Welsh Language: Marketing, the Consumer-Citizen and Language Behavior." *Current Issues in Language Planning* 6(1): 64–72.

McEwan-Fujita, Emily. 2005. "Neoliberalism and Minority-Language Planning in the Highlands and Islands of Scotland." *International Journal of the Sociology of Language* 171: 155–171.

May, Stephen. 2001. *Language and Minority Rights: Ethnicity, Nationalism and the Politics of Language*. Harlow, UK: Longman/Pearson Education.

May, Stephen. 2003. "Misconceiving Minority Language Rights: Implications for Liberal Political Theory." In *Language Rights and Political Theory*, edited by Will Kymlicka and Alan Patten, 123–152. Oxford: Oxford University Press.

Meillet, Antoine. [1918] 1928. *Les Langues dans L'Europe Nouvelle*. 2nd ed. Paris: Payot.

Neff van Aerstaeler, JoAnne. 2006. "Language Policies in Spain: Accommodation or Alteration." In *Along the Routes to Power: Explorations of Empowerment through Language*, edited by Martin Putz, Joshua A. Fishman and JoAnne Neff-van Aertselaer, 179–198. Berlin: Mouton de Gruyter.

Nelson, Daniel. 1980. *Frederick W. Taylor and the Rise of Scientific Management.* Madison: University of Wisconsin Press.

Persico, John. 1992. *The TQM Transformation: A Model for Organizational Change.* White Plains, NY: Quality Resources.

Rose, Nikolas. 1999. *Powers of Freedom: Reframing Political Thought.* Cambridge: Cambridge University Press.

Shore, Cris, and Susan Wright. 2000. "Coercive Accountability: The Rise of Audit Culture in Higher Education." In *Audit Cultures: Anthropological Studies in Accountability, Ethics and the Academy*, edited by Marilyn Strathern, 57–89. London: Routledge.

Spolsky, Bernard. 2009. *Language Management.* Cambridge: Cambridge University Press.

Strathern, Marilyn. 2000. *Audit Cultures: Anthropological Studies in Accountability, Ethics and the Academy.* London: Routledge.

Swift, Jill. A., Joel E. Ross, and Vincent K. Omachonu. 1998. *Principles of Total Quality.* 2nd ed. Boca Raton, FL: St. Lucie Press.

Thompson, Arthur A. Jr., and Alonzo J. Strickland III. 1984. *Strategic Management: Concepts and Cases.* 3rd ed. Boston: Irwin McGraw Hill.

Urla, Jacqueline. 1989. "Reinventing Basque Society: Cultural Difference and the Quest for Modernity, 1918–1936." In *Essays in Basque Social Anthropology and History* (Basque Studies Program Occasional Papers Series. No. 4), edited by William Douglass, 149–176. Reno, NV: Basque Studies Program.

Urla, Jacqueline. 2008. "Kafe Antzokia: The Global Meets the Local in Basque Cultural Politics." In *Recasting Culture and Space in Iberian Contexts*, edited by Sharon R. Roseman and Shawn S. Parkhurst, 253–270. Albany: State University of New York Press.

Urla, Jacqueline. forthcoming. *Reclaiming Basque: Language, Nation, and Cultural Activism.* Reno: University of Nevada Press.

Williams, Glyn, and Delyth Morris. 2000. *Language Planning and Language Use: Welsh in a Global Age.* Cardiff: University of Wales Press.

5 Literary Tourism

New Appropriations of Landscape and Territory in Catalonia[1]

Joan Pujolar and Kathryn Jones

2002 was declared by the *Generalitat de Catalunya*—the Catalan government—as the 'Year of Verdaguer,' an invitation to all public institutions and nongovernmental groups to commemorate the centenary of the death of poet Jacint Verdaguer (1845–1902). Verdaguer symbolizes the *Renaixença* (the rebirth or renaissance) of Catalan letters in the nineteenth century. In one of the hundreds of initiatives connected with the celebration, artist Perejaume[2] was commissioned to create a lasting monument in the village of Folgueroles, Verdaguer's birthplace. Figure 5.1 is the result: in a small park, the Folgueroles brook was channeled so that its course reproduced the signature of the poet.

The signature can be seen, at least in part, from a variety of hills surrounding the low ground where it lies. The intention of the author, as we will see, was to highlight the contribution of Verdaguer's role to the formation of particular representations of the Catalan landscape that have become part of popular culture. Thus the Folgueroles landscape is made to physically bear the author's signature as if he had authored its very hills, plains, fields, meadows, woods, paths, roads, cottages, villages, pools and rivers.

In this chapter, we shall attempt to explain how such an artistic work became both meaningful and relevant at this particular time and place. We will show how it was made in the context of a contemporary social movement to reclaim and reinterpret the Catalan landscape in a way that symbolizes nationhood. This symbolization is done by mobilizing language and literature as national emblems through a variety of social practices usually aimed at the construction and preservation of the Catalan literary heritage (tour guides, museums, festivals and celebrations). We will argue that this movement constitutes a response to globalization in terms of both reclaiming the collective memory of place and reasserting the relevance of Catalan language and identity. This response presents an inbuilt ambivalence between (a) an attempt to adapt traditional discourses about place and nation in the context of a heritage industry that commoditizes landscape and identity for global consumers, and (b) a desire to resist the patterns of linguistic practice

Figure 5.1   Verdaguer *signs* the landscape. Photo by Toni Anguera. Source: Fons de la Fundació Jacint Verdaguer.[3]

and cultural consumption that globalization fosters and which are perceived as a threat for Catalan identity, particularly for the use of the Catalan language and the consumption of Catalan literature. In short, it is an attempt to sustain discourses about (national) *pride* by adopting discourses about (economic) *profit* in ambivalent and contradictory ways.

This chapter draws on a comparative study about identity tourism (Pitchford 2008) conducted in three linguistic minority contexts: Catalonia, Wales and the Acadian and Franco-Ontarian areas of Canada. We shall focus on Catalonia here because it is the site where discourses about landscape and literature have undergone a wider development, both historically and contemporarily; however, we shall also point at parallel phenomena taking place in Wales and elsewhere (Canadian approaches to landscape have been somewhat different, as we will also show). We have gathered the data mainly through visits to particular tourist sites, interviews with workers of these sites and documentation obtained on site or through their increasingly sophisticated websites. The museums dedicated to the writers Jacint Verdaguer and Josep Pla (1897–1981) in Catalonia have been the key sites, as they (both the writers and the sites themselves) have historically played a central role in the development of the discourses analyzed; however, we also draw significantly from information available in the two most important projects connected with this movement—the *Espais Escrits* (www.espaisescrits.cat) and *Endrets* (www.endrets.cat) projects[4]— as well as press reports and other information from various public and private institutions. We are going to be deliberately vague about some sources in order to protect the identity of interviewees and employees of the sites, as it would be too obvious to many potential readers even with the use of pseudonyms. A simple web search would suffice to locate them. Although this may diminish the colors of the narrative, we hope it will not impact on the clarity of the analysis.

To understand the significance of contemporary discourses about language, landscape and nation, it is important to situate the phenomena analyzed in a historical perspective. So we shall begin with a historical appraisal of the representations of landscape in literature with an emphasis on the Catalan case. After this, we shall also trace the history of the two Catalan literary houses and how they gradually became inscribed as part of the "heritage industry" (Hewison 1987). To do so, we shall bring into the analysis Harvey's (1989) ideas about processes of time–space compression and his reflection on how socioeconomic changes bring about new forms of perceiving and constructing space and territory. Finally, we shall discuss how Catalan literary sites currently negotiate their position in the cultural, political and economic fields; how they resolve the tensions involved in using different languages in the context of tourism; and how landscape is mobilized to respond to the contradictory demands they face as they seek to reproduce traditional discourses about national identity and adapt to the requirements of the tourist industry.

LANDSCAPE, LITERATURE AND THE NATION IN HISTORICAL PERSPECTIVE

There is a well-established tradition of literary production whereby representations of landscape and territory were mobilized already in the eighteenth and nineteenth centuries to signify national character (Ebbatson and Donahue 2005; James 1981; Siddall 2009; Williams 1975). In Catalonia, as in Wales, such developments emerged later, in the context of the nineteenth-century literary *renaissances* that took place amongst many linguistic minorities (Morgan 1983; Roma i Casanovas 2004). It was part of a wider movement of romantic inspiration that became bound up with the development of the political and cultural infrastructures of nationalism. The landscape and literature movement taking place in Catalonia today has clear continuities with this tradition and maintains its connections with developments found elsewhere: (a) in Wales, the Cae'r Gors Kate Roberts Heritage Centre, created in 2001 in Rhosgadfan, emphasizes aspects of the author's writings that connect with the local geography (see www.caergors. org); (b) in Italy, a network called *I Parchi Letterari* 'Literary Parks' developed during the 1980s and created the association *Paesaggio Culturale Italiano Srl* in 2009 (Torrents 2007). In this section, we shall present a brief historical overview of the Catalan literary apprehension of landscape within this wider European context.

The very notion of landscape is historically connected with the transformation of the territory or the land into a commodity. Williams (1975) locates the process in eighteenth-century England as a growing middle and upper class could increasingly look into the territory "from a distance," in contrast with the experience of farmers and other agricultural workers. The "birth" of the landscape was accompanied, particularly in Britain, with the new scientific spirit, as a significant number of people began hiking around the "countryside" to gather all types of botanical, zoological and geological information that fed into the debates over evolution and national history. In Catalonia, the signification of landscape for national identity appears to have developed in the second half of the nineteenth century in the context of the literary renaissances that developed in connection with the rise of Romantic nationalism (Roma i Casanovas 2004). We find parallel developments in Wales, as when the English-language writer T. J. Ll Pritchard and many of his contemporaries are said to have explicitly sought to imbue the Welsh landscape with meaning by connecting particular places with Welsh traditions and legends (Morgan 1983).

Harvey's insights into "the condition of postmodernity" are useful to understand how modern apprehensions of the territory are bound up with the economic and technological transformations brought about by capitalism and its correlates of industrialization, urbanization and the development of nation-states. Harvey (1989) identifies specific historical moments or phases of "time–space compression" that involve changes in the apprehension of time and place resulting from the successive changes in transport and communication technologies and their associated modes of production. He argues that we should not assume that these processes are unique to our contemporary period. He points to the second half of the nineteenth century as a moment undergoing a specific process of time–space compression following a characteristic crisis of capital accumulation in 1848 Europe, which was slowly resolved by the development of new forms of transport, communication and management of time in industrial production and investment. Contemporary globalization, he argues, is another such moment. From this perspective, it is interesting to note that Harvey's phases coincide with the timing of the various moments of Catalan preoccupation with landscape. The late nineteenth century, Harvey claims, brought about new representations and forms of control over territories, dislocated existing geographies, accelerated urbanization and changed cultural perceptions of place. It brought about the opposing trends of internationalism (as in Marxism) versus new forms of localism and parochialism that fed into emerging nationalisms up to the Second World War, the period that Hobsbawm (1992) characterizes as the apogee of nationalism.

> The ideological labour of inventing tradition became of great significance in the late nineteenth century precisely because this was an era when the transformations in spatial and temporal practices implied a loss of identity with place and repeated radical breaks with any sense of historical continuity . . . Modernism . . . While celebrating universality

and the collapse of spatial barriers, [it] also explored new meanings for space and place in ways that tacitly reinforced local identity. (Harvey 1989, 272)

As traditional forms of life were becoming obsolete, "historical preservation and the museum culture experienced strong bursts of life" (272). It is also important to bear in mind that not only space but *time* was important in the equation in the sense that places often achieved their significance in terms of their value in (national) history and memory.

The second phase identified by Harvey starts in the 1960s with the popularization of the car, the development of mass tourism and the cultural industries, followed in the 1990s by a marked acceleration fuelled by new communication technologies, the globalized economy and its correlates of relocalization of production, financial flows and immigration.

Seen from this viewpoint, the reclaiming of the landscape as a cultural icon with identity value can be presented both as a result of and as a reaction to socioeconomic processes that dislocate (literally, detach from place) identities and their associated cultural practices, including the use of languages. Discourses about landscape constitute a reaction to the diminishing relevance of place in the production and reproduction of both local cultural practices and national identities. In this context, it is important to appreciate that literary discourses about landscape are not an isolated phenomenon stemming from nostalgic solitary artists, but part of wider social movements.

Roma i Casanovas (2004) has extensively traced the emergence of the notion of "landscape" in Catalonia from the sixteenth to the twentieth centuries, where the British interest in the territory for scientific exploration and leisure arrived later than in Britain. After a few exceptions in the form of exploring priests and monks from the monastery of Montserrat, the late nineteenth century saw the emergence of the *excursionista* movement. The *Associació Catalanista d'Excursions Científiques* 'Catalanist Scientific Excursion Association' was created in 1876 in a period of rapid articulation of political nationalism. It later became the Centre Excursionista de Catalunya (see www.cec.cat) and played a fundamental role in the cataloguing, publicization and development of Catalan folklore, monumental heritage, flora, fauna, history, geology and so on (Camarasa 2000). It is not possible to overstate the importance of this tradition in the construction of modern knowledge about the Catalan territory and its economic and cultural resources, a process entirely led by a Catalan-speaking middle class, which was not always politically united but largely shared a commitment to Catalonia as a separate cultural community. Most names big and small in the various scientific fields have been members and often have actually conducted their research (or initiated their vocation) through *Excursionista*, Boy Scout and similar associations. Many works now exhibited at the *Museu Nacional d'Art de Catalunya* in Barcelona were identified, recovered and restored by parties who hiked to distant villages and chapels built at the top of mountains.

The poet Jacint Verdaguer (1845–1902) was part of this movement, and his works were deeply implicated in the production of particular forms of interpreting, sensing and moving within the territory. His masterpiece, "L'Atlàntida" (1877), is a kind of tectonic epic about the sinking of the island of Atlantis, where many of the characters are mythical figures that impersonate or manipulate islands, mountain ranges or seas. Barely second comes his poem "Canigó" (1886), named after the mountain peak, which is a more conventional epic about the origins of the Catalan nation in the Middle Ages. Many of his works present some concrete place or geographical accident as embodying some national, moral or religious value.

However, writing about landscape, place and national character in Catalan literature is not exclusively a nineteenth-century phenomenon. It makes a fairly continuous strand that begins with Jacint Verdaguer's romanticizing epic poems, continues with *modernista* Joan Maragall (Fradera 2009), moves into the deceptively realist prose of Josep Pla and reemerges in the contemporary period with the repertoire of "walks" by Josep Maria Espinàs[5] (1927–), to name but a fraction of the literary names involved. Josep Pla (1897–1981), to whom our second site is devoted, shines with a distinctly strong light in the constellation of landscape writing in Catalonia. He wrote nonfiction prose almost exclusively and was an exceptional witness and participant in the invention of a well-known geographical entity: the *Costa Brava*. He worked for many years for Francesc Cambó, the undisputed leader of Catalan nationalists for the first thirty years of the century. Cambó allegedly took part in a dinner of Catalan politicians where the term *Costa Brava* was created as a tourist destination in 1908 (Playà 2008). Pla was the first to write (in Spanish; publishing in Catalan was forbidden in Spain from 1939) the tourist guides that were reprinted for decades (later in Catalan versions), a task which he combined with conventional journalism and the writing of his *dietari*, a work of memoirs in the form of a diary which deals mainly with the landscape and geography of the Empordà region, the everyday life in small villages and the local food (Pla 1945). In his writings, there are numerous references to the importance of the landscape and climate to fashion national character and he has a particular argument to make that the beauty of the landscape stems from its economic productivity. His gaze over the landscape differs in important ways from the barren landscape of mainland Spain idealized by the Spanish literati of the *Generación del 98*, as well as from the earlier epic and nostalgic appropriations associated, amongst others, with Verdaguer (Figueras 2004; Fuster 1967).

In any case, one important aspect of the Catalan material is precisely the thematization of Catalanness, national character and national emblems. Although patriotic literature (as well as a certain ethnocentrism and/or national partisanship) can admittedly be found everywhere, our literature

survey suggests that the explicit thematization of national identity generally occupies very different positions in the literary fields expressed in
dominant or minority languages. This is not to say that most literary
works of minority authors discuss national identity (actually, they don't),
but that their patriotic production occupies a special position in popular
and learned memory that is consistent with their own role as national figures often accredited with having significantly contributed to the formation of a literary corpus and a written standard that accorded legitimacy
to the claims to nationhood (this is clearly Verdaguer's case). Thus, in the
first versions of the *Espais Escrits* website in 2005, visitors were invited
to watch a video in which a poem of Verdaguer written in 1901 was
recited against the background of a 3D satellite perspective of the Catalan territory travelling from the mountains to the city (Verdaguer 2005).
The poem features one mountain peak asking another whether it believes
that the *nissaga catalana* 'the Catalan lineage' is dwindling, to which the
other responds that it is not, but rather that it loses its strength as it climbs
down from its original dwellings in the mountains and into the cities.[6] We
have not found comparable texts dealing with English or British identity
in these terms in the studies available (Bhabha 1990; Corse 1997; Ebbatson and Donahue 2005; Edensor 2002), not even in Williams' (1975)
impressive survey. Ebbatson and Donahue (2005) in particular need to
engage in a very sophisticated hermeneutic to show that poems of Ten-
nyson, Arden, Hardy or Jefferies involve the construction of particular
visions of Englishness or Britishness. Even the title "England, My England" by Lawrence is reportedly metonymic of the social implications of
war. They do acknowledge that some English literature projects a colonial
gaze over Wales that is comparable to portrayals of Ireland or of overseas
possessions where the wilderness of the land or the "backwardness" of the
natives are opposed to England's orderly, modernized spaces and figures
(Ebbatson and Donahue 2005). Blake's "Jerusalem," while exceptionally
similar to Verdaguer's poem in its thematization and problematization
of English identity, cannot be said to characterize his whole work in this
sense and was not inscribed in a comparable political and cultural movement in which this theme was central. Thus the thematization of national
identities seems to occur rather in contexts of serious identity crisis, such
as 1898 Spain or among minorities.

Thus, Catalan literature has a long tradition of writing about the landscape and of representing the landscape as an expression of national identity, and this tradition is centrally inscribed in the process of modernization
of the Catalan language and culture, as well as the development of the forms
of knowing and managing the territory brought about by industrialization.
From this perspective, the contemporary development of the Catalan literary heritage, and its new forms of constructing and apprehending the
landscape in the context of tourism, appear as one way to negotiate change
and continuity in the face of contemporary socioeconomic transformations

that are comparable to the ones taking place in the nineteenth and early twentieth centuries. In the next section, we shall explain how the idea of Catalan literary heritage eventually developed.

THE DEVELOPMENT OF THE
LITERARY HERITAGE IN CATALONIA

There is a long tradition that binds literature with tourism, as is made evident by the early twentieth-century boom of literary "pilgrimages." Virginia Woolf (1994) criticized, already in 1904, the fashion of visiting places connected with literary works, including the former residences of authors. This phenomenon was complemented with the so-called "literary geographies" or "literary atlases" that became very popular in the 1920s and 1930s (Herbert 1996, 2001). Indeed, Iribarren's (2007) account of the travels of a Catalan intellectual in Britain in the 1920s and 1930s suggests that literature had a prominent role at the time to define the touristic interests of the educated classes. The development of cultural and heritage tourism, however, has recently led to a quantitative increase and a qualitative diversification (Herbert 1996, 2001) and has inscribed these activities within the field of economic initiative and strategic planning. Little is known about this earlier period of literary tourism in Catalonia, but nowadays it clearly constitutes a burgeoning field of activity.

The sites analyzed here refer back to 1964, with the formal creation of the *Agrupació Amics de Verdaguer* 'Society Friends of Verdaguer' and 1973, when Josep Pla donated his sizable library to a private foundation that eventually became the Fundació Josep Pla in 1990 (he died in 1981). Evidence of the activities by the *Amics de Verdaguer* can be found in 1960, reportedly encouraged by a Barcelona resident with family connections in Folgueroles, Miquel Saperas, then secretary of *Orfeó Català*,[7] one of the emblematic institutions of the *Renaixença* devoted to the development of popular music, which was tolerated by the Francoist regime because it was controlled by the conservative bourgeoisie. However, the *Amics* reportedly contained varied political affiliations and actively worked against the moves of the regime to appropriate the figure of the writer. The specific events that led to the process are not known, but the timing is consistent with the beginning of an economic recovery after a period of disastrous autarkic policies under Franco, which involved the development of mass tourism and the resulting boom of the construction industry parallel to the rearticulation of political and economic opposition movements to the dictatorship. The figure of Saperas, a Barcelona resident that is active in a small rural village of the interior, is typical of a time when city dwellers were appearing in increasing numbers in beaches and villages, and begun buying land and building second residences. The *Amics* gathered funds by popular subscription to buy, through the municipality, the childhood residence of the poet, although in the end they had to buy the adjacent one, which opened in 1967 as a museum.[8]

Josep Pla's case is somewhat different in that he had moved back to live in his hometown after moving to Barcelona to study and working as a journalist for many years. His association with the conservative nationalists who sided with Franco during the war had imbued him with a certain stigma, although he was welcomed by most opposition political and cultural groups. He was, in any case, a nationalist clearly committed to a hegemonic and autonomous Catalan cultural field. In 1973 he decided to donate his sizable library to a private foundation that eventually became the *Fundació Josep Pla* in 1990.

Coming back to Harvey's (1989) trajectories of time–space compression, the 1960s and 1970s mark the beginning of the second phase, characterized by a crisis of the Keynesian-Fordist model of production and capital accumulation in which some elements of the later period of "flexible accumulation" were appearing, such as the rapid growth of the service sector combined with new patterns of mass consumption of "short-cycle" cultural and manufactured products (i.e., products such as fashion objects that need to be quickly replaced to ensure sustained demand). It is the period connected with the rise of mass culture, mass tourism, counterculture, the revival of minority movements, and the development of civil rights movements in a context of rapid economic growth in Europe and North America. Many authors locate the appearance of postmodernity at this time, one of its many implications being the rise of the cultural industries and, among them, the "heritage industry" in tourist contexts (Hewison 1987).

In the various contexts we have analyzed, the development of the heritage industry seems to go at different paces. Among Acadians in Canada, the Caraquet Chamber of Commerce came up in 1965 with the idea to build a typical Acadian Village as a tourist attraction as a project inserted in an overall strategy of economic development in Acadian areas (http://www.villagehistoriqueacadien.com/historique.cfm). The site finally opened in 1977. This emerged in the context of the political mobilizations that led to the election of Acadian Louis Robichaud as regional premier of New Brunswick in 1960. The Québecois *Révolution tranquille* took hold in the same period, and similar heritage initiatives were taking place in other Acadian areas such as the Evangeline Region in Prince Edward Island (Pujolar 2006). In relation to Nationalist and Culturalist sectors in Catalonia (and Wales for that matter), there is no evidence that the actors of this period were in anyway contemplating their initiatives as inscribed in projects of economic development. Rather, they were investing in the articulation of a Catalan cultural field in which money was supposed to be spent rather than earned. If any practical function was attributed to the Verdaguer and Josep Pla sites, it was largely that of documentation for scholars.

The idea and the very concept of literary heritage would come later in the 1990s, and it is reasonable to partially attribute the development to the decline of agriculture and industry in the Catalan hinterland brought about by globalization and tertiarization. During the 1980s, the traditional textile mills gradually disappeared, starting in the upper valleys of the Pyrenees; small villages and towns started to lose population, and local administrations started talking about the need of *dinamització territorial* 'local development', and specifically of *turisme rural*. Spain's entry into the European Community in 1986 seems to have accelerated the process as local industries increasingly faced international competition. This is consistent with the evidence found in numerous studies that attest in multiple forms how many linguistic minorities started investing in tourism, cultural heritage and local development in the 1990s as globalization gathered speed (Boudreau and White 2006; Heller 2003, 2004; Le Menestrel 1999; McLaughlin 2007; Moïse 2006; Pitchford 2008; Pritchard and Morgan 2001; Pujolar 2006; Torrents 2007).

This marks the moment in which the literary sites analyzed were eventually built, opened and inserted in the context of tourism. The foundation *Patronat Casa Museu Verdaguer* was established in 1991 with the support of the municipality and took the present form as the *Fundació Jacint Verdaguer* in 2006. In 1992, the municipality decided to employ a part-time curator and the house had regular opening hours. Two nationwide commemorations, the 1995 *Segle Romàntic* 'Romantic Century' and the 2002 *Any Verdaguer* 'Verdaguer Year', brought unusual numbers of visitors and imaginative celebrations (such as the one depicted at the beginning of this chapter), and this raised further interest from local politicians in terms of its possible benefits for tourism. The history of the *Fundació Josep Pla* is similar. At first it consisted basically of the author's own library that could be visited twice a week (it had no telephone or computer). In 1994 the municipality decided to buy the author's birthplace, refurbish it and carry out a museization project. 1997 was the *Any Pla* and the site became an unusual focus of political interest both locally and nationally. In Wales, The Friends of Cae'r Gors (in reference to the Marsh Field surrounding Kate Roberts' birthplace) was also created in 1995, and actively sought funding until it managed to open the center in 2001 thanks to a lottery fund.

The significance of the events taking place at this time was very well captured by one of the interviewees:

Extract 1
Entrevistada 1: realment va ser un un èxit allò desbordant • i també va va servir una mica de consciència per per dir bé la fundació té tot el sentit que existeixi no? Un centre de patrimoni literari que s'ocupi doncs de custodiar i de • i de difondre l'obra de l'escriptor • • punt o sigui una cosa tan simple com aquesta que en aquells moments • ara ja és una idea definida i un concepte que • que comença a estar clar però que en aquells moments ni existia el concepte de patrimoni literari no? I llavors la idea va ser tenir una doble línia d'actuació que per una banda

hi hagués • resposta a la demanda del turisme cultural i per l'altra resposta a la demanda dels estudiosos • de la literatura no?

Interviewee 1: it was a real success, somewhat overwhelming, and it
also helped to create some awareness that the foundation made total
sense, right? A center of literary heritage in charge of the custody and-
and the dissemination of the writer's work. This is it; something as
simple as that; but which at the time . . . Now it is an established idea
and a concept . . . that begins to sink in clearly; but at the time the
very concept of *literary heritage* did not exist, right? And then the idea
was to have a double line of action: on the one hand to respond to the
demand of cultural tourism and on the other to respond to the demand
of literature scholars, right?

The extract is explicit about the emergence of new categories and new
social practices in connection with literary sites. The transformation, in
this case, runs parallel to a professionalization of the sector, as people who
had for years participated in the sites as voluntary workers (most of them
women) tied to local cultural associations were finally employed by the
foundations and local authorities. Most workers, both senior and junior,
are trained philologists. By the late 2000s, the two sites had at least one
director accompanied by polyvalent support staff members who could
work as administrative assistants, librarians, tourist guides and educational assistants for visiting schools. The extract also portrays with clarity
the duality of purpose that is constitutive of these sites nowadays. From
an earlier focus on preservation of documentation and artifacts because
of their cultural value, cultural tourism became interesting to participants
both as a source of funding and also as a new form of disseminating particular representations of literature, culture and the national imaginary.
It is in this context that we see the development of the concept of literary
landscape, which we shall address in the next section.

LANGUAGES AND LANDSCAPE IN THE
CULTURAL AND TOURIST MARKETS

Given the duality of objectives mentioned (the cultural and the touristic),
we shall now spell out various forms of positioning that literary sites developed in Catalonia. As cultural institutions, they took up the role expected
of them as curators of the memory of national writers. As organizations in
need of funding, they sought the support of both public administrations
and private donors whenever possible. To do this, they claimed their value
as cultural infrastructures, tourist attractions, or both. They organized
activities consistent with one objective or the other, or with both. Choices
naturally involved tensions and compromises. In this section, we analyze

how the sites negotiated the tensions involved in this duality. However, prior to this, it is important to be aware of a number of determining factors faced by those who made decisions as to the funding, the institutional status and the activities of the sites. So we shall first analyze the position of literary heritage sites in the cultural field, in local politics and the tourist market. This will allow us to understand both the constraints faced and the strategies deployed by those who run the sites. Finally, we shall examine two key aspects in which tensions played out: (1) the use of languages and (2) the development of new discourses about landscape (in which language was also given a primary role).

The literary and academic focus was very present at both Catalan foundations. In the statutes of the Verdaguer Foundation, cultural tourism appeared as a third objective, after that of preserving the property assets and disseminating the work of the author through the production of activities for schools, seminars, research and publications. The educational activities offered to schools were advertised prominently, as well as numerous seminars, talks, conferences, roundtables, book presentations and temporary exhibits. Other activities allowed participants to engage with the authors through the website in the form of blogs, the "[p]oem and image of the month" or a weblog. The activities changed over time, so that one year exhibits and round tables could be dedicated to some biographical aspect of the writer, while the next could be about the relationship between the writer and a prominent historian, and so on. Most of these activities required participants to visit the sites, or at least the villages where they are located, or their surroundings (such as the guided literary walks). Activities addressed to a general public were organized on Fridays and Saturdays to allow for the presence of numerous people from Barcelona who had their second residence near Palafrugell or Folgueroles. There was also a significant repertoire of events taking place in Barcelona or elsewhere in collaboration with many other actors (universities, cultural institutions), evidence that the foundations had successfully positioned themselves as key participants in matters related to the authors in the Catalan cultural field.

From an economic perspective, the basic fact is that the sites needed external funding. According to the *Coordinadora Catalana de Fundacions* (a nonprofit, independent, umbrella organization of private foundations), the 2008 operating budget of the Verdaguer foundation was 163680€, while that of the Josep Pla foundation came to 205860€. Revenue from an average of 5,000 visitors at 3€ could barely reach even a tenth of the overall budget, which means that the sites were far from achieving sustainability through tourism; this indicates that their funding has been obtained mainly from municipal authorities from the moment of their inception.

The *Generalitat*, the autonomous Catalan government, has also recently begun to contribute through the *Institució de les Lletres Catalanes*, although not as a stable source (an application for a grant has to be submitted each year). Universities can also make small contributions, and funds for specific activities can be obtained from the *Caixes* (typically Catalan cooperative financial institutions that operate largely as banks but who spend their profits on projects of social interest). Beyond this, the private sector, even in the tourist industry, has been largely absent. Only the *endrets* project seemed to have managed to obtain contributions from the two major publishing houses in Catalan, Enciclopèdia Catalana and Edicions 62. The absence of the Department of Tourism was, from this perspective, significant. In 2006, the Minister of Tourism visited the *Casa Museu Verdaguer* and declared that it was bound to be the main distinctive tourist resource in the area. However, no substantial commitment from his department came in the following years. Political backing from the *Generalitat* seemed to be discretional and subject to the visiting itineraries of ministers.

This lack of interest was in contrast with recent developments in tourist policies in Catalonia, where attention to cultural aspects has increased in the last two decades, particularly after the emergence of Barcelona as an important tourist destination. Literary heritage has, however, been secondary (at best) behind top attractions such as Modernist art and architecture, conventional art museums or special cases such as the sites devoted to Dalí, Miró, Picasso or Tàpies.

Following the "cultural" tab in the Turisme de Catalunya website in late 2010,[9] we found a "Catalonia is culture" guide, featuring "Literature" as a theme on page 33. The examples given were, however, of works originally written in Spanish that had recently been translated and widely read internationally, mostly located in Barcelona, where the local tourist board produced a number of tourist routes based on both Catalan and Spanish literary works. On the same webpage there was a special mention of the *Espais Escrits* network, and a text pointing out to visitors the importance of literature written in Catalan. To find the sites connected with Catalan literature, one had to explore further the *Espais Escrits* website.

Thus, from the perspective of tourist resources, Catalan literary sites were basically a complementary resource that appeared only in general inventories. Literature written in Spanish was given more prominence even when there were no specific foundations, museums or associations devoted to them. This is significant if we bear in mind that, between 2003 and 2010, the Catalan Ministry of Tourism was located in a department controlled by Catalan nationalists who insisted on the value of Catalan cultural heritage in tourism as a strategic asset to complement the traditional "sand and sun" model. For instance, the ministry promoted a network of ten brand-new tourist centers distributed across the territory featuring different cultural themes. One of them was located precisely in Palafrugell, where the *Fundació Josep Pla* is located. However, the theme chosen for this centre was "cuisine" and the tender documentation for the museization project only mentioned Josep Pla marginally because he often referred to local cooking and socializing about food in his writings. Those working in the sites pointed out the contradictions of a policy that paid lip service to the value of cultural heritage but showed little commitment to resources that, in principle, should be seen as key elements of the Catalan cultural tradition.

The attitudes of the private tourism sector were similar. The foundations were making efforts to bring about joint projects with owners of hotels and restaurants, or to train those working in tourist offices and hotels so that they recommended the sites. They generally felt that their efforts were met with very little interest, except at special moments such as in centenaries and commemorations. While the local population reached 2,205 (in Folgueroles) and 22,365 (in Palafrugell), the sites had a regular turnover of 4,000 to 5,000 visitors; the directors aimed to raise the figure up to 10,000, beyond which the buildings would probably need renovations. These are significant numbers for the towns concerned, but small numbers as compared with the millions that visit the Costa Brava, just ten miles from Palafrugell. The *Fundació Josep Pla* has made some bids to attract the interest of international visitors with temporary exhibits such as "*Pels camins de l'Empordà. Günter Grass— Josep Pla*" (Pathways around the Empordà), an exhibit featuring drawings by Günter Grass, made when he visited the Empordà region as a tourist, and which were presented against texts of Pla's that had some connection with what was depicted. A few German tourists appear to have turned up at the exhibit, but certainly not in large numbers.

The management of the language choices in the sites was one key indicator of the tensions and ambivalences brought about by their cultural and touristic aims. Language choice was a sensitive issue for two main reasons, because of the status accorded to Catalan as emblem of national identity, and because literature is an eminently linguistic product that is difficult to consume without access to either original texts or translations. In fact, in linguistic terms, literature makes a costly "high-tech" product. It is a powerful discourse in terms of its symbolic legitimacy and its aesthetic workmanship, particularly when it can be enlisted in particular contexts for audiences to participate in complex significations connecting narratives, images, places and histories. Whereas much tourism is devoted to activities and objects where language can be treated as a simple auxiliary resource that can easily be adapted (i.e., translated) for the benefit of the audience, in literature language is the very object of attention, contemplation or veneration, the substance of the product offered, and so translation is very often problematic. Additionally, the work of national authors acquired (part of) their social and political significance out of the very fact that they were written in the national language. The promoters of sites had a trajectory of participation in struggles over the development of an independent cultural field through the national language. The association *Amics de Verdaguer*, for one, had seen its legalization delayed for years due to a conflict with Franco's *governador civil*, who required the bylaws to be written in Spanish and all formal proceedings to be conducted in this language. Those I interviewed were admittedly very young children (if born at all) when these events took place, but they had actually grown up within or in close contact with the groups that had started the project, and had no doubts about the continuity of their commitments in this respect.

The sites mainly attracted visitors from Catalan-speaking regions and some Spanish speakers, especially in the case of Josep Pla, who had a significant readership in the rest of Spain. This also indicates that the predominant profile of the visitors had to do, generally speaking, with the audiences that the authors had had and the constituencies in which the authors had a name. Catalan writers, from this perspective, cannot be compared with figures such as Shakespeare, Hans Christian Andersen or Roald Dahl, who are widely known internationally and whose houses or sites of memory attract international visitors. Moreover, the writers were primarily connected—in the eyes of both their publics, their *Amics* and the managers of the sites—with Catalan political claims to nationhood, as we pointed out earlier; this was not an element toward which international visitors could be expected to feel a comparable form of involvement to that of local visitors. Thus, although all the stakeholders were willing to attract more visitors, foreigners included, the task had added difficulties. To these difficulties, one must add the practicalities of ensuring an adequate visibility of the Catalan language, and hence the management of translation in ways that did not defeat the purpose. It goes without saying that these difficulties probably affected the ability of site promoters to draw support and funding from both private and public sources, as well as the position that the sites were given in the tourist sector generally.

In relation to language choice, the Catalan websites of the literary houses provided partial translations in Spanish, English, German and French. However, in these languages, only fixed and sometimes outdated information was provided. Those who run the sites recognized that they did not have the necessary resources to provide sufficient information for non–Catalan-speaking visitors. The permanent exhibits in the houses were generally prepared to receive visitors speaking Spanish, French and English through written support material. In the physical sites, Catalan was always more visible (in the upper position, in bigger or bold font, etc.), and there were no versions of the multimedia material (videos, recordings) in other languages. In guided tours, while all tour guides were capable of delivering their explanations in Spanish, even in these cases they produced a lot of switching or quotes in Catalan accompanied with translations and comments. Catalan somehow had to be made visible. In one of the sites, tour guides were instructed to use Spanish only with groups coming from non-Catalan speaking regions of Spain; as a result, with Spanish-speaking Catalan residents they politely resisted implicit or explicit requests to change the language. At the Fundació Verdaguer, they also placed a special emphasis on the local accent which, in Catalonia, is regarded as a characteristically authentic one. They considered that the local accent and vocabulary conveyed part of the literary force of the texts. The Catalan sites displayed copies of the translations of the authors' works in other languages.

The language issue was also sensitive in other similar sites we have studied, where we have found slightly different ways of addressing the same problem, that is, ensuring the higher visibility of the home language. At the Cae'r Gors Kate Roberts Heritage Centre in Wales, for instance, the website was linguistically ambivalent, although the Welsh "language" flag featured more centrally and larger than all the other five flags representing the other language versions (French, German, English, Hebrew and Japanese). Further exploration revealed a significantly different trajectory for Welsh speakers and for speakers of other languages. The Welsh version provided detailed information about the center's history, staff and activities; while the versions in other languages simply gave access to the programs for visitors in PDF format. These programs were all bilingual, all in Welsh (more visible) and in each of the languages separately. In the town of Bouctouche in New Brunswick (Canada), tourists can visit a reproduction of a traditional Acadian village called *Le Pays de la Sagouine*, which opened in 1992 after the success of the play *La Sagouine* by Antonine Maillet. The site had evolved from giving English a restricted space (in 2004 visits in English could only be done on Fridays) to being fully bilingual (both in the website and with the availability of guided tours in 2008). Otherwise, when we visited the site, we found some elements that would probably be difficult to adapt to non-French speakers. Professional actors in the guise of village dwellers engaged in conversation with groups of visitors about the different accents and characteristic expressions of different French-speaking regions. Artistic performances such as plays and songs were also primarily in French.

The consumption of setting and landscape is present in the Kate Roberts Heritage Centre in Wales, where the visit focuses on presenting the spaces of the traditional *tyddyn* 'small holding' and emphasizes the location of the site in the mountains of Caernarfon. Landscape is not a concept exploited at *Le Pays de la Sagouine*, and it appears to be comparatively less relevant to the Acadian experience, literary or not (see Winspur 2006). The village of la Sagouine can arguably be presented as a specific landscape: the small fishing village with the seascape. However, it is tellingly an artificial village, not a historical one, and the website features statements by Antonine Maillet claiming that Acadian identity must be located in time rather than space. In any case, the Catalan emphasis on landscape appears as a specifically local and imaginative attempt to reconcile the contradictory demands placed on the sites. First, it provides new ways of disseminating literature. Second, it has many potential uses in tourism. Third, it has a continuity with local, long-established cultural traditions of uses and representations of the territory, as we showed already. Fourth, it largely requires the use of the Catalan language and thus contributes to reproduce the national imaginary (particularly as local literature in Spanish is rare, except for recent works by some writers from Barcelona). Literary routes or trails are budding everywhere, as tourists (usually retired people) and school pupils are routinely invited to walk villages and cities and natural parks accompanied by readings of all types of literary texts. Josep Pla and Jacint Verdaguer tours are offered to visitors along the streets of their village/town of birth to places that were significant in their lives or to monuments. In the two cases, there are also outings offered in the immediate vicinity to places of significance in their work: fountains connected with traditional religious celebrations, the original manor house of the family, small chapels, a light-house with views of the Costa Brava. The visit to the places of significance is normally accompanied by the reading of texts.

In 2005, a group of literary houses of the type analyzed created the network *Espais escrits*. This provided a distinct institutional visibility to the idea of literary landscape and geography. At the same time, it allowed to make explicit its national scope. First, it became the first institution that covered all literary sites in the Catalan-speaking territories (not just Catalonia, but also Valencia, the Balearic Islands and the Roussillon), thus establishing an implicit link between nation as territory and nation as landscape. Until March 2011, the website displayed a map of the *Països Catalans*, the 'Catalan Territories.' Second, it provided a distinct place for Catalan literature among similar institutions in Europe, such as the *Fédération des maisons d'écrivains*, the *Arbeitsgemeinschaft Literarischer Gesellschaften* or, not the least important, the Spanish *Associación de Casas-Museo y Fundaciones de Escritores*. The network began by organizing a series of seminars on *patrimoni literari i territori*, 'literary heritage and territory,' the seventh edition taking place in 2011 (www.espaisescrits.cat).

However, *Espais Escrits* is just one key actor within a much wider and burgeoning movement to reclaim the Catalan landscape as an identity icon: new trails, monuments and public plaques and props, sites and books about literary places and trails, literary atlases or geographies are being continuously created. A recent survey by Camps and Viladegut (2009) yielded the significant number of sixty books, all of them published after 1990. Literary guided tours have been the staple offer of the sites analyzed for years, but they are also organized by tourist offices, museums, cultural associations and community centers. An additional important initiative is the *endrets* project, subtitled as *Geografia Literària dels Països Catalans*, an online database of a near-encyclopedic ambition that connects literary texts and particular places (www.endrets.cat). The exploitation of the idea of landscape in connection with literature and tourism is not unique to Catalonia, as similar developments can be found throughout Europe and North America, as we mentioned earlier. However, the extent of the mobilization is probably unparalleled, and must be understood in the context of the long historical trajectory of Catalan involvement in the cultural appropriation of the territory. The text that featured for a period in the *endrets* website could hardly be more explicit as to the agenda:

La paraula, feta art, i el paisatge es juxtaposen en una simbiosi que aixeca acta notarial d'una llengua i un país mil·lenaris; fa prendre consciència d'allò que tenim i permet valorar-ho en la justa mesura; i ens encoratja a encarar el futur per mantenir-hi una posició preeminent al costat de les altres llengües i cultures.

The word, turned into art, and the landscape join in a symbiosis that represents an affidavit of a language and a millenary country; it raises awareness of what we have and allows us to value it in its fair measure; and it encourages us to face the future to maintain a preeminent position besides other languages and cultures. (Translated by Joan Pujolar, retrieved on 29/10/2010)

The *endrets* project includes the publication in book form of various "Literary Geographies" in the form of a guide in which even GPS coordinates of the places are given. The first volume devoted to the province of Barcelona (Soldevila 2010) was presented at the headquarters of the Institut d'Estudis Catalans (the Catalan Academy) with the participation, in addition to the author, of the president of the IEC Salvador Giner, former premier of Catalonia Jordi Pujol, the minister of culture Joan Manuel Tresserras, Mr. Joan Triadú (the symbol of cultural resistance during the Franco dictatorship) and the actor Lluís Soler. The staging expresses the wish to present it as an initiative of national importance. It was, by the way, a noticeably all-male event, so that one cannot help to note the contrast between the seemingly male-dominated and hierarchical *endrets* project, basically focused on the production of a gigantic database, and the clearly female-run network *Espais Escrits*, focused precisely on the networking itself at all levels and with a less spectacular staging (although they are also promoting their own literary database at www.mapaliterari.cat). In any case, the initiatives of *Espais Escrits* or the publication of the *Atles literari de les terres de Girona* (http://www.ddgi.cat/atlesWeb/faces/index.jsp) have not received as much political attention as Endrets so far.

CONCLUSIONS

In a well-known Catalan coastal resort, a group of local cultural institutions decided to organize activities to promote the reading of literature. So they hired two actors who, styling themselves as Don Quixote and Sancho Panza, walked along the beach and talked and joked with the thousands of tourists bathing under the summer sun. The tourists there were supposed to draw some entertainment from their general familiarity with Cervantes' characters. To participate in the fun, they did not need to know much about Spanish literature, let alone the difference between the Catalan and Spanish languages and literatures, or about the actual places that might lay some claim as scenes of Don Quixote's adventures (not that resort, in any case).

This anecdote is fairly representative of the distance that separates those who wish to use tourism to disseminate particular representations of the Catalan language, culture and nation, on the one hand, and, on the other, actors who (even in the context of cultural initiatives) may have different ideas as to how to use literature to engage with tourists.

We also recently visited another place of memory dedicated to Verdaguer, the *Santuari de la Mare de Déu del Mont* (www.marededeudelmont.com), a sanctuary at the top of a mountain in the Pyrenees, where a statue of the writer with pen and notebook sits in front of a stunning view of the mountains, with the Canigó popping up far away on the horizon on a clear day. There we were reminded of another theme in Verdaguer's work that literary houses and discourses about landscape and nation usually play down or erase altogether: Catholicism. Indeed, Verdaguer was a priest, and his work was clearly inscribed in the conservative strand of Catalan nationalism that emerged precisely from the seminar where he studied.

These two additional scenes remind us that contemporary representations of language, culture, literature, landscape and nation are the specific product of decisions and positions taken by actors with very different trajectories and interests and inserted in different markets. Just as Catalan culture has a problematic or marginal position in global tourist markets, Verdaguer's Catholicism does not command the same legitimacy as in the past in the Catalan cultural and political fields.

The mobilization of literature to reproduce traditional (though now secular) discourses on language and identity has a long trajectory. The traditional enthusiasm of literary pilgrims for the scenes, relics and mementos of authors and works also provides a natural line of work for the inscription of literature in tourist activities. These were the means through which those who run Catalan literary houses were carving out new positions to gain access to new resources. Attention to landscape, territories or specific places "outdoors" is also a classic feature of tourism. The construction of territory as "landscape," as sensuous experience that can be packaged for consumption lies at its very origins. In a time of increasing mobility, time–space compression affects not only the control of nation-states over their territory, but also the availability of the territory to *signify* the nation as economic activities, bodies and cultural practices become increasingly delocalized (Appadurai 1996). Thus the territories around the big urban centers have become the subjects of policies of "economic development" or "*dinamització territorial*." One of the options left for those with attachments to territories of whatever kind is precisely to turn the territory into a commodity and make it into "landscapes" or sites of "memory," that is, marketable objects for mobile consumers. In this context, the uses of the territory developed through ecotourism, activity tourism, agrotourism and other modalities make economic sense in the same way as those developed by the Catalan literary houses analyzed here. According to Edensor (2002), such developments are often used to (re)deploy nationalist discourses, typically of a conservative character as the artificial, technological and culturally diverse city is set in contrast with a natural and racially unpolluted countryside. Tourism is the typical space where these images of the territory are produced, distributed and consumed.

Catalan literary sites were not, from this perspective, substantially different from many other types of tourist sites all over the world. What was specific to the sites analyzed here was their close connection with cultural nationalism, in which literature and literary authors had been instrumental in the modernization of the Catalan language and culture while producing specific representations of landscape and territory. It was from this perspective that, just as literary authors could be credited as founders of the national language, they could at the same time be credited as creators of the national landscape and thus—as artist Perejaume expressed in his project—sign the landscape in the same way that they had signed their poems and narratives. Thus the momentous social movement taking place in Catalonia around the geography of literature is accomplishing many things: it reaffirms the status of Catalan as "the" language of the land, it reaffirms the place of (national) literature in contemporary society,[10] and it reminds visitors of the meanings and experiences historically connected with the places through which they now move at increasing speed and in which they spend less and less time.

However, if many tourists to Barcelona end up visiting the scenes, however fictional, of authors who write in Spanish, sun bathers engage with Don Quixote or, in Wales, visitors prefer the English-language strand of Welsh literature, or *Le Pays de la Sagouine* has to get an English version, we can also begin to see the limits in the conditions of possibility for the reproduction of modern ideologies over language and identity in Catalonia and similar contexts. Traditional narratives of uniform, monolingual national communities may well survive in particular niches; however, they do so in an extremely fragmented market where they do not have a hope of engendering political hegemonies. They become just marginal voices inside the myriad of activities possible in the tourist market. Both politicians and tourist entrepreneurs, as they make decisions to promote some tourist attractions over others, tend to treat literature, language or identity as elements of limited relevance.

The discourses produced in these literary sites represent one of the ways in which nationalist discourses or traditional forms of belonging inscribed in past "structures of feeling" (Williams 1975) seek to reproduce themselves and also to adapt to new times. They seek, at the same time, to legitimate claims to political autonomy and to secure access to economic resources under the new conditions presented by the globalized economy, that is, to reconcile modernist discursive formations with late capitalism. As new resources are constantly channeled to develop specific territories as tourist destinations, social actors and groups connected with cultural policies not traditionally included in tourist routes have strong incentives to enter the circuit. However, they face difficult choices in a marketplace characterized by multilingualism, in which the target audience is increasingly global rather than local, and in which both political and economic actors are more attentive to global flows than to local needs. From this perspective, the efforts of Catalan literary sites to attract both visitors and resources meet with limited success, so that the actual constituency of these new discourses over language, literature and territory remain on the home ground of local cultural politics.

We have sought to show how literature is mobilized in Catalonia in the context of the heritage industry. The sites analyzed served to display particular representations of national identity in which language played a key role. This was done by drawing upon the significance that landscape and territory has for the national imaginary. The literary representations of landscape and territory, together with strategies to display other national symbols, especially language, are some of the ways in which such sites draw from traditional resources to construct identity in ways that are potentially relevant to new forms of consuming nature, culture and identity in tourism. Identity tourism recontextualizes discourses and practices of the cultural sector formerly used to mobilize political hegemonies locally to elaborate products for consumption in a fragmented and globalized marketplace. However, the returns of the investment are low, and this expresses some of the difficulties that local cultural communities face in their attempts to reproduce identity and adapt to globalization.

NOTES

1. This chapter is based on the research Project "Language, Culture and Tourism: Identity Discourses and the Commoditization of Languages in Global Markets" funded by the Dirección General de Investigación of the Ministerio de Educación y Ciencia in Spain: Ref. HUM2006–13621-C04–04/FILO.
2. See http://lletra.uoc.edu/en/author/perejaume for more information about the artist.
3. The work is visible via Google maps through the coordinates 41.937129,2. 324004. Reproduced with the permission of the Fundació Jacint Verdaguer.
4. *Espais Escrits* means literally 'written spaces.' *Endrets* is a neologism constructed out of the word *indrets* 'places' or 'sites.'
5. See http://en.wikipedia.org/wiki/Josep_Maria_Espinàs for a list of Josep-Maria Espinàs works in travel writing.
6. See http://www.folgueroles.com/poema-aplec-gleva-verdaguer.asp.
7. See http://www.palaumusica.org.
8. Interestingly enough, Kate Roberts' house in Wales was also saved from oblivion and probable destruction at the same time. It was bought by a private individual and transferred to a group of trustees belonging to Plaid Cymru in 1965; a small tribute fund was created in 1967 which allowed for minor restorations to be made.
9. http://www.turismedecatalunya.com/cultura/index.asp
10. Some Catalan literary scholars have also developed an interest in landscape and literary routes because of the pedagogic potential and as a way to reclaim

a position for the study of literature in the educational curriculum, where it has recently lost weight (see Camps and Viladegut 2009).

REFERENCES

Appadurai, Arjun, 1996. *Modernity at Large: Cultural Dimensions of Globalization*, Minneapolis: University of Minnesota Press.

Bhabha, Homi K. 1990. *Nation and Narration*. London: Routledge.

Boudreau, Annette, and Chantal White. 2006. "Turning the Tide in Acadian Nova Scotia: How Heritage Tourism is Changing Language Practices and Representations of Language." *The Canadian Journal of Linguistics/La revue canadienne de linguistique* 49(3): 327–351.

Camarasa, Josep M., 2000. *Cent anys de passió per la natura. Una història de la Institució Catalana d'Història Natural. 1899-1999.* Barcelona: Institut d'Estudis Catalans.

Camps, Josep, and Miquel Viladegut. 2009. "Les rutes literàries com a integració de les arts en l'enseyament de la literatura." Accessed April 10, 2011. http://www.aulamariustorres.org/activitats/index.php#5a_jornada.

Corse, Sarah M. 1997. *Nationalism and Literature: The Politics of Culture in Canada and the United States*. Cambridge: Cambridge University Press.

Ebbatson, Roger, and Ann Donahue. 2005. *An Imaginary England: Nation, Landscape and Literature, 1840–1920.* Farnham, UK: Ashgate Publishing.

Edensor, Tim. 2002. *National Identity, Popular Culture and Everyday Life.* Oxford: Berg.

Figueras, Narcís. 2004. "El paisatge selvatà en la literatura." *Quaderns de la Selva* 16: 115–127.

Fradera, Josep M. 2009. *La pàtria dels catalans. Història, política, cultura.* Barcelona: RBA Editores.

Fuster, Joan. 1967. *L'home, mesura de totes les coses.* Barcelona: Edicions 62.

Harvey, David. 1989. *The Condition of Postmodernity: An Enquiry Into the Origins of Cultural Change.* Oxford: Wiley-Blackwell.

Heller, Monica. 2003. "Globalization, the New Economy and the Commodification of Language and Identity." *Journal of Sociolinguistics* 7(4): 473–492.

Heller, Monica. 2004. "Paradoxes of Language in the New Economy." *Babylonia* 4(4): 29–31.

Herbert, David T. 1996. "Artistic and Literary Places in France as Tourist Attractions." *Tourism Management* 17(2): 77–85.

Herbert, David T. 2001. "Literary Places, Tourism and the Heritage Experience." *Annals of Tourism Research* 28(2): 312–333.

Hewison, Robert. 1987. *The Heritage Industry: Britain in a Climate of Decline.* London: Methuen.

Hobsbawm, Eric J. 1992. *Nations and Nationalism Since 1780: Programme, Myth, Reality.* Cambridge: Cambridge University Press.

Iribarren, Teresa. 2007. "Literatura i turisme: Hores angleses de Ferran Soldevila." In *Diaris i dietaris*, edited by Joan Borja, Joaquim Espinós, Anna Esteve and M. Àngels, Francés, 241–251. Paiporta: Denes.

James, Louis. 1981. "Landscape in Nineteenth Century Literature." In *Victorian Countryside*, edited by Gordon Mingay, 150–165. London: Routledge.

Le Menestrel, Sara. 1999. *La voie des cadiens. Tourisme et identité en Louisianne.* Paris: Belin.

McLaughlin, Mireille. 2007. "Touring Indigeneities: On the Tensions of Producing Canadian, Québécois and Native Tdentities on the Franco-European

Commercial Fair Circuit." Paper presented at the annual meeting of the American Ethnological Association (AES) and the Canadian Anthropology Society (CASCA), June, Kingston, Ontario, Canada.

Moïse, Claudine. 2006. "Le tourisme patrimonial: la commercialisation de l'identité franco-canadienne et ses enjeux langagiers." *Langage et société* 118(4): 85–108.

Morgan, Prys. 1983. "From a Death to a View: The Hunt for the Welsh Past in the Romantic Period." In *The Invention of Tradition*, edited by Eric J. Hobsbawm and Terence Ranger, 43–100. Cambridge: Cambridge University Press.

Pitchford, Susan. 2008. *Identity Tourism. Imaging and Imagining the Nation*. Bingley, UK: Emerald Group Publishing Ltd.

Pla, José. 1945. *Guía de la Costa Brava*. Barcelona: Ediciones Destino.

Playà, Josep. 2008. "100 anys de la Costa Brava." *La Vanguardia*.

Pritchard, Annette, and Nigel J. Morgan. 2001. "Culture, Identity and Tourism Representation: Marketing Cymru or Wales?" *Tourism Management* 22(2): 167–179.

Pujolar, Joan. 2006. *Llengua, cultura i turisme. Perspectives a Barcelona i a Catalunya*. Barcelona: Turisme de Barcelona.

Roma i Casanovas, Francesc. 2004. *Del Paradís a la nació: La Muntanya a Catalunya, Segles XV–XX*. Cossetània Edicions.

Siddall, Stephen. 2009. *Landscape and Literature*. Cambridge: Cambridge University Press.

Soldevila, Llorenç. 2010. *Geografia Literària 1. Comarques barcelonines*. Barcelona: Editorial Pòrtic.

Torrents, Carlota. 2007. *A la recerca d'un model europeu de xarxes de patrimoni literari*. Barcelona: Generalitat de Catalunya. Accessed April 10, 2011. http://www.espaisescrits.cat/downloads/cat/Models_europeus.pdf.

Verdaguer, Jacint. 2005. *Poesia, 1*. Barcelona: Proa.

Williams, Raymond. 1975. *The Country and the City*. Oxford: Oxford University Press.

Winspur, Steven. 2006. "L'Acadie comme addresse. La poésie de Raymond LeBlanc et Hermenegilde Chiasson." In *Regards croisés sur l'histoire et la littérature acadiennes*, edited by Madeleine Frédéric and Serge Jaumain, 87–100. Bern: Peter Lang Publishing.

Woolf, Virginia. 1994. *The Essays of Virginia Woolf*. London: Chatto & Windus.

6 Pride, Profit and Distinction

Negotiations Across Time and Space in Community Language Education

Adrian Blackledge and Angela Creese

INTRODUCTION

Western societies have become more diverse in recent times, as numbers and territorial origins of migrants have expanded. This phenomenon has resulted in new demographic patterns of migration and postmigration, termed "superdiversity," and characterised by "a dynamic interplay of variables among an increased number of new, small and scattered, multiple origin, transnationally connected, socio-economically differentiated and legally stratified immigrants who have arrived over the last decade" (Vertovec 2007a, 1024). In recent years transnationalism has become one of the key ways of understanding contemporary migrant practices (Vertovec 2007b). In this chapter we demonstrate that the "language" associated with the home territory may become a key feature of maintaining and reproducing "cultural heritage." That is, pride in the "national language" of the home country is a dimension of pride in the nation and the culture, as at least some language users, at least some of the time, hold passionate beliefs about the importance and significance of a particular language to their sense of "identity" (Blackledge and Creese 2010).

In this chapter we ask why national ideologies retain their productivity as modes of production of capital of distinction, not only on the diaspora market but also in the struggle over who defines what counts as legitimate "Bengaliness" in the UK. In language classes in complementary schools ("community language schools" or "heritage language schools") the national language is offered to the next generation as a gift of inheritance. At the same time, the linguistic repertoires of the receivers of the gift are multiple, flexible, and diverse, as they access resources from myriad sources in their multilingual, digital worlds, and the "national language" may play only a small part in those repertoires.

Complementary schools are both institutional spaces for the reproduction and transmission of heritages and languages, and spaces in which negotiation and, at times, contestation of these heritages and languages plays out. The various stakeholders—students, teachers, parents, administrators, principals—articulate a range of rationales for their investment of time and resources in the schools. In this chapter we will see language in flexible use and up for grabs, language traded, exchanged, bartered, wrangled over, and negotiated in the symbolic spaces of complementary schools.

Adopting a theoretical and analytical perspective that combines the ethnographic with the linguistic, we are able to tell a story that connects a cacophony of linguistic practice with histories and territories, with traditions and heritages, with pedagogies and ideologies, and with the changing worlds of digital communication and globalization. That is, our analytical gaze takes us beyond the immediate, to other times and other spaces. Those other times and spaces include the tangible pasts of narrated events in the making of nations, exemplified by stories of martyrdoms, liberation struggles and heroic deeds. They also include artifacts associated with the construction of the "home" territory: traditional folk tales, festivals, food and flags. They include histories of migration, and at times multiple migrations. And they include local time and space, as young people live out their lives in the complex cosmopolitan worlds of their cities and use a vast array of linguistic resources that constantly change and develop, and that derive their linguistic features from a wide range of sources, including those associated with religious texts, the "homeland" national heritage, popular cultural forms, academic English, nonstandard English, and many more. These complex linguistic repertoires bear the traces of past times and present times, of lives lived locally and globally. These are the voices of young people whose "communities"—their teachers and parents—want them to experience and to learn something of a "culture," a "heritage," a nation or territory, which now lies at a distance.

We suggest that at times "pride" in the national language becomes a form of "distinction," as certain sets of linguistic resources (e.g., the national language) are considered to be of greater value than other sets of linguistic resources (e.g., the vernacular language). Furthermore, speakers of some sets of linguistic resources may come to be regarded as of greater value than speakers of other sets of linguistic resources. In these cases, we argue, even in transnational settings the (transnational) state may have an important role in the legitimation of certain ways of speaking above others. Thus those who are able to access certain sets of linguistic resources gain a "profit of distinction" (Bourdieu 1991, 55) over those who are either unable or unwilling to do so. Heller and Duchêne argue that rather than accepting ideological positions in which there is competition over languages, "perhaps we should be asking instead who benefits and who loses from understanding languages the way we do, what is at stake for whom, and how and why language serves as a terrain for competition" (2007, 11). In this chapter we report research that addresses this issue, and demonstrates that the flexible, heteroglossic language practices of multilingual speakers in transnational settings coexist with pride in certain languages defined as symbols of national, cultural and heritage identity. We further demonstrate that beliefs about differences in the value of certain sets of linguistic resources may be used to construct social distinctions between the users of those resources.

PRIDE

Here we focus on *pride* in relation to the circulation of linguistic resources in postmigration settings. We argue that certain sets of linguistic resources may be viewed as carriers of "cultural heritage." We further propose that the same sets of linguistic resources may be constructed as being closely related to "national identity." Related to the second point, we also consider the role of language in processes of "transnationalism."

Heritage

In recent times the scope of definitions of "heritage" has broadened considerably from concern for the preservation of buildings and historical sites to include historical areas, towns, environments, social factors and "intangible heritage" (Ahmad 2006, 299; Smith 2006, 54; UNESCO 2003, Article 2:2). Patrick (2007) points out that appeals for the protection of forms of "intangible heritage" have played an important role in campaigns for language rights. Whether we are dealing with traditional definitions of "tangible" or "intangible" heritage, we are engaging with sets of values and meanings, including emotion, memory and shared knowledge (Smith 2006). Bourdieu and Passeron suggest that "inheritance always implies the danger of squandering the heritage" (1979, 25). However, it cannot be assumed that the preservation and transmission of "heritage" is straightforward. Simply the process of "passing on" resources will alter them. Tunbridge and Ashworth argue that there is rarely a simple relationship between a group of people and "heritage" resources: "The same piece of heritage can be interpreted and received by different groups in quite different ways" (1996, 92). Rather than being a static entity, "heritage" as a process of meaning making may "help us bind ourselves, or may see us become bound to, national or a range of sub-national collectives or communities" (Smith 2006, 66) as particular resources come to act as powerful symbols of, or mnemonics for, the past (Lipe 2007). Smith proposes that the idea of "heritage" is "used to construct, reconstruct and negotiate a range of identities and social and cultural values and meanings in the present" (2006, 3). She argues that "heritage" is a set of practices involved in the construction and regulation of values, a discourse about negotiation, about using the past, and collective and individual memories, to negotiate new ways of being and to perform identities. People engage with "heritage," appropriate it and contest it (Harvey 2007). "Heritage" may become a site at which identities are contested rather than imposed unproblematically. That is, those who seek to preserve and pass on certain sets of resources may find that the next generation either rejects imposed subject positions, contests the validity or significance of resources or appropriates them for other purposes. In our research we found that certain sets of linguistic resources were valued by some as gifts of inheritance, and by others as sites of negotiation.

A dimension of "cultural heritage" is the national. Castles points out that more than 100 million people reside outside the country of their birth. He asks what nationalism means for people who settle in one country without abandoning their cultural belonging to another. Castles suggests that the nation-state "is based on the obliteration of minority cultures" (2005, 312), and that immigrant groups are often caught between an urge to maintain "immigrant cultures and languages" and a pragmatic acceptance of assimilation that can lead to marginalization and loss of community solidarity. He concludes that "the nation-state model . . . cannot offer an adequate basis for societal belonging in the age of globalization and migration" (2005, 314), and argues that continuing attempts to base citizenship on membership of an imagined cultural community leads to political and social exclusion and the racialization of differences. May and Fenton note that many states are multinational, comprising a number of national minorities, or polyethnic, comprising a range of immigrant groups. If nations are people who see themselves as those already "in place," ethnic minorities are people who may be seen, however begrudgingly, as being in situ, but who still remain, by the exclusivist definitions of nation so often applied, invariably "out of place" (May and Fenton 2003, 14). However, Pujolar argues that describing the contemporary world as "postnational" does not mean that nationality, nationalism or nation-states are no longer relevant or are receding in favor of an international, transnational or cosmopolitan era. In fact there are "strong arguments to contend that nationalism is on the increase" (Pujolar 2007, 90). Many states seek to regulate immigration, and arguments against immigration are invariably expressed in nationalist language (Essed 2000; van Dijk 2000).

It is sometimes taken for granted that the concept of "diaspora" is oppositional to nations and nationalism. In recent years *transnationalism* has become one of the key ways of understanding contemporary migrant practices (Vertovec 2007b). The social relations of migrants and refugees are not confined within nations but are "transnational," hence a diaspora is a specific form of transnational community (Cox and Connell 2003, 330). Glick Schiller, Basch and Blanc-Szanton (1992) argued that immigrants are increasingly becoming transnational. In recent years, the extent of transnational engagement has intensified. The degrees to and ways in which today's migrants maintain identities, activities and connections linking them with communities outside the host country are unprecedented (Vertovec 2007a). Levitt and Glick Schiller (2004) argue that assimilation and enduring transnational ties are neither incompatible nor binary opposites. Anderson refers to "long-distance nationalism" to suggest that a strong allegiance binds members of an ethnic diaspora to their homeland (1998, 74). Glick Schiller and Fouron define long-distance nationalism as "a claim to membership in a political community that stretches beyond the territorial borders of a homeland" (2002, 4). Vertovec (2009) refers to "dimensions of transnational competence" and suggests that within many families whose lives are stretched across migrant sending and receiving contexts, transnational patterns of everyday activity have become normative.

DISTINCTION

Bourdieu argued that every material inheritance is, strictly speaking, also a cultural inheritance. Each class condition is defined "by everything which distinguishes it from what it is not and especially from everything it is opposed to; social identity is defined and asserted through difference" (Bourdieu 1984, 172). Bourdieu's argument here is that by passing on tastes and distastes, and sympathies and aversions associated with a particular social class, a sense of belonging to that class is also transmitted. Furthermore, in order to pass on the inheritance of belonging, it is necessary to define what one is *not*. That is, in order to endow the next generation with the sense of "who we are," it is crucial to pass on a sense of "who we are not." Bourdieu argued that this sense of continuity is enacted through the reproduction of "distinction" in education; in ways of speaking; in cultural values; and in judgments about taste (including art, literature, cinema, clothes, food, etc.). A family heirloom, for example, not only bears witness to the age and continuity of the lineage and so "consecrates its social identity, which is inseparable from permanence over time" (1984, 77); it also contributes in a practical way to transmitting the values, virtues and competences which are the basis of legitimate membership in a certain social class. A certain way of "doing" language and culture "confers the self-certainty which . . . bourgeois families hand down to their offspring as if it were an heirloom" (1984, 66).

For Bourdieu "heritage" is reproduced through "class" and "education," in the reproduction of distinction: "an unacquired merit which justifies unmerited attainment, namely heritage" (Bourdieu and Darbel 1991, 110). Bourdieu argues that in education there is an assumption of a community of values between pupil and teacher which occurs where the system "is dealing with its own heirs to conceal its real function, namely, that of confirming and consequently legitimizing the right of the heirs to the cultural inheritance" (1993, 299). He further argues that only when the heritage has taken over the inheritor can the inheritor take over the heritage. This appropriation of the inheritor by the heritage takes place "under the combined effect of the conditionings inscribed in the position of inheritor and the pedagogic action of his predecessors, themselves possessed possessors" (Bourdieu 2000, 152).

One of the ways in which some groups pass on to the next generation the distinction between themselves and other groups is in the transmission of certain "ways of looking, sitting, standing, keeping silent, or even of speaking" (Bourdieu 1991, 51).

Bourdieu demonstrates that an important aspect of "cultural inheritance" is the competence necessary to speak the "legitimate language." It is this competence to speak the legitimate language that translates social distinctions into "distinction." Such legitimate competence can function as linguistic capital, "producing a *profit of distinction* on the occasion of each social exchange" (Bourdieu 1991, 55).

The value of legitimate language lies in its distance from simple, common ways of speaking. In making this argument Bourdieu demonstrates that the state has an important role in the legitimation of certain ways of speaking above others (which therefore become illegitimate). When the state refers to *the* language it refers to the standard variety, the official language, which is bound up with the state, and "this state language becomes the theoretical norm against which all linguistic practices are objectively measured" (Bourdieu 1991, 45).

Through examination and legal sanction some linguistic performance becomes more legitimate than other linguistic performance. In order for the official language or variety to impose itself as the only legitimate one, "the linguistic market has to be unified and the different dialects (of class, region or ethnic group) have to be measured against the legitimate language or usage" (Bourdieu 1991, 45). This linguistic unification is both the producer and the product of political domination.

Here Bourdieu is largely referring to processes of social stratification in a society (twentieth-century France) divided by social class. Although we cannot unproblematically transpose this theoretical model to the UK in the twenty-first century, much of Bourdieu's analysis resonates with the ways in which Standard English acts as the language of political domination, and the means by which that domination is reproduced, notably in education, and in policy for managing migration. However, in superdiverse, transnational societies it is no longer (if ever it was) sufficient to interrogate social distinctions merely along class or "ethnic" lines. Instead we must take a more nuanced approach, paying attention to distinctions where they arise in the complex interrelationships of constantly changing neighborhoods.

We have argued elsewhere (Blackledge and Creese 2008, 2010) that for some linguistic minority groups in the UK (a variety of) the "community" or "heritage" or "national" language is taught to children in complementary schools as an important dimension of their inheritance. That is, for some people the language becomes the carrier of the "culture" associated with the territory from which the group migrated. In this chapter we will demonstrate that many of those associated with these informal educational institutions are motivated by a *pride* in their language and culture, passing on "their" language as a gift of inheritance. At the same time, however, we will show that not all of those associated with the schools share the same beliefs and values about these sets of linguistic resources. Rather, teaching of the community language at times becomes a site of negotiation, and at times the means by which social difference is translated into distinction. We will argue that alongside *pride* in language learning resides the production of the *profit of distinction*.

METHODOLOGY AND RESEARCH DESIGN

The research reported in this chapter investigated linguistic practices and identities in four cities in England.[1] The research project is a comparative sociolinguistic study of four interlocking case studies with two researchers working in two complementary ("heritage language," "community language," "supplementary") schools in each community. These are non-statutory schools, run by their local communities, which students attend in order to learn the language normally associated with their ethnic heritage.

The case studies focused on Gujarati schools in Leicester, Turkish schools in London, Cantonese and Mandarin schools in Manchester, and Bengali schools in Birmingham. The project design is of four linking, ethnographically informed case studies. Our research colleagues in the team were Taşkin Baraç, Arvind Bhatt, Shahela Hamid, Li Wei, Vally Lytra, Peter Martin, Chao-Jung Wu and Dilek Yağcioğlu-Ali. Each case study identified two complementary schools in which to observe, record and interview participants. We also collected key documentary evidence and took photographs. Two key participant children were identified in each school. These children were audio-recorded during the classes observed, and also for thirty minutes before and after each class. Key stakeholders in the schools were interviewed, including teachers and administrators, and the key participant children and their parents. In all we collected 192 hours of audio-recorded interactional data, wrote 168 sets of field notes, made 16 hours of video-recordings, and interviewed 66 key stakeholders.

The specific aims of the project were

1. to explore the social, cultural and linguistic significance of complementary schools both within their communities and in the wider society;
2. to investigate the range of linguistic practices used in different contexts in the complementary schools; and
3. to investigate how the linguistic practices of students and teachers in complementary schools are used to negotiate young people's multilingual and multicultural identities.

We have reported the findings of each separate case study elsewhere (Creese et al. 2007a, 2007b, 2007c, 2007d) and provided a detailed analysis and discussion of the research in a separate volume (Blackledge and Creese 2010). However, the present paper extends these discussions, with specific reference to the notions of pride, profit and distinction in superdiverse settings.

In the present discussion we focus exclusively on the two Bengali schools in Birmingham, the second largest city in the UK after London, and the city with the highest proportion of "black and ethnic minority" residents.

LANGUAGE AND PRIDE

Language as National and Cultural Heritage

Our first example comes from an interview with the founder and administrator of one of the Bengali schools. In the course of the interview the administrator made a forceful and emotional statement following a question in which we queried the rationale for teaching Bengali to children in Birmingham. He began his answer in Sylheti, and continued in English:

Example 1
ei bhaashar jonno 1952 te amaar theke dosh haath dure Barkat, Salam maara jaae 1952 te <*because of this language in 1952 ten yards away from me Barkat and Salam were killed in 1952*> I was also a student in year 10. From Sylhet to Dhaka was 230 miles, we marched there Sylhet to Dhaka 230 miles with slogans. We want our mother language, it is a raashtro bhasha <*state language*> how will I forget about my mother language? my brothers gave their life for this language. I will never forget it while I'm alive. (administrator interview, School A)

For the school administrator the "mother language" was a vital symbol of the founding of the Bangladeshi nation. More than fifty years earlier he had witnessed the incident in which the "language martyrs" were killed while demonstrating against the imposition of Urdu as the national language by West Pakistan, and these events had informed his view that British-born children of Bangladeshi heritage should learn and maintain the Bengali language. The historic incident, which marks the Bangladeshi calendar as "Ekushey February," continues to be celebrated as a key moment in the collective memory of the Bangladeshi nation, and in the Bangladeshi community in UK (Gard'ner 2004).

It is immediately clear that for the school administrator the Bengali language holds considerable purchase in terms of his identity and nationhood (May 2005). In our conversations with parents and teachers in and around the Bengali schools in Birmingham we frequently heard the view that the next generation should learn Bengali because "we are Bengali." For many of the participants passing on "the mother language" was a symbolic means of transmitting their heritage. It is clear that not only are spatiotemporal dimensions crucial to the meanings evident here, but also the indexical nature of language (Blommaert 2010; Silverstein 2003), as one thing (here the Bengali language) points to another (Bengali/Bangladeshi heritage/culture).

One of the teachers told us that there was a clear association between learning Bengali and affiliating to the heritage of Bangladesh:

Example 2
from the national concern you should know Bengali, national Bengali the basic thing I'm not saying that he or she should be highly qualified in Bengali, national Bengali just the national thing, the basic thing. They should know like the alphabets, how to read. Sometimes if somebody speaks with them the national language they should be able to know what they've been saying. (teacher interview, Bengali school)

We constantly saw individual participants positioning themselves in relation to the "ethnic, linguistic, and cultural loyalties" (Pavlenko 2007, 177), which they chose to emphasize. One of the senior teachers in the same school argued that learning Bengali was associated with maintaining knowledge of Bangladeshi "roots": "We may have become British Bangladeshi or British Indians but we don't have fair skin and we cannot mix with them. We have our own roots and to know about our roots we must know our language." For both of these Bangladeshi-born teachers, teaching and learning Bengali was an important means of reproducing their "heritage" in the next generation. We heard an explicit rationale from administrators, teachers and parents that a key aim of the school was for the children to learn Bengali because knowledge of the national language carried features of Bangladeshi/Bengali "heritage."

The rationale of the schools was put into practice in the classroom through a pedagogy that frequently introduced "heritage" content in the context of teaching Bengali. Here "heritage" included narratives of national belonging, and the introduction of national symbols of Bangladesh. In Example 3, video-recorded in the Bengali classroom, the teacher picks out a symbol of Bangladeshi nationality, the national anthem. As he has the national anthem as the ring tone for his cell phone, he plays it to the class. He continues to list Bangladeshi national symbols (T: Teacher; R: Researcher):

Example 3
T: ei. eitaai aamaader jaatio shongeet othobaa national anthem. ekhon aamaader Bangladesher ko-e ektaa jinish aache jaatio bol-e.
      <This, this is our national anthem. now, we have a few things in Bangladesh which are our national symbols.> jaatio shongeet *<national anthem>*
      jaatio kobi *<national poet>*, jaatio phul *<national flower>* baa jaatio baa national fol *<or national or national fruit>* baa national paakhi *<or national bird>* Bangladesher jaatio fol ki? *<what is the national fruit of Bangladesh?>*
Ss: [no response]

T: water lily, water lily, water lily Bangla, water lily, shapla. etaa aamaader jaatio ful *<this is our national flower>* jaatio paakhi (.) doel *<national bird>*
[pauses and addresses R] doel-er Englishtaa ki apa? *<what is the English for doel, apa?>*

R: [unsure, hesitates] dove

T: er por-e jaatio kobi, poet, national poet, national poet Kazi Nazrul Islam *<after this national poet, poet, national poet, national poet Kazi Nazrul Islam>*. (classroom video-recording, School B)

Here the process of teaching Bengali is intimately interwoven with the process of teaching symbolic representations of Bangladesh, as knowledge of the national/cultural symbols, like knowledge of the Bengali language, comes to represent Bengali "heritage."

In some cases the students themselves articulated pride in their achievements as learners of Bengali. At times their enthusiasm for learning Bengali was manifested in a competitiveness with each other. The following example is from the beginning of one of the lessons we recorded, as a ten-year-old boy, Tamim, competes with a girl Saleha, of the same age:

Example 4

Tamim: Saleha, Saleha, look where are you. I'm in the last page boishaakhjoishto aashin karrtik ograhoyon.[reading names of Bengali calendar months] are you there? ko kho go gho . . . [reading out the consonants]
Boishaakh joishto aashaar [names of Bengali months] red blue green yellow violet pink. that's easy, these are easy. the days of the week. you're not on ko kho, you're on o aa. boishaakh joishto. see you don't even know. I know how to say it fast

Saleha: maasher naam *<the names of months >* January, February, March

Tamim: boishaakh, joishto. (audio-recording, School B)

Here Tamim exhibits pride in his learning, competing with Saleha and insisting that he is further on in his learning than she is. When Saleha responds with the names of the months it is in English. Although the students were not always so enthusiastic about their Bengali language learning, this was not an uncommon attitude among the young learners.

The complementary school students were not only proud of their Bengali learning. Another feature of their learner identities was a keen awareness of their level of attainment in their mainstream education. Tamim (and his sister Tabeya) told us that he was "cleverer" than students two years older than him:

Example 5
Tamim: me and my friend we are the top in our whole school
Tabeya: whole school
Tamim: but first my friend, she is the top in year four, then I'm the
second. we are still better than some of year six. we are better than most of year six. there's about thirty children, thirty
or something like that. at the whole of year six, the whole of
the school we'd come about fifth or sixth. we're cleverer than
some of year six. (interview, School B)

A further dimension of (some of) the students' pride in their learning
achievement was their attitude to reading the Qur'an in Arabic. In all of the
families in the study, children were reading the Qur'an, or had completed
their reading of the Qur'an. In Alamghir's family in particular there was a
high level of commitment to this practice:

Example 6
Alamghir's mother proudly tells us that one of her sons, Zakir, goes
to the madrassah and is hoping to be a Hafiz-e-Qur'an (someone who
learns the entire Qur'an by heart). She seems very proud, and considers
it to be a noble and honourable act. (Fieldnotes School A)

On a number of occasions when we visited the house, Zakir was dressed
in traditional Bangladeshi costume and was ready to go to the madrassah.
Reading the Qur'an with a tutor seemed to be regarded by the parents as
nonnegotiable, and was privileged above Bengali learning. Tamim spoke
enthusiastically about this practice:

Example 7
Tamim: my Dad says, you know the Qur'an, after I finish it, I am
going to get an English version of the Qur'an so that I can
understand every word of it.
Researcher: so now what you read you don't understand?
Tamim: no, but sometimes, there are common words and my
mosque teacher, he reads it out and if he reads it triple
times and we know it has a meaning to it and he knows
the meaning, tells us the meaning and then something like
a fact or something. (interview, School B)

Not for a moment put off by the researcher's question here, Tamim
seems to be very positive about the experience of reading the Qur'an. In
Example 8 the Arabic tutor has come to the children's home to provide
a private study lesson, and is reciting Arabic words for the students
to repeat:

Example 8

Tutor: qaribun, qareebun, qareeb [reads along with Tabeya often repeating the same words] re- yaa ze- yaa qaa ri- bun

Tabeya: six times forsi <*I read it six times*>

Tutor: qaf zabar qaa, re zer ri, be pesh bu, nun, qareebun. [spells the Arabic words; repeated many times] laam zabar laa [repeated many times]

Tamim: laam zabar laa. aami khaali ekhtaa mistake khorsi, ekhtaa mistake khorsi sir <*I made only one mistake, only one mistake sir*>. (home audio-recording, School B)

Here the tutor is teaching the children to spell the words in Arabic by repeating after him. In making his claim to proficiency in Qur'anic Arabic, Tamim uses Sylheti and English together.

In these examples we see that learning Bengali has a symbolic status as a means of transmitting Bengali/Bangladeshi cultural heritage to the next generation. In some cases, and at some times, the students were proud of their achievements as learners of Bengali. Predominantly English speakers who also had some level of proficiency in Sylheti, they were engaged in learning to read the Qur'an in Arabic, and were proud of their achievement in academic English in their mainstream school.

LANGUAGE AND DISTINCTION

In conducting our fieldwork we found clear evidence that it is not sufficient to take one "ethnicity" or "country of origin" as our unit of analysis. That is, we found that our participants made distinctions within the "ethnic group," and these distinctions were often represented as linguistic differences. What people believed about their language (or other people's languages), and the situated forms of talk they deployed, revealed divergent and contested views about the value and status of particular linguistic resources. We saw that attitudes to, and practices of, linguistic repertoires were tied in complex relation to distinctions made between speakers of those repertoires.

When we interviewed the administrators and teachers in the schools they spoke emphatically about the need for children to learn Bengali, the standard, literate language of Bangladesh. This was frequently held to be oppositional to Sylheti, which was the spoken variety used by the families of students attending the Bengali schools. Whereas Bengali was the language of the educated elite in Bangladesh, particularly Dhaka, Sylheti was the language of rural Sylhet in northeast Bangladesh. One of the school administrators (of a different school from that in Example 1) was emphatic that Bengali was not the same as Sylheti, and that Sylheti should not be

allowed to "contaminate" the standard form. He was concerned that Sylheti forms were beginning to appear in the spelling and grammar of Bengali
newspapers in UK, introducing "thousands of spelling mistakes—Bengali
newspapers I have seen in many places the spelling was wrong, sentence
construction was wrong." For the administrator nonstandard resources
were "contaminating the language." He made this point about the necessity for children to learn standard Bengali:

Example 9
I am always in favour of preserving languages and all these things. but
it doesn't mean that this should contaminate other languages and give
this more priority than the proper one. we have to preserve the proper
one first, and at the same time we have to encourage them to you know,
use their dialect. but we shouldn't make any compromise between these
two. (administrator interview, School B)

The argument that the Bengali language should remain "pure" and
uncontaminated by other languages was not uncommon among people
we met in and around the schools. The administrator of the other school
stated,

Example 10
bhasha to bolle Bangla bhasha bolte hobe Sylheti kono bhasha naa
<*when you talk about language it means Bengali, Sylheti is not a lan-
guage*>. (administrator interview, School A)

For several respondents "Bengali" constituted a more highly valued set
of linguistic resources than "Sylheti," and was regarded as the "proper"
language. Patrick suggests that in arguing in support of a particular language, "speakers can be locked into fixed or essentialised notions of identity,
'authenticity' and place, which provide no recognition of mobile, postcolonial speakers" (2007, 127). It was clear that for some of our respondents,
not all linguistic resources were equally valued, and while some sets of
linguistic resources were considered to be "a language," others were not.
In this sense there was a constant reinvention of "language" on the part of
some participants.

Those who spoke "Sylheti" were often criticized by "more educated"
people who spoke "Bengali." They were characterized by the administrator of one of the schools as members of the "scheduled," or "untouchable"
caste: people without rights or resources in the Indian subcontinent:

Example 11
publicraa ki dibe amar aapne especially bujhben amader desher je shob
lok aashche ora kon category lok aashchilo, mostly from scheduled
caste, gorib, dukhi krishokra aashchilo. oder maa baba o lekha pora

interested naa oder chele meye raa o pora lekha interested naa. oraa baidhitamolok schoole jete hoe primary schoole sholo bochor porjonto jete hoe, ei jonne schoole jaai.

<*what will the public contribute? you [the researcher, Shahela Hamid] especially will understand what type of people came from our country. they belonged to the category of scheduled caste, they are the poor, the deprived, farmers. their parents were not interested in education nor are the children interested. they go to school because it's compulsory*>. (administrator interview, School B)

Here Sylheti speakers are referred to as the "scheduled caste." Regarded as the least-educated group in society, with no resources of any kind, they are considered to be the lowest of the low (Borooah 2005; Borooah, Dubey and Iyer 2007; Kijima 2006). Here linguistic features were viewed as reflecting and expressing broader social images of people. Irvine and Gal suggest that people's ideologies about language often "locate linguistic phenomena as part of, and evidence for, what they believe to be systematic behavioural, aesthetic, affective, and moral contrasts among the social groups indexed" (2000, 37). One of the teachers argued that children should learn Bengali for "moral reasons." Irvine and Gal propose that a semiotic process of *iconization* occurs, in which linguistic features that index social groups appear to be iconic representations of them, as if a linguistic feature depicted or displayed a social group's inherent nature or essence. Bourdieu and Darbel argue that some more powerful groups provide "an essentialist representation of the division of their society into barbarians and civilized people" (1991, 112). Here the fact of speaking "Sylheti," rather than "Bengali," appeared to index the Sylheti group in particularly negative terms.

While some speakers in our study considered "Sylheti" to be quite different from "Bengali," others regarded the two sets of resources as indistinguishable. As we have seen, there were several instances of participants commenting on the differences between Sylheti and Bengali in terms of social status and value, but not everyone agreed about the extent to which these sets of linguistic resources were distinct. While the administrator of one of the schools argued that Bengali and Sylheti were "completely different," a student's mother said they were "thoraa different" <*a little different*>, while other parents also held this view, saying they were "little bit different thaake" <*only*> and even "the same." Here there was clear disagreement about the nature and extent of the differences between the sets of linguistic resources used by the students' parents at home and the literate version of the language taught in the complementary school classrooms. That is, there was disagreement about the permeability of the boundaries between languages. These differences of perception were likely to be ideological. Those who argued that the "languages" were completely different from each other were speakers of the prestige language, unwilling to allow the lower status language to contaminate their linguistic resources. Those who argued that the "languages" were almost the same as each other were speakers of Sylheti, which was held to index the lower status, less-educated group.

We asked one of the key participant children, eleven-year-old Masuda, and her cousin Maria, about the languages they use at home. In this extract from field notes they pointed out that unlike most of their fellow students, their families are not from Sylhet:

Example 12
Masuda says "we speak the proper Bengali", while Maria says "no, we speak a little bit lower class, a little bit". Masuda disagrees: "no, we do speak high class". Masuda says her father is from Dhaka. They say they are learning to join Bengali letters, and talk me through an elaborate technical explanation of how letters are joined in Bengali, and how this affects meaning and sound. They say they are "not bad, quite good" at reading Bengali, "but we were brought up to speak and read English, so we are a bit confused, a little bit." (Field notes, School A)

The children were not asked about associations between Bengali and social status, but here they have a clear sense that it is possible to speak "high class" or "low class." They also have a sense of their own achievement in learning Bengali.

On many occasions children demonstrated their awareness of differences between Sylheti and Bengali. The following example is from field notes taken during the first week of observation in School B. The teacher (Al) is working with the older group of children:

Example 13
Al administers to the older children what appears to be an ad hoc and informal test of Bengali vocabulary. The children are enthusiastic about this, clearly enjoying their multilingualism. The group of girls is a little boisterous, but Al appears unworried by this. When he asks them to compose a sentence in Bengali one of the girls, Tabeya, says in English: "we don't use this language." Al is amused, and asks them to compose a sentence in Sylheti. There is a discussion about linguistic differences between Sylheti and Bengali in the phrase "I have a friend." Tabeya says: "We say aamaar shoi aasoin (Sylheti), but you say "aamaar ekti shoi aase" (Bengali)." She also gives an example in English, Sylheti and Bengali: "aamaar ekti friend aase." The notable thing here is that the Bengali phrase is accompanied by much eye-rolling and eyebrow-raising from the speaker, and intonation which indicates that speaking the phrase in Bengali is associated with a different social class from the Sylheti phrase. That is, Bengali appears to be associated with putting on airs, showing off, or sophistication. (Field notes, School B)

In saying "we don't use this language" the collective pronoun appears to refer to the children and their families, distinguishing them from the teacher. Here the children, and Tabeya in particular, show an understanding that Sylheti and Bengali are different from each other, and also that they index different social groups and values. However, even in this instance where linguistic differences are explicitly marked by children, and acknowledged by teachers, the simple dichotomy between Sylheti and Bengali breaks down: Tabeya borrows the Bengali word "shoi" in her Sylheti sentence and uses the more polite form of the Sylheti verb "aasoin" in her sentence. Despite the clear ideological differences between Sylheti and Bengali for many of our participants, the varieties were frequently mixed in their linguistic practices.

On many occasions the research participants interactionally evidenced their awareness of differences (perhaps mainly in status and value) between "Sylheti" and "Bengali." The following example was recorded at the dinner table in the family home of one of the students:

Example 14
Mother: khitaa hoise? Tamim, khaibaani saatni?
                   <what is the matter? Tamim, would you like some relish?>
Father: aaro khoto din thaakbo
                   <how many more days is that [voice recorder] going be with you?>
Tamim: aaro four weeks *<four more weeks>*
Father: (XXXX)
Student: no they said any. if you talk all English
Father: ginni, oh ginni [calling his wife using a highly stylised Bengali term of endearment]
Mother: ji, hain go daakso kheno *<yes, dear why are you calling me?>* tumaar baabaa shuddho bhasha bolen *<your father is speaking the standard language>*
Father: paan dibaa *<can I have some paan>* aapne aamaar biyaai kemne *<how are you my relation?>* (home audio-recording, Bengali case study)

Here the Sylheti-speaking parents play the roles of Bengali speakers, appropriating an exaggerated, literary version of "high" Bengali, and adopting the airs and graces that they see as characteristic of the Bengali-speaking group. The terms of endearment used here ("ginni," "hain go") are forms of parody (Bakhtin 1973, 1984, 1986), exaggerations beyond common usage, as speakers of Bengali are caricatured in mock-sophisticated discourse. This brief interaction is situated in a whole hinterland of language ideological beliefs and practices, as the couple acknowledges differences between Bengali and Sylheti as sets of linguistic resources, and the conditions which differentially provide and constrain access to linguistic resources. The impromptu role-play light-heartedly, but not half-heartedly, "parodies another's socially typical . . . manner of seeing, thinking and speaking" (Bakhtin1994, 106). Here the repetition of a notional "high-class" discourse is both creative (Pennycook 2010) and evaluative (Vološinov 1973). In "the space provided by private life . . . the laws of price formation which apply to more formal markets are suspended" (Bourdieu 1991, 71). This does not, of course, mean that the usual hierarchies are truly transgressed, but rather provisionally suspended (if at the same time reinforced), to be reimposed outside of the private realm.

We heard further nuanced distinctions between certain sets of linguistic resources. In an interview with Shazia and Tamim, aged ten and eleven years respectively, the children mentioned a drama activity, based on a story of new arrivals from Bangladesh. In talking to the researcher (R) they described this group as "freshies" (cf. also Martin, Creese, Bhatt, and Bhojani 2004):

Example 15
R: what do you mean "freshie", what does that mean?
Tamim: freshie as in a newcomer
R: is that bad to say to somebody?
Tamim: yea it's kind of like a blaze but it's also a word to describe a new person coming from a different place
Shazia: it's not a good thing
Tamim: it's kind of both. if you say it as in trying to tease somebody, "freshie", and we say it as in erm trying to say erm, as in they're newcomers and they come from a different country for the first time
R: could you tell if someone was "freshie"?
Shazia: well from Bangladesh it's not always their skin colour, it's sometimes how they talk
R: how do you talk "freshie"?
Tamim: it's kind of like they don't know that much English
Shazia: they might just show off in their language but if you ask them a question in English they just
Tamim: they're like "what", "what", you know
Shazia: they say strange words in their language and if you ask them a question in English they just say "what" in their language. (student interview, School B)

Shazia and Tamim narrate their identity in opposition to that of the newly arrived children, repeatedly referring to "their" language, which they see as different from the language they speak themselves. Here "what, what" is spoken with an intonation which appears to represent some confusion on the part of the newly arrived group. Here is another form of parody, as the British children represent the new arrivals as inferior to themselves, and make indexical links between linguistic resources and membership of the in-group. Although the students speak the same "language" as the new arrivals in daily interactions with their parents, they nevertheless indicate that "how they talk" is one of the defining ways in which the "freshies" are different from them. That is, the way the new arrivals talk distinguishes them from the British-born children, and this distinction is more than linguistic.

A further means by which the students distinguished themselves from others was in their policing of their teachers' use of English. On a number of occasions students engaged in mockery or mimicry of their teachers' pronunciation of English, or their grammatical usage, lexical choice, or spelling. In Example 16 the children mock the teacher's pronunciation:

Example 16
Mr J writes the Bengali word "baash" and its English equivalent "bamboo." However, the children giggle at his expense and imitate the way he pronounces "bamboo." (Field notes, School B)

This was a relatively common feature of the Bengali classrooms.

A further aspect of the students' language repertoire was their attitude to academic English at their mainstream school. The students demonstrated that they were very much aware of their academic standing in their peer group. Tamim had a clear sense of the possibilities of profiting from his academic distinction:

Example 17
Tabeya: he wants to be a scientist.
Tamim: I'm not sure, because if I don't have a good job, if I don't go to a good university, I might not have a good job, if I go to a good university then I might have a good job
Tabeya: he might get a chance to be a scientist because you know his best friend, his dad is a scientist.
Tamim: not that, that's what I think
Tabeya: you know his best friend, he manages at least every science test, he manages to get half a mark or one full mark more than his friend.
Tamim: in some of them, not all of them, I used to beat my friend in science. (student interview, School B)

Here Tamim is already, at the age of ten, thinking about his future employment prospects and his university education. A moment before this he had asked the researchers whether Oxford University was "the top university in the whole world." Tamim talks about going to extra classes for tuition to help him with the forthcoming examination for entry to Grammar School.

During a conversation with us at his home before going to Bengali class the same day, he had told us about his various extracurricular academic commitments, saying that he takes extra tuition for the Grammar School test and homework club:

Example 18
I've a whole bag I'll show you. Here I've got stuff I have got folders, maths and English. This is my diary, well we have to do paper 5 to 6. I work on 9 to 10. I work 2 hours a day. (field notes, School B)

Tamim showed us a diary, in which he had scheduled his academic activity for each week, including Grammar School tuition (a day each week), Qur'anic Arabic tuition (five sessions each week), homework club (once a week) and Bengali class (once a week). In addition, he had to complete homework from his Primary School teacher. These are students full of aspiration and confidence, seeing themselves as high achievers with successful careers ahead. They were not from academic families, however. While Masuda's parents were educated professionals (albeit relatively low-paid community worker and part-time school teaching assistant), Tamim's father and mother were a restaurant worker and housewife, respectively, his father travelling many miles every evening to a neighboring city to work, and returning late at night.

Of course the young people's Englishes were not confined to the sphere of academic learning. There is little space here to discuss their interest in, and practices of, globalized digital linguistic resources. In this brief example the two sisters Rumana and Aleha are singing along to Hindi pop music just before leaving home for Bengali school.

Example 19
Rumana: [singing along to music] rock your body, rock your body, rock your body, rock your body, tumhare bina <*without you*> chaenna aaye <*there's no peace*> rock your body
Aleha: Rumana, come on. I'm going amma, salam alaikum <*mother, salam alaikum* > salam alaikum abba, zaairam aami <*salam alaikum father. I'm going*>. (home audio-recording, School B)

A dimension of the girls' linguistic repertoire here is that Hindi is not a language straightforwardly associated with their "national cultural heritage," but comes to them as a resource from popular culture. Aleha then uses the Arabic-derived "salam alaikum" alongside English and Sylheti as she leaves for school. Tamim also spoke of his interest in popular music:

Example 20
Tamim: I like Bhangra
R1:   really?

Tamim: I like Bhangra with rap

R2:   oh they have all kinds of crossover Bhangra music now don't they

Tamim: I like rap like Fifty Cent I mean

R2:   do you like Eminem?

Tamim: yes he's all right

R1:   so is that OK? I mean rap and all that is all right?

Shazia: erm yea

R: your dad doesn't?

Shazia: he doesn't really erm if it's in front of him he will shout but erm if we stopped it it's all right.

Tamim: RAP anyway I don't hear rap at home I might just hear it a bit cos I hear it from my friend's dad in his cars and everything because

R1:   is your friend Pakistani or Indian?

Tamim: English . . . I mean Bengali. (student interview, School B)

Here ten-year-old Tamim associates himself with firstly Bhangra, then "Bhangra with rap," and finally "rap like Fifty Cent." This appears to represent a negotiation of an increasingly daring subject position. Whereas listening to Bhangra music may be regarded as relatively mainstream and conservative, "Bhangra with rap" moves toward an increasingly American pop culture position, and "rap like Fifty Cent" is likely to represent a "Gansta Rap" identity. Tamim is happy to be associated with "my friend's dad," and the researcher assumes that his friend must be of Pakistani or Indian heritage, as it may be surprising for a good Bangladeshi to listen to this kind of music. In the final utterance in this excerpt, Tamim's pause between "English" and "I mean Bengali" may suggest that nationality, ethnicity and even language are not the salient categories for him at this moment—rather, he is more interested in positioning himself as a cool, streetwise consumer of contemporary, global music.

For some of our participants, some sets of linguistic resources were very considerably privileged above other, similar sets of linguistic resources. While resources that were described as "standard" or "proper" or "real" or "book" Bengali had come to represent the "heritage" of the Bangladeshi nation, sets of resources described as "Sylheti" were associated with the uneducated poor, who were held to be disinterested in schooling and unmotivated. Similarly, sets of linguistic resources associated with Bangladesh were distinguished from very similar resources associated with Britain (or Birmingham, or even a specific local neighborhood in Birmingham). However, we also saw that these distinctions were contested by others, who denied that clear differences existed, or made fun of the assumption that these differences were constitutive of differences in social status. That is, there were disagreements about what constituted (a) language, and about the ideological links between speakers and the sets of linguistic resources that they called into play. Academic literacies also played an important role in the young students' aspirations and their sense of themselves. They had a clear sense of how the profit of distinction may be earned, even where it may not be granted as a gift of inheritance.

What we have seen is that nuanced linguistic differences, some of them agreed upon and others not, come to act as subtle distinctions between groups and individuals. While some sets of resources are ideologically viewed as representing dimensions of nation, heritage and culture, these same sets of resources also come to represent their speakers as superior to speakers of other sets of resources. Blommaert takes Foucault's notion of "orders of discourse," together with Silverstein's (2003) "indexical order," to propose the term "orders of indexicality," in which "some forms of semiosis are systematically perceived as valuable, others as less valuable and some are not taken into account at all, while all are subject to rules of access and regulation as to circulation" (Blommaert 2010, 38). Orders of indexicality are stratified and systematically give preference to some modes of semiosis over others. It is such systematic perceptions that determine that speakers of "Bengali" are presupposed to be of higher class or caste than speakers of "Sylheti." These structures, constituted in discourse, create difference that in turn may be turned into inequality (Blommaert 2010, 41).

PRIDE, PROFIT AND DISTINCTION

In the stories of martyrdoms and heroic deeds that we often heard in and out of the Bengali classrooms, beliefs about, and values attached to, certain linguistic features and repertoires were crucial to our understanding. Linguistic practices were always local, but at times they moved between localities, were "translocal" (Blommaert 2010), traveling (to put it crudely) in an ideological triangle between inner-city Birmingham, a village in rural Sylhet and Dhaka, the capital city of Bangladesh. But locality was more than this, as digital communication made available resources that superseded territorial boundaries, offering linguistic resources that resided solely in none of these localities, and may have been more at home on the streets of New York City or Mumbai.

When a family sits at the dinner table, or a student sits in a classroom, and makes fun of those same discriminatory discourses, they are not only entertaining themselves and others but also engaging with discourses which have become sedimented through repeated acts of sameness (Pennycook 2010), many times, in many places. When Tabeya makes a lighthearted assertion about some lexical difference between Bengali and Sylheti, it may be that is all she is doing. But her statement is accompanied by a bodily demonstration of her keen awareness of the ideological differences between those lexical items. What we saw consistently was that in and around Bengali complementary schools in Birmingham pride was taken in the Bengali language, which for some was a crucial means by which to offer the gift of inheritance. At times the students did not unproblematically accept the gift of the language, preferring to contest, manipulate, appropriate and otherwise negotiate the resource being offered. For all that, they often spoke of their pride in their language learning, and in their ability to read and write the language of their (or their parents') heritage. Parents, teachers and administrators spoke, if not with one voice, of the importance of learning Bengali in relation to "national" and "cultural" belonging.

How do we understand this grassroots movement that organizes itself to teach pride not in the nation where the young students are *in situ*, but rather in the territory which many of them have rarely, if ever, visited? As we noted earlier, it is sometimes taken for granted that the concept of "diaspora" is oppositional to nations and nationalism, as the social relations of migrants and refugees are not confined within nations but may also be "transnational" (Cox and Connell 2003, 330). However, Dirlik (2004) argues that nationalism discourse in diaspora is often overlooked. There is of course great diversity within as well as between groups in diaspora, and "a diaspora discourse that reifies cultural identity . . . is complicit in the racialization of identity, which may serve some interests but has oppressive consequences for others" (Dirlik 2004, 499). This may be "long-distance nationalism" (Anderson 1998, 74), as some people in diaspora remain affiliated to their home territory. We saw exposition in pedagogy of pre-existing memories, myths, symbols and traditions (Smith 2005) in the reinvention of the nation. In fact we saw teaching of nationality and nationalism that was explicit, frequent and direct. At times what we heard in these Bengali complementary schools appeared to exemplify what Dirlik calls "diaspora discourse that reifies cultural identity" (2004, 499). For school administrators, parents and teachers, national and ethnic affiliation appeared to be presented as a straightforward, unambiguous and unproblematic choice.

Teaching of national heritage in the complementary schools was not the same phenomenon as the discursive flagging of nationalism in contexts where national belonging of the dominant "national" group is unstintingly reproduced in the repeated discourses of banal nationalism (Billig 1995, 93). This is not the nationalism of the nation-state, backed by power and capital. Rather, it is the nationalism of the "out of place" (May and Fenton 2003, 14), a nationalism that has to be taught precisely because it is not flagged daily in constant discursive acts of misrecognition. Teachers, and some parents, were emphatic about the importance of teaching affiliation to, and pride in, the homeland.

For the students, born in Britain to immigrant or second-generation parents, the teaching of national belonging did not appear to produce any sense of being "caught between" national identities. Rather, they were "determined to extend their possibility to make a multitude of identifications available" (Haglund 2005, 164). There was no conflict in learning

Bengali while wearing an England football shirt. Many students expressed their pride in being "Bangladeshi," and their pride in their ability to learn the national language, and in their knowledge of aspects of the collective memory and mythology of the national homeland.

In doing so, however, they were quite prepared to turn on its head the imposition of Bengali as a pure, uncontaminated artifact of inheritance. Here the notion of a "pure" Bengali became a constitutive piece of a system in which pride and profit were related. Learning Bengali offered an additional dimension to the young people's linguistic repertoires, alongside (*inter alia*) academic English, Bhangra, American/global rap, Sylheti (but not "freshie" Sylheti), Qur'anic Arabic, bits and pieces of Hindi, and many more. In these repertoires pride and profit coexisted.

In our observations, interviews, audio-recordings and video-recordings, we saw that distinctions were made between sets of linguistic resources, and that some sets of resources were held to index those who used them. That is, some ways of speaking (and reading and writing) produced a profit of distinction. Notwithstanding the fact that there was little consensus about "actual" differences between the sets of linguistic resources we are calling "Bengali" and "Sylheti," pride functioned as capital of distinction and therefore as a form of profit.

One of the particularly striking aspects of the voices we heard was the way in which sets of linguistic items were indexically linked to their speakers. We encountered powerful discourses, "systemic patterns of indexicality which were also systemic patterns of authority, of control and evaluation, and hence of inclusion and exclusion" (Blommaert 2010, 38). These patterns of indexicality appeared to have become sedimented over time, over generations, in other times and other spaces, and were now "relocalized" (Pennycook 2010) in Birmingham as discriminatory discourses. These positions resided at one and the same time, in one and the same place. Sets of linguistic resources were both objects of pride and means of producing and reproducing distinction.

NOTES

1. The research we draw on here was supported by the following research grant: *ESRC (RES-000–23–1180)* "Investigating Multilingualism in Complementary Schools in Four Communities."

REFERENCES

Ahmad, Yahaya. 2006. "The scope and definitions of heritage: From tangible to intangible." *International Journal of Heritage Studies* 12(3): 292-300.
Anderson, Benedict. 1998. *The Spectre of Comparisons: Nationalisms, Southeast Asia, and the World*. London: Verso.

Bakhtin, Mikhail M. 1973. *Problems of Dostoevsky's Poetics*. Translated by R. W. Rotsel. Ann Arbor, MI: Ardis.

Bakhtin, Mikhail M. 1984. *Problems of Dostoevsky's Poetics*. Edited and translated by Caryl Emerson. Manchester, UK: Manchester University Press.

Bakhtin, Mikhail M. 1986. *Speech Genres and Other Late Essays*. Edited by Caryl Emerson, and M. Holquist. Austin, TX: University of Austin Press.

Bakhtin, Mikhail M. 1994. "Problems of Dostoevsky's Poetics." In *The Bakhtin Reader: Selected Writings of Bakhtin, Medvedev, Voloshinov*, edited by Pam Morris, 110–113. London: Arnold.

Billig, Michael. 1995. *Banal Nationalism*. Sage: London.

Blackledge, Adrian, and Angela Creese. 2010. *Multilingualism: A Critical Perspective*. London: Continuum.

Blackledge, Adrian, and Angela Creese. 2008. "Contesting 'Language' as 'Heritage': Negotiation of Identities in Late Modernity." *Applied Linguistics* 29(4): 533–554.

Blommaert, Jan. 2010. *The Sociolinguistics of Globalization*. Cambridge: Cambridge University Press.

Borooah, Vani K. 2005. "Caste, Inequality, and Poverty in India." *Review of Development Economics* 9(3): 399–414.

Borooah, Vani K., Amaresh Dubey, and Sriya Iyer. 2007. "The Effectiveness of Jobs Reservation: Caste, Religion and Economic Status in India." *Development and Change* 38(3): 423–445.

Bourdieu, Pierre. 1984. *Distinction: A Social Critique of the Judgement of Taste*. London: Routledge.

Bourdieu, Pierre. 1991. *Language and Symbolic Power*. Cambridge: Polity Press.

Bourdieu, Pierre. 1993. *Sociology in Question*. London: Sage.

Bourdieu, Pierre. 2000. *Pascalian Meditations*. Cambridge: Polity Press.

Bourdieu, Pierre, and Alain Darbel. 1991. *The Love of Art: European Museums and their Public*. London: Polity Press.

Bourdieu, Pierre, and Jean-Claude Passeron. 1979. *The Inheritors*. Chicago: University of Chicago Press.

Castles, Stephen. 2005. "Citizenship and the Other in the Age of Migration." In *Nations and Nationalism: A Reader*, edited by Philip Spencer and Howard Wollman, 301–316. Edinburgh: Edinburgh University Press.

Cox, Jeremy, and John Connell. 2003. "Place, Exile and Identity: The Contemporary Experience of Palestinians in Sydney." *Australian Geographer* 34(3): 329–343.

Creese, Angela, Arvind Bhatt, and Peter Martin. 2007a. *Investigating Multilingualism in Gujarati Complementary Schools in Leicester*. Birmingham, UK: University of Birmingham.

Creese, Angela, Adrian Blackledge, and Shahela Hamid. 2007b. *Investigating Multilingualism in Bengali Complementary Schools in Birmingham*. Birmingham, UK: University of Birmingham.

Creese, Angela, Vally Lytra, Taskin Baraç, and Dilek Yağcıoğlu-Ali. 2007c. *Investigating Multilingualism in Turkish Complementary Schools in London*. Birmingham, UK: University of Birmingham.

Creese, Angela, Chao-Jung Wu, and Li Wei. 2007d. *Investigating Multilingualism in Chinese Complementary Schools in Manchester*. Birmingham, UK: University of Birmingham.

Dirlik, Arif. 2004. "Intimate Others: [Private] Nations and Diasporas in an Age of Globalization." *Inter-Asia Cultural Studies* 5(3): 491–502.

Essed, Philomena. 2000. "Beyond Antiracism: Diversity, Multi-identifications and Sketchy Images of New Societies." In *The Semiotics of Racism*, edited by Martin Reisigl and Ruth Wodak, 41–62. Vienna: Passagen Verlag.

Gard'ner, James Maitland. 2004. "Heritage Protection and Social Inclusion: A Case Study from the Bangladeshi Community of East London." *International Journal of Heritage Studies* 10(1): 75–92.

Glick Schiller, Nina, and Georges Fouron. 2002. *Georges Woke Up Laughing: Long Distance Nationalism and the Search for Home.* Durham, NC: Duke University Press.

Glick Schiller, Nina, Linda Basch, and Christina Blanc-Szanton. 1992. *Towards a Transnational Perspective on Migration: Race, Class, Ethnicity and Nationalism Reconsidered* (Annals of New York Academy of Science Vol. 645). New York: New York Academy of Sciences.

Haglund, Charlotte. 2005. *Social Interaction and Identification among Adolescents in Multilingual Suburban Sweden.* Stockholm: Centre for Research on Bilingualism.

Harvey, David. 2007. "Heritage Pasts and Heritage Presents. Temporality, Meaning and the Scope of Heritage Studies." In *Cultural Heritage*, edited by Laurajane Smith, 1–29. London: Routledge.

Heller, Monica, and Alexandre Duchêne. 2007. "Discourses of endangerment: Sociolinguistics, Globalization, and Social Order." In *Discourses of Endangerment. Ideology and Interests in the Defence of Languages*, edited by Alexandre Duchêne and Monica Heller, 1–13. London: Continuum.

Irvine, Judith, and Susan Gal. 2000. "Language Ideology and Linguistic Differentiation." In *Regimes of Language: Ideologies, Polities and Identities*, edited by Paul Kroskrity, 35–84. Santa Fe, NM: School of American Research Press.

Kijima, Yoko. 2006. "Caste and Tribe Inequality: Evidence from India, 1983–1999." *Economic Development and Cultural Change* 54: 369–404.

Levitt, Peggy, and Nina Glick Schiller. 2004. "Conceptualising Simultaneity, A Transnational Social Field Perspective on Society." *International Migration Review* 38(3): 1002–1039.

Lipe, William. 2007. "Value and Meaning in Cultural Resources." In *Cultural Heritage*, edited by Laurajane Smith, 286–306. London: Routledge.

Martin, Peter, Angela Creese, Arvind Bhatt, and Nirmala Bhojani. 2004. *Final Report on Complementary Schools and their Communities in Leicester.* Leicester, Birmingham, UK: University of Leicester/University of Birmingham.

May, Stephen. 2005. "Language Rights: Moving the Debate Forward." *Journal of Sociolinguistics* 9(3): 319–347.

May, Stephen, and Steve Fenton. 2003. "Ethnicity, Nation and 'Race': Connections and Disjunctures." In *Ethnonational Identities*, edited by Steve Fenton and Stephen May, 1–20. Basingstoke, UK: Palgrave Macmillan.

Patrick, Donna. 2007. "Language Endangerment, Language Rights and Indigeneity." In *Bilingualism: A Social Approach*, edited by Monica Heller, 111–136. Basingstoke, UK: Palgrave Macmillan.

Pavlenko, Aneta. 2007. "Autobiographic Narratives as Data in Applied Linguistics." *Applied Linguistics* 28: 163–188.

Pennycook, Alastair. 2010. *Language as a Local Practice.* London: Routledge.

Pujolar, Joan. 2007. "Bilingualism and the Nation-State in the Post-National Era." In *Bilingualism: A Social Approach*, edited by Monica Heller, 71–95. Basingstoke, UK: Palgrave Macmillan.

Silverstein, Michael. 2003. "Indexical Order and the Dialectics of Sociolinguistic Life." *Language and Communication* 23: 193–229.

Smith, Anthony. 2005. *The Antiquity of Nations.* Cambridge: Polity Press.

Smith, Laurajane. 2006. *Uses of Heritage.* London: Routledge.

Tunbridge, John E., and Gegory J. Ashworth. 1996. *Dissonant Heritage. The Management of the Past as a Resource in Conflict.* Chichester: Wiley.

UNESCO. 2003. *Convention for the Safeguarding of the Intangible Cultural Heritage*. Paris: UNESCO.

van Dijk, Teun A. 2000. "On the Analysis of Parliamentary Debates on Immigration." In *The Semiotics of Racism: Approaches in Critical Discourse Analysis*, edited by Martin Reisigl and Ruth Wodak, 65–84. Vienna: Passagen Verlag.

Vertovec, Steven. 2007a. "Super-Diversity and Its Implications." *Ethnic and Racial Studies* 30(6): 1024–1054.

Vertovec, Steven. 2007b. "Introduction: New Directions in the Anthropology of Migration and Multiculturalism." *Ethnic and Racial Studies* 30(6): 961–978.

Vertovec, Steven. 2009. *Transnationalism*. London: Routledge.

Vološinov, Valentin Nikolaevich. 1973 [1929]. *Marxism and the Philosophy of Language*. Translated by Ladislav Matejka and I. R. Titunik. London: Seminar Press.

7 War, Peace and Languages in the Canadian Navy[1]

Michelle Daveluy

INTRODUCTION

The military context is often thought of as an environment in which talk is counterproductive to the completion of tasks at hand. Perhaps such a description may fit industrial workplaces, where workers are unable to speak over noisy machinery that requires their full attention for proper operation (Boutet 2008; Heller and Boutet 2006), but this is not the case among military personnel. Fieldwork shows rather that between intense activities involving collective work (Hutchins 1990, 1995), soldiers and sailors spend a lot of time waiting for orders to be uttered and plans to be determined. Meanwhile they chat. Much of this time is devoted to complaining and storytelling, interactive activities that Irwin (2002) considers constitutive of a battalion's sense of history and identity.[2]

Research reported here was conducted between 2003 and 2008 (Daveluy 2006a, 2006b, 2006c, 2007a, 2007b, 2008a, 2008b). It addresses language issues in the context of military affairs at the two Canadian Navy bases: on the East Coast in Halifax, Nova Scotia, and the West Coast in Esquimalt, British Columbia. I had the opportunity to sail onboard the Navire Canadien de Sa Majesté VILLE DE QUÉBEC (hereafter NCSM VILLE DE QUÉBEC) and Her Majesty's Canadian Ship VANCOUVER (hereafter HMCS VANCOUVER). These two ships are frigates manned by crews of up to 225 shipmates. These crews are highly diverse, as staff is drawn from all over Canada. Women serve in the Canadian Forces, and some are posted on the NCSM VILLE DE QUÉBEC and the HMCS VANCOUVER; in both cases they represent about 5 percent of the crew. Data was collected in 2004 in Halifax, and at sea, on training missions, in July 2005 and February 2008.

My work on the Canadian Forces needs to be contextualized: I do not work for the Canadian Forces; I am not trained in, nor do I study, military outcomes. I am interested in the language component of the working conditions of the 60,000 Canadians who have voluntarily chosen to enroll (see Daveluy 2007a for a more detailed discussion). In terms of methods, sailing onboard Canadian Navy ships entails complete nonstop immersion in the group of interest. Escaping the object of study is not an option in the middle of an ocean. As opposed to fieldwork on land, there are no personal quarters of any sort on a ship. The Canadian Forces insisted my work would be enhanced by personally experiencing life at sea. It was indeed the most productive approach to my research interests. I shadowed sailors of all ranks, trades and departments during their work activities; conducted a number of interviews; and was invited several times to visit the three rank-segregated spaces where personnel relax when off duty.

I argue that in the military context, parameters usually associated with the new economy date back to the Cold War era (Moskos, Williams and Segal 2000). In Canada, this period was followed by decades of peace-making missions that foregrounded the participation of Canadian military personnel in international activities led by the United Nations. The fact that the country is at time of writing involved in war efforts in the Middle East corresponds to changes in the work environment of the military staff. However, most armed forces in the world reproduce to a certain extent the civilian national language ideology (Bauman and Briggs 2003), and inter-national joint operations or deployments in various parts of the world bring together apparently incompatible (even irreconcilable) language practices. The predominance of English for safety and efficiency purposes is often pre-sented as an unavoidable outcome, but research shows that multilingualism (bilingualism specifically in Canada) is simultaneously valued even though not always overtly promoted, in particular at the institutional level.

The language policy of the Canadian Forces is set up in such a fash-ion that risk management remains an individual affair. Indeed, unilingual individuals working in a language they do not know particularly well face dangerous situations in the conduct of their daily tasks. This was always the case, but Canada's recent involvement in war activities has increased both the risk level and public awareness of it (see Daveluy 2008b). Even though the collective nature of work in the military context fits the team model well, the primary concern here is on language-related skills, trans-mission of information and preservation of traditional knowledge, rather than the military organizational structure per se. The complexity of the language dynamics military staff deals with at work is the main focus. I documented a variety of activities ranging from the transmission of infor-mation through the chain of command, public speech through entire ships (pipes), interpretation and translation from French to English and vice versa, tasks involving writing (by hand and on keyboards), and nonverbal naval communication (boatswain calls and flag messages).

My work shows that the Canadian Forces are advantageously drawing from the ideology of official bilingualism in times both of war and of peace. I present how pride in a national order sustains profitable management of language use in the context of military operations. The detailed descrip-tion of language-related activities during training exercises in the Canadian Navy that follows shows that military personnel is information focused, and more globally oriented in their communication strategies since the adoption of the Canada Command system in 2004. However, the participation of the Canadian Forces in war rather than peace efforts since 2007 does not seem to have drastically changed the language dynamic fostered by official bilingualism, at least in the Navy. Language-wise it is risky business as usual. Even though the current war effort corresponds to lower emphasis on language issues in military priorities, the Canadian Forces remain legally bound to the country's official bilingualism (Department of National Defence & Canadian Forces (DND and CF) 2004). As a result, the language policy of the Canadian Forces incorporates French and English minorities in terms of (a) recruitment and (b) language use during work activities. Still, as in most military contexts in the world, matters pertaining to operational efficiency and security take precedence over language principles, however they may be formulated. Research I conducted in the Canadian Navy documents how the language policy of the Canadian Forces is implemented considering the stated constraints of the military context, as well as the impact the language policy has on daily social and linguistic practices.

The military culture of risk management is presented first. Then, the language policy of the Canadian Forces is described. The third section focuses on communication in the military context. Finally, data obtained onboard Canadian Navy ships is discussed in detail.

THE MILITARY CULTURE OF (RISK) MANAGEMENT

According to Moskos, Williams and Segal (2000), military forces have recently moved away from nation-state ideologies to become fully post-modern. This transformation is associated with a trend toward professionalization within armed forces all over the world. Enrolling individuals have shifted from an institutional to an occupational culture. In the process, heroic leaders have turned themselves into efficient managers (Nuciari 2003). Ann-Marie MacDonald, a military brat and world-famous author, provides a fictional example illustrating how this played out in Canada:

> The Cold War has escalated, marshalling unprecedented destructive force, most of which operates as an elaborate deterrent and requires a large bureaucracy to administer it. This is a war that is not so much waged as managed.
>
> He pulls a frayed textbook from the shelf: *Principles of Management: A Practical Approach*. We can do better than that. He has begun to assemble his own management text, a compilation of the latest articles coming out of the States, places like Harvard and Michigan. The world is changing rapidly and the military, being among the largest corporations in the world, can either lead or lumber behind like a dinosaur. Leaders today have to understand teamwork. That's the key to all the latest advances in science and technology . . .
>
> Jack is not alone in believing that the military chain of command is not simply a series of orders and knee-jerk responses, but a model for the flow of information and accountability. Air force types—especially

if they are veterans—tend to share this thinking. But it's important to codify and teach it so that it's not dependent on unwritten traditions and individual temperaments. (MacDonald 2003, 41)

The quote hints at the replacement of the warrior figure by the soldier-scholar image, in particular among officers for whom knowledge has gained the greatest value within the ranks. The following excerpt further highlights long-established priorities in the military context, including the importance of communication in risk management:

> "Think of the military as a corporation," says Jack. "What business are we in? We're in the peace business. Who are our stakeholders? The people of Canada. Our aim is to defend the country. In order to achieve that aim we must identify various objectives: to join with our allies in managing the threat of Soviet expansion; to monitor and respond to perilous situations within our own borders and around the world; to assess risk in the light of present-day weapons of mass destruction. What becomes key? Communication." He pauses and looks around. The men are relaxed on several chairs scavenged from neighbouring offices. Listening intently. "You may have a crack pilot, but if his ground crew used the wrong wing nut because the engineer submitted the right form to the wrong department whose initials changed last week and he is orderly bored with paperwork, you've got a potentially lethal domino effect." (MacDonald 2003, 129)

In fact, soldiers appear to fit Urciuoli's notion of *worker-self-as-skills-bundle*: not only is the worker's labor power a commodity, but the worker's very person is also defined by the summation of commodifiable bits (Urciuoli 2009, 211). This is at least how I interpret a conversation during one of those numerous moments one has to patiently share with mates during military operations. Onboard a Twin-Otter transiting from Eureka, on Ellesmere Island, a Canadian soldier tells me, talking about a friend serving in the Air Force who speaks Icelandic: "He is a valued commodity right there." I must admit I am not clear Icelandic in itself is highly valued comparatively to other languages in military affairs, except perhaps from an Icelandic perspective. The principle though is that languages are considered as much of an asset among military personnel as they are in other contemporary work environments.

Still, this is not to say military forces are completely freed from national ideologies. To the contrary, during the period of time that followed the end of the Cold War, studies on Canadian military language issues have been restricted to policy analysis, a topic that will be addressed in the following section. What is different in the Canadian Forces nowadays is that among those who are currently serving, most grew up and were trained during peace-making times and the transition to the war effort was a shock to many of them. Anne Irwin (2007) documented changes in how soldiers facing death in Afghanistan use the recurrent *Good to go?* in their daily interactions. Usually a simple security check routinely uttered prior to troop movement, she claims it is now used to inquire about a soldier's psychological well-being as much as his or her state of preparedness to physically go from point A to point B. In the current context, postings in remote places like Eureka, on the top of the world where it is dark half of the year and excessively cold, may be gaining currency (value) among Canadian military personnel. The chances of facing death or the enemy remain much slimmer there than in conflict zones. The language policy of the Canadian Forces, which is presented next, frames current working conditions and risks military personnel faces on a daily basis.

THE LANGUAGE POLICY OF THE CANADIAN FORCES

The language policy of the Canadian Forces (Asselin 2005, 2006) is implemented through four different types of units: English units, French units, English or French units, and, finally, French and English units. Although the Canadian Forces are officially bilingual as a whole, English is the language of the Canadian Navy, when considered as a single unit. In many respects, however, each of the two naval bases constitute autonomous units: the Pacific and the Atlantic Maritime Forces, respectively. For a long time, the Halifax base was a bilingual unit (including both English or French + English and French components), while the Esquimalt base has always been an English unit. The language status of the Halifax base has recently been changed from bilingual to English. The NCSM VILLE DE QUÉBEC is the only French unit in the Canadian Navy; it is stationed in Nova Scotia. The HMCS VANCOUVER is an English unit on the West Coast.

However, no matter what the language of a unit in the Canadian Forces, there is a cap on the number of speakers of French and English at any given time. This cap is set at a maximum of 80 percent of the unit staff that can speak the language of the unit. As a result, there is always a sizeable proportion of the staff that does not speak the language of the unit where they are posted. There are a number of pragmatic reasons justifying the existence of this limit. These reasons include difficulties encountered in recruiting French speakers in the Canadian Forces in general, but also human resources constraints related to the skill sets that are required to maintain equipment and capacity in any given unit. At the same time, other reasons, of a much less pragmatic nature, were also invoked by policy makers to endorse such an implementation strategy of official bilingualism. Indeed, the presence of nonspeakers of the language of the unit was also suggested as a means to prevent the development of parallel ethnolinguistic forces within the Canadian military (Letellier 1987a, 1987b).

In units like the frigates where I conducted research, this means that there is always up to forty-five shipmates who do not speak the language of the ship. One of the most striking results obtained in my ethnography of communication onboard Canadian Navy ships is that, even in such complex circumstances, the language most likely to be used onboard the NCSM VILLE DE QUÉBEC remains French, in particular for work-related activities.

To sum up, communication across units in the Navy occurs in English, while the language used within the confines of the NCSM VILLE DE QUÉBEC is French. Joint activities with other ships from either the Pacific or the Maritime Forces take place in English. Finally, all units, including the NCSM VILLE DE QUÉBEC, use English in emergency situations: a safety measure, one is told when enquiring about how that can be considering the language policy of the Canadian Forces.

The actual global geopolitical situation and Canada's participation in ongoing world events have recently modified institutional discourse about the language policy of the Canadian Forces. The language policy I have described was developed through a long process of negotiations between government agencies and the military representatives in times of peace (Bernier and Pariseau 1991, 1994; Direction des langues officielles 2004; DND and CF 2004; Lettellier 1987a, 1987b; Pariseau and Bernier 1987, 1988). In that context, languages had an instrumental value, and ensuring demolinguistic representation in the Canadian Forces was advantageous in terms of recruitment from the institution's perspective. Military personnel could then present their native tongue as an asset financially rewarded through bonuses for those who performed well in language proficiency tests. To ensure fair representation of the official minorities in the ranking system of the Canadian Forces, bilingualism was a criterion overtly used for promotion.

Since Canada's recent involvement in global conflicts, the linguistic *modus operandi* of the Canadian Forces has been altered. In the context of frequent deployments to theaters of actions that are much more dangerous than Canadians have had the experience of in the last forty years or so, the language agenda is now presented as a civilian issue rather than a military priority.

However, practices do not seem to have been noticeably impacted by those recent changes. A longer-term assessment is necessary, but it is clear to me that the claim that bilingualism is not a promotion criterion anymore in the Canadian Forces had not yet trickled down the ladder when I conducted research. It is in fact difficult to see how it will ever trickle down the ladder. Services offered in French and opportunities to work in French may be restricted in relation to the war effort, but the claimed changes to the language policy must be understood in the context of the limited implementation of the previous agreed-upon policy. Individual bilingualism was and, I believe remains, rewarded. As for the use of French as a language for work purposes, it remains as limited as it previously was. In my opinion, the current institutional stand on official bilingualism fits very closely with the already existing state of affairs in the Canadian Forces as far as languages are concerned. As previously stated, language is a risky business from a military perspective, but managing risks is part of the military agenda. Furthermore, bilingualism ensures profitable outcomes in Canada, if only in terms of recruitment in a country where mandatory military service does not exist.

Perhaps the fact that, at the same period of time, the American Navy implemented a reward system for the use of languages other than English is a good counterexample to consider. American sailors are individually financially compensated for using languages other than English during deployments (Associated Press 2007; Daveluy 2007b; Powell and Lowenkron 2006; Scruto 2007). In this approach language appears as a skill among many, and military personnel can be viewed as language workers similar to those described by Heller (2003) (see also Boutet, this volume). In fact, then, languages remain highly relevant in contemporary conflicts, and the recent positioning of the senior Canadian military administration should not be overemphasized until systematically studied. As far as I am concerned, it remains highly likely languages will regain some importance shortly in the Canadian Forces, if only because of current pressures on enrolment levels that must be maintained for the missions to which the country is already committed.

Given the implementation strategy endorsed by the Canadian Forces for its language policy, communication occurs in ways that are not necessarily within the range of usual expectations for human interactions. How this plays out in the Canadian Navy is described next, starting with relevant parameters of communication among military personnel.

COMMUNICATION IN THE MILITARY CONTEXT

In military contexts, communication is often associated with extreme instances of interaction, like being yelled at, in particular during training, or silently motioning troop action prior to attacking the enemy. Even though these two poles of interaction do occur, the most important portion of military activities that I witnessed is information oriented. Seeking information, transmitting it through the chain of command and acting upon it summarizes most of the time devoted to work in the military context I observed. As clearly shown by Hutchins (1990) in his description of the fixed cycle in port maneuvers, teamwork is essential in this information management process. Tasks are compartmentalized in a way reminiscent of the production line in industries. Each step in a procedure contributes to the accomplishment of the task at hand. Individuals are trained to accomplish a number of specific steps in a given sequence. Each individual is responsible for a clearly identified step, or series of steps, in the sequence. In such a system, individual skills are necessary, but not particularly valued, as the collective objective is paramount.

However, it would be a mistake to consider interaction is at a minimum under these circumstances. On a ship, only those assigned to the machines room work in a noise level typical of an industrial environment. In all other departments, working conditions are such that communication is unhindered. It is important to acknowledge, then, that interaction during work shifts includes casual exchanges as well as highly formulaic speech, used specifically while transmitting information through the chain of command.

Frequently, communication through the chain of command is also oversimplified into the utterance of orders, from the top down, followed by automatic responses. However, most of the time, interaction I observed leading to the utterance of orders was collaborative rather than emerging from a single, isolated source. In fact, most if not all orders are the culmination of a more or less extensive, at least bidirectional, information management process. In transmitting information up the chain of command, redundancy is a key factor. For example, a sound heard on sonar is reported to one's immediate superior who then crosschecks the fact (often with another team member) prior to channeling the information either within the group under his or her command or to the next level of command. Speaking loudly and clearly is the norm in the military context so that critical information is often heard by many more individuals than one's immediate superior. In such cases, hearing information does not trigger a reaction at the next level of command. Only confirmed information transmitted through proper channels does, and it always does. Information management within a cell occurs in serious but plain language, while the actual transmission of the information through the chain of command is repeated from one level to the next, bracketed by formulaic expressions. Through the chain of command, then, redundancy and repetition are prominent.

Down the chain of command, when an order is verbally issued, the opposite occurs: members of the ranks who may be busy anywhere on the ship instantly react to a keyword as soon as it is heard on the public address system. Movement is automatic, and a chain of reactions takes place until the appropriate summoned team gathers for the specific purpose announced throughout the ship. Casual conversations are often interrupted in the middle of a sentence as soon as the public address system is turned on. I witnessed individuals intensely listening to the system prior to actual words being uttered or even transmitted. In some instances, announcements are repeated a number of times, and at least one interview ended when a participant first warned me that he was likely to have to run soon, as per the message aired as we were talking. Shortly after, he stood, smiled and left as soon as the search and rescue call was made. In fact, he kept track of his work commitments throughout our conversation. Had I not been an untrained outsider, there would have been no need to explain his behavior and sudden departure.

In short, sailors constantly monitor their auditory environment to make sure not to miss a cue for action, while simultaneously training themselves to carefully select the source of information they respond to, since some require immediate attention while others don't. In sum, communicative competence for a sailor is twofold: they must be efficient at quickly reacting to an order, while never reacting to information crossing their auditory range until relevance is established. In that sense, avoidance behaviors are telling. For example, to preserve themselves from discussions they should not be overhearing, sailors will matter-of-factly change direction or simply turn their back on ongoing exchanges they should not be part of.[3]

The following section provides evidence from daily interactions onboard Canadian Navy ships that further illustrate communication within a fairly small group of people who cannot escape each other's company. Data obtained in the only French unit of the Canadian Navy is presented first.

ONBOARD NCSM VILLE DE QUÉBEC

My research focuses mainly on the relationships between French and English native speakers expected to work primarily in French onboard the NCSM VILLE DE QUÉBEC. How unilingual English speakers negotiate this linguistic market is of particular interest. Differences among French native speakers are also highly relevant. Depending on their origin (Québécois, Acadians, etc.) and their degree of bilingualism, diverging views emerge regarding the benefits and costs associated with the use of French onboard the frigate. Tension definitely exists among various types of French speakers working together onboard the NCSM VILLE DE QUÉBEC. Acadians tend to view themselves as bilinguals by definition, while Québécois position themselves as French monolinguals who have to learn English to work in the Canadian Forces. In a context where bilingualism is related to promotion, competition between these two groups is palpable. Acadians expect to be recognized for the language abilities they provide to an institution that openly advocates endorsing bilingualism, while Québécois stand their ground and continue lobbying for more French in the Forces. In one case, language is viewed as an intrinsic talent; in the other, it is a developed skill. From the institutional perspective both add value to the system (Heller 2003, 2005).

At sea onboard the NCSM VILLE DE QUÉBEC, data elicited during nonwork activities (off watch) show important differences according to rank and age with regards to language use. For officers, bilingualism is particularly critical for advancement. Interestingly, they use French almost exclusively when they are not on duty, making their mess a French environment. Indeed, because of the predominance of English as the language of work in the Navy, officers have more opportunities to display their ability in French while socializing in the mess than they have while working. For noncommissioned officers, English is often used when off work, and numerous comments were volunteered about this situation. French native speakers told me that, first and foremost, it is a matter of politeness to use English with unilingual colleagues. However, many also remember the era when English was exclusively used in the Navy, and they claim they do not want to reproduce the unilingual pattern they were subjected to as French unilingual speakers at the beginning of their career. As for the members of the ranks, unilingual speakers tend to hang together, creating a bilingual environment of mutually exclusive French or English sections in the cafeteria.

It is important to note both English and French noncommissioned officers have lived the language transition in the Navy very intensely. For example, a unilingual English speaker explained he filed a request to be sent to French classes twenty-two years in a row without ever being given the chance to learn it. He claims to have lost interest in French now that he is reaching retirement. However, the language status of the NCSM VILLE DE QUÉBEC does not prevent him from accepting to be repeatedly posted on the ship. He is one of the English monolinguals openly praising the VILLE DE QUÉBEC for its pleasant atmosphere. He sums it up as, "You know, work hard, play hard. They do that well here."

Onboard the NCSM VILLE DE QUÉBEC, competence was particularly clearly evidenced during communication through the public address system. Most messages, referred to onboard as "pipes," are produced in French. For standard, regularly required pipes, poorly designed manuals, inaccurately translated from English, are used (Benschop 2006). However, many pipes are unique and must be drafted on the spot, according to specific circumstances. In these cases, consensus about how to phrase the pipe must be reached rapidly. Formulaic sentences that fit the need should be known from training, but in many instances training occurred in English and staff is not necessarily familiar with appropriate equivalents in French. On the bridge, I witnessed negotiation about how to phrase information occurring prior to pipes on numerous occasions. To complete a pipe, knowledge of both French and English is essential, but translation skills are also an asset. Pipes are equivalent to public performances in many ways. Delaying issuing an order may have consequences, but a poorly worded pipe may also confuse coworkers and hinder efficient completion of the task at hand. Poor performance on the public address system can additionally result in exposure to ridicule in the form of teasing, jokes and comments made directly to the individual afterward.

Another area of stress clearly identified onboard the NCSM VILLE DE QUÉBEC is the written usage of the French language. Many shipmates were uncomfortable when encouraged to use French for internal written documents. Some claimed this directive duplicated their workload, since sooner or later a translation of these documents was highly likely to be required as well. Writing them directly in English appeared to many as a sound strategy. However, it is also important to acknowledge that comfort levels regarding writing French vary greatly among Canadians. In general, Québécois perform fairly well in this regard because they have been schooled in French, while only younger Acadians have received similar formal exposure to the language in an academic setting. I already alluded to the competition between these two groups of French speakers in the Canadian Navy, a competition that extends to writing abilities. Challenges associated with the preservation of a language in the absence of a standardized written code are well documented (e.g., see Hoffman 2008). I suggest that limited writing skills at the individual level in the military context should be further explored in that specific perspective. However, as I explain next, the contemporary importance of writing in the military context became clearer to me onboard an English unit.

ONBOARD HMCS VANCOUVER

Onboard the HMCS VANCOUVER, I came to realize that writing skills are an issue in the Navy in general, rather than a language-specific matter. In this English unit, it became apparent that comfort levels in typing on recent equipment vary greatly and constitute a challenge for many experienced sailors. Trained to read and verbally communicate information appearing on radar screens, many sailors are limited when the time comes to type this same information on the keyboards of computers that are now routinely used in operation rooms and various other departments.

The type of exercise I was invited to attend onboard the HMCS VANCOUVER prompted me to spend more time in the combat room than the bridge, as I previously did onboard the NCSM VILLE DE QUÉBEC.[4] When I mentioned to the Second-in-Command onboard the HMCS VANCOUVER that I felt the configuration of the combat room was quite different from my recollection of the one onboard the NCSM VILLE DE QUÉBEC, he explained a section had indeed been redesigned to have more, and more modern, computers. These computers were used to monitor the web during operations to track information that could be of use to locate enemy submarines that it was the objective of our mission to detect. Nowadays, the Canadian Forces have fully adopted a communication protocol, Canada Command, which heavily relies on real-time monitoring of civilian and military media in the decision making process leading to actions. Back in 2008, onboard the HMCS VANCOUVER, the Second-in-Command insisted it was a single unit affair to dedicate resources to that effect rather than a policy of the entire military organization.

Skill-wise this means that sailors trained to read radar screens or listen to sonar equipment and then loudly provide relevant information were now collaborating with mouse and keyboard users who can quietly inform their superiors. If there was any breech of communication between the Captain and his web analysts, nobody but them was aware of it, while any similar situation for others in the combat room could lead to comments, reprimands and reminders on how to appropriately proceed which are provided in front of the entire audience. In a competitive environment like the military context, having the opportunity to protect one's reputation from public scrutiny is advantageous. Web analysts are then privileged, since mistakes on their part remain unnoticed by their teammates. Within ranks, there is also a generation gap since younger crewmembers that are comfortable with modern technology are in a position to perform better than experienced sailors who may not be so well acquainted with web communication.

On the other hand, it is also onboard the HMCS VANCOUVER that I was able to better understand the importance and role of nonverbal activities in the Navy. In a long conversation, the English unilingual member voluntarily repeatedly posted onboard the NCSM VILLE DE QUÉBEC painstakingly explained to me that piping was the essence of sailing. "If all systems fail, that's what we can rely on." Indeed boatswain calls and flag messages are very simple technologically, but they require fairly complex skills to master. I realized what he meant years later, witnessing young sailors practicing their boatswain calls and flag communication onboard the HMCS VANCOUVER. It became clear to me that younger sailors were expanding their skill range while at sea. The fact that they were truly enjoying themselves doing it does not change the reality of the value of these skills when senior sailors would evaluate them for promotion.

Individual interests match the collective here. In terms of language ideologies, there is plenty of evidence that language preservation and use are associated with the practice of traditional ways of life. In that sense, sailors wanting and making the point to preserve apparently arcane ways of communicating like boatswain piping are very much like Inuit claiming that the proper use of Inuktitut and its maintenance in the contemporary world entail hunting skills and an intimate knowledge of the land. Perfectly honed sailors do master both modern and traditional ways of communicating critical information.

CONCLUSION

The military as a field relies heavily on political discourse about rights and citizenship, making pride rather than profit a more readily relevant theme in this milieu. However, data collected in the Canadian Navy provides evidence of the relationship between discourses associated with both pride and profit. The language policy of the Canadian Forces clearly addresses issues pertaining to the rights of citizens voluntarily choosing to make a living in a job sector the state has a vested interest in. Still, in a country where military service is not mandatory, ethnolinguistic representation of official minorities certainly contributes to the Canadian military agenda in either war operations or peace missions. As a canonical agency of the nation-state, the military draws its legitimacy from civilian priorities, in this case official bilingualism. The ethnography of communication at sea shows precisely how tensions between national priorities and military constraints are mediated through language use in the conduct of routine activities for work purposes as well as off duty.

To sum up, current adequate communicative competence in the Canadian Navy includes written as well as oral skills in the language of one's unit. Without a language policy overtly specifying it, it also seems to me successful sailors are at least to some extent proficient in both speaking and writing English as well as French, not to mention naval skills like boatswain calls and flag communication. Nowadays, then, writing and reading in a number of languages are valuable assets in the Canadian Forces, while interaction through the chain of command remains associated with formal verbal ways of communicating segmented information. It is important to keep in mind that sailing in a unit where language is less salient an issue provided the opportunity to better understand the value language skills have in the military context. A wide range of language skills contributes to information gathering and management in the Canadian Navy. These include traditional naval communication skills, and abilities in speaking and writing the two official languages of Canada, but the capacity to rapidly translate between French and English is also an asset.

The relationship between both profit and pride discourses in the Canadian Navy is further illustrated in the use of language in the framework of the business model of teamwork for cohesiveness and efficiency purposes. For example, a supervisor claimed ethnolinguistic competition within a trade is an asset for enhanced efforts by French and English teams in his department. From the members of the ranks in that specific trade, language affiliations extended beyond work, as they insisted teammates were also friends, not mere coworkers. In practice, then, the business model meets language use and affinities in complementary fashion, sustaining rather than eliminating each other

The language skills required for work in military organizations like the Canadian Forces provide evidence of some features clearly associated with the new economy. In short, the well-traveled sailor matches in many ways the characteristics of the delocalized transient worker who, isolated from kin, develops multilingual skills for practical reasons. By definition, military personnel are mobile in the sense that postings are usually for a few years only in various locations within national boundaries in a vast country. Sailors appear particularly mobile because they spend considerable periods of time at sea all over the world. Their workplace is particularly evocative of nonplaces (Augé 1992). Exposure to the world and its linguistic diversity is required as well, as it feeds their specific professional identity within the military milieu.

Canadian military personnel (and their families; see Asselin 2007) are to a great extent uprooted, delocalized and relocalized within their own country, in a similar fashion to migrants crossing geographical or symbolic borders, or both. Language identity and discursive practices illustrate the complexity of their life as transient individuals belonging to communities in flux. I have argued elsewhere that French and English native speakers working for the Canadian Forces are extremely mobile speakers who are not well accounted for in current theories and models about linguistic communities, including those regarding linguistic minorities (Daveluy 2008a). Until very recently their mobility has been used to exclude them from sociolinguistic analysis, even though the type of work they do fits the framework of the globalized new economy.

Still, work for military forces has always been about putting one's life on the line. In Canada, this eventuality has recently gained weight because of the shift from so-called peacetime work to frequent deployments to euphemistically called "reconstruction zones." The mediation of the risk all military personnel is subjected to has always been dealt with through information management. For a long time, secrecy surrounding information management in military affairs was strict, but that is not necessarily always the case nowadays. In the current electronic era, norms pertaining to secrecy have had to be relaxed, considering that some of the relevant information for military purposes is sometimes also easily available to all citizens in the world. Scholars, then, should feel at ease to focus on the working conditions of military personnel in order to better account for the complexity of communication and language use in the military context. This would provide the opportunity to consider alternate discourses at play in the Canadian Forces.

Indeed, the security discourse certainly requires further work in order to clarify how it is related to the discourses associated with pride and profit respectively. In fact, pride, profit and security are all at stake in the construction of monolingual units for unilingual speakers of either official languages of the country. Security is addressed through a number of recurrent themes, including "safety" and "efficiency." Safety for all, ensuring all shipmates make it in dangerous circumstances, is a matter of pride in the military ethos. Jeopardizing individual rights, like in the use of English in emergency situations, even though unilingual French speakers are by definition involved, is not considered contradictory in terms of efficiency. To the contrary, it is conceived as an unavoidable component of risk management. Minimizing risk for all does not mean eliminating risk for all. The discourse of security then clearly entails elements of both pride and profit in daily practice.

I have strategically decided not to address cases of miscommunication, but it would certainly be inappropriate to suggest the phenomenon is absent in the Canadian Navy. In military interactions, authority is also contested much more often than general wisdom would like it. Highlighting which language skills are valued, at least covertly in the Canadian Forces, my objective was to underline challenges unilingual military personnel, of either official language, face on a regular basis. It should be noted it remains impossible to enroll in the Canadian Forces as a bilingual individual. Those who attempt to do so are specifically told that language and gender are the same and a recruit has to choose one for each category (Daveluy 2006b). Such a procedure certainly ensures that satisfactory demolinguistic representation of official minorities is obtained in the Canadian Forces. The reality is, though, that unilingual sailors do not necessarily need to be deployed to dangerous theatres to put their lives on the line, since their security is routinely jeopardized because of their limited ability to cope with information management as it currently occurs in the Canadian Forces.

Considering Canadian military personnel as language workers of the neoliberal order, as I suggested at the outset of this chapter, allows us to identify tensions characteristic of this specific discursive shift. The military is not clear as to whether it considers speaking French a right, a skill or, given the pressure to recruit more sailors for the expanding role of the Canadian military, a technique for recruitment. Nonetheless, the military shows clearly that when the logic of ethnonationalism (making sure francophones are represented in the forces, that there is one workspace where French is the language of work) encounters the logic of military security and the logic of rational management (securing an efficient and productive workforce in the interests of the stakeholders, the Canadian people) English emerges again as the dominant language, albeit not one that can simply take over entirely. This very same tension also offers opportunities for sailors who can easily translate between French and English to acquire at least some symbolic capital, although friction between Acadians and Québécois shows that for some workers, symbolic capital may not be enough; instead, the hope is for something like better chances at employment or promotion, or, alternatively, protection from adverse career consequences for unilingual francophones. Further, for some, the acquisition of symbolic capital may not be worth the responsibilities that come with it. In any case, by considering the military as a worksite, we can illuminate some of the central issues in the transition from the welfare to the neoliberal state, and the limits of ethnonationalism in the management of increasingly globalized conflicts and military responses.

NOTES

1. A preliminary version of this paper was presented at the 17th *Sociolinguistics Symposium* in 2008, in a session organised by Monica Heller and Alexandre Duchêne (see Daveluy 2008b). Another version was discussed at the workshop *Language, Ideologies and the New Economy* at the Institut de plurilinguisme in Fribourg, Switzerland in 2009. Financial support to attend the workshop was awarded by the Swiss National Research Foundation within

the Research Program "Language, Identities and Tourism" (principal investigators: Professors Alexandre Duchêne and Ingrid Piller). Thanks to Monica Heller and Alexandre Duchêne for inviting me to contribute to these activities. The research onboard Canadian Navy ships was funded by the Social Sciences and Humanities Research Council and the University of Alberta.

2. Limited sociolinguistic analysis of interaction among military personnel is available. Still quoting Elkin (1946), most scholars do mention the prominent use of acronyms in military jargon, the prevalence of vulgar speech in interaction often involving males exclusively and the omnipresence of sexual connotations in discourse. Many focus on ritual behavior, like Jaffe (1988) did with saluting in the American army. Few study the impact languages can have in military daily practice. Olynyk, Sankoff and D'Anglejan (1983) is an exception; they analyzed the consequences of using French or English during military training. Irwin (1993, 2002, 2007) also contributes important information based on her ethnographic study of an army battalion over extensive periods of time. Particularly relevant to my own research is Hutchins' (1995) systematic documentation of the collaborative nature (Goodwin 1995; Malinowski 1935) of the work necessary for maneuvering ships in and out of ports in the American Navy. Like Bernhard Altermatt and his colleagues in Switzerland, where four if not five languages are at stake in military affairs, my work specifically contributes the bilingual component of the Canadian case to better understand the role languages play in the military.

3. To me, such behaviors belong to a series of understudied interactive strategies found in a number of sociolinguistic situations. For example, in societies which do not compartmentalize activities on a generational basis while maintaining an age- or experience-related hierarchy in terms of turn taking and floor privileges, several individuals must regularly ignore ongoing interaction that they should not be actively involved in. They are routinely passively attending exchanges that they are not strictly participating in. Communication in small-scale societies (in Pacific Islands, among hunter-gatherers like the Inuit, etc.) fits this model, which remains unexplained even though theoretically rich.

4. It is difficult to determine if the few years between my sailing experiences explain the changes I witnessed in terms of secrecy on each ship or if it has to do with official policy or perhaps even individual managerial approaches. In the darkness of the combat room, not noticing the person I was shadowing had left, I was once escorted out and reminded not to spend time there alone considering the particularly sensitive nature of this area. This occurred onboard the VILLE DE QUÉBEC while, years later, the Captain of the HMCS VANCOUVER insisted nothing was confidential on his ship, a somewhat surprising stance, and encouraged me to come and go onboard as I saw fit. Interestingly, his crew was not necessarily of the same opinion. A number of times, lower rank individuals requested me to delete pictures I had taken in their presence, alleging I had captured confidential information. They did not appear concerned about their own appearance on my photographs. They were, rather, protecting the circulation of critical information like names and code numbers of ships in convoys. When reminded the Captain had authorized me to take as many pictures as I wanted, they systematically responded this permission did not apply in the case at hand. I always complied when requested to erase pictures because it was clear to me staff had more at stake than myself. Were anyone blamed in a contentious situation, repercussions would have been much greater for the sailor involved than for me. Once before I had witnessed a case of management of

confidentiality across the ranks, onboard the VILLE DE QUÉBEC. I interpreted it as a strategy on the part of a high-rank individual to refuse a request for information I had made. In front of me, he asked one of his assistants if a breech of confidentiality would occur were my request granted. They openly discussed the issue in my presence. In the process, I understood this was not so much a matter of seeking advice from a lower-ranked individual, an unlikely strategy in the military context, but a way to deny a request while making the decision appear nonpersonal.

REFERENCES

Asselin, Gabriel. 2005. *Les plaintes au Commissariat aux langues officielles et les Forces canadiennes.* Research Report, Department of Anthropology, University of Alberta.

Asselin, Gabriel. 2006. "Linguistically-Defined Environments: Continuity and Isolation in Linguistic Communities of Canadian Navy Bases." Paper presented at the annual meeting for the Society for Applied Anthropology, British Columbia, Vancouver, March 2006.

Asselin, Gabriel. 2007. *Ni civiles ni militaires. Les familles francophones de la base des Forces Canadiennes Esquimalt, en Colombie-britannique.* Master's thesis. Department of Anthropology, University of Alberta.

Associated Press. 2007. "Language Corps." *New York Times.* Accessed May 10, 2007. http://www.nytimes.com/2007/05/10/washington/10brfsLANGUAGECORP_BRF.html?scp=1&sq=May%2010,%202007%20LAnguage%20Corps&st=cse

Augé, Marc. 1992. *Non-lieux. Introduction à une anthropologie de la surmodernité.* Paris: Seuil.

Bauman, Richard, and Charles L. Briggs. 2003. *Voices of Modernity: Language Ideologies and the Politics of Inequality.* Cambridge: Cambridge University Press.

Benschop, Diana. 2006. "Reading between the Lines." Paper presented at the annual meeting for the Canadian Anthropology Society / Société canadienne d'anthropologie (CASCA), Montréal, Québec, Canada, May 2006.

Bernier, Serge, and Jean Pariseau. 1991. *Les Canadiens français et le bilinguisme dans les Forces armées canadiennes. Tome II 1969–1987. Les langues officielles: la volonté gouvernementale et la réponse de la Défense nationale.* Ottawa. Service historique de la Défense nationale. www.gc.ca/hr/dhh/publications

Bernier, Serge, and Jean Pariseau. 1994. *French Canadians and Bilingualism in the Canadian Armed Forces, Volume II, 1969–1987: National Defence's Response to the Federal Policy* (Socio-Military Series No. 2). Ottawa: Directorate of History of the Department of National Defence.

Boutet, Josiane. 2008. *La vie verbale au travail. Des manufactures aux centres d'appels.* Toulouse: Editions Octares.

Daveluy, Michelle. 2006a. "Communicating Among Linguistic Communities Onboard a Canadian Navy Ship." In *Papers from the 20th APLA conference,* edited by Margaret Harry, Stephanie Lahey and Christa Beaudoin-Lietz, 27–34. Halifax: Saint Mary's University in Halifax.

Daveluy, Michelle. 2006b. "The Ethnography of Language Communities Onboard a Canadian Navy Ship." Paper presented at the annual meeting for the Canadian Anthropology Society/Société canadienne d'anthropologie, Montréal, Québec, Canada, May 2006.

Daveluy, Michelle. 2006c. "Communicating Across Linguistic Communities Onboard a Canadian Navy Ship." Paper presented at the annual meeting of the Society for Applied Anthropology, Vancouver, British Columbia, Canada, March 2006.

Daveluy, Michelle. 2007a. "Anthropological Research on the Military: Risks, Challenges, and Rewards." Paper presented at the Department of Anthropology Speakers Series, University of Alberta, Canada.

Daveluy, Michelle. 2007b. "Langues, mobilité et sécurité dans les forces armées canadienne et américaine." Paper presented at the Colloque du trentième anniversaire de la revue Anthropologie et Sociétés, Université Laval, Québec, Canada, November 2007.

Daveluy, Michelle. 2008a. "Language, Mobility and (In)Security: A Journey Through Francophone Canada." In *Social Lives in Language: Sociolinguistic and Multilingual Speech Communities*, edited by Naomi Nagy and Miriam Meyerhoff, 27–42. Amsterdam: Benjamins.

Daveluy, Michelle. 2008b. "Whose Life is on the Line? The Ongoing Repositioning of French and English Minorities in the Canadian Navy." Paper presented at the Sociolinguistics Symposium 17, Amsterdam, Netherlands, April 2008.

Department of National Defence and Canadian Forces. 2004. *2003–2006 Official Languages Strategic Plan / Plan stratégique des langues officielles*. Accessed October 10, 2011. http://www.forces.gc.ca/hr/dol_strat/frgraph/OLStratPlantb_f.asp

Direction des langues officielles. 2004. *Bilan de la Défense nationale sur les langues officielles de 2003–2004*. Ottawa: Ministère de la Défense nationale.

Elkin, Frederick. 1946. "The Soldier's Language." *The American Journal of Sociology Human Behavior in Military Society* 51(5): 414–422.

Goodwin, Charles. 1995. "Seeing in Depth." *Social Studies of Science* 25: 237–274.

Heller, Monica. 2003. "Globalization, the New Economy, and the Commodification of Language and Identity." *Journal of Sociolinguistics* 7(4): 473–492.

Heller, Monica. 2005. "Language, Skill, and Authenticity in the Globalized New Economy." *Revista de sociolinguistica*. Accessed March 30, 2011. http://www6.gencat.net/llengcat/noves/hm05hivern/heller1_2.htm

Heller, Monica, and Josiane Boutet. 2006. "Vers de nouvelles formes de pouvoir langagier? Langue(s) et identité dans la nouvelle économie. " *Langage et société* 118: 5–16.

Hoffman, Katherine E. 2008. *We Share Walls: Language, Land, and Gender in Berber Morocco*. Oxford: Blackwell Publishing.

Hutchins, Edwin. 1990. "The Technology of Team Navigation." In *Intellectual Teamwork: Social and Technological Foundations of Cooperative Work*, edited by Jolene Galegher, Robert E. Kraut and Carmen Egido, 191–220. Hillsdale, NJ: Lawrence Erlbaum.

Hutchins, Edwin. 1995. *Cognition in the Wild*. Cambridge: MIT Press.

Irwin, Anne Lucille. 1993. "Canadian Infantry Platoon Commanders and the Emergence of Leadership." MA thesis. University of Calgary.

Irwin, Anne Lucille. 2002. "The Social Organization of Soldiering: A Canadian Infantry Company in the Field." PhD dissertation. University of Manchester.

Irwin, Anne Lucille. 2007. "Life Outside the Wire: Discourses of Wellness." Lecture given at University of Alberta, Edmonton, Canada.

Jaffe, Alexandra. 1988. "Saluting in Social Context." *The Journal of Applied Behavioral Sciences* 24(3): 263–275.

Letellier, Armand. 1987a. *Réforme linguistique à la Défense nationale: La mise en marche des programmes de bilinguisme 1967–1977*. Ottawa: Service historique, Ministère de la Défense nationale.

Letellier, Armand. 1987b. *DND Language Reform: Staffing the Bilingualism Programs, 1967–1977* (Socio-Military Series No. 3). Ottawa: Directorate of History of the Department of National Defence.

MacDonald, Ann-Marie. 2003. *As the Crow Flies.* Toronto: Vintage Canada.

Malinowski, Bronislaw. 1935. *Coral Gardens and Their Magic: A Study of the Methods of Tiling the Soil and of Agricultural Rites in the Trobriand Islands.* London: Geroge Allen & Unwin.

Moskos, Charles C., John A. Williams, and David R. Segal, eds. 2000. *The Postmodern Military. Armed Forces after the Cold War.* Oxford: Oxford University Press.

Nuciari, Marina. 2003. "Models and Explanations for Military Organization: An Updated Reconsideration." In *Handbook of the Sociology of the Military,* edited by Giuseppe Caforio, 61–85. New York: Kluwer Academic/Plenum Publishers.

Olynyk, Marian, David Sankoff, and Alison d'Anglejan. 1983. "Second Language Fluency and the Subjective Evaluation of Officer Cadets in a Military College." *Studies in Language Acquisition* 5: 213–236.

Pariseau, Jean, and Serge Bernier. 1987. *Les Canadiens français et le bilinguisme dans les Forces armées canadiennes. Tome I 1763–1969. Le spectre d'une armée bicéphale.* Ottawa: Service historique de la Défense nationale.

Pariseau, Jean, and Serge Bernier. 1988. *French Canadians and Bilingualism in the Canadian Armed Forces, Volume I, 1763–1969: the Fear of a Parallel Army* (Socio-Military Series No. 2.) Ottawa: Directorate of History of the Department of National Defence.

Powell, Dina, and Barry Lowenkron. 2006. National Security Language Initiative (NSLI) launched January 5, 2006. *White House Briefing.*

Scruto, Andrew. 2007. "More Language Bonuses Offered to Sailors." Posted Friday March 23, 2007, 6:41:07 EDT. http://www.navytimes.com/news/2007/03/navy_language_bonus_070322w/

Urciuoli, Bonnie. 2009. "Skills and Selves in the New Economy." *American Ethnologist* 35(2): 211–228.

8 Frontiers and Frenchness
Pride and Profit in the Production of Canada

Monica Heller and Lindsay Bell

MAKING THE NATION IN FRANCOPHONE CANADA: FIXING PRIDE, MOVING PROFIT

In 1911, Louis Hémon, from Brittany, set out across the Atlantic in the time-honored European quest for the pure, the good and the true among the French-speaking Catholic descendants of French colonists in New France. He went as far up the Saguenay River into nature as he could, washing up on the shores of Lac Saint-Jean in mid-northern Quebec. The farming family in the village of Péribonka that took him in became the inspiration for the iconic novel *Maria Chapdelaine*; published in 1916, this text was translated into dozens of languages, inspired several films and served as required reading in high schools and colleges.

In the fashion of modern nationalism, the novel constructs French Canada as necessarily linked to the biological reproduction of a community tied to place, in particular a place close to nature. This is the ideological foundation of Canadian discourse and practice in the ethnolinguistic organization of social, political and economic relations. But if we look more closely at the novel (and the conditions of its production) we can see how it works to make fixity out of mobility and community out of labor—the same work, we argue, that is still being done a hundred years later, in ways which show the complex intertwinings and co-constructions of pride and profit now as in the past.

The novel begins with the tragic death of François Paradis, Maria's intended. As men did at the time, he has gone off into the forest to work in logging in the winter; indeed, François has renounced farming, and lives the (supposedly free) life of the logger, hunter and trapper, one of the symbolic models of French Canadian masculinity. In the forest night, he hears Maria call to him and sets off in a snowstorm to rejoin her, only to freeze to death. Maria is then courted by two men: Eutrope Gagnon, an older farmer (who represents the alternative ideological model of the farmer/settler), and Lorenzo Surprenant, a scion of the village who has returned with money in his pockets from the New England textile mills to find a wife to take back over the border. Maria chooses Eutrope, the farmer, even though he is less attractive both in looks and status, because that choice allows her to literally contribute to the reproduction of Péribonka, which is, of course, the right thing to do.

What do we have here? An image of the fixed community, concocted by a foreigner thousands of kilometers away from home, a community whose origins (never discussed in the novel) emerge out of European colonial expansion, and its sequel in the francophone elite's attempts to colonize the north as a bulwark against the English, but where subsistence farming cannot actually guarantee a livelihood: community reproduction, rather, requires the mobility of men, either into the forest in the winter or off to New England altogether. (Indeed, as Morissonneau 1978 points out, it requires selling the products of labor, whether of food or lumber, in a market dominated and controlled by anglophones. The attempt to produce autonomy actually produced economic subordination.)

By the 1930s, the Saguenay region will furnish labor for aluminum plants and hydroelectricity; its surplus population, like that of other similar regions, will continue to seek work in industrialized cities in the United States and Canada, or will be harnessed to the building of transportation infrastructures and primary resource extraction projects across the country. Indeed, Hémon himself left Péribonka to follow the railhead west, only to be killed in 1913 by a train on the tracks of Chapleau, a small northern Ontario town settled by Québécois and other francophone railway builders, lumberjacks, and mill workers.

The Saguenay and similar regions continue to produce its Marias, both literally in the form of people invested in a sense of local, ethnolinguistically homogenous community, and discursively in the form of contributions to political projects of territorial state nationalism. (Today, the farm Hémon lived on is the site of a museum dedicated to the specificity of francophone Saguenay and its cultural productivity; to learn anything about the history of mills where people work, you need to find the small museum tucked away in a desanctified Anglican church in a nearby town, dedicated to the English family that developed regional industry and employed the francophone workers who remain unmuseified.)

In this chapter, we will explore some of the ways the intertwining of pride and profit that characterized the production and reproduction of Péribonka as an icon of French Canada persist today, as well as how the conditions of late capitalism appropriate them in somewhat different form. *Maria Chapdelaine* signals a gendered and classed process of erasure of the labor mobility required for community reproduction, in favor of an image of fixed, rooted and homogeneous communities. This process, we argue, is still with us although, one hundred years later, its relative success has led to the expansion of the pride-related francophone labor market, in the form of francophone institutions legitimated through an appeal to the rights of a marginalized and exploited nation. Further, that market is increasingly embedded in tertiary sector economic activities (tourism, arts, culture, translation, communication) that commodify language and identity directly.

The co-construction of pride and profit remains central to the ethnolinguistic categorization that organizes Canadian society, but current conditions shift their articulation in ways which call into question the traditional forms of gendered divisions of labor, and that lay bare the erasure of labor mobility in the construction of the francophone nation. Drawing on fieldwork conducted in 2009 among francophone workers and residents in Yellowknife and Hay River, the two major urban centers of Canada's Northwest Territories (NWT), we will show that this process, while evident everywhere, is nonetheless gradual and uneven, positioning social actors differentially in terms of their interest in maintaining hitherto dominant discourses of francophone Canada. We focus mainly on the discursive descendants of *Maria Chapdelaine*, contemporary francophone mobile workers from across eastern Canada, whose labor holds up an increasingly fragile fiction of fixed community.

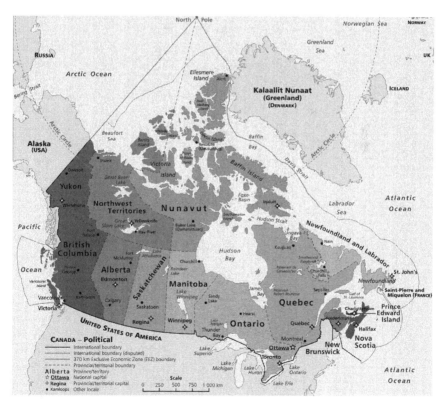

Map 8.1   Political divisions of Canada and places mentioned in text.

ETHNOLINGUISTIC CATEGORIZATION, CLASS RELATIONS AND THE CANADIAN FRONTIER

Three crucial aspects of Canadian socioeconomic organization require explicitation here. The first is that Canada has been constructed as a frontier from the time of European colonial expansion (Wolf 1982). The second is the harnessing of ethnolinguistic difference in the organization and legitimation of labor relations in the extraction and processing of primary resources that characterize frontier economies. This second aspect laid the foundation for the third dimension of Canadian socioeconomic organization relevant to our story, the construction of ethnolinguistically defined semiautonomous markets. Together they help us understand the relevance of "Frenchness" to Canadian social reproduction and the kinds of pride–profit tensions that reproduction entails.

European capitalist expansion depended on frontiers for acquiring natural resources and expending surplus populations (Harvey 2005). Canada acted as such a frontier zone initially for France (1534–1763) and for Britain (from 1763 to Canadian independence in 1867 and arguably well beyond that date). As with all frontiers, the Canadian frontier moved inexorably; in this case, over the last four hundred years it moved west and north, as resources got tapped out or devalued, and as settled populations increased. Indeed, the frontier is still on the move today. The NWT, the focus of the research discussed here, is part of a broader circumpolar frontier valued for its reserves of oil, gas and minerals and for its romantic narrative of unspoiled nature (Emmerson 2010; Jakobsson 2009).

The boom-and-bust, resource-based economy of the moving frontier always requires flexible labor. In sparsely populated North America, getting labor to the resource requires variable forms of mobility, since the reproduction of that labor force also paradoxically requires agriculturally based settlements. Late nineteenth-century industrialization introduced new forms of articulation between settlement and labor mobility. Further, cultural differences and linguistic proficiency have been used since New France to organize the fur trade, and since the British Conquest to legitimate anglophone economic and political domination, and the relegation first of francophones, and then of immigrant groups, to lower strata of an economy based largely on primary resource extraction and transformation, and later on manufacturing (Porter 1965).

All strata of the laboring population in the frontier-oriented economy have been defined in ethnoracial, ethnocultural and ethnolinguistic terms. In the fur trade, the indigenous populations largely supplied the furs, while francophones occupied all other roles until the British conquest. At that point, they were relegated to the roles of "coureurs de bois," "voyageurs"[1] and sometimes trading post agents, next in line to the fur providers in the chain of extraction, transformation and exchange in the service of the British Hudson's Bay Company.

Similarly, francophones occupied subordinate labor positions in other resource extraction activities central to the Canadian economy: lumber, fishing and mining. These activities were crucial to any attempt to establish agricultural settlements (like Péribonka), which were doomed without other sources of income. Canadian soil is for the most part not very fertile, and is arduous to clear and develop. As a result, the social organization of eastern Canadian agriculture tended to produce day laborers or small farmers whose existence was precarious, and who were easily attracted to the two main options available to them: entry into the expanding manufacturing industries of the northeast, especially in New England and Montréal, or participation in the elite-led colonization efforts to the north and west, which produced places like Péribonka. Much historical research has shown the extent to which geographical mobility has been to the production and reproduction of ethnolinguistic difference in this process, and to the production of francophone Canada in particular (see notably Frenette 1998; Ramirez 1991).

Historically, then, francophones were concentrated in peripheral regions whose reproduction as fixed communities depended on the mobility of at least some sectors of their populations, sometimes single men, but often, as Ramirez (1991) showed, as entire families, friendship groups or in various forms of kin- or community-based chain migrations. In the mid to late 1800s, the destination of choice was the textile mills of New England, in a migration that actually continued into the early twentieth century. Industrializing southern Quebec and Ontario also drew workers, as did the construction of the railway and the opening of mines and lumber industries in northern Ontario in the late nineteenth and early to mid-twentieth centuries.

Similar processes drew people farther west, following paths already long laid down by the fur trade. In some cases, mobility led to settlement, but frequently there was movement back and forth, or some members of a community or family might be mobile, thereby sustaining kin and community at home. Home also provided a safe haven against the precarity of the kinds of resource activities connected to mobility, as resources may be seasonal, are exhausted or increasingly globalized capital looks elsewhere for cheaper sources of goods or labor.

At the same time, crosscutting political arrangements set up a space for the development of an alternative francophone sphere, which has served as a means of contesting anglophone domination and the place of francophones in Canadian political economy (Frenette 1998; Martel and Pâquet 2010; Morissonneau 1978). The francophone elite of the nineteenth and twentieth centuries was invested in resisting anglophone domination through the construction of an idea of a homogeneous French Canadian nation, tied to the soil (Morissonneau 1978). The construction of this national idea involved both the erasure of the kinds of mobility referred to previously, as well as encouraging a different kind of mobility, one tied to the idea of colonization, that is, of the occupation of regions far from anglophone hegemony where francophones could dream of establishing autarkic communities.[2]

This traditionalist spiritual nationalism served as the basis of a more recent (post–First World War) state territorial nationalist modernity that produced a privileged quasi-national market, regulated through the use of French, and legitimated through the kinds of pride discourses connected to patriotism, and linked particularly, but not exclusively, to Quebec. In French Canada, in fact, this linkage of pride and profit has been explicitly expressed in hortatory slogans, from the Quebec of the 1950s and 1960s ("Achat chez nous!" / Keep your purchases at home, or perhaps, buy from your own kind), to present day New Brunswick ("J'achète en français" / I buy in French). This market is both a production and a consumer market, and is structured in ways that provide employment to francophones.

This is accomplished in two ways. First, mastery of French has become a criterion of employment for a job market that functions substantially in French. Second, the national "pride" market is predicated on the dominant ways in which nations are legitimated, that is, through the construction of a culturally and linguistically (if not to say biologically) homogeneous population rooted for centuries on a particular, delimited territory. The proposition of a fixed francophone community requires realization, and this has taken place through the development of a number of institutions (schools, media and cultural associations prominent among them) dedicated to the construction of this population. These institutions provide employment for francophones in both their linguistic and identity capacity, as agents of national construction. They also set up a tension between an ostensibly fixed community that legitimates francophone nationalism (however soft) and the realities of labor mobility that exist alongside them and, indeed, are necessary to their reproduction.

This logic was taken up by the Canadian federal government in an attempt to counter Québécois independentist claims that French could only survive within the bounds of a sovereign Québécois state. Federal language policy, and indeed the legitimacy of the Canadian state as representative of all its citizens, is predicated on the notion that an anglophone minority community in Quebec and a minority francophone community in the other provinces can exist and flourish (enjoy "linguistic vitality" is the conventional expression) in the same way as the majorities can, as fixed populations, with their own traditions and institutions. Federal policy was therefore largely responsible for the creation of a parallel francophone institutional market (mainly in the form of schools and cultural associations) across Canada.

This national modernity is, of course, as many other chapters in this book demonstrate, the source of the value of authenticity that itself has become commodified in such sectors as heritage tourism. But that value also operates as a criterion of selection in areas such as customer service, where the ideology of the native speaker remains a powerful source of value in the weighing of linguistic proficiencies or of quality of service. As a result, the institutions that are set up to serve a natural, existing population (but that they must in fact create) end up attracting all kinds of people with slim claims to francophone authenticity but who are interested in access to the valuable linguistic and symbolic resources distributed there.

Throughout this history, pride and profit have been inextricably linked. The old and new forms of labor mobility sustain each other, as they have sustained their own erasure in the discursive construction of the category "francophone." Today, however, some of the contradictions we have pointed to above become more and more difficult to ignore, calling into question the basis of legitimacy of the use of ethnolinguistic categories to make or resist inequality. We find these contradictions emerging most clearly precisely in those areas where old and new forms of labor mobility encounter each other: in the quasi-industrial corners of the service economy, as in the canonical domain of the call center (Boutet 2008; Dubois, LeBlanc and Beaudin 2006); in heritage tourism (Heller and Pujolar 2009; Pujolar, this volume); and in frontier economies (involving activities such as mining, construction or transportation) like that of the NWT (Coates and Morrison 1994). Here, we will use the example of the NWT to explore those contradictions and how they articulate pride and profit for francophone Canada.

CO-CONSTRUCTING PRIDE AND PROFIT ON THE CANADIAN FRONTIER[3]

The region we focus on here, the NWT, is inscribed in the long Canadian history of tension between fixity and mobility, pride and profit. It partly represents the final frontier, as proximate circles of mobility (New England, industrialized areas of eastern and central Canada) involve increasingly tapped-out resources or the off-shoring characteristic of late capitalism. Workers must go farther and farther afield. But it also links itself to the patriotic saga of the fur trade and the valiant explorers of the Canadian north, whose stories contribute to the national myth of Canada and, not coincidentally, to its current claims to sovereignty in the region (Leroux 1989).

The data we present here are based on ethnographic fieldwork conducted mainly by the second author in 2009, with some help over a brief period in June 2009 by the first author, in the context of a broader four-year (2008–2012) project on francophone labor mobility linking the NWT to the oil sands of Alberta, to northern Ontario and Quebec, and to francophone New Brunswick (see note 2). Our fieldwork was concentrated in the two major urban areas of the NWT, Yellowknife (the capital) and Hay River (a transportation hub), where francophone institutions are concentrated. (Bell was also a teacher in the francophone elementary school in Hay River in 2004). It consisted of seven formal interviews with the participants and directors of the major francophone institutions (one school, the Yellow-knife and Hay River branches of the lobbying and cultural association, the community economic development organization, the community newspaper and radio) and with seventeen francophones who happened to be in the area for work (either looking for it or recruited to it) in aviation, horticulture, communications, the military, transport, the Coast Guard, national media, construction and tourism, or who were looking mainly for adventure and travel and finding ways to pay their way. We spoke informally to many more in the context of events we attended that were organized by one or more of the francophone institutions, and we looked at their media and documentation. We also attended Hay River community events along with most segments of the town's population (such as the annual lobster festival held in the town's arena[4]).

Mobilizing Land and Labor in a Frontier Economy

The NWT is among the few remaining sectors where the old forms of labor mobility are patently obvious. In the rest of Canada, heavy industry has been off-shored, computerized and downsized; mines and pulp and paper mills close daily. The cod fishery on which much of Atlantic Canada depended was closed due to overfishing in 1992, and there are cheaper sources of lumber and minerals in other parts of the world. Manufacturing has suffered the same fate as elsewhere in the First World. The Arctic, however, remains vital for four reasons: security, transportation, oil and gas, and diamonds. Global warming holds promise for easier access to undersea oil and gas, and the opening up of hitherto impassable waterways. Along with Alberta's oil sands and the mines and agriculture of British Columbia, Canada's Far North has become the place to go for unskilled, semiskilled and skilled labor from the eastern areas of the country which have always supplied them.

Additionally, the NWT participates fully in the pan-Canadian construction of the idea of "francophone community." As of the early 1970s, the nationalist framework formed in Quebec was exported to francophones living in other regions of Canada in an alliance between the Canadian state and regional francophone elites cast adrift by Québécois nationalism (Heller 2011). The task of preserving and producing linguistic duality across the country transformed existing elite networks (usually aligned with the Catholic church; Choquette 1977, 1987) into state institutions charged with reproducing "community." This was achieved in large part through the creation of francophone institutions, most notably schools. In the NWT, the Federation Francoténoise (FFT) was formed in the 1980s by ex-Québécois who mobilized around the issue of education, leading to the construction of two francophone schools. These schools remain at the center of heated debates locally, as the mobility and complicated trajectories of students and staff undermine the legitimizing logic of preserving a "fixed community," which we will discuss further.

As mentioned previously, political and economic shifts in the 1990s led to a vision of language as a valuable economic resource. Around the same time, state funding for institutions like the FFT retracted. Taken together, these changes produced the emergence of new institutions across Canada and in the NWT aimed at promoting economic vitality as a means to linguistic vitality (Silva and Heller 2009). In the NWT, this translated into the FFT developing an economic development plan entitled "Bâtir un pays—Planification 2002–2005 en matière de développement économique de la collectivité francophone des Territoires du Nord-Ouest" (Building a nation: Planning 2002–2005 in terms of economic development of the francophone community of the NWT) (Fédération franco-ténoise 2002). From this, the Conseil de développement économique des Territoires du Nord-Ouest (CDÉTNO) was formed. The two institutions have since been marked by conflict as tensions between pride and profit make for discrepant ideas about what it means to "do being" francophone (cultural preservation vs. economic development), as has been the case across the country.

The extreme mobility of NWT francophones exacerbates these tensions as it undermines the foundational ideology of a fixed population on which the FFT's legitimacy depends. In fact, it is not just the legitimacy of the FFT that is at stake, but the legitimizing discourse of Canadian dualism— the Canadian federal government's language policy commits it to the promotion of the vitality of linguistic minority communities (anglophone in Quebec, francophone everywhere else), as a means of countering Québécois nationalist claims that French can survive only in a sovereign Quebec. This can be illustrated vividly by a recent report produced by the federally funded Institut canadien de recherche sur les minorités linguistiques/Canadian Institute for Research on Linguistic Minorities (ICMRL), titled *La Francophonie boréale: La vitalité des communautés francophones dans les territoires* (Robineau et al. 2010). This report looks for signs of vitality, notably in legal protections and the development of institutions, and treats as a problematic paradox the fact that the francophone population is composed mainly of migrants, many of whom are not even residents of the NWT. Nonetheless, it concludes, the community has many resources and is beginning to establish itself. The emphasis is clearly on working toward a fixed population, recognizable by its institutions. The contradiction, of course, is that all the francophones the ICRML met were from somewhere else, as were all those we spoke to in our own research.

Les Franco-Ténois

The francophones that we met in the NWT arrived there via two different routes. The first route is reminiscent of the long-established forms of labor mobility described in the iconic novel *Maria Chapdelaine*. The second route links the archipelago of francophone institutions now spread across Canada. These routes intersect in ways that produce pride–profit tensions for francophone institutional spaces, families and even individuals.

Modern-Day *"Maria Chapdelaine"*

In the NWT in the summer time, there is always construction along the Mackenzie Highway. Talk of an oil pipeline going from the Beaufort Sea southward has prompted investment in infrastructure, in particular the construction of bridges across the mighty Mackenzie and other small rivers along the highway. A man in a hard hat holds up a stop sign. We pull up beside him for an estimate of how long we might have to wait here. Our eagerness to move along to the capital city subsides when we see the name Antoine LeBlanc on his hard hat; Monica makes Lindsay roll down the window, and leans out to ask "on va avoir à attendre longtemps?" (will we have to wait long?). We get the hoped-for friendly response in French, and use the time to set up an arrangement for Lindsay to return and talk.

Antoine is the foreman of a twelve-man crew from New Brunswick hired to build bridges in the NWT. While Lindsay waited to meet with him in the diner at the work crew's base camp, she spoke with four other crewmembers about her research purposes. They seemed curious as to why a young woman might have come to such an out of the way place to speak with their boss. "On mène une recherche sur la migration de la main d'œuvre francophone. On essaie de comprendre qui va où et pourquoi" (We are doing research on migration of francophone labor. We want to understand who goes where and why), Lindsay tells them. The oldest at the table laughs as he looks to his colleagues to confirm, "Comment dit-on 'money talks'?" (How do you say [in French] "money talks"?).

Antoine's team includes his own two sons, and other men, almost all New Brunswick francophones, handpicked by him to take this contract. They live in a motel, which they see very rarely as they are on the road to the site by 5 a.m. and not back until 7 p.m. They are supposed to work four weeks on (on site) and two weeks off (back home), but the pressure to get the project done before the cold sets in, and the temptation of time-and-a-half, means that it will be more like six or seven weeks before they take a break to go home.

Antoine and his sons speak to Lindsay in French, with the exception of the word "labor" (/le'bər/), which they use to denote entry-level work in their field. (Antoine says, "quand ça [le projet] commence je dis 'je veux ces gars-là', j'ai déjà travaillé avec ces gars-là' . . . mais parfois il en prend des nouveaux, ben c'est plus comme des « labor », des journaliers, et ils viennent et apprennent" (when it [the project] starts, I say "I want those guys there, I have already worked with those guys," but sometimes it takes new people, more like "labor" [sic], laborers, and they come and learn). His son adds, "J'ai commencé comme journeyman, le 'labor,' maintenant je suis rendu à apprenti" (I started as a "journeyman" [sic], "labor" [sic], now I have made it to apprentice).

They describe the company they work for as "anglaise" (English), and all three learned English on the job (as Antoine's wife says about him, when he started working for that company: "la seule chose qu'il savait c'était yes pis no" / the only thing he knew was yes and no). (This is an expression we hear often from Acadian workers about their first experience working for Anglophone companies. [5]) Part of being "labor" apparently involves not only acquisition of technical skills (learning how to build bridges), but also linguistic ones (learning to deal with the bosses and other work teams in the region in English, although as Antoine describes, his control over selection of crew members tends to mean they work in francophone crew units within a larger team).

For a number of years, Antoine, who never finished high school, was able to work at bridge sites closer to home in New Brunswick, but for the past two years he and his crew have been sent north. He says he doesn't mind, because on his two weeks off he has a lot of time to spend with his wife, Manon. The money in the NWT is good; he and his sons use it to buy property and even luxury goods for themselves and their families in northeastern New Brunswick, as well as putting some money aside for retirement.

As it happens, the region where they live is one we have been interested in for some time; like the Saguenay (and the northern Ontario home of the Charlebois family we describe next), it is a "bastion traditionnel," a key site of discursive production of francophone community-ness. Also like those regions, it has long relied on primary resource extraction (mainly lumber and fish) and their industrial transformation, coupled with temporary or permanent labor migration. And as is the case with most "traditional bastions," it is in economic crisis, seeking to turn its cultural capital into a new economic base (through heritage and cultural tourism as well as popular culture).

During a stay in the area the LeBlanc family lives in, Monica and Hubert (another member of our research team) met up with Manon. Manon works in human resources at a large national chain hardware store. The company's head offices are in Ontario, and its working language is English. However, spearheaded by the economic interests of an emerging francophone bourgeoisie based in Quebec, francophones have constituted themselves as a niche market, who need to be spoken to in French if you hope to sell them anything. Manon's bilingualism, acquired in early adulthood through her own efforts to capitalize on available opportunities, allows her access to employment in the service sector; she speaks English to her out-of-province bosses, and French to her coworkers and local clients. The local branch of the chain makes money because of people like Antoine, who spend part of their income on things like home renovations (the LeBlancs also bought a sports car, although many workers buy high-end trucks with their earnings).

Manon misses her husband and sons, but tries to stay cheery. She spends time with her daughter and daughters-in-law; enjoys her car and her house; sometimes goes to the nearby cultural capital to take in a show. She and Antoine use his off time to visit relatives who moved away earlier in more permanent forms of labor migration, all of whom live in English-dominant parts of New Brunswick and Ontario (and who form part of her English-learning strategy). Still, in Manon's eyes, this life mode is temporary: "on va faire ça pour un couple d'années," "on se place pour la retraite" (we'll do this for a few years; we're positioning ourselves for retirement). Manon, then, a little bit like Maria Chapdelaine, does being francophone much more than do the men in her family. Like Maria, she finds it hard, but, as she says "au bout de la ligne on va être recompensés" (at the end of the line, we will get paid back).

Our second Maria Chapdelaine does not need to stay home in order to reproduce Frenchness. Camille Charlebois arrived in Hay River in 2004 to teach Grade 2 in the recently opened French-language elementary school, an example of the institutional spaces central to ideologies of fixed francophone communities. Camille's move north was part of a family strategy, which, Ramirez (1991) reminds us, was an alternative model of mobility in the nineteenth and twentieth centuries among North American francophones. Camille came with her husband Robert, and they were soon joined by other family members.

Great-grandparents on both sides of the Charlebois family had moved from Quebec to Hearst, in northern Ontario, as part of the nineteenth-century opening up of the region in a combined effort to drive a railway through Canada to the Pacific (thereby heading off American incursions northwest and setting up delivery modes for western grain), to gain access to the lumber and mineral deposits of the region, and to prevent surplus labor from being siphoned off by U.S. industry and lost to the French Canadian nation (Frenette 1998). (Hearst is not far from where Louis Hémon met his untimely end, and indeed, had Maria Chapdelaine married Lorenzo, her rich textile worker, she might have tried to convince him to try his luck later in precisely this region, when the Catholic Church went into New England to try to convince errant souls there to come back to the north, the land, and the Franco-Catholic fold.)

The Charlebois ancestors were dairy farmers; a move to industrial production in the 1960s and 1970s meant more milk to those who could afford equipment. One side of the family was able to make this move; the other had to sell out and move into the lumber industry. Currently, the pulp and paper mills which have sustained the population have collapsed; while neither Camille nor Robert were directly employed in that industry, the economic crisis made it difficult for them to make ends meet.

Camille had been working in the area for some time as a teacher in French-language minority schools, exactly the kind of institution produced by political lobbying for the rights of fixed communities. Finding a job, however, meant having to be ready to move around the area, a life-mode hard to sustain since her family could not always follow, and in that area distances are long and the roads often treacherous. Camille spotted an ad in her local paper for a job at a francophone school in the NWT, and knew this could provide a means for her and Robert to have jobs in the same town.

In her own job interview, Camille asked about the likelihood of her husband finding employment. He had experience in carpentry, small engine repair and welding. The interview team laughed and reassured her that there was always work in the north for people with those skills. She and her family arrived, and quickly her husband was hired at a construction firm. Seeing the limits for earning potential as labor in that firm, he took up a business opportunity to purchase the local recreational vehicle sales and repair shop. The idea of Hay River appealed to him also in terms which could have been used by his great grandparents to explain their attraction to northern Ontario: he likes "la paix", "ça prend la forêt" (he needs peace and the forest).

Since then, Martin, Raymond and Stéphane, three young members of the Charlebois family, have followed Camille and Robert. Martin, the youngest of the three, explained, "Ben, c'était pas compliqué, il y avait plus d'ouvrage à Hearst, il y en avait pas, pas en touT. C'est mort. La ville est en train de devenir fantôme" (Well, it's not complicated, there was no work in Hearst, there wasn't any, none at all. It's dead. The town is becoming a ghost town).

With no work to be had at home, they needed to look elsewhere, and Camille and Robert provided a safety net; indeed, Martin's account of what happened when the plant he worked in closed focuses on the importance of connections for finding work in places like Alberta or British Columbia: "ils vont s'en aller où ce qu'ils connaissent du monde" (they'll go where they know people). Martin found work in Hay River as a mechanic's helper in a garage and later took up a position in his uncle's shop. Raymond found work in the diamond mines.

Thanks to family connections, Stéphane initially tried his luck in construction jobs in the interior of British Columbia. When the work dried up, his cousins invited him north, where he worked a variety of jobs and then joined the shop crew, supplementing his income with small renovation or repair jobs evenings and weekends.

The men all learned English in part through school, but mostly on the job. Because of their unease in English, none of them like to answer the phone, but it is a big part of their job providing service calls to the wider region. While none of them imagines spending the rest of their days in Hay River, or even in the NWT, they have been there for three to six years, with no concrete projects for returning to Ontario. Still, they go back to Hearst for regular visits, and Robert envisions joining other family members in running a business guiding tourist bear hunters at a lodge they own. One of his nephews assures us that the northern Ontario economy will pick up again ("ça va reprendre"), and then he'll go back.

It is Camille who is most directly implicated in the production of French-ness. She teaches in an institution designed to reproduce it, although, in many ways, it actually has to produce it. She has drawn Robert into this space: he served as school trustee for some time. But Robert's work is not connected to the discursive space of francophoneness. What is more, for the Charlebois, it is Camille who provides the stable salary and benefits of a middle-class economy; the men have jobs linked to an increasingly precari-ous frontier economy.

For the Charlebois and LeBlanc families, pride and profit are inter-linked, but in ways rather different from how the process works for people more centrally involved in the francophone institutional market. Their live-lihoods, especially those of the women, depend on it more (in the case of Camille) or less (in the case of Manon) directly. The men depend on solidarity networks defined by Frenchness, and through which they find work or survive bleak times. Their value as "good" labor is also ethnicized, in contrast notably to the category "aboriginal,"[6] but also in articulation with other ethnolinguistic categories, whether regional ("Newfie," "Cape Bretoner") or immigrant. The relation to profit operates via Frenchness as a labor category, not as a form of cultural capital in its own right. At the same time, this labor category acts to legitimize institutionalized franco-phone spaces, on the grounds that their autonomy is necessary for bettering the life chances of people like Martin or Antoine's sons.

Profiting from Pride

Institutions of the francophone market (schools, media, cultural associa-tions and government agencies) are meant to serve and represent all kinds of francophones, including the Leblancs and the Charlebois. However, those institutions construct francophones as a fixed, homogeneous popula-tion, which it clearly is not. One result is the marginalization of working class mobility and the privileging of middle-class ideologies of language, identity and nation. In this section, we discuss how middle-class franco-phones arrive on the frontier to profit from the national pride legitimating those institutions. Their own mobility must be discursively erased or recon-figured as part of a general process of erasure necessary to the production of the idea of fixed community.

Yellowknife and Hay River share a francophone newspaper, a radio sta-tion and branches of the cultural centre, as well as the CDÉTNO. The stories of some of the people who work there help illustrate the ways in which they constitute a labor market for a mobile population, while producing an image of a fixed and historically rooted one. This labor recruits differently, though, from the one people like Antoine and the Charlebois men are involved in; while theirs uses kin, friends and neighbors to recruit by word-of-mouth, the institutional market uses state or paragovernmental agencies. The role of the state, in fact, is central in the reproduction of this market.

In the radio station, we find Denis, a young Québécois not long out of journalism school. Looking for his first job in 2004, he almost went to the Congo, but came to Yellowknife instead on a six-month contract, and ended up staying four years. His contracts, and those of others, are generally related to the federal government's youth employment grants, which aim at keeping people between eighteen and thirty-five years of age in the job market. Many francophone cultural centers and media around the country are staffed in this way. By 2008, his colleague, another Québécois, had gone off to South America, and Denis went on holiday and then back to Quebec, where he worked as a self-employed translator and editor and went back to university. He says it is almost impossible to find work in journalism in Quebec; he has come back to Yellowknife for the summer, for more experience, because northern issues interest him and make sellable articles for the Quebec market, and for the pleasure. He is one of a dozen or so young Québécois who live off the grid near the lake, in a kind of environmentalist alternative community. Both the newspaper (where he used to work) and the radio (where he works now) are government-funded and gain revenue from advertising from federal agencies that by law must publish everything in both official languages.

At another agency, one employee, Claudine, is a young woman from France who had come to Montréal on a university exchange and ended up immigrating. In journalism like Denis, she has gone from internship to internship, many involving stays in other parts of Canada, or overseas, but has not been able to find steady employment in Montréal, which is where she would like to be based. She found the job posting for her current position, a two-year renewable contract in public relations, on an Internet site, and was in Yellowknife shortly after: "j'ai une opportunité, je la prends, c'est comme ça que je marche" (I have an opportunity, I take it, that's how I work). She dreams of eventually moving on, possibly into the NGO sector, possibly in South America, but with Canada as her home base.

Another employee, Andrea, is a young bilingual artist from the Saguenay, who learned English from her anglophone mother. As is the case for other sectors, it is easier to break into the arts in the Far North than elsewhere. She and her partner, a horticulturalist turned artist, had planned to tour the northern arts scene, and go to British Columbia and then California to learn about organic farming, but needed to finance the trip. They found it impossible to do so in the east, and came to Yellowknife when a friend of her partner's told them about a couple who own the only landscape-gardening center in the city, and who often hire young francophones for the summer (the wife of the couple is francophone, and has an effective recruitment network through her current and ex-employees—Andrea and her boyfriend thus profit from both typical modes of labor recruitment, word-of-mouth for her boyfriend, state agencies for her). Andrea went to an event organized by the FFT the first night she got to town, and two days later had a contract for the summer. Part of her work is meant to contribute to developing francophone tourism products, including cultural heritage ones.

None of the young people are driven by a commitment to the development of the NWT francophone community, although the activities they engage in are oriented to just that. The institutions set up by the state offer them possibilities for breaking into their fields, engaging in mobile (and sometimes alternative) lifestyles, and, in some cases, perfecting their English. Nonetheless they experience the tension between pride and profit in their own life trajectories. For example, Andrea agrees that to really claim to have had the experience of being in the north you need to spend a winter there, as Claudine and Denis have, and she intends to come back to do so after her stay in California.

Institutional spaces also draw on older sources of workers. The cultural center in Yellowknife is staffed by two women in their fifties. One is the spouse of a military officer who has been posted for a few years to the Department of Defense offices in Yellowknife; when we met, they were about to move back to Ottawa, the capital, and their home base. The other had worked for a number of years in the cultural sector in northeastern New Brunswick; in the last few years of her career, she said (as many people do) that she was seeking to fulfill a lifelong dream of the Far North, as well as adding to her pension. It is possible that funding changes to the cultural sector might also have influenced her move, as neoliberal policies shifted money away from traditional activities and towards economic development.

In all these spaces, the tension between pride and profit, while present, tends to get resolved in much the same way as Robineau et al.'s (2010) study of community vitality did, namely, by highlighting efforts to make community despite mobility and mixity. Mobility and mixity become either obstacles to be overcome, or are simply ignored in favor of historical continuity and ties to place.

On the other side of the Great Slave Lake, we see a slightly different picture of the world of cultural associations, one that poignantly reveals how difficult it can be to manage the tension between pride and profit institutionally and individually. In the next section, we meet Carole, the outgoing employee of the Hay River branch of the francophone cultural center.

SITES OF TENSION

Institutions: Pride as Profit for Whom?

After many years moving between Alberta and Quebec, Carole met her (anglophone) trucker husband on his run between northern Alberta and Hay River. She was reluctant to leave Alberta, but he insisted the family should be together. Carole fell into her job when she followed her husband to Hay River in 2004. The francophone cultural association that was looking for someone to run it quickly recruited her.

Carole was about to step down from this role when we met her; she was exhausted by years spent writing grant proposals for programs with eligibility requirements that did not always match the realities of Hay River, followed by writing reports to the government granting agencies, rather than doing any of the cultural work the association was supposed to do. In addition, she said, no one ever actually showed up any longer for any of the events they were able to organize.

Carole accounts for this by explaining that for many years, the association mobilized the community around getting access to French-language television, and then establishing a French-language school. Once the school was opened as a full-fledged school in 2001, it occupied all the social space for doing being francophone in the town. Carole feels the center needs a new mission; "quel est notre rêve maintenant?" (what is our dream now?), she asks. She suggests, for example, that the center could provide services to adolescents and the elderly, but, she feels, "la relation a pas été bâtie . . . il faut gagner leur confiance" (the relationship hasn't been built . . . we need to gain their trust). Somehow, those who wish to categorize themselves as francophone are now doing so through the school; other members of the population don't affiliate with the idea of francophone community that the centre represents. They are in Hay River to work, not to build a community.

Like the center, the school experiences a problem of absence of some legitimate participants; some Hay River francophones do not send their children there. More dramatically however, in 2007 the school's admissions policy became an object of public, and now legal, debate. Some people in town feel that not all of the school's two hundred students are legitimately francophone, and therefore shouldn't be admissible. The issue is important because funds are tied to enrollment levels: the more students the anglophones feel they are losing to the French school, the more resources go to the French school rather than the English ones.

The Hay River school conflict is similar to others that have occurred over several decades across Canada (Heller 1994) and lays wide open the ways in which institutions founded to develop the pride of a putative population serve to profit some members of its middle class, but also other kinds of people altogether. Consistent with what we see in other parts of English Canada, high interest in French schools by non-French speaking parents reflects the importance bilingual capital is seen to play on the Canadian job market. As elsewhere in Canada, bilingualism in Hay River operates as a mode of class distinction, with predominantly middle-class parents choosing to enroll their children in programs providing official language instruction (English for francophones and French for Anglophones). As the school has grown, demands for newer facilities have been met by hostility from local Anglophone elites who claim the students of the francophone school are "not real francophones." The battle over space and funding is now a legal matter being disputed in court.

Francophone institutional spaces are thus complicated sites of tensions between pride and profit. These tensions have consequences for the institutions themselves: some struggle to stay open, while the unexpected success of other institutions paradoxically undermines their legitimacy. These tensions have consequences for individuals as well; employees like Carole are called on to resolve irreconcilable contradictions, parents have to navigate political mine fields over the question of where to send their children to school and working-class francophones confront subtle forms of class prejudice when they do show up. Institutions, however, are not the only site where pride–profit related tensions emerge. In the next section we look at those who decidedly distance themselves from the autonomous francophone market and its institutions.

Global Citizens

For some of the young people we met, the construction of autonomous francophone markets (notably in Quebec) emerged as an obstacle to the realization of their professional and personal goals. We met Simon at the garden center where Andrea's boyfriend had just been hired for the summer. Simon is from northwestern Quebec. He says he inherited his wanderlust from his parents who had also spent summers of their youth working in western Canada and who always encouraged him to travel. He shares with most of our participants the romance of the north, its solitude and its endless forest. But he also found Quebec stifling, too small and crowded for someone interested in solitude and space. In particular he resented having to navigate oppositional tensions between political camps, the independentists (or, referencing biker gang terminology, what he called the "full patch bleus") and the federalists ("full patch rouges").[7] He was particularly incensed that Quebec's language policy had made it difficult for him to acquire English, the form of capital most important to realizing his dreams of mobility and global citizenship. Although his Frenchness enabled him to get to Yellowknife (recruited through the same informal network as Andrea's boyfriend), once arrived he made the strategic decision to distance himself from the francophone institutions that exist precisely to serve people like him.

While Yellowknife attracts a certain kind of would-be global citizen like Simon, it also serves as an important destination for young professionals in need of experience in competitive fields. This is particularly true of quasi-state regulated fields like aviation. Waiting to board the plane bound for Hay River, Monica watched as Jacinthe loaded passenger luggage onto a truck. Jacinthe next turned up on board the flight as the bilingual flight attendant. It turned out that these duties were part of her training toward becoming a pilot. Like Simon, she had recently arrived from Quebec, where she had earned her initial credentials, and quickly found herself having to look outside Quebec to acquire the experience she needed to become a licensed pilot within a reasonable amount of time: the opportunities were simply not available in the overcrowded Quebec market. For Jacinthe, leaving Quebec meant acquiring professional experience as well as improving her English. Aviation is a global profession largely standardized in English. Jacinthe's goal is to fly. She doesn't much care where she is based or what language she speaks. The move to Yellowknife is just one stop on what is likely to become a highly mobile trajectory.

During our research we met many other people whose stories were comparable to Simon's and Jacinthe's. The trope of "global citizen" contains two elements: lifestyle and professional advancement. People like Simon often search for adventure and proximity to nature and find frontier work to make that happen. People like Jacinthe, in fields like aviation, engineering, journalism or education, find themselves in the north as part of increasingly far-flung mobile career trajectories. In both cases, language is mainly important insofar as it allows them to build and navigate these networks. The construction of pride-based categories and spaces is too restrictive and requires counterbalancing with strategies of mobility and multilingualism.

MARIA CHAPDELAINE IN THE TWENTY-FIRST CENTURY

Linking the opening story of Maria Chapdelaine with the stories of NWT francophones, we could argue that interlocking categories of gender, class and Frenchness are being reproduced as variations on the older story. At the same time, our fieldwork revealed interconnected tensions that define the present moment, and that have the capacity to undermine future reproductions of the mobility/fixity contradiction and its concomitant tensions between pride and profit on which French Canada and the state depend.

First, the globalized new economy destabilizes the reproduction of the category "francophone" in its modernist nationalist sense in a number of ways. While francophone institutions adapt by adopting the language and practices of service and product, this move ends up serving some people as a springboard into the global multilingual economy, and others as a bridge to acquisition of French as a form of capital of value in the current marketplace, confusing criteria of inclusion and exclusion, and of performance of Frenchness. For others, of course, such as Camille, these institutions offer at least a slim advantage as sources of a livelihood harder and harder to come by in the intense competition of the neoliberalized economy.

Next, our Marias point to a tension between francophone and global markets. The ability of the Québécois elite to produce a niche market has created jobs for people like Claudine, Andrea, Denis, Manon and Camille. Their Frenchness is the access point to employment in white-collar jobs. The sustainability of the market they service depends not only on the investment of its participants in its distinctiveness, but also on its added value for a globalized consumption of authenticity. It also depends on the continued circulation of francophone labor. In Camille's case, a teaching job in the NWT depended on a francophone population having moved to the area during a lead/zinc boom in the area in the 1980s. For Manon, the hardware store depends on sales from worker's wages earned on the frontier: local salaries and employment opportunities cannot provide sufficient disposable incomes for extensive home renovations. Yellowknife's status as a capital brings in bilingual state employment and the francophone institutions which signal state commitment to official bilingualism.

Third, our François/Lorenzos point to a tension between francophone as a cultural category and francophone as a labor category. All of the primary workers we interviewed in the NWT tended live their ethnolinguistic identity both in terms of relationship to home, and as a category organizing social relations among workers (although they readily form relations of solidarity with other Canadian workers—the "Newfies," the "Nova Scotians"—against foreign temporary labor). They may have an Acadian flag in the garage they use for relaxing with friends on their rare evenings off, they go home for holidays, they plan their future on the plot of land they bought there, but they don't use the local francophone institutions to socialize, look for work or access any other services. While their Frenchness gets sustained by the Marias, their nonparticipation in these institutions undermines the very spaces producing work for other Marias, as well as for the Claudines, Andreas and Denis. In an era of accountability, we consistently saw that francophone service centers in boomtowns existed under constant threat of closure (two actually did close during our fieldwork). Not only are ethnonational niche markets fragile; the mobile workers who help sustain them find themselves in increasingly precarious labor positions in globalized industries.

The link between ethnolinguistic categories as constitutive of markets and simultaneously of labor categories has been productive in Canada for a long time. What is less clear is whether current political economic conditions allow for the sustainability of the ideology and practice of Frenchness on which more than francophones have come to depend. The contradictions between pride and profit threaten to undermine the discursive legitimacy of a principle that has long been central to the social organization of Canada.

NOTES

1. Coureurs de bois (literally, runners of the woods) were usually the first link in the chain between indigenous suppliers and European consumers of furs. Voyageurs (literally voyagers) manned the canoes which transported trade goods, trade agents and other Europeans.
2. In fact, the francophone elite had long debated the relative merits of embracing versus fleeing industrial modernity, although the proponents of industry tended to seek collective strategies for wresting control of regional industry

from the hands of English-speakers, rather than seeking to transform themselves as entrepreneurs (Frenette 1998; McLaughlin and Heller 2011).

3. This research is funded by the Social Sciences and Humanities Research Council of Canada, the Wenner-Gren Foundation for Anthropological Research and the Northern Scientific Training Program. We thank the participants in the research, and our team members Michelle Daveluy (Université Laval), Mireille McLaughlin (Université d'Ottawa) and Hubert Noël (Université de Moncton). We also thank Marcel Martel (York University) for his indispensable advice.

4. Lobster is an iconic food of Atlantic Canada. "Lobster Fest" is a fundraising event organized by the local chapter of the Knights of Columbus, a Catholic men's charitable association. Its popularity is testimony to the salience of the presence in Hay River of people from Atlantic Canada. Like them, the lobster is flown in from the East coast.

5. Actually, many of them said: "les seuls mots que je savais étaient yes pis no pis toaster", *toaster* being fairly well integrated into Canadian French vocabulary.

6. Another central component to Canadian sociopolitical organization is the marking of some spaces and populations as indigenous. To understand the salience of processes of (racial, cultural and linguistic) differentiation with regard to Canadian indigeneity, see Kulchyski 2005.

7. Membership in such gangs is signalled with patches worn on jackets. As initiation progresses, the patch moves from partial to "full." Blue and red have long been used to symbolize oppositional political allegiances. In Canada, traditionally, blue has been associated with conservative political parties and red with liberal ones. However, more recently blue has come to also signify Quebec (and independentism) and red Canada (or federalism).

REFERENCES

Boutet, Josiane. 2008. *La vie verbale au travail. Des manufactures aux centres d'appel.* Toulouse: Octares.

Coates, Kenneth, and William Morrison. 1994. *Working the North: Labor and the Northwest Defense Projects, 1942–1945.* Fairbanks: University of Alaska Press.

Choquette, Robert. 1977. *Langue et religion: Histoire des conflits anglo-français en Ontario.* Ottawa: Presses de l'Université d'Ottawa.

Choquette, Robert. 1987. *La foi gardienne de la langue en Ontario 1900–1950.* Montréal: Bellarmin.

Dubois, Lise, Mélanie Le Blanc, and Maurice Beaudin. 2006. "La langue comme ressource productive et les rapports de pouvoir entre communautés linguistiques." *Langage et société* 118: 17–42.

Emmerson, Charles. 2010. *The Future History of the Arctic.* New York: Public Affairs.

Fédération franco-ténoise. 2002. *Bâtir un pays—Planification 2002–2005 en matière de développement économique de la collectivité francophone des Territoires du Nord-Ouest.* Yellowknife: FFT.

Frenette, Yves. 1998. *Brève histoire des Canadiens français.* Montréal: Boréal.

Harvey, David. 2005. *The New Imperialism* (Clarendon Lectures in Geography and Environmental Studies). New York: Oxford University Press.

Heller, Monica. 1994. *Crosswords: Language, Ethnicity and Education in French Ontario.* Berlin: Mouton de Gruyter.

Heller, Monica. 2011. *Paths to Post-Nationalism: A Critical Ethnography of Language and Identity.* Oxford: Oxford University Press.

Heller, Monica, and Joan Pujolar. 2009. "The Political Economy of Texts: A Case Study in the Structuration of Tourism." *Sociolinguistic Studies* 3(2): 177–202.

Hémon, Louis. 1916. *Maria Chapdelaine. Récit du Canada français.* Montréal: J.-A. Lefèvre.

Jakobsson, Sverrir. 2009. *Images of the North: History-Identities-Ideas.* Amsterdam: Rodopi.

Kulchyski, Peter. 2005. *Like the Sound of a Drum: Aboriginal Cultural Politics in Denedeh and Nunavut.* Winnipeg: University of Manitoba Press.

Leroux, Denis. 1989. *Leroux Beaulieu et les autres ou La petite histoire des francophones dans les Territoires du Nord-Ouest.* Yellowknife: Éditions Fédération francoténoise.

Martel, Marcel, and Martin Pâquet. 2010. *Langue et politique au Canada et au Québec. Une synthèse historique.* Montréal: Boréal.

McLaughlin, Mireille, and Monica Heller. 2011. "'Dieu et patrie': ideologies du genre, de la langue et de la nation au Canada francophone." In *Langage, genre et sexualité,* edited by Alexandre Duchêne and Claudine Moïse, 253–274. Québec: Nota Bene.

Morissonneau, Christian. 1978. *La Terre promise: Le mythe du Nord québécois.* Montréal: HMH Hurtubise.

Porter, John. 1965. *The Vertical Mosaic: An Analysis of Class and Power.* Toronto: University of Toronto Press.

Ramirez, Bruno. 1991. *On the Move: French-Canadian and Italian Migrants in the North Atlantic Economy, 1860–1914.* Toronto: McClelland and Stewart.

Robineau, Anne, Christophe Traisnel, Éric Forgues, Josée Guignard Noël, and Rodrigue Landry. 2010. *La Francophonie boréale: La vitalité des communautés francophones dans les territoires.* Moncton: Canadian Institute for Research on Linguistic Minorities.

da Silva, Emanuel, and Monica Heller. 2009. "From Protector to Producer: The Role of the State in the Discursive Shift from Minority Rights to Economic Development." *Language Policy* 8(2): 95–116.

Wolf, Eric. 1982. *Europe and the People without History.* Cambridge: Cambridge University Press.

9   The Making of "Workers of the World"

Language and the Labor Brokerage State

Beatriz P. Lorente

On July 31, 2007, the Technical Education and Skills Development Authority (TESDA), the government agency in charge of managing and supervising technical education and skills development in the Philippines, launched the Language Skills Institute (LSI). The LSI was mandated to offer courses in English, Spanish, Mandarin, Korean, Nihongo, Italian, Russian and "other languages as may be needed" (TESDA 2007). A national LSI would be located in Manila, and there would be at least one regional LSI in each of the fifteen regions of the country.[1] To make the language courses accessible to most Filipinos, scholarships under the President Gloria Macapagal Arroyo Training for Work Scholarship Project would be offered, so that those who were interested could become "world class" for "free" (TESDA 2007). Speaking at the launch, the then Director General of TESDA, Augusto Boboy Syjuco, gave the reason for setting up such an institute:

> In a globalizing labor market, the usual knowledge, skills and attitude that our workers possess are no longer sufficient. We need to provide interventions to allow them to gain workplace communication skills not only in English but also in other languages, especially those spoken in the usual destinations of our Overseas Filipino Workers (OFWs). With the right knowledge, skills, attitude, language skills and culture orientation, our OFW should henceforth be called Pinoy Workers of the World (Pinoy WOW). (Syjuco 2007)

That a national government would take pride in establishing and funding language institutes where its citizens could learn the necessary "workplace communication skills" in the languages of the countries they are likely to migrate to for work (i.e., "the usual destinations of our Overseas Filipino Workers") is not surprising, given that the Philippines can be considered to be a labor brokerage state, that is, it is a state that—through institutional and discursive practices—"mobilizes its citizens and sends them abroad to work for employers throughout the world while generating a 'profit' from the remittances that migrants send back to their families and loved ones" (Rodriguez 2010, x).

The Philippines is the world's largest "exporter" of government-sponsored temporary contract workers in terms of both magnitude and geographic scope (Tyner 2004). At the time that the LSI was launched in 2007, of the more than 8.7 million Filipinos overseas, 4.1 million were temporary labor migrants or overseas Filipino workers (OFWs). They were working mainly as household service workers, professional nurses, waiters, bartenders, cleaners, electrical wiremen, caregivers, plumbers, pipe fitters, welders and flame-cutters in more than two hundred countries and territories worldwide (Commission on Filipinos Overseas 2007). [2]

The country is highly dependent on their remittances. Remittances from overseas Filipinos are the country's premier foreign exchange earner, easily dwarfing foreign direct investments and exports. In 2006, while foreign direct investments only amounted to US$2 billion, and export earnings came to about US$3.7 billion, remittances from overseas Filipinos hit US$12.8 billion, accounting for almost 11 percent of the GDP (BBC News 2007; Chipongian 2007).[3] It has been estimated that remittances support half of the country's population (Kanlungan Center Foundation 1999), keeping the economy of the perennial "sick man of Asia" afloat, and generating consumption-led economic growth in spite of recession and high unemployment (Department of Labor and Employment 2005).

Syjuco's reference to a "globalizing labor market," where "workplace language skills" and knowledge of the languages of the destination countries are necessary in order to ensure the continued competitiveness of migrant Filipino workers, broadly reflects how, in the globalized new economy, language is a key resource for distinguishing as well as adding value to products, as new markets are sought and niche markets are developed (Duchêne and Heller in press; Heller 2010). As a labor brokerage state, the Philippines' success in accumulating profit relies on it being able to assemble, standardize and flexibilize a sought-after commodity: "Pinoy workers of the world"—short-term, contractual and incredibly mobile workers—who are "resilient," "loyal," "equipped with extensive educational training," have a "natural ability to adapt to different work cultures" and are "ideally suited in any multi-racial environment given a facility with the English language" (Philippine Overseas Employment Administration 2006b). As can be gleaned from the rationale for the launch of the LSI, as well as from the preceding descriptions of Filipino workers, language is an important part of this assemblage.

This chapter seeks to explore the particular ways in which language is instrumentalized by a labor brokerage state in this labor enterprise of producing "workers of the world" who can be marketed globally, and yet are flexible enough to meet the needs of local labor markets. What is being commodified here is labor; the Philippine strategy for accumulating profit is not to produce standard workers per se but standard workers who can "fit" anywhere in the world. The ways in which "Pinoy workers of the world" are represented calls attention not just to how the Philippines, as a labor brokerage state, is commodifying its labor force for the global labor market, but also to how the state legitimizes such activities. As Tyner has thoughtfully pointed out,

> To view the Philippine state as simply bowing to the spatial logic of capitalism potentially obfuscates the contradictory and contested activities of the state. Although capital accumulation, such as the desire for remittances, is a primary catalyst for state intervention, the state must also cope with the equally important political repercussions of social relations and the fundamental problem of sustaining legitimacy in the eyes of its citizenry. The balance of these often contradictory interventions significantly influences state legitimacy and informs the discourses of migrant labor. (2004, 2)

The data for this chapter are drawn mainly from secondary sources, that is, newspaper articles and official documents published and circulated by relevant government institutions in the Philippines. A number of these sources were compiled between 2001 and 2006, in the course of an ethnographically informed study of Filipino domestic workers in Singapore (Lorente 2007). Since 2007, I have been regularly updating and adding to these secondary data sources, as well as learning about new developments, by systematically conducting searches on the Internet, and by visiting the Philippine Overseas Employment Administration (POEA) and the Overseas Workers Welfare Administration (OWWA) in Manila on trips to the Philippines in May 2008 and December 2009.[4]

This chapter first traces the beginnings of labor migration in the Philippines as a way of fleshing out how the Philippines evolved into a labor brokerage state. Second, it examines how language has been and is being mobilized as a resource in this labor enterprise, both in terms of representing migrant Philippine labor, as well as in terms of intervening in attempts to standardize and flexibilize the language skills of migrant Filipino workers. Finally, it looks at how the state defines its role, as it balances the need for profit with the need to legitimize its actions with its citizenry. This is done by looking at the particular case of the new requirements for would-be migrant household service workers.

THE PHILIPPINES AS A LABOR BROKERAGE STATE

Labor migration from the Philippines began in the 1970s as an attempt to resolve deteriorating social and economic conditions in the country, brought about largely by the restructuring of the Philippine economy toward commercial agriculture and export-oriented industrialization (EOI) under the auspices of Ferdinand Marcos' economic development-oriented "New Society."[5] The rise of labor migration from the Philippines is well chronicled in numerous migration studies on the Philippines (for annotated bibliographies, see Perez and Patacsil 1998; Yukawa 1996).

The Philippines was not a newcomer in global labor circuits. During the Spanish colonial period (1521–1898), Filipinos worked for Spanish galleons; the first known instance of Filipino "labor migration" occurred during the galleon trade between Manila and Acapulco from 1565 to 1815. Employed as laborers (and likely also as prostitutes) on board the ships, Filipinos abandoned ship in Acapulco as early as the sixteenth century, migrating to other parts of Mexico. By 1763, a Filipino community had settled in Louisiana, in what would become the longest-standing permanent settlement of Asians in the United States (Fujita-Rony 2003). During the American colonial period, the first wave of Filipino migrants began at the beginning of the twentieth century and was structured largely by the colonial relations between the Philippines and the United States (see Takaki 1998). The ones who left were mainly Filipino men, many of them from northern Luzon; they filled temporary labor needs in agriculture in Hawaii and on the U.S. West Coast (Yukawa 1996). The second wave was made up mostly of Filipino professionals, many of whom were in the medical profession (see Choy 2003); they went to the United States after major reforms in U.S. immigration law in 1965 opened the door to a steady and significant flow of Filipino permanent migration to the United States.

However, apart from the nature of the work and geographical destinations of OFWs, labor migration since the 1970s has also been characterized by the deliberate intervention of the state in the structures and processes of migration. The evolution of such state-sponsored labor migration can be traced to the shift from a strategy of import substitution in the aftermath of political independence in 1946, to a strategy of EOI from the late 1960s to the Martial Law Period from 1972 to 1981 (Gonzalez 1998; Tyner 2000). "One key to the Philippines' economic strategy was the discursive marketing of an 'internationally attractive labor force', i.e. a cheap and docile workforce prevented from unionizing or striking" (Tyner 2004, 30). To produce such a labor force, the Philippine government restructured domestic labor market conditions through the 1974 Labor Code (also known as Presidential Decree or PD 442). The code

> permit[ted] employers to pay new employees only 75 percent of the basic minimum wage during a six-month "probationary" period . . . By releasing workers after this period, multinational corporations effectively instituted a high turnover rate . . . Denied access to traditional economic forms of subsistence production, yet more fully incorporated into the waged labor force, many Filipinos found employment opportunities unavailable in the Philippines, or untenable due to low wages. (Tyner 2000, 136)

Labor export was seen by the state as a means of resolving such unemployment and underemployment problems, while, at the same time, promoting Philippine development and alleviating balance of payment problems through remittances. In this way, the extremely destabilizing restructuring of the labor market that was an essential part of the country's export-led development strategy effectively made Philippine labor one of the "natural resources" that the country could export.

The 1974 Labor Code also laid the foundations of labor migration (specifically in Articles 17.1 and 17.2) by mandating that the Philippine state would promote "the overseas employment of Filipino workers through a comprehensive market promotion and development program and, in the process . . . secure the best possible terms and conditions of employment of Filipino contract workers on a government to government basis" (Tyner 2004, 33).

With its labor force effectively considered as exportable "commodities," the Philippines was one of the first Asian countries to respond to the labor needs of the oil-rich countries in the Middle East in the 1970s. What was intended to be a temporary solution to domestic unemployment and balance of payment problems, "continued and expanded beyond the Middle East in response to the increasing demand for Filipino workers on the one hand, and the development of institutions and policies in the Philippines that enabled the state to seize opportunities in the global labor market on the other" (Asis 2005, 26). Overseas employment has become a cornerstone of administrations from Marcos to Aquino, figuring as an essential aspect of national development goals as elucidated in Medium-Term Philippine Development Plans (Tyner 2004). In this regard, the role of overseas labor migration in the Philippines has fundamentally shifted

> from a temporary solution to the critical low employment rate in the domestic market to an employment strategy that recognizes the role of overseas remittances in alleviating poverty, spurring investment and cushioning the impact of worldwide recession when private capital dries up. (POEA 2005b, 3)

Officially, the Philippine state only "manages" labor migration; it does not promote it. A Department of Labor and Employment (DOLE) "White Paper" released in 1995 emphasized,

> Many people see opportunities abroad and want to benefit from them. And there are labor-market gaps in the global economy that are best filled by labor migration. The challenge to Philippine policymaking today is not one of exporting the country's labor surplus; it is *managing* effectively the *natural* process of labor migration—which will continue even if we ban the outflow of our workers. (DOLE 1995 in Guevarra 2003, 115)

This report was later incorporated in the Migrant Workers and Overseas Filipino Act (RA 8042) of 1995. It is important to note that the Philippine state's portrayal of itself as "managing" labor migration is buttressed by a discourse that "proposes that opportunities abroad are *natural* processes of globalization and that the desires and aspirations of Filipinos to work overseas are *natural* responses" (Guevarra 2003, 115).

In managing this supposedly natural process of labor migration, the most important government institution has been the Philippine Overseas Employment Administration (POEA), which oversees this official "management" of overseas workers. The Philippine state, through the POEA, aggressively promotes migrant Filipino workers (Tyner 2000). It has a marketing division that conducts market research on the locations where OFWs may go, and the nature of the possible employment opportunities in these places. The POEA also seeks to develop "friendly markets" for OFWs in the form of "inbound marketing programs," where Filipino "skills and talents" are showcased to foreign principals and employers invited to visit the Philippines, and "outbound marketing missions" where POEA representatives are sent to existing and prospective labor destinations to explore opportunities and secure contracts (Guevarra 2003).

The POEA works in tandem with the DOLE, the TESDA and the OWWA. For example, in 2005, the POEA implemented the DOLE Labor Opportunities Program (DOLOP), which was designed as an "in-bound marketing activity to promote the services of OFWs and showcase their skills and talents" (POEA 2005b, 15). The TESDA is in charge of providing technical education to Filipinos, and now offers training courses that are designed to cater to the needs of overseas labor markets. As will be discussed later, prospective domestic workers are now required to get a TESDA certificate in household services in order to be deployed overseas. The OWWA is the government agency responsible for providing welfare assistance to registered OFWs and their dependents. The POEA also licenses and regulates the thousands of privately owned overseas employment agencies in the country.

The POEA's "management" of international labor migration has become the "model for other labor-sending economies for the past two decades" (POEA 2005b, 3). More importantly, it is in this way that the export of labor from the Philippines represents the unprecedented convergence of interests between states and international capital, with the recruitment and deployment of migrant labor centrally organized and 'guaranteed' by the state (Aguilar 2002).

Patterns of Labor Migration from the Philippines

As an employment strategy, overseas labor migration could be considered to be enormously successful, if one were to look at the sheer number of OFWs that have been deployed by the state. The number of OFWs has increased exponentially since labor migration was instituted in 1974. In 1975, only 12,501 migrants were recorded as having left the country (Kanlungan Center Foundation 1999). Ten years later, 372,784 Filipinos left the country as migrant workers. By 2005, the POEA claimed to have deployed almost a million OFWs (see Table 9.1) and the number has increased since then.

The majority of OFWs are in the Middle East and Asia (see Table 9.2), in countries like Saudi Arabia, United Arab Emirates (UAE), Hong Kong,

Table 9.1 Annual Deployment of Overseas Filipino Workers, 1984–2009[6]

Year	Overseas Filipino Workers	Growth Rate (%)
1984	350,982	
1985	372,784	6.21
1986	378,214	1.46
1987	449,271	18.79
1988	471,030	4.84
1989	458,626	−2.63
1990	446,095	−2.73
1991	615,019	37.87
1992	686,461	11.62
1993	696,630	1.48
1994	718,407	3.13
1995	653,574	−9.02
1996	660,122	1.00
1997	747,696	13.27
1998	831,643	11.23
1999	837,020	0.65
2000	841,628	0.55
2001	867,599	3.08
2002	891,908	2.80
2003	867,969	−2.7
2004	933,588	7.56
2005	988,615	5.9
2006	1,062,567	7.5
2007	1,077,623	1.42
2008	1,236,013	14.7
2009	1,422,586	15.1

Sources: Kanlungan Center Foundation (1999), Philippine Overseas Employment Administration (2005a, 2005b, 2009).

Table 9.2   Top 10 Destinations of Land-Based Overseas Filipino Workers (Rehires and New Hires), 2009

Country	2009
1. Saudi Arabia	291,419
2. United Arab Emirates	196,815
3. Hong Kong	100,412
4. Qatar	89,290
5. Singapore	54,421
6. Kuwait	45,900
7. Taiwan	33,751
8. Italy	23,159
9. Canada	17,344
10. Bahrain	15,001

Source: Philippine Overseas Employment Administration (2009, 18).

Singapore and Taiwan. These Middle Eastern oil-rich countries and affluent Asian economies demand a flexible and low-cost labor force to sustain their economic growth and support their own labor force. OFWs are also heading to North American and European destinations, such as Italy and Canada, where there are significant care deficits.

Also, the groups in which most OFWs have been classified in recent years highlight one of the defining characteristics of labor migration from the Philippines: the feminization of migrant labor. This has been brought about not just by the international division of labor, but more particularly by the international division of *reproductive* labor, wherein migrant women from developing countries like the Philippines perform the caretaking and household work of class-privileged women in industrialized countries (Parreñas 2000, 2001). This international division of reproductive labor is underpinned by the shift of reproductive work from the household (where it is considered to be an integral component of the roles of women as wives and mothers) to the market (where it is considered "unskilled"), as a result of global economic restructuring. Among the "tigers" of East and Southeast Asia (which include Singapore), the movement of local women into waged labor was the result of state-led industrialization (in the 1970s) and economic liberalization (in the 1980s). This has worsened the care deficit in countries that lack institutional child and elderly care, and where the provision of care is considered to be a family affair. "All this has set in train strong market forces demanding transnational, flexibilised workers to fill the cracks and crevices in the domestic sphere, an arena often neglected by the state and treated as dispensable in terms of the globalising logic" (Huang, Yeoh, and Abdul Rahman 2005, 2). This is reflected in the current "niches" of migrant Filipino labor; Table 9.3 lists the top ten occupational groups of new OFWs as of 2009.

Table 9.3   Deployed Overseas Filipino Workers (New hires, Top 10 Occupational Groups by Sex), 2009

Occupational Group	Male	Female	Total
1 Household service workers	1,888	69,669	71,557
2 Nurses professional	1,599	11,866	13,465
3 Waiters, bartenders and related workers	4,978	6,999	11,977
4 Charworkers, cleaners and related workers	2,140	7,916	10,056
5 Wiremen electrical	9,709	43	9,752
6 Caregivers and caretakers	507	8,721	9,228
7 Laborers and helpers general	7,105	994	8,099
8 Plumbers and pipe fitters	7,702	20	7,722
9 Welders and flame cutters	5,870	40	5,910
10 Housekeeping and related service workers	908	4,219	5,127
Total deployment	42,406	110,487	152,893

Source: Philippine Overseas Employment Administration (2009, 19).

As can be seen in Table 9.3, an overwhelming majority of the new hires were deployed as household service workers, that is, domestic workers. Practically all of them are women. In fact, Filipinos constitute one of the largest groups of transnational domestic workers, and, indeed, one of the largest and widest flows of contemporary female migration (Parreñas 2001). It is estimated that about half of the total number of OFWs are women, and that two thirds of them are domestic workers (Tyner 1999).

The patterns of labor migration from the Philippines are highly indicative of the country's rather peripheral position in the global division of (reproductive) labor. The Philippine labor enterprise profits from establishing and dominating such niches in the global labor market.

LANGUAGE IN THE PHILIPPINE LABOR ENTERPRISE

Language has always played an important role in the Philippine labor enterprise, so much so that the position of the Philippines as a labor-sending state could be considered to have influenced Philippine language policy significantly (Gonzalez 1998). In 1974, when the bilingual education policy (BEP) instituting Filipino and English as the media of instruction was put in place (Tupas 2007), with the provision that steps would be taken toward the development of Filipino as the common national language, the Philippine economy was already well into the process of becoming more fully incorporated into the global economy as a source of low-waged labor.

It was in this same year that the first batch of government-sponsored Filipino contract workers was deployed to the Middle East, an early indication of how the search for a national linguistic symbol of unity would soon be overtaken, or had already been overtaken, by the insertion of the Philippines into the world system as a labor-sending country. The almost indisputable argument was that English was necessary if the country were to participate and fully benefit from the global economy. Arguably, in this light, the biggest losers were the Filipinos, whose wages had been eroded by their incorporation into the global labor market, and whose varying levels of English competence differentially affected their entry as (mainly) low-waged workers in an export-oriented, labor intensive light industry financed by foreign capital (Tollefson 1991).

In fact, already in the 1970s, the Philippine government had restructured the education system, in accordance with the perceived needs of EOI. Restructuring the education sector was a vital complement to the changes that had been made to the labor sector. Major changes to the Philippine educational system can be traced back to Martial Law. According to Tollefson,

> Various presidential decrees transformed the elementary and high school curricula into "work-oriented" programmes to prepare youth for participation in commercial and industrial enterprises . . . The goal was to ensure that the educational system would "equip high school students with specific skills needed for industry and agriculture" . . . In addition, beginning in 1976, the World Bank funded [the] publication and distribution of millions of new textbooks and manuals through the Ministry of Education, Culture and Sports that were designed to help the system of education respond to the new economic policy. (1991, 149)

These changes to the Philippine educational system were reinforced further through the institutionalization of the National College Entrance Examination (NCEE), which became the country's main educational stratifier:

> With standards set by the central government, the NCEE determined who among the high school graduates could go on to college, earn their degrees and most possibly become white-collar workers. Those who did not pass could either enroll in technical education certificate courses or start working on low-paying jobs because by then they would have been taught vocational skills in high school through institutionalized technical programmes. (Tupas 2004)

These changes in Philippine educational policy translated to a renewed emphasis on English and a shift towards vocational and technical English training. The Marcos government's strong support of English was due primarily to its crucial role in meeting the labour requirements of the Philippine economy. (Tollefson 1991, 150)

The three main labor needs at that time were consistent with the country's policy of EOI financed and managed by foreign capital. They consisted of (1) a large pool of workers for unskilled and semitechnical jobs in light manufacturing, assembly and the like; (2) office staff and middle managers able to work under the managers of transnational corporations investing in the Philippines; and (3) a service industry for foreign businesses, including maintenance crews, hotel staff and domestic workers (Tollefson 1991). What the formal education system then produced was a multitiered skills-oriented population whose proficiencies in English were ordered accordingly (Tupas 2001, 2004), with most students being educated for low-paying jobs requiring only basic English (Tollefson 1991).

These differences reproduced the already glaring social and economic disparities in the Philippines. Those who learned English well and who had the skills to take up the better-paid white-collar jobs were inevitably graduates of elite schools, with most of them coming from the well-off and landed families in the Philippines. Those who did not learn English well were usually from the impoverished areas of the country; they usually did not go on to college and they ended up in the large pool of semiskilled and unskilled workers in the manufacturing and service sectors. As Tollefson pointedly states, "the policy of using English in schools thus serves a dual purpose: it helps to ensure that a great number of students fail, and it produces the necessary number of graduates with appropriate English skills" (1991, 151). When overseas labor migration was formalized by the government in 1974 as a viable employment alternative and as a strategy of capital accumulation, many OFWs came from the group of semiskilled and unskilled workers.

The Philippine education system's pattern of producing a hierarchy of labor, with corresponding levels of English skills meant for an externally defined labor market, has intensified or even worsened with the institutionalization of overseas labor migration. As Toh and Floresca-Cawagas (2003) point out, the quality of education in the Philippines has continuously deteriorated over the years, and the educational system is unable to respond realistically and relevantly to social, economic and political demands in the country. This is most evident in the disparity between the degrees of most college graduates and the demand for such skills or expertise in the domestic labor market (along with the failure to create such demand), leading to a rise in the number of educated underemployed and unemployed who, in turn, may be funneled into overseas labor migration.

Former president Arroyo articulated this push toward matching the goals of Philippine education with the demands of the global labor market. In a

2002 speech during Migrant Workers' Day, Arroyo argued that the increasing number of OFWs did not constitute a brain drain, because they benefited the country economically. As such, she urged the education system to "produce and produce" the workers that are "in demand" overseas:

> Kaya pag sinasabi nila brain drain, sabi ko, hindi, naglilingkod doon naglilingkod pa rin dito dahil hindi kinakalimutan 'yung mga pamilya, 'yung pamayanan, at sa ganung paraan pati 'yung bansa natin ay nakikinabang. *Ang importante kung ano 'yung nakikita nating demand sa mga skills, ang ating school system ay dapat produce nang produce. Kung malaki ang demand sa nurses, produce more nurses; kung malaki ang demand sa I.T. workers, produce more I.T. workers kasi kailangan din natin sila dito, kailangan sa ibang bansa.* Kaya pakinabang kung nandoon, pakinabang kung nandito sila, so produce more because there is an overall increase in demand.

> So when they say brain drain, I say, no, they are serving there but they are still serving here because they do not forget their families, their communities, and in this way our country also benefits. *The important thing is when we see the skills that are in demand, our school system should produce and produce. If there is a big demand for nurses, produce more nurses; if there is a big demand for I.T. workers, produce more I.T. workers*, because we need them here and other countries need them. They're an advantage there and they're an advantage here, so produce more because there is an overall increase in demand. (Arroyo 2002; emphasis and translation mine)

Standardizing the Language Skills of Flexible Workers of the World

This dependence of the Philippine labor market on the demands of external markets is evident in how the Philippine government has continued to emphasize and support policies and skills training programs aimed at maintaining Filipinos' competitive edge in terms of linguistic resources. This has been true in the case of English, as proficiency in what is considered as the global lingua franca supposedly makes Filipinos "ideally suited (for) any multi-racial working environment" (POEA 2006b). This is also true in the case of the "other languages," apart from English, that are spoken in the destination countries of OFWs:

> Learning another language or as many languages as possible as needed in the workplace is analogous to sprinkling a little spice to an otherwise already sumptuous dish to make it more palatable and appetizing. Workplace language skills will add to the competitive advantage of our Pinoy workers . . . multi-lingual, skilled, valuable, effective, sought after, successful and the country's pride. (TESDA 2007)

Given that competitiveness in the global labor market has practically been equated with English proficiency, it is not surprising that, at least until recently, there have been dire warnings that Filipinos are losing their "competitive edge" over other countries because of their supposedly declining levels of English competence (Manila Times 2003; Philippine Daily Inquirer 2004). A similar discourse is emerging in relation to outsourcing, and more specifically to the call center industry. Call centers are seen as the country's "emerging sunshine industry" (Jobstreet 2003a, 2003b). In its attempt to attract businesses, the Philippines has been emphasizing the English proficiency of its workforce and most especially, the Filipinos' familiarity with American culture and linguistic variety because of the country's colonial history. These are supposedly the country's advantages over India (see Salonga 2010).

It seems, though, that concrete steps were and are being taken to ensure that Filipinos maintain their "competitive advantage." Efforts to rectify the perceived loss of English competence have ranged from the implementation of "English-only zones" and "English hours" at universities in Manila (Quismundo 2004), to English "refresher classes" for seamen and "English in the workplace" sessions for Filipinos working in the U.S. dependency of Saipan (Department of Foreign Affairs 2002).

On a larger scale, during the Arroyo presidency from 2001 to 2010, there were explicit pronouncements of a "return to English," affirming just how the economic necessity of sustaining labor migration from the country has been and continues to be the most striking development in language policy and planning in the Philippines (Gonzalez 1988, 1998, 2004; Sibayan and Gonzalez 1996). In her first State of the Nation address in 2001, Arroyo made proficiency in English the major policy goal of the Department of Education. In January 2003, she followed this up by mandating a "return to English" as the main medium of instruction in Philippine schools.

In September 2005, the House Committees on Higher Education and on Basic Education endorsed and sought the immediate approval of House Bill 4701 (HB 4701), which, among other things, would make it mandatory for English to be the official medium of instruction in *all* academic subjects in high school (Rosario 2005). This bill was passed almost a year later on September 21, 2006.

Even with the very recent introduction of the Multilingual Education bill (MLE), which proposes the use of mother tongues as the primary medium of instruction in all subjects from preschool up to the end of elementary education (Gunigundo 2010) , the status of English as being absolutely essential for the continued competitiveness of Filipino workers has remained largely unchanged and unquestioned. In fact, supporters of MLE have been careful to point out that using the mother tongue in the lower grades would help children learn English better in the upper grades (Tupas 2009).

While the continued maintenance of the grip of English in the Philippines may be the most visible impact of labor migration on the linguistic economy and language policies of the country, due to the country's dependency on the continued "competitiveness" and therefore continued remittances of overseas Filipinos, it is increasingly not the only one. There seems to be a shift in how English is positioned as the "competitive advantage" of OFWs. While, by and large, English proficiency is still portrayed as the exclusive linguistic capital of OFWs, it is also starting to be depicted as the *minimum* linguistic capital of OFWs. This shift is legitimized by the Philippine state in a discourse of "people empowerment," understood as the provision of language teaching in the languages that will enable Filipinos to access and take full advantage of overseas work opportunities. This shift can perhaps be best illustrated with the new guidelines for household service workers that the POEA issued in 2007.

LANGUAGE AND COMMUNICATION SKILLS FOR SUPERMAIDS

On February 5, 2007, the POEA issued new guidelines for the "Reform Package affecting Household Service Workers" (HSWs). Under these new guidelines, HSWs with visas issued after December 16, 2006 would have to meet the following requirements: a minimum age of twenty-three, a minimum entry salary of US$400, a TESDA NC2 certificate for Household Services[7] and attendance at an OWWA country-specific language and culture orientation. After getting their NC2 certification, would-be HSWs could then take the "supermaid course." The "supermaid course" was intended to train Filipino HSWs to become "home managers" who can competently "plan and organize work, use mathematical concepts and techniques to respond effectively to difficult/challenging behavior, provide care and support to children, maintain a healthy and safe environment, respond to emergency and provide care to pets" (TESDA 2006b).

The notion of "supermaids" was introduced by Arroyo in August 2006, during a roundtable discussion on job and livelihood opportunities for Filipino domestic workers who were returning to the Philippines from war-torn Lebanon at that time. The president said the government had put in place livelihood and training programs to upgrade the skills of Filipinos going abroad as domestic workers so that they would not just be ordinary domestic workers but—in the then president's words—"supermaids" (Dalangin-Fernandez 2006).

In its Governing Board Resolution 8 for the series of 2006, the POEA outlined the rationale for introducing the new requirements for would-be HSWs: "migrant workers for deployment require the highest degree of protection owing to their gender and the vulnerable state of their employment" (POEA 2006a), and "the State recognizes that the ultimate protection to all migrant workers is the possession of skills and familiarity with the country and language of their employers and host governments" (POEA 2006a). In seeking acceptance for these new requirements, the POEA further argued that "the certification one gets from this training would enable a household help to apply for a higher job level in hotels . . . HSWs must welcome the training program. We are adding more value to the skills of our HSWs" (Marcelo 2007). Upgrading the skills of domestic workers would translate to Filipinos being given a premium by employers, that is, "they would be able to earn more" (Marcelo 2007).

The introduction of these new guidelines was met by a storm of protest from recruitment agencies and workers. At least 8,000 workers, most of them women applying for overseas jobs as domestic workers, held a protest rally on January 15, 2007, at the Liwasang Bonifacio and in front of the DOLE offices in Intramuros, Manila, protesting the new guidelines (GMA News 2007). In Hong Kong, about 5,000 FDWs marched on the streets on January 28, 2007, to demand the immediate scrapping of the new POEA guidelines (Philippine Daily Inquirer 2007).

Recruitment agencies, workers and migrant NGOs protested the $400 minimum wage, arguing that this would effectively price Filipinos out of the market for domestic workers. The groups also complained about the steep costs of the TESDA NC2 training and the OWWA country-specific language and culture orientation, the fees for which ranged from P5,000 to P10,000, and the additional amount of time (approximately twenty-seven days) it would take for them to complete the training.

Domestic workers and some migrant groups also questioned the government's capacity to enforce the salary guidelines and its motivation for collecting more fees for additional certificates, the general sentiment being that this was another "money-making scheme" of the government. DOLE and the POEA responded by highlighting that the guidelines were intended to raise the working conditions of disadvantaged Filipino household service workers globally, and that the issue had been "hijacked" by recruitment agencies who stood to lose their profitability because of the "no placement fee" guidelines (DOLE 2007). The $400 minimum salary would help secure a premium niche for Filipino "supermaids" and hopefully, better working and living conditions for them (Manila Times 2007). The additional training which Filipinos would go through would also enable them to apply for "higher level" service jobs in, for example, hotels and restaurants.

With regard to the new language and communication requirements set by the POEA for both the NC2 and the supermaid course, there are three interesting points to note: (1) the ability to communicate in English is considered to be a "minimum requirement"; (2) "workplace communication skills" (presumably in English, and on top of the basic ability to communicate in English) is one of the basic modules in the TESDA training program; and (3) some knowledge of a "foreign" language other than English is considered to be necessary, as seen in the requirement that prospective domestic workers undergo a country-specific language and culture training with the OWWA.

The Filipino "supermaid," as constructed by these new POEA guidelines, is an English-knowing multilingual, knowledgeable of the language (e.g., Cantonese for Hong Kong, Arabic for the Middle East, etc.) and culture of the household she is going to work for, and with competent "workplace communication skills."

The discourse of English being the "competitive edge" of Filipino migrant workers is translated into English being a "minimum requirement" at the local scale where would-be housemaids, housekeepers and cleaners are trained for deployment. As Tollefson (1991) has already pointed out, that English competence can be made a "minimum requirement," and that there is no lack of Filipinos lining up to leave the country, are the results of a large labor surplus in the country. As a minimum requirement, it would seem that the ability to communicate in English is no longer sufficient to sustain the "competitiveness" of FDWs.

On top of being able to communicate in English, FDWs are also supposed to have the ability to "participate in workplace communication." The "Competency-Based Curriculum Exemplar" for the Household Services National Certificate 2 (NC2) (TESDA 2006a) is generic when it comes to the kind of communication skills which are considered to be valuable for service workers. The module, "participating in workplace communication" is supposed to cover the following:

> Parts of speech; sentence construction; effective communication; communicating with the employer; communicating with other members of the household; familiarizing with common places and terminologies; basic mathematics; technical writing; types of forms; recording information. (TESDA 2006a)

The assessment criteria include

> [s]pecific relevant information is accessed from appropriate resources; effective questioning, active listening and speaking skills are used to gather and convey information; appropriate medium is used to transfer information and ideas; appropriate non-verbal communication is used; appropriate lines of communication with superiors and colleagues are identified and followed; defined workplace procedures for the location and storage of information are used; personal interaction is carried out clearly and concisely. (TESDA 2006a)

These assessment criteria place an emphasis on the transfer of information, on "obtaining and conveying workplace information" according to what is "appropriate" and/or according to "defined workplace procedures." There is also a literacy component where the emphasis is on completing relevant work-related documents, that is, filling out forms and recording information. The final component is participation in workplace meetings and discussions where their "own opinions are clearly expressed and those of others are listened to without interruption," "workplace interaction are conducted in a courteous manner appropriate to cultural background and authority," "questions about simple routine workplace procedures and matters concerning conditions of employment are asked and responded." These suggest that the communication skills that are considered to be valuable are "passive"; they are not about constructing or questioning knowledge or procedures.

The introduction of a communication skills element in the curriculum for household service workers points to how the new work order with its linguistic demands (Cameron 2002) has, at least discursively, come to be inserted in the economy of labor migration from the Philippines. It is indicative of global developments (or the new work order) where linguistic and communication "skills" have come to dominate forms of work, and in the case of the Philippines, forms of migrant labor. As Cameron points out,

> Whereas the industrial economy required large numbers of manual workers, who were colloquially referred to as "hands" and whose language skills were seen as largely irrelevant, the new capitalism is different. For one thing it is dominated by forms of work in which language-using is an integral part of every worker's functions. [It has been] suggested that the traditional "manual/non-manual" distinction was in the process of being superseded by a new division of labour, in which an elite class of "symbolic analysts"—creative professionals skilled in the manipulation of words, numbers, images and digital bits—would dominate a much larger and less privileged group providing routine services, either "in person" or behind the scenes. While the work done by these service providers is not necessarily any more creative or demanding than traditional manual work, it does put more pressure on literacy skills . . . and more generally, interpersonal communication skills. (2002, 72)

Apart from knowing English and having workplace communication skills, Filipino "supermaids" are also constructed to be knowledgeable in the language and culture of the destination country. This means being able to understand Cantonese if they are heading to Hong Kong, Arabic if they are going to any of the countries in the Middle East, and possibly Mandarin Chinese if they are going to Singapore. Six language and culture familiarization courses are currently being offered: Arabic, Hebrew, Italian, Cantonese, Mandarin and English. The twenty-hour course lasts for three days. Of these twenty hours, only sixteen actually go to training in language and culture; four hours are devoted to a stress management workshop that seeks to prepare would-be domestic workers for problems they may face with the families they leave behind in the Philippines, and with the families they will work for in their various destinations. In 2007,

129,159 OFWs ready for deployment underwent the country-specific language and culture training as part of their pre-departure orientation seminar. In 2008, 60,979 would-be foreign domestic workers were trained in basic spoken and written Arabic, Cantonese, Mandarin, Italian, English and Hebrew, ostensibly to help them in their day-to-day interactions with their foreign employers (OWWA 2009).

In the booklet used for the language and culture familiarization program, the following topics are covered: introduction to the destination country and culture (i.e., religion, government system, traditions and food), introduction to the language of the destination country including alphabet and numbers, greetings, and vocabulary lists for vegetables, fruits, tastes, kinds of meat and parts of the body, parts of the home, household chores and family members. Expressions and words used for caring for the sick and describing common illnesses are also given, as is a list of specific cultural do's and don'ts in the destination country.[8] Obviously, the OWWA orientation will not be sufficient to make would-be "supermaid" HSWs proficient in the language of their destination countries, but this development reinforces the image of migrant Filipino workers as being "flexible" and able to work with anyone, whether or not they speak English.

The image of the "supermaid" that emerges suggests that for the Philippine state it may no longer be enough to depend on English as the competitive edge of OFWs. It would seem that competitiveness in the global market increasingly demands English speakers with workplace communication skills and linguistic competence in the language of their destination country. This emergence of workplace communication skills and multilingualism (i.e., English and the language of the destination country) as a means of making Filipino workers distinctive in the global labor market may be attributed to increased competition from other labor-sending countries, such as Indonesia and Sri Lanka, in the niches which the Philippines has traditionally dominated (Huang, Yeoh, and Abdul Rahman 2005). In Singapore, for example, Indonesia is already the country's biggest supplier of foreign domestic workers (Basu 2011).

Faced with more affordably priced competition, the Philippine state's response has been to skillify its migrant workers in a bid to move them into "high value jobs" or to premium positions in the marginalized occupational niches where they may gain a profit from being distinctive from the rest of the competition. The Philippine state is also reconfiguring, in the process, what globally marketable, flexible and profitable workers would be. Their supposed proficiency in English, the global lingua franca, indexes them as being globally marketable, and their certified knowledge of the "necessary" language and culture of their destination countries makes them made-to-order in a standardized way for the niches in the local labor market where they will work. Apart from the new guidelines for prospective foreign domestic workers, this discourse is also becoming evident in recent POEA Annual Reports, which proudly report on the increase in the number of professionals and skilled workers in the total deployment of new hires, and which highlight the organization's "momentum of searching and generating high value jobs in international labor markets for Filipinos who take the option to seek employment outside the country" (POEA 2007, 5).

This skillifying of migrant Filipino workers and of Filipino domestic workers in particular serves not only to ensure the profitablity of the Philippine labor enterprise, it is also through this that the Philippine state legitimizes its actions in the eyes of its citizenry. The move into "high value" jobs is framed as the responsibility of the state, because "the possession of such skills by Filipino workers abroad is their best protection from any abuse or maltreatment" (Marcelo 2007); as the duty of the state as it should enable its citizens to take advantage of opportunities to work overseas should they choose to take the option; and as a source of national pride:

> With the vast opportunities being offered by the seemingly smaller and borderless world, the Pinoy workers' proven competence, ability, trainability and adaptability simply put them on a competitive edge. The growing need for language-adept workers can be easily filled by our Pinoy workers who take pride in having the capacity and learning ability to learn languages easily. (TESDA 2007)

CONCLUSION

This chapter has examined how, as a labor-sending state, the Philippines has emerged as a site of production that binds origins and destinations, that is, it is a location where bodies are transformed into globally marketable, made-to-order and profitable migrant labor for particular niches in the global labor market. The Philippine labor enterprise's project of ensuring the competitiveness of its migrant workers has material consequences: it reproduces inequalities within the state and reinforces the state's role as the provider of made-to-order, readily deployable, flexible workers in the global labor market. This chapter has also shown some of the mechanisms by which the Philippine state intervenes in the labor-market-related migration trajectories of its citizens. These mechanisms call attention not just to how states as power institutions, construct particular representations of Filipino labor, but also to how states legitimize the "export" of migrant bodies for profit through the "empowerment" and continued "professionalization" of OFWs by ensuring that they have the supposed access to the linguistic resources they need in order to be more "globally competitive."

This skillifying of the linguistic skills of migrant Filipino workers and in particular of Filipino domestic workers hints at a rather interesting construction of "workers of the world": their supposed possession of translocally valid language resources—in this case, workplace communication skills, English and the languages spoken in their target destinations—not only give them a "global" appeal in the labor market, but also distinguish them as "authentically" Filipino. They are not just any worker of the world; they are "Pinoy workers of the world." This particular assemblage, where linguistic resources that are framed as being globally mobile are used to index a national identity, hints at the complex and troubling encounters between the brokerage state's desire for profit, via the accumulation of remittances from its migrant workers, and its need to sustain legitimacy by constructing these very migrant workers as national sources of pride.

NOTES

1. Currently, the foreign language courses offered at the LSI are Arabic (which also includes Saudi/Gulf Culture), English, Korean, Mandarin, Japanese and Spanish (which is referred to as "Spanish Language for Different Vocations"). There are a total of thirty-three LSIs across all of the regions of the country.

2. As of 2009, there were 8.5 million overseas Filipinos, representing about 9.2 percent of the country's population of 92 million. Of these 8.5 million overseas Filipinos, 4 million are permanent migrants whose stays overseas do not depend on work contracts; the majority of these migrants are in the United States; 3.8 million are temporary migrants, and around 650,000 are irregular migrants. Permanent migrants are immigrants or permanent residents whose stays do not depend on work contracts. Temporary labor migrants or OFWs are persons whose stays overseas depend on their work contracts, which may range from six months to two years; they are expected to return to the Philippines at the end of their employment. Irregular migrants are those who are not properly documented, without valid residence or work permits, or who are overstaying in a foreign country. In a special category are the sea-based workers or seafarers; there were more than 330,000 Filipino seafarers 'overseas' in 2009.

3. Remittances from overseas Filipinos seem to hit new record highs every year. In the first half of 2010 alone, remittances through bank channels amounted to US$9.062 billion.

4. I visited the POEA in May 2008 in order to get a sense of how would-be overseas Filipino workers (OFWs) were processed. I visited OWWA in December 2009 with the intention of observing a country-specific language and culture familiarization program. I managed to talk to an OWWA administrator about the program, get hold of the booklet used for the Arabic language and culture familiarization program and to watch, albeit briefly, a class for would be domestic workers heading to Arabic-speaking countries. Although the data from my observations and interview are not used in this chapter, they were invaluable in helping me contextualize and concretize the data from my secondary sources.

5. Marcos launched his vision of the this "New Society" at the same time that he declared Martial Law on September 21, 1972. This "New Society" emphasized individual and national discipline and the sacrifice of personal liberties for economic development (Tyner 2004).

6. Annual deployment figures only manage to 'catch' those who are leaving the country to work abroad for the first time. They do not include return labor migrants.

7. The TESDA training regulations for prospective foreign domestic workers first came to my attention in May 2005 when I came across copies of the draft training regulations at the Bayanihan Center in Singapore where I was

volunteering in a skills upgrading program for Filipino domestic workers. In the cover letter which was addressed to Philippine labor attaches in Hong Kong, Singapore and Malaysia, the undersecretary of DOLE requested the validation of TESDA's draft training regulations for domestic workers by the labor attache, ten employees of Filipino domestic workers and twenty-five Filipino domestic workers.

8. This is based on the Arabic language and culture familiarization program booklet that I got hold of in December 2009. The OWWA administrator I briefly spoke to said that the topics were standard and that the other language and culture familiarization programs followed them.

REFERENCES

Aguilar, Filomeno V. 2002. "Beyond Stereotypes: Human Subjectivity in the Structuring of Global Migrations." In *Filipinos in Global Migrations: At Home in the World?*, edited by Filomeno V. Aguilar, 1–38. Quezon City: Philippine Migration Research Network and Philippine Social Science Council.

Arroyo, Gloria Macapagal. 2002. *Speech on Migrant Workers' Day.* 7 June. Accessed February 15, 2006. http://www.ops.gov.ph.

Asis, Maruja M. B. 2005. "Caring for the World: Filipino Domestic Workers Gone Global." In *Asian Women as Transnational Domestic Workers*, edited by Shirlena Huang, Brenda S. A. Yeoh and Noor Abdul Rahman, 21–53. Singapore: Marshall Cavendish.

Basu, Radhu. 2011. "Where Have the Indonesian Maids Gone?" *The Straits Times*, March 26, D2–D7.

BBC News. 2007. "Filipino Remittances Hit $12.8bn," February 15. Accessed February 18, 2007. http://news.bbc.co.uk/go/pr/fr/-1/hi/business/6364143.stm.

Cameron, Deborah. 2002. "Globalization and the Teaching of 'Communication Skills'." In *Globalization and Language Teaching*, edited by David Block and Deborah Cameron, 67–82. London: Routledge.

Chipongian, Lee C. 2007. "OFW Remittances Hit $12.8 B in 2006," *Manila Bulletin*, February 16. Accessed February 16, 2007. http://www.mb.com.ph/BSNS2007021687228.html.

Choy, Catherine Ceniza. 2003. *Empire of Care: Nursing and Migration in Filipino American History, American Encounters/Global Interactions.* Durham, NC: Duke University Press.

Commission on Filipinos Overseas. 2007. *Stock Estimate of Overseas Filipinos 2007.* Accessed December 15, 2010. http://www.cfo.gov.ph/pdf/statistics/Stock%202007.pdf.

Dalangin-Fernandez, Lira. 2006. "Arroyo: Philippines to Send 'Super Maids' Abroad Soon." *Philippine Daily Inquirer*, August 3. Accessed February 15, 2007. http://globalnation.inquirer.net/news/news/view_article.php?article_id=13304.

Department of Foreign Affairs. 2002. "Philippine Consulate General in Saipan Offers English Training Seminars." Accessed May 17, 2002. http://www.dfa.gov.ph/news/pr/pr2002/may/pr82.htm.

Department of Labor and Employment (DOLE). 2005. "Remittances of OFWs Contribute 9.2 Percent to Country's GNP." Accessed August 27, 2005. http://www.dole.gov.ph/news.

Department of Labor and Employment (DOLE). 2007. "Gov't Debunks Issues Concocted by Vested Interest Groups vs. Standards to Prevent Abuses on HSWs," February 12. Accessed February 16, 2007. http://www.dole.gov.ph/news.

Duchêne, Alexandre, and Monica Heller. in press. "Multilingualism and the New Economy." In *Routledge Handbook of Multilingualism*, edited by Marilyn Martin-Jones, Adrian Blackledge and Angela Creese. London: Routledge.

Fujita-Rony, Dorothy B. 2003. *American Workers, Colonial Power: Philippine Seattle and the Transpacific West, 1919–1941*. Berkeley: University of California Press.

GMA News. 2007. "More Rallies vs Hiring Policy for Pinoy DH." Accessed January 17, 2007. http://www.gmanews.tv/story/27059/More-rallies-vs-hiring-policy-for-Pinoy-DH

Gonzalez, Andrew. 1988. *The Role of English and its Maintenance in the Philippines: The Transcript, Consensus, and Papers of the Solidarity Seminar on Language and Development*. Manila, Philippines: Solidaridad Publishing House.

Gonzalez, Andrew. 1998. "The Language Planning Situation in the Philippines." *Journal of Multilingual and Multicultural Development* 19(5–6): 481–525.

Gonzalez, Andrew. 2004. "The Social Dimensions of Philippine English." *World Englishes* 23(1): 7–16.

Gonzalez, Joaquin L. 1998. *Philippine Labour Migration: Critical Dimensions of Public Policy*. Singapore: Institute of Southeast Asian Studies.

Guevarra, Anne Romina 2003. "Manufacturing the 'Ideal' Workforce: The Transnational Labor Brokering of Nurses and Domestic Workers from the Philippines." PhD diss., University of California at San Francisco, San Francisco.

Gunigundo, Magtanggol. 2010. *House Bill 162*. Accessed October 1, 2010. http://mlephil.wordpress.com/2010/09/04/h-b-no-162-gunigundo-multilingual-education-bill/.

Heller, Monica. 2010. "Language as Resource in the Globalized New Economy." In *The Handbook of Language and Globalization*, edited by Nikolas Coupland, 349–365. Malden, MA: Wiley-Blackwell.

Huang, Shirlena, Brenda S. A. Yeoh, and Noor Abdul Rahman, eds. 2005. *Asian Women as Transnational Domestic Workers*. Singapore: Marshall Cavendish.

Jobstreet. 2003a. "IT Outsourcing Seen to Boost Jobs, Economy." Accessed May 29, 2003. http://ph.jobstreet.com/career/jobs123/ind3.htm.

Jobstreet. 2003b. "Call Centers—RP's Emerging Sunshine Industry." Accessed May 29, 2003. http://ph.jobstreet.com/jobs123/ind1.htm.

Kanlungan Center Foundation, Inc. 1999. *Fast Facts on Filipino Labor Migration*. Quezon City: Kanlungan Center Foundation, Inc.

Lorente, Beatriz P. 2007."Mapping English Linguistic Capital: The Case of Filipino Domestic Workers in Singapore." PhD diss., National University of Singapore, Singapore.

Manila Times. 2003. "Filipinos' English Skills on the Decline," October 23. Accessed October 24, 2003. http://www.manilatimes.net/national/2003/oct/23/top_stories/20031023top3.html.

Manila Times. 2007. "Superpay for Supermaids," January 25. A4.

Marcelo, Patricia. 2007. "Labor Execs Stick to Skills as OFW Protector." Accessed January 19, 2010. www.ofwjournalism.net/previousweb/vol6no5&6/prevstories6505.php.

Overseas Workers Welfare Administration (OWWA). 2009. *Language Training and Culture Familiarization Program*. Accessed September 15, 2009. http://owwa.gov.ph/article/articleview/238/1/19/.

Parreñas, Rachel Salazar. 2000. "Migrant Filipina Domestic Workers and the International Division of Reproductive Labor." *Gender and Society* 14(4): 560–580.

Parreñas, Rachel Salazar. 2001. *Servants of Globalization: Women, Migration, and Domestic Work*. Stanford, CA: Stanford University Press.

Perez, Aurora E., and Perla C. Patacsil. 1998. *Philippine Migration Studies: An Annotated Bibliography*: Philippine Migration Research Network.

Philippine Daily Inquirer. 2004. "RP Workforce Losing Edge in English." May 3, 2004. Accessed May 11, 2004. http://money.inq7.net/features/view.features.php?yyy=2004&mon=05&dd+03&file=4.

Philippine Daily Inquirer. 2007. "5T Pinoy Maids March in Hong Kong vs. New Deployment Rules." January 29. Accessed February 15, 2007. http://globalnation.inquirer.net/cebudailynews/news/view_article.php?article_id=46222.

Philippine Overseas Employment Administration (POEA). 2005a. *Deployment of Overseas Filipino Workers, 1984–2002*. Accessed September 8, 2005. http://www.poea.gov.ph.

Philippine Overseas Employment Administration (POEA). 2005b. *Annual Report 2005*. Accessed February 15, 2007. http://www.poea.gov.ph/ar/AR2005.pdf.

Philippine Overseas Employment Administration (POEA). 2006a. *Governing Board Resolution No. 08, Series of 2006*. October 24. Accessed February 16, 2007. http://www.poea.gov.ph/GBR/2006/gbr08_2006.pdf.

Philippine Overseas Employment Administration (POEA). 2006b. *Filipino Workers: Moving the World Today*. December 12. Accessed February 18, 2007. http://www.poea.gov.ph/about/moving.htm.

Philippine Overseas Employment Administration (POEA). 2006c. *OFW Global Presence: a Compendium of Overseas Employment Statistics 2005*. Accessed February 15, 2007. http://www.poea.gov.ph/stats/OFW_Statistics_2005.pdf.

Philippine Overseas Employment Administration (POEA). 2007. *Annual Report 2007*. Accessed April 18, 2011. http://www.poea.gov.ph/ar/ar2007.pdf.

Philippine Overseas Employment Administration. 2009. *2009 Compendium of OFW Statistics*. Accessed February 1, 2011. http://www.poea.gov.ph/stats/2009_OFW%20Statistics.pdf.

Quismundo, Tarra. 2004. "'English-Only Zones' Set in Manila." *Philippine Daily Inquirer*, September 1.

Rodriguez, Robyn Magalit. 2010. *Migrants for Export: How the Philippine State Brokers Labor to the World*. Minneapolis: University of Minnesota Press.

Rosario, Ben R. 2005. "Bill on English as Medium in Schools Endorsed." *Manila Bulletin*, September 27.

Salonga, Aileen Olimba. 2010. "Language and Situated Agency: An Exploration of the Dominant Linguistic and Communication Practices in the Philippine Offshore Call Centers." PhD Diss., National University of Singapore, Singapore.

Sibayan, Bonifacio P., and Andrew B. Gonzalez. 1996. "Post-Imperial English in the Philippines." In *Post-Imperial English: Status Change in Former British and American Colonies, 1940–1990*, edited by by Joshua A. Fishman, Andrew W. Conrad and Alma Rubal-Lopez, 139–172. Berlin: Mouton de Gruyter.

Syjuco, Augusto Boboy. 2007. "Inauguration of the TESDA Language Skills Institute." July 31. Accessed December 12, 2009. http://www.titoboboy.com/speech01.html.

Takaki, Ronald T. 1998. *Strangers from a Different Shore: A History of Asian Americans*. Updated and rev. ed. Boston: Little Brown.

Technical Education and Skills Development Authority (TESDA). 2007 *Crossing the Language Divide*. Accessed December 12, 2009. http://www.tesda.gov.ph/page.asp?rootID=9&sID=224&pID=9.

Technical Education and Skills Development Authority (TESDA). 2006a. *Competency Based Curriculum Exemplar: Household Services NC II*. Manila: Technical Education and Skills Development Authority.

Technical Education and Skills Development Authority (TESDA). 2006b. *Competency Based Curriculum Supermaid (Home Manager)*. Accessed February

15, 2007. http://www.tesda.gov.ph/uploads/file/PGMA%20guidelines/Curriculum%20Supermaid%20Course.pdf.

Toh, Swee-Hin, and Virginia Floresca Cawagas. 2003. "Globalization and the Philippines' Education System." In *Globalization and Educational Restructuring in the Asia Pacific region*, edited by Ka Ho Mok and Anthony R. Welch, 189–231. Houndmills, UK: Palgrave Macmillan.

Tollefson, James W. 1991. *Planning Language, Planning Inequality: Language Policy in the Community*. London: Longman.

Tupas, Topsie Ruanni F. 2001. "Linguistic Imperialism in the Philippines: Reflections of an English Language Teacher of Filipino Overseas Workers." *The Asia-Pacific Researcher* 10(1): 1–40.

Tupas, Topsie Ruanni F. 2004. "Anatomies of Linguistic Commodification: The Case of English in the Philippines vis-à-vis Other Languages in the Multilingual Marketplace." Paper presented at the Singapore Association for Applied Linguistics Symposium on The Mother Tongue Issue in Multilingual Communities, August 14.

Tupas, Topsie Ruanni F. 2007. "Go Back to Class: The Medium of Instruction Debate in the Philippines." In *Language, Nation and Development in Southeast Asia Roundtable*, edited by Lee Hock Guan and Leo Suryadinata, 17–38. Singapore: Institute of Southeast Asian Studies.

Tupas, Topsie Ruanni F. 2009. "Language as a Problem of Development: Ideological Debates and Comprehensive Education in the Philippines." *AILA Review* 22: 23–35.

Tyner, James A. 1999. "The Web-Based Recruitment of Female Foreign Domestic Workers in Asia." *Singapore Journal of Tropical Geography* 20(2): 193–209.

Tyner, James A. 2000. "Migrant Labour and the Politics of Scale: Gendering the Philippine State." *Asia Pacific Viewpoint* 41(2): 131–154.

Tyner, James A. 2004. *Made in the Philippines: Gendered Discourses and the Making of Migrants*. London: RoutledgeCurzon.

Yukawa, Joyce. 1996. *Migration from the Philippines, 1975–1995: An Annotated Bibliography*. Quezon City, Philippines: Scalabrini Migration Center & Fondazione Giovanni Agnelli.

10 Language Workers
Emblematic Figures of Late Capitalism[1]

Josiane Boutet

INTRODUCTION

Globalization engenders contradictions between two opposing economic and social processes: on the one hand, we observe a strong tendency to standardize, homogenize and despatialize activities, delocalization or offshoring being its most explicit manifestation; on the other, we also see resistance, largely through the cultivation of unique branding, regionalization and localization. Standardization concerns the production and consumption of tangible as well as cultural goods, including language, leading to, notably, the generalization of English as medium of communication. Processes of localization can be observed at the economic level, for example, in microcredit bank loans; on the political level, various nationalistic claims play that role; and, on the linguistic level, we observe the defense of "small" or minority languages.[2]

Languages and language activity are part of the process of economic globalization. Because of globalization, language is mired in contradictions between a fundamentally identity oriented and geographically centered historical conception, inherited in large part from the ideology of the Age of Enlightenment and the French Revolution ("one language, one country, one nation"), on the one hand, and, on the other, their present-day economic status, as commodities whose value can be assessed and paid for, thereby constituting a profit base for commercial companies (Grin et al. 2010). In other words, languages both continue to be considered identity attributes, and thus one of the bases for nationalist claims all over the world, while simultaneously being caught up in processes of commodification in which identity values no longer hold sway, and emerging as resources and a source of profit for businesses (Heller 2003; Heller and Boutet 2006; Heller and Duchêne 2007). Take the example of North Africa: in Tunisia and Morocco, opposition movements fight, sometimes violently, to hold on to their minority Berber languages, to transmit and teach them, to assign them a public function in competition with Arabic languages. But at the same time, the rapid corporate outsourcing to these countries gives economic precedence to the languages of those companies, particularly French (due to their colonial history). To work in a call center in Tunisia, one must be able to speak perfect French. The employer does not care what the first language(s) of the teleoperators might be, Arabic or Berber (I shall return to this). Globalization is on the way to imposing, even on the speakers themselves, a managerial conception of languages and language activity, no longer seen as a "source of pride" but a "source of profit." The brutal introduction on the economic market[3] of languages and language activity is accompanied by the arrival of a new group of wage earners, whom I call "language workers" (Boutet 2008, 141–173).

The specific forms of exploitation characteristic of late capitalism produces *one* of the existing configurations of the combination between language activity and work activity. Since the Industrial Revolution at the end of the eighteenth century, successive organizations of labor have imagined and framed wage earners' verbal expression according to different configurations. From labor in nineteenth-century mines, textile mills and factories, to the modern work carried out in call centers, the contribution of language has varied greatly. In order to describe and understand its role, and to analyze labor from the point of view of language, I have proposed the theoretical and descriptive notion of "the language part of work" (*la part langagière du travail*, cf. Boutet 2001).

Human labor entails triggering physical and muscular, perceptive, cognitive, psychological, relational and social capacities that vary according to the task. Human labor may also imply activating linguistic capacities, in the sense of knowing how to read, write and communicate in one or more than one language. I called "the language part of work" the implementation of the linguistic competencies needed to do a job. Depending on the professional sector, craft, modalities, prescription, functions and usages, the linguistic forms of the language part of work will differ. How can one compare lawyers and journalists, for whom the written word represents nearly the totality of their work activity, with masons, or train conductors, for whom language is only one component of the activity, associated with muscular activity, physical movement, professional gestures and body positions? The language component is therefore variable from a synchronic as well as from a diachronic point of view. It is part of *a history* of relations between work activity and language activity.

At this point I wish to stress, in a necessarily sketchy manner, three broad historical configurations of the language part of work. In the first configuration, language and languages do not contribute to carrying out the job and are, on the contrary, thought to be mutually incompatible. I will be presenting and analyzing archives of workshop rules and regulations (*les règlements d'atelier*). The analysis of this historical body of material shows how a system of industrial workers' speech (*parole*) developed that was made up of constraints, prohibitions and sanctions, a system that Frederic W. Taylor (1911) was to reproduce in his prescriptions and methods for the scientific organization of labor at the beginning of the twentieth century. A second configuration grew out of a first form of exploitation, and consisted of an industrial treatment of the language part of work. As early as the end of the nineteenth century, in the wake of the technical innovations concerning the telephone, the advent of new service activities led to language work, and notably to the emergence of the occupation of "les dames du téléphone" (telephone ladies). The third configuration is contemporary; it is characterized by an extreme merchandizing of the natural resource that the human faculty of speech represents. By analyzing call centers, I will be exposing the present-day specificities of the language part of work, in the form of a three-fold standardization: of voices, of discourses and of languages.

THE LANGUAGE PART OF WORK DURING THE INDUSTRIAL REVOLUTION

In *Discipline and Punish* (1977), Michel Foucault illustrated the continuity that exists among convents, army, schools, hospitals, prisons and industrial workshops. In all those institutions, the same sort of control, organization, architecture, and regulations dominated. At the end of the eighteenth century, the philosopher Jeremy Bentham in particular noted those interrelations; thanks to factory blueprints, he was able to develop the plan of panoptic prisons that permitted the constant sub rosa surveillance of prisoners. Though never actually built on those plans, panoptic prisons and, more generally, panoptic systems were, as Foucault demonstrated, constitutive of institutions of the Industrial Revolution. Workshop rules emerge in the context of the Industrial Revolution and of the development of an economic model that was no longer artisanal but industrial, and were inherited from the rules of the army, convents and schools. Foucault comments on the rules of Christian schools as follows:[4]

> The meticulousness of the regulations, the fussiness of the inspections, the supervision of the smallest fragment of life and of the body will soon provide, in the context of the school, the barracks, the hospital or *the workshop*, a laicized content, an economic or technical rationality for this mystical calculus of the infinitesimal and the infinite. (Foucault 1977, 140; my emphasis)

By posting workshop rules and regulations on the walls, the directors of textile mills, plants, mines, sawmills, printing shops and factories dictated and regulated the way workers were supposed to behave during working hours, any lapse being followed, as we shall see, by strictly codified sanctions. During the nineteenth and the first part of the twentieth centuries (until 1936 in France), workshop rules functioned like a private domestic police force. As such, they were posted in every area where there was production. The law of March 22, 1841, made it mandatory to post the internal regulations in production areas. What is more, they had to be filed with the local sheriff, police or mayor. Litigation concerning the respect of internal regulations could go as far as the jurisdiction of the *Conseils des Prud'hommes*.[5]

Thanks to research carried out by sociologist Alain Cottereau (in Biroleau 1984), the French Bibliothèque Nationale has kept and catalogued a body of 354 workshop rules, covering (in a nonrepresentative manner) the period ranging from 1798 to 1933.[6] The documents are most often workshop wall posters. The number of articles in the 354 documents varies and, consequently, the precision of the rules set forth is also variable: from five to several dozen articles, as in the rules and regulations of the Bessé paper mill in 1846, which include five chapters and fifty-six articles.[7] Though they are not among the most common articles, prohibitions specifically aimed at free speech are nevertheless present in approximately one third of the rules (i.e., about one hundred posters). The various modes of verbal activity, the various language practices of male and female workers are mentioned, such as "whistling, chatting, swearing, shouting, using subversive language" and, depending on the company, diversely sanctioned, from a fine to temporary redundancy:

> Article 23. . . . Deburrers are expressly forbidden from talking with caretakers, or risk a fine that will not exceed seventy centimes in case of a first offence, two weeks' suspension in case of recurrence . . .

> Article 25. Any preparation worker who leaves the job to go talk with a co-worker at another loom or in another shed, will be fined ten centimes for the first offence, twenty-five for the second, two weeks' suspension the third time. (Mr Bureau's Textile Mill, Nantes, 1843)[8]

Prohibitions of a Moral Nature

Some of the prohibitions were meant to pick out and punish those language practices that endanger honesty, decency and tranquility in the work place. "Chatting" or "talking with one's neighbor" were sometimes tolerated, but "shouting, insulting, picking a fight, obscenity" were forbidden. The following excerpts from the rules and regulations of the Bessé paper mill in 1848 contain an impressive array of behavioral prohibitions, including verbal prohibitions such as "quarrelling, insulting, shouting," "uttering licentious words" or reading "aloud":

> Article 40. It is forbidden . . .
> To have meals on the premises;
> To smoke tobacco there;
> To quarrel or fight;

To insult anybody;
To shout;
To sing at the top of one's lungs;
To sing or pronounce licentious words;
To be indecently dressed;
To read, either to oneself or aloud;
To amuse oneself in ways that disturb others and are detrimental to the job.

A recurrent theme among the moral prohibitions is being insulting, injurious, speaking rude words, or being "fresh" to one's superiors, as in the Sondernach Cotton Mill in 1856:

Article 3 In case a worker takes the liberty of stealing, damaging a piece of work, or being impertinent to his masters, he will be expelled on the spot.

The punishment in case of insubordination, that is, lack of respect toward the hierarchy, whether in word or deed, was invariably exclusion, as at Mulhouse Gas factory in 1851:

ART. 3. Workers owe respect, submissiveness and obedience to their superiors and to the employees assigned to supervising and directing their work.

Any worker who speaks rude and injurious words against the foremen or other firm employees while on the job will be dismissed immediately and without notice.

Indecent language, whether uttered against another worker or a foreman, is always prohibited, but the system of punishments distinguishes among them carefully: there are fines for insulting a colleague, but a higher fine, or even, frequently, immediate dismissal in case of insults directed against those in charge:

ART. 8
Quarrels, rude or insulting words against a worker, male or female, or an apprentice, will be fined from 0 fr. 25 to 1 franc accordingly; in case of physical violence, the fine may be raised to 5 francs.

ART. 9
Insults, threats or violence against a foreman or other person in charge of demonstrating or directing the job may incur a fine ranging from *one* to *five francs* or immediate dismissal, accordingly. (Large French optical and eye-glass firm, Ligny, 1900)

Workshop rules and regulations give us a glimpse of workers who shout, insult and use bad language. And also, beyond badly behaved and uncouth workers who utter "rude, injurious, unseemly words," we get a glimpse of workers capable of "plotting, disturbing the peace, making seditious remarks," that is, workers using collective speech to find ways of organizing and resisting the exploitation they endured. As a counterpoint, the image of the model worker—as the bosses would like him to be—emerges: a worker who neither quarrels, nor shouts, swears or sings seditious or licentious songs, who respects his employers and does not insult them, who speaks like an honest man. But the portrait of the real workers is also conjured up: they shout, quarrel, swear, utter seditious words, disturb the peace with indecent songs and language, answer back, and insult their superiors.

Prohibitions Regarding Production Processes

Prohibitions concerning workers' language do not concern only wage earners' lives and moral behavior, but also the work itself. "Speaking, conversing, chatting, singing" are regularly associated with "leaving one's job, going to another workshop." Wage earners' spatial mobility in the workshops, moving about, *conversing*, are often expressed as being in a cause and effect relationship. In order to do the job they were entrusted with, they must remain at their loom, at their post, and not move about the firm to converse:

> ART. 15. Workers are forbidden to leave their job to converse with other comrades, or sing or whistle, or run the risk of being fined 50 centimes. (Workshops Charles Fiechter, Mulhouse, 1866)

It is also stipulated that the worker must concentrate on his job and nothing else, whether the prohibition bears on their verbal activity . . .

> *Discussions, arguments or protesting, which are* UNFAILINGLY DAMAGING FOR THE RAPIDITY AND CORRECT EXECUTION OF WORK, *are formally prohibited*. (Printing shop of the journal *Moniteur Universel*, 1850, Paris)

. . . or on nonverbal activity, such as *"sewing, doing one's hair or getting ready to leave"*:

> Article 6. Order and absolute silence must always be observed in the workshops. It is strictly forbidden, or run the risk of being dismissed, to sing, read, sew and do anything except the job entrusted to the worker. (Textile mill, Lille, 1866)

Prohibitions concerning production are also aimed at the way the job is done. A job well and carefully done implies not speaking so as to avoid being distracted, and remaining attentive, as stipulated in the regulations of a mechanical weaving factory in the Ain Region in 1849:

> Article 4. No worker, male or female, is to leave the loom or go from one workshop to another, for whatever reason, or converse with his/her neighbor. Everyone must pay strict attention to their job.

We are confronted here by a conception of verbal expression, which, in whatever form, is seen exclusively as unproductive, idle chatter that disturbs or hinders labor activity. Each person must pay strict attention to their own work:

> ART. 8—It is forbidden to prevent workers from doing their job by talking with them, or risk paying a fine of 50 centimes. (J. Welter Atelier, Mulhouse, undated)

> ART. 8 Workers are forbidden to talk among themselves in ways that prevent them from doing their job, or risk paying a fine of 10 centimes; those who talk in the stairwells or latrines will be fined likewise. (Duval Textiles, Nantes, 1857)

Workshop rules show that the language part of human activity was envisaged exclusively as contradictory with work activity: it hinders, slows down and distracts workers. It might be said that the language part of work had not yet been acknowledged by employers, though in some very few cases, the rules do mention speech that might be useful for work, and thus permitted:

> Article 7. A fine of fifty centimes will be inflicted upon any worker, male or female, who talk together, *except for what pertains to their job.* (Delcoury Linen mill in Wazemmes, 1856; my emphasis)

The same may be said for the expression "conversation *foreign* to the job at hand," which implies that conversations that are useful for that job may also exist:

> ART. 6. *Any conversation foreign to the job at hand* is forbidden in the workshops: offenders will be punished by fines ranging from fifty centimes to one franc. (Compass plant in Cousances-aux-Bois, 1866; my emphasis)

Consider also the following restrictive formula:

Art. 2.—Spinners and piecers are expressly forbidden to converse with their neighbors or leave their looms, *except when the job calls for it* (Maquet Mill workshops in Harmel, 1855, my emphasis)

But for a few rare examples, workshop rules and regulations only exhibit a view of workers' speech as being morally evil and counterproductive. Later developments in the scientific rationalization of labor (Taylor 1911), and Fordism during the early part of the twentieth century repeated that conception, and until the end of the *"Trente Glorieuses"* in Europe,[9] language activity in factories was seen as liable to disrupt the physical component of labor, and as potentially slowing down productivity. Language was not considered likely to participate in accomplishing a task; its productive role had not yet been imagined, and, in that sense, the language component of industrial labor had yet to be recognized.

FIRST INDUSTRIAL CONFIGURATION OF THE LANGUAGE PART OF LABOR: THE "DAMES DU TÉLÉPHONE"

Throughout the nineteenth century, it was mainly the small farmers or craftsmen leaving the countryside to sell their workforce in the cities or working class suburbs who became part of a proletariat; they progressively penetrated other sectors of the economy, notably the service sector. When one pictures the service sector toward the end of the nineteenth century, one immediately thinks of household services, servants, maids and other domestic employees, or else state employees such as postmen or ticket vendors in the train stations, that is, services that were organized in a traditional rather than industrial fashion. Yet, as of the end of the nineteenth century, a whole service sector had been organized according to the industrial model. In France, such was the case of the telephone service and the large, hand-operated phone centers, between the end of the century to the 1960s; after that time, transmitting had become automatic and telephone operators were no longer in demand.

The work of the "telephone ladies" (*les dames du téléphone*) was conceived of and organized following industrial methods of organization: rationalization, surveillance, timing, the scientific selection of wage earners, and repetitive and routine (including articulatory movements). As of 1918, Fontègne and Solari, labor scientists specialized in professional guidance, closely examined the operators' work in situ (i.e., not in the lab). They studied the women's gestures, their rapidity, responses to visual signals, and vocal messages: gestures were repetitive and continuous; the operators processed ca. 150 calls an hour, up to 350 during peak time. It seemed that the labor activity of these "lady employees" in the early twentieth century was characterized by a tightly controlled organization:

The administration's control and marking system encouraged competition. Posted at regular intervals, female controllers (one for every ten to twelve operators) made sure the system was running smoothly. Some of them went up and down the rows, with note-pads and watches, methodically checking the number of calls the operators dealt with, noting their mistakes, and "assessed" the women's performance. Another group of female controllers listened in on the operators to supervise the quality of communications. The operators were thus under constant pressure to accelerate the calls they put through. (Frader 2006, 134)

The psychiatrist Le Guillant produced a clinical study of the various problems caused by that activity (1956). Among them, he stressed the ways conditions of life at work perturbed life outside of work:

> Operators frequently use by mistake, in daily life, expressions that refer to the job but that come to them automatically. The most frequent, which they say very often and on many occasions, for instance when somebody addresses them suddenly, is: "Hello, please hold on". When entering a place, they declare, *e.g.*: "Paris, 380." Or else they say, when flushing the toilet: "Finished, no-one there." Quite often they laugh about it together, but quite often too, it makes them break into tears. In the metro, when the conductor has pushed the button to start the train, they state their names in loud, clear voices. At the ticket window they subconsciously ask for "two units" instead of two metro tickets, and get angry if made to repeat their request; 20% of the persons examined show they are have in fact been contaminated by those professional phrases (Le Guillant et al. 2006 [1950], 135–136).

Professional expressions suddenly turn up in social situations in which they are completely incongruous and out of place; the expressions escape them, but they are linguistic automatisms rather than Freudian slips, the clinical consequence of a mechanical language activity, controlled and overseen in industrial fashion. We will see next that the work presently being done in call centers is on its way to generating clinical disturbances which, though not exactly the same, are nevertheless comparable.

Though telephony was organized according to industrial methods, there was one major difference with industry, that is, what the rationalization of labor was aiming at. It was not *the physical movement and muscular force*, the flexibility and speed of workers' bodies that were uppermost, as in factories of the Industrial Revolution first, and then in taylorism, but the *articulatory movements* of the women employed by the telephone company and what they entailed in terms of phonation, audition and, more generally, linguistic competencies. Those linguistic and communicative capacities were reduced as we saw to injunctions, orders and very short and repetitive sentences with no organization in the way of discourse patterns: "Hello, one moment please, hold the line"; "Hello, number 12, you have number 8 in Paris," and so on.

The future coupling of telephony with information technology gave way to a new profession, the teleoperator, and a new configuration of the language part of work, characterized by the extreme standardization of professional communications at every level of language: voice, prosody, lexicon, syntax and regional accents (Roy 2000).

SECOND INDUSTRIAL CONFIGURATION OF THE LANGUAGE PART OF WORK: CALL CENTERS

The globalized economy of information (Ducatel et al. 2000; Gorz 2003) has been accompanied by the expansion of teleworking,[10] growing numbers of call centers (in banks, tourism, mail ordering, telecommunications, administration),[11] and the IT off-shoring of a great many service activities (Lanciano-Morandat et al. 2005; Russel 2008). Expansion was made technically possible by crossing the old telephone technology with modern Information Communication Technologies (ICT), today known as the union of telephony and information. This service sector, at the avant-garde of technology, is rapidly growing, both in the industrialized world and the emerging economies (e.g., North Africa, India, Brazil). Call centers may be internal to corporations, as was the case in one of those that I surveyed and mention subsequently. They may also be outsourced, in cases where the service is subcontracted. In that case, the order may emanate from a single company or from several, and the service becomes a multiclient center. Outsourcing can also be off-shoring, that is, geographic, as in the case of Tunisia.

On the physical and perceptual level, work in call centers is characterized by visual activity (on the screen), and by listening and permanent pressure on the ear, due to high decibel levels. Mentally and emotionally, employees are confronted by short, juxtaposed tasks (calls sometimes not exceeding sixty seconds), rapid rhythms and constant surveillance—either by the physical presence of the coach walking up and down through the rows, or by a system of listening in—as well as by potential aggressiveness and verbal violence on the part of the clientele (see INRS website, www. inrs.fr/htm).

Work in call centers has a third characteristic: the language activity carried out there. Though an absolutely central dimension, it should be noted that it is rarely taken into account by sociologists (Buscatto 2002) or economists (Gadray 2003; Gadray and Zarifian 2002) who study those services, or by management: "Communication skills are crucial, but rarely recognized or validated in any formal way. Employees as well as employers bear the consequences" (Bonnafoux et al. 2005, 10). Yet, the activity is entirely linguistic (and both oral and written). Thus, some linguists and sociolinguists have made it their job to describe those skills by observing and recording people on the job (Boutet 2001, 2008; Dubois et al. 2006; Roy 2000).

The labor activity of many wage earners includes both a language component and a nonlanguage component, as in the case of nurses, whose work entails both linguistic (conversations with patients, transmissions, orders, discussions, written prescriptions, etc.) and nonlinguistic activities (various forms of care, home visits, handling the patients, etc.). In call centers, on the contrary, language activity is the entirety of the job, making it one of the "language professions" Marcel Cohen referred.[12] In an anthropological perspective, he showed that human societies have developed techniques of the voice or of the written word that vary historically and culturally. He defined language professions as follows: "Exercising language, remunerated in one way or another, regularly or temporarily, is the occupation of many men in very varied conditions" (1956, 215). He continued, more precisely: "Language professions bring into play relations of value and hierarchy, the special application of intellectual faculties, particular relations to more or less complex material tools, in very different conditions depending on the society" (215). He distinguished "voice technique" and "writing technique."

Concerning professions that make a central use of writing techniques, Cohen described the practices and techniques of engravers, typographers, or pen pushers such as clerks, secretaries, stenographers, and so on. Concerning voice techniques, Cohen reminded us that in many societies, the voice must be learned in order to be used professionally, as in singing, whistling, shouting or speaking. Many professions thus make use of the techniques of the spoken voice: "Priests or sorcerers of different categories, lawyers, political orators, teachers, army officers, narrators and actors, auctioneers, *telephone operators*, TV speakers, etc." (Cohen 1956, 215; my emphasis). The telephone operators of yesteryear as well as the teleoperators of today make use of the techniques of the spoken voice. But, beyond being a language profession, work in call centers today is mainly characterized by an extreme standardization of vocal productions: standardized voices, formatted discourse, and reduction of linguistic variability. Let us look at each one in turn.

Standardized Voices

The management of call centers, which usually takes its cue from marketing and training services, take teleoperators' voices very seriously. As one training service executive put it:

> We work a lot on phone attitudes. The expression "you can hear the smile" is not a glib saying, on the contrary, it's absolutely fundamental. We show them how, by the tone of their voice—that is one of the

exercises they learn at the *École clientèle*—they can influence the emotional context of a conversation . . . Their voices are their most powerful tool for producing contrasting feelings.[13]

For management and training in the call centers, smiling is one of the elements prescribed in telephone work.

The smile is not the only object prescribed in training and control. A whole set of vocal qualities are required. As far as women are concerned, they are asked to express charm, a gift for listening, patience, empathy and sweetness with the clients—they must be seductive (Cameron 2000). As one company doctor, Dr. Arnaudo, remarked about a company specialized in selling banking by phone: "Here, as in most commercial professions, *persuasion calls for seduction.* And that hypothesis seems all the more plausible, and seduction all the more central in these telephone activities, as the tele-actresses dispose of no other support for their persuasion" (2005, 105). All such qualities, transmitted by the voice alone, are what companies call "the commercial sales hook."

In job interviews, as well as in training periods and during monitoring by the coach, management requires standardized voices and formatted speech. It should be stressed that such commercial voice standardization is also liable to be perfectly counterproductive, for clients as well as for companies. Too much formatting may result in stereotyped voices—the "airport voice" that Yvan Fonagy analyzed as being a *"cliché prosodique"* (1983)— that the clientele may rapidly find unbearable. This is also the case of the "sales voice" *cliché prosodique*: very fast speech, few lengthening phrases, a rather monotonous intonation, and very few pauses of a linguistic nature, but rather short breath intakes in syntactically unpredictable places, often accompanied by glottal stops or breaths (Boutet 2008, 156–161). The standard voice imposed by management is not without consequence for wage earners' mental health, their vocal expression being monitored even on the most intimate and personal level, its quality. As ergonomist François Daniellou put it:

> Tele-operators' subjectivity is constantly being threatened. They are asked to express it in order to guarantee the quality of the relationship, to smile because "you can hear the smile" on the phone. But at the same time, it's a formatted, normalized sort of subjectivity that has nothing in common with the whirlpool of desire, anxiety and debates about values that inhabits them. (2006, 46)

A Formatted Professional Discourse

Today, call centers are not all identical as to the management of professional discourse. Depending on the products or services they offer, on the company organization of the call center (internal, external, offshore), depending on the country, the labor activity and communicative competencies required and implemented vary. However, it is possible to point out two extremes: some call centers are patterned on a strictly industrial model, with a rationalization of calling time (forty to sixty seconds per call). Others differ from that model by developing counseling activities, supervised of course, but requiring both more time and a greater personal commitment on the part of the wage earner.

We can broadly distinguish between two broad types of professional communications in the skills and language acts involved in a counselor's language activity: in a selling-and-marketing type approach, there are "outgoing" calls whereby a product or service is being sold are the teleoperator's initiative. The calls known as "incoming" are the client's initiative: he/she calls to buy something (e.g., as in tourism), obtain information from an administration, get advice or solve a problem. The two types of professional communications do not entail the same language activities on the part of the wage earner. Outgoing calls are totally standardized, leaving no room at all for the employee to be autonomous; incoming calls give them a certain amount of leeway.

Some call centers function with outgoing calls alone. The consultant's language activity is generally organized on a taylorized model, their professional dialogues strictly channeled by way of scripts, time control—calls last an average of ca. sixty seconds in such centers—and a rigorous supervision of their communications. Consultants' verbal activity and language practices are restricted threefold: by time, by the obligation to follow the script point by point, and by the supervision of the "coaches" listening in to calls. When a quality approach exists, it is in the form of procedures established by protocols, even by software scripts to assist in decision making. Standardized communicative activity with the client leads certain services to work "with the bases of knowledge and diagnostic procedures (tree sequences of questions to ask the client) that allow them to give the client a quick response without possessing any particular technical know-how. Model building thus allows establishing simple and rationally codified procedures which also permit recruiting a workforce for their personal rather than their formal qualities, therefore being able to cope with a large turnover." (Bonnafoux et al. 2005, 8)

The industrial formatting of discourse that all these IT tools permit, is however not (as yet?) completely widespread. True, the financial structures of management tend to impose scripts and set arguments so as to get the best return out of one's wage earners' working time. But when call centers operate on incoming calls (the clients' initiative), the consultants' language activity is not the same. They are no longer simply voices reciting a script and functioning like vocal robots, but speaking beings engaged in interactions in which they bring to play their own resources and language competencies. It is no longer only a matter of proposing a sale or offering a client information, but of advising, discussing, solving a problem on the telephone. In the various call centers I observed,[14] which were specialized in both consulting and marketing, I was able to observe that the consultants brought into play a large diversity of language skills and acts: they informed, solved problems, reassured, convinced, argued. Their technical skills were visible in the dialogues, for example, giving expert advice on technical systems, solving technical problems, understanding how an installation functions, producing technical diagnoses.

In the following excerpt, for example, the consultant was patiently explaining to an inexperienced woman how to program her electric heating system:

C.:   vous fermez les portes euh les fenêtres vous mettez à fond votre convecteur ou vos convecteurs dans la pièce si vous en avez plusieurs hein

Cl.:   oui

C.:   une fois que votre thermomètre va vous indiquer votre température de confort c'est-à-dire euh 19 20 degrés hein—sauf si pour/ vous êtes peut-être plus frileuse ou moins frileuse—vous adaptez votre température en fonction de votre besoin hein

Cl: oui

C.:   hein personnel—donc quand votre thermomètre vous indique 19 20 degrés c'est ce qu'on préconise euh vous baissez tout doucement votre thermostat—jusqu'à ce que celui-ci se désenclenche— alors euh vous entendez un petit clic—ou alors c'est une lumière qui s'éteint ça dépend les les appareils

Cl.:   dans les—non là y a pas de lumière y a y a un thermostat euh sur le mur enfin que je connais rien du tout là—ça fait comme une petite pendule . . .

C.:   donc je pense que c'est—peut-être simplement un thermostat d'ambiance qui peut-être règle vos convecteurs mais là j'avoue que—je pourrais pas vous le confirmer à 100 pour 100

Cl.:   ben oui oui

C.:   je vais essayer de de de me renseigner quand même—en l'occurrence je pense que vos convecteurs se règlent de façon manuelle hein comme je vous l'ai expliqué

Translation

C.:   you have to close the doors uh the windows you turn your convector up high in the room or convectors if you've got several, er

Cl.:   yes

C.:   once your thermometer shows you've reached a comfortable temperature, that is uh 19–20 degrees, eh—except if you're maybe less prone to the cold–you adapt the temperature to your needs, er

Cl.:   yes

C.:   er personal—so when your thermometer shows 19–20 degrees that's what we recommend uh you lower your thermostat gently—until it turns on—you uh you hear a little click—or else there's a light that goes off it depends on the the equipment

Cl: in the—no there there isn't a light there's there's a thermostat uh on the wall well I don't know anything about it—it's like a little clock . . .

C.:   so I think it's—maybe just a thermostat that maybe turns your heater on but I admit—I can't promise 100 percent

Cl.:   well yeah yeah

C.:   I'm going to try to to to find out anyway—as it is I think you have to turn on your electric heater by hand er the way I explained before.

In such work, where the industrial model leaves them a certain degree of initiative and autonomy, telecounselors use their language resources and their skills to deal with the professional interaction as best as possible: guiding the client, giving, appropriate answers, analyzing the request, coordinating the dialogue, adapting to the client's language and technical level, and informing him/her correctly and precisely.

Reducing Linguistic Particularities

Given the worldwide economy, an increasing number of consultants in call centers must now bring into play not only monolingual communicational skills, but also bilingual or plurilingual competencies (Duchêne 2009; Labrie et al. 2000). Such capacities may have developed in very different sociolinguistic situations, leading to quite different levels of language mastery and forms of bilingualism. They may have been acquired in a bilingual social context, the case for example of French-speaking Canadians in New Brunswick, who, as French speakers, find themselves in a minority situation. A bilingual workforce exists there whose French, until recently, was neither appreciated nor put to any professional use. That bilingual French–English competence, which English speakers rarely possess,[15] is what the bilingual call centers exploit (Dubois et al. 2006; Roy 2000).

A totally different sort of exploitation of employees' bilingual skills is to be found in offshore, unilingual call centers. Only one of the plurilingual wage earner's languages is called for on the job. The others (the wage earner's first language and national and official languages of the countries where the companies have settled), within the prescription of professional communications and contrary to what we saw in New Brunswick, are not considered working languages. The plurilingual repertoire of the teleoperators is not put to use in all its diversity. Only one language is the working language, and it is usually not the wage earner's first language. The working language—the wage earner's second language—is most often English,

French or Spanish. That is the situation in many offshore call centers, as it is in India or Tunisia. Many English-speaking companies have set up their call centers in India: in 2007 it was estimated that 1.6 million wage earners, an educated and young population (between twenty and thirty years old), were working in that sector. India's linguistic situation[16] is characterized by a great number of vernacular languages, spoken by the poorest and most dominated Indians, and by a socially discriminating use of English. As A. Montaut wrote, "One thus returns to the original schism between the elite of dominants and the mass of dominated: if English, as Di Bona noted [1998, p. 370], continues to be the *lingua franca* of politics, education and commerce in India," it is due to a "persistent schism between the world of success and the world of those left behind . . . To know English means to belong to the elite, not to know it means being relegated to the provincial margins of intellectual life" (2004, 82). In a country where only the urban elites speak English, offshore companies thus take advantage of a qualified and cultivated workforce but pay much lower salaries than in the home country.[17] Bilingualism with English, a heritage of British colonization, concerns the urban population alone; call centers are therefore set up in a few capitals such as Bengaluru, Mumbai, New Delhi or Hyderabad. In contrast with call centers in New Brunswick, wage earners' bilingualism or plurilingualism is not given full value in the case of India, since only the English language is called for on the job (whether or not that language happens to be one of the languages acquired in the family, or a second language learned in an institutional situation). Family language or languages do not represent a resource for the company.

The same may be said of the French call centers opened in Tunisia. In 2007, it was estimated that 150 French call centers and 10,000 teleoperators were working there; the sector showed a rate of growth of 60 percent. Again, the workforce is young, college educated, strongly feminized and bilingual (Morlet, forthcoming). Contrary to the British colonization in India that reserved the use of English for the elite, during the period of the French Protectorate (1881–1956) the French imposed and spread the French language throughout the entire population via the administration and especially through French schools. Generations of bilingual Tunisians thus grew up with both Tunisian Arabic and French. After independence, the country chose Arabic as its sole official language, opting for progressive arabization and to maintain French as a second language, today taught as of the third year of primary school. Though French is no longer the first language of the vast majority of Tunisians, it has acquired the status of preferred second language. Consequently, most students are bilingual, representing a reserve supply of French-speaking college graduates for French companies. Their only second language becomes a working language. Tunisian Arabic or Berber are excluded from job prescriptions—but not from actual work situations, since peer communication continues in their first language.

In all these cases, there is an identical prescription for bilingual skills: management imposes similar constraints on various sorts of bilingualism.

The prescription could be summed up by the injunction "make them think you're a native speaker!" Wage earners' bilingualism must be well balanced, their speech show no regional accent, no interference, no borrowings; in short, none of the phenomena normally produced by plurilingual speakers. Every trace of one's own national and linguistic origin must be kept out of sight. In the case of the French call centers in Tunisia, aside from the obligation to speak the French of France, managements' prescription goes so far as to impose changing first names: Latifa, a young Tunisian woman, says into the phone: "Hello, I'm Pauline, can I help you?"; Abdallah, a young Tunisian man, must present himself as "Patrick" (this has of course been by now well documented for call centers in India as well). For the employees, such personality loss does not go without saying. Speaking a second language without any accent is, as everybody knows, nearly impossible, daily placing the wage earner in a situation of professional frustration and failure. What is more, when offshore companies work for several clients (multiclient centers), employees must not only sell several different products in the same day but also assume different identities one after the other, playing separate roles under different aliases. Health in the workplace is severely compromised, and wage earners suffer from stress and identity problems (Morlet, forthcoming).

CONCLUSION

More than one hundred years after the invention of the rationalization of manual labor and piecework, the worldwide economy of information and communications has made it possible to rationalize the processes of articulation. The logics of standardization, of voice, of discourse and of languages, if pushed to their limits, would lead to the disappearance of employees in this sector: they would be replaced by vocal robots, as is already the case in many companies where guiding the client is done by a voice server. Many economic and social factors however impede that process: the low cost of labor (especially in off-shoring), unemployment and the world crisis, as well as considerable turnover, a weak, not to say inexistent, rate of unionizing, and the predictable resistance of the clientele. A technological element tops it off: the fact that automatic translation, though one of the first sectors developed in artificial intelligence, is still not operational.

Worldwide call centers function according to a new capitalist organization of human labor that exploits all of a person's competencies, down to the so-called natural capacity to speak one or more languages. That is the reason some sociologists have termed call centers "service factories" where work is

> hyper-taylorized since Frederick Winslow Taylor's principles of time control are pushed to the extreme, as are too the principles of the prescription and control of its execution, of the strict division of labor between the prescriber-controller and the worker who does the job: as

soon as the teleoperator is "logged on", all his/her activities (including potentially his/her telephone conversations) are recorded, and the technologies being used allow "real time", precise control. (Di Ruzza and Franciosi 2003, 132)

The French CGT (Confédération Générale du Travail), the most important trade union, speaks of "workers of the new economy." I myself categorize these (mostly young and educated) employees as "language workers," although their subjective positioning rarely goes in that direction. Most international research converges around the idea that the sector does represent a contemporary version of taylorism, though neither the content of work, nor the level of recruiting (the majority being taken on with post-secondary education), nor the forms of duress, not even the salaries—which in the emerging countries are vastly superior to local salaries—seem to resemble menial factory labor. This doubtless is what informs the subjective perception of the job by some wage earners who say they are "not factory workers," but rather who feel they are on the same side as the "white-collar workers" in modern companies at the cutting edge of IT. In this, we see a serious social contradiction between the objective reality of the exploitation these employees undergo and their awareness of the actual situation. In the context of a worldwide economy, the outbreak of strikes in France in this sector at time of writing no doubt indicates the rise of a collective consciousness among such language workers.

NOTES

1. Translation: Gabrielle Varro, with the collaboration of Jeremy Paltiel and Monica Heller
2. European linguistic policy has followed that trend by adopting the European Charter for Minority Languages (*Charte européenne des langues minoritaires*). For an analysis of United Nations policies on linguistic minorities, see Duchêne 2008.
3. One must remember that in thirty years we have changed over from Pierre Bourdieu's metaphorical use of "linguistic market" to a literal use of the term "market".
4. Schools founded by Jean Baptiste de la Salle toward the end of the eighteenth century. Foucault commented on the *Traité sur les obligations des frères des Ecoles Chrétiennes* by J.-B. de la Salle, 1783.
5. This social jurisdiction emerged toward the beginning of the nineteenth century. Its purpose is to settle litigation between wage earners and employers. The judges are elected (not professional magistrats). The elected representatives of wage earners and elected representatives of employers are at parity in the Councils.
6. *Règlements d'atelier. 1798–1933* (microfiches, call number: 14 179, 1–354). For a catalog of these fiches: Anne Biroleau, 1984, *Les règlements d'atelier, 1798–1936*, Paris, Bibliothèque Nationale, introduction by Alain Cottereau.
7. Without being exactly repetitive, the rules and regulations are nevertheless very similar, and the sections are often the same: conditions for hiring and firing;

labor organization; log-book kept up to date; quality of work; work time (breaks, meals, bells); how to use tools and machines; cleaning the workshop and cleanliness thereof; workers' funds; workers' behavior (prohibitions concerning drinking, smoking, talking, bringing in strangers, relieving oneself, etc.).

8. I have tried as much as possible to preserve the layout of the regulations as it appeared in the various posters. For the French originals, see the appendix.

9. The "Thirty Glorious Years" were a period of full employment and economic growth. They represented European reconstruction after the Second World War and lasted until the first oil crisis, that is, from 1944 to 1973. The first oil crisis in 1973 caused all the developed countries to reconsider the models of productive organization, in particular taylorism. Consequently, a series of reorganization of systems of production followed one upon another, robotics and computerized labor became generalized and the predominance of industry continued to decrease to the benefit of the service sector. In France, the professional group of employees thus became the majority: 8 million employees vs. 6 million workers.

10. In France, call centers had their economic boom toward the end of the 1990s, later than in North America or Great Britain.

11. In France in 2005, the sector numbered 260,000 wage earners (of whom 70,000 were externalized, that is, subcontracted) and 3,500 call centers. Wage earners in this sector represented 0.75 percent of the active population (vs. 5 percent in the United States). The workforce is strongly feminized (68 percent), young (86 percent are under thirty-five) and educated (over half have done two years of college (Bac + 2); see Bonnafoux et al. 2005.

12. Chapter IV, "Language Professions" (*Les métiers du langage*), pp. 214–226.

13. *Ecole-Clientèle* training program, quoted by Calderon (2005, 85).

14. Survey in eleven call centers across France (three hundred dialogues and over thirty hours of audio-recording) in a large French electric company.

15. According to Dubois et al. (2006, 18), 72 percent of New Brunswick French speakers are bilingual, vs. 15 percent of English speakers.

16. Concerning the actual place and status of English in India, aside from Montaut cited here, see also Chapter 4 in Sonntag (2003).

17. It is of note that job offers in call centers in India are not limited to English-speaking companies. French companies also recruit there, a fact that has led one of the largest Alliance Française (New Delhi) to propose professional French language courses adapted to the needs of the call centers.

REFERENCES

Arnaudo, Véronique. 2005. "L'art du phoning entre séduction et dérapages. Histoire d'un 'harcèlement' sexuel au service de la performance." *Travailler* 13: 95–112.

Biroleau, Anne. 1984. *Les règlements d'atelier, 1798–1936*. Paris: Bibliothèque Nationale.

Bonnafoux, Sylvain, Paul el Gammal and Stéphane Roux. 2005. *Le travail dans les centres d'appels*. Paris: CNAM.

Boutet, Josiane. 2001. "La part langagière du travail. Bilan et évolution." *Langage et Société* 98: 17–42.

Boutet, Josiane. 2008. *La vie verbale au travail. Des manufactures aux centres d'appels*. Toulouse: Octares.

Buscatto, Marie. 2002. "Les centres d'appels, usine moderne? Les rationalisations paradoxales de la relation téléphonique." *Sociologie du travail* 44: 99–117.

Calderon, Juan. 2005. "Le travail face à la restructuration productive: le cas d'un centre d'appels." *Formation Emploi* 96: 11–24.

Cameron, Deborah. 2000. *Good to Talk? Living and Working in a Communication Culture.* London: Sage Editions.

Cohen, Marcel. 1956. *Matériaux pour une sociologie du langage.* Paris: Albin Michel.

Daniellou, François. 2006. "Le sourire doit s'entendre." In *Le travail intenable. Résister collectivement à l'intensification du travail,* edited by Laurence Thery, 39–48. Paris: La Découverte.

Di Ruzza, Renato, and Colette Franciosi. 2003. "La prescription du travail dans les centres d'appels téléphoniques." *Revue de l'IRES* 43: 121–147.

Dubois, Lise, Mélanie Leblanc, and Maurice Beaudin. 2006. " La langue comme ressource productive et les rapports de pouvoir entre communautés linguistiques. " *Langage et Société* 118: 17–42.

Ducatel, Ken, Juliet Webster, and Werner Herrmann, eds. 2000. *The Information Society in Europe: Work and Life in an Age of Globalization.* Lanham, MD: Rowman & Littlefield.

Duchêne, Alexandre. 2008. *Ideologies across Nations: The Construction of Linguistic Minorities at the United Nations.* Berlin: Mouton de Gruyter.

Duchêne, Alexandre. 2009. "Marketing, Management and Performance. Multilingualism as Commodity in a Tourism Call Centre." *Language Policy* 8: 27–50.

Fonagy, Yvan. 1983. *La vive voix. Essais de psycho-phonétique.* Paris: Payot.

Foucault, Michel. 1977. *Discipline and Punish: The Birth of the Prison.* Translated by Alan Sheridan. New York: Pantheon Books.

Frader, Liliane. 2006. "Depuis les muscles jusqu'aux nerfs: le genre, la race et le corps au travail en France, 1919–1939." *Travailler* 16: 111–144.

Gadray, Jean. 2003. *Socio-économique des services.* Paris: La Découverte.

Gadray, Jean, and Philippe Zarifian. 2002. *L'émergence d'un modèle de service.* Rueil Malmaison: Editions Liaisons.

Gorz, André. 2003. *L'immatériel.* Paris: Editions Galilée.

Grin, François, Claudio Sfreddo, and François Vaillancourt. 2010. *The Economics of the Multilingual Workplace.* Oxford: Routledge.

Heller, Monica. 2003. "Globalization, the New Economy and the Commodification of Language and Identity." *Journal of sociolinguistics* 7(4): 473–492.

Heller, Monica, and Alexandre Duchêne. 2007. "Discourses of Endangerment: Sociolinguistics, Globalization and the Social Order." In *Discourses of Endangerment: Interests and Ideology in the Defense of Languages,* edited by Alexandre Duchêne and Monica Heller, 1–13. London: Continuum.

Heller, Monica, and Josiane Boutet. 2006. "Vers de nouvelles formes de pouvoir langagier? Langue(s) et identité dans la nouvelle économie." *Langage et Société* 118: 5–16.

Labrie, Normand, Nathalie Bélanger, Roger Lozon, and Sylvie Roy. 2000. "Mondialisation et exploitation des ressources linguistiques: Les défis des communautés francophones de l'Ontario." *La revue canadienne des langues vivantes* 57(1): 88–117.

Lanciano-Morandat, Caroline, Hiroatsu Nohara, and Robert Tchobanian. 2005. *French Call Centre Industry Report 2004.* LEST - Laboratoire d'économie et de sociologie du travail - CNRS : UMR6123 - Université de Provence - Université de la Méditerranée & Russell Sage Foundation. Accessed June 20, 2011. http://halshs.archives-ouvertes.fr/docs/00/43/01/00/PDF/French-CC-report.pdf

Le Guillant, Roelens, et al. 2006 [1956]. "La névrose des téléphonistes." In *Le drame humain du travail. Essai de psychopathologie du langage,* 131–148. Ramonville, Eres.

Montaut, Annie. 2004. "L'anglais en Inde et la place de l'élite dans le projet national." *Hérodote,* 4(115): 63–89.

Morlet, Thierry. forthcoming. *L'ergonomie face au développement des systèmes de travail off shore: l'exemple de la Tunisie.* Toulouse: Octares.

Roy, Sylvie. 2000. "La normalisation linguistique dans une entreprise: Le mot d'ordre mondial." *La revue canadienne des langues vivantes* 57(1): 118–143.

Russel, Bob. 2008. "Call Centres: A Decade of Research." *International Journal of Management Reviews* 10(3): 195–219.

Sonntag, Selma K. 2003. *The Local Politics of Global English: Case Studies in Linguistic Globalization.* Oxford: Lexington Books.

Taylor, Frederick Winslow. 1911. *The Principles of Scientific Management.* New York: W.W. Norton and Company Inc.

ANNEX

Article 23. . . . Il est expressément défendu aux débourreurs de causer avec les soigneuses, sous peine d'une amende qui ne pourra excéder soixante-dix centimes pour la première fois, et s'il y a souvent récidive, il sera mis en quinzaine de congé. . . .

Article 25. Tout ouvrier de préparation qui quittera son travail pour aller causer avec l'ouvrier d'un autre métier ou d'une autre salle, sera mis à l'amende de dix centimes pour la première fois, vingt-cinq centimes la seconde, et en quinzaine de congé la troisième fois.

Article 40. Il est défendu . . .
D'y prendre aucun repas ;
D'y fumer du tabac
De s'y quereller ou de s'y battre ;
D'injurier qui que ce soit ;
D'y proférer des cris ;
D'y chanter à tue-tête ;
D'y chanter des chansons ou d'y faire entendre des paroles licencieuses ;
D'y être vêtu d'une manière indécente ;
De s'y livrer à aucune lecture, soit en particulier, soit à voix haute ;
D'y prendre des amusements de nature à troubler l'ordre et à nuire au travail.

Article 3 En cas que l'ouvrier se permettrait de voler, gâter expressément un ouvrage quelconque, ou dire des impertinences à ses maîtres, il sera mis à l'instant hors de l'établissement.

ART. 3. Tout ouvrier doit respect, soumission et obéissance à ses supérieurs et aux employés préposés à la surveillance et à la direction des travaux.

L'ouvrier qui profèrerait des paroles grossières et injurieuses contre les contremaîtres ou autres employés de l'usine dans l'exercice de leurs fonctions, serait renvoyé sur le champ et sans avertissement.

ART. 8

Toutes disputes, paroles grossières ou insultantes envers un ouvrier, ouvrière ou apprenti seront passibles d'une amende de 0 fr. 25 à 1 franc suivant le cas ; s'il y avait voies de fait, l'amende pourrait être portée à 5 francs.

ART. 9

Les injures, menaces ou violences envers un contre-maître ou toute autre personne chargée de montrer ou diriger le travail, sont passibles d'une amende de *un* à *cinq francs* ou du renvoi immédiat, selon le cas.

   (Grande fabrique française de verres de lunettes et d'optique, Ligny, 1900)

ART. 15. Il est défendu aux ouvriers d'abandonner leur travail pour causer avec leurs camarades, ainsi que de chanter ou de siffler sous peine d'une amende de 50 centimes. (Ateliers Charles Fiechter, Mulhouse, 1866)

Toute   discussion,   altercation   ou   contestation,—NUISANT INFAILLIBLEMENT A LA CELERITE ET A LA BONNE EXECUTION DU TRAVAIL, *sont formellement défendues.* (Imprimerie du Moniteur Universel, 1850, Paris)

Article 6. L'ordre et le plus grand silence doivent toujours régner dans les ateliers. Il est strictement défendu, sous peine d'amende, de chanter, lire, coudre et de s'occuper de toute autre chose que du travail qui a été confié à l'ouvrier. (Atelier de textile, Lille, 1866)

Article 4. Aucun ouvrier ou ouvrière ne devra pendant les heures de travail quitter son métier ni aller d'un atelier à l'autre, sous quelque prétexte que ce soit, ni causer avec son voisin ou sa voisine, chacun devant s'occuper attentivement de son travail.

ART. 8—Il est défendu d'empêcher les ouvriers qui travaillent par des causeries et d'arrêter sa besogne par là, sous peine d'une amende de 50 centimes. (J. Welter Atelier, Mulhouse, undated)

ART. 8 Il est défendu aux ouvriers de causer entre eux de manière à nuire au travail, sous peine de 10 centimes d'amende ; il y aura la même amende pour ceux qui feront la conversation dans l'escalier ou dans les latrines. (Duval *Textiles*, Nantes, 1857)

Article 7. Seront punies d'une amende de cinquante centimes tout ouvrier ou ouvrière qui converseront ensemble, *sauf pour ce qui est relatif à leur besogne.* (Filature de lin de Delcoury à Wazemmes en 1856 ; je souligne)

ART. 6. *Toute conversation étrangère au travail* est interdite dans les ateliers : tout contrevenant sera puni d'une amende de cinquante centimes à un franc. (Manufacture de compas à Cousances-aux-Bois en 1866 ; je souligne)

Art. 2.—Il est expressément défendu aux fileurs et rattacheurs de causer avec leurs voisins ou de quitter leurs métiers, *à moins que ne l'exige le besoin du service* (Filature des ateliers Maquet à Harmel en 1855)

11 Silicon Valley Sociolinguistics?

Analyzing Language, Gender and *Communities of Practice* in the New Knowledge Economy[1]

Bonnie McElhinny

INTRODUCTION

In an article in *The Systems Thinker*, Juanita Brown and David Isaacs argue for "Conversation as a Core Business Process." It is time for managers to recognize, they argue, that "'the grapevine' is not a poisonous plant to be cut off at the roots, but a natural source of vitality to be cultivated and nourished" (1996–1997, 1). "Conversations," they insist, "are as much a core business process as marketing, distribution, or product-development" (1). A key method through which companies can harness this organizational intelligence is through "the discovery" of communities of practice, "self-organizing networks [which] are formed naturally by people engaged in a common enterprise—people who are learning together through the practice of their real work" (2). The phrase "community of practice" (henceforth, *CofP*) is generally said to have been coined by Jean Lave and Etienne Wenger in 1991 in their book *Situated Learning: Legitimate Peripheral Participation*, a study of the social organization of learning in a variety of professional groups that were inducting and training new members, and perpetuating routines for set tasks (see also Wenger 1998).[2] Although, as we will see, CofPs have been defined somewhat differently in different settings, Eckert defines a CofP as

> an aggregate of people who come together around some enterprise. United by this common enterprise, people come to develop and share ways of doing things, ways of talking, beliefs, values—in short, practices, as a function of their joint engagement in activity. . . . It is not the assemblage or the purpose that defines the community of practice; rather, a community of practice is simultaneously defined by its membership and the shared practice in which that membership engages. (2000, 35)

One of the central theoretical goals of materialist feminism is to understand "why representations of identity are changing. . . . and how these changes in identity are connected to historical shifts in the production of life under late capitalism" (Hennessey and Ingraham 1997, 9). In this chapter, I take up this challenge by considering CofP, a way of understanding identity and interaction that has become widely used in linguistic anthropology (especially in feminist analyses) to challenge structural-functionalist accounts of social relations, bounded notions of speech community and essentialist accounts of identity (Eckert and McConnell-Ginet 1992, 1995; Holmes and Meyerhoff 1991). CofP has also, however, circulated widely in corporate circles, as an innovative strategy for institutional reorganization. Drawing on Emily Martin's (1994) work on how ideologies of flexibility play into neoliberal visions of bodies and corporate culture, I offer a critical overview of recent writings on CofPs by business consultants and in business journals, considering when and how representing the self as performed may contribute to the formation of a subject more adequate to a globally dispersed, multinational corporate culture (Hennessey 1993, 6), and when it may be used to challenge reified notions of identity and social relations in ways that envision alternatives to such cultures. The notion of CofP can be seen as an attempt to meet the late capitalist challenge of developing new tools, new definitions of community, and new definitions and forms of interaction that go beyond the traditional focus on fixed places, moments and groups described by Heller and Duchêne (this volume). This chapter thus contributes to a growing body of literature on language ideologies that considers how "different images of linguistic phenomena gain social credibility and political influence," both within linguistic disciplines and beyond (Gal and Woolard 2001, 2). It considers how globalization might not just lead us to new topics for analysis, but also new methods for managing and organizing knowledge, and asks us to consider in detailed ways how sociolinguistic scholars and corporations are all trying to elaborate new ideologies of personhood, community and organizational structure, and what the differences and similarities between those might be. Finally, the chapter asks when academic analytic notions might be complicit with hegemonic ideologies about globalization and when they might contest them.

The article in *The Systems Thinker* (Brown and Isaacs 1996–1997) is just one of dozens of articles in corporate organizational circles which has taken up, tested, developed and trumpeted the notion of CofP in the past twenty years as a tool to "support strategic conversation as a key business leverage" (2), and as a strategy for enhancing organizational performance and making the most of intellectual capital (see the following especially salient citations for examples of the use of the notion in a range of realms: Agresti 2003; Bond 2004; Brown and Duguid 1991; Cox 2005; Endsley, Kirkegaard and Linares 2005; Gongla and Rizzuto 2001; John 2006; Kimble, Hildreth and Wright 2000; Lesser and Everest 2001; Lesser and Storck 2001; Liedtka 1999; McDermott 1999; Mitchelle, Wood and Young 2001; Swan, Scarbrough and Robertston 2002; Vlaenderen 2004; Wenger 1998; Wenger, McDermott and Snyder 2002; Wenger and Snyder 2000). In the spring of 2006, CofP had 26 million hits on Google. Articles carefully parse the differences between *project teams, formal work groups, informal networks* and *CofP* (cf. Wenger and Snyder 2000) as well as other relevant units of social interaction, as they consider how to improve service and product delivery. CofPs are now seen as key to the knowledge management strategies of such influential organizations as the World Bank, DaimlerChrysler, American Management Systems, IBM Global Services, the Mexican Conservation Learning Initiative, Medico, and the European Aerospace, Defence and Space Corporation. Business school scholars elaborate on how to "build business value through communities of practice" and how to "link competitive advantage with communities of practice" (Liedtka 1999). The elaboration of the value of CofP becomes the elaboration of certain ideologies about *conversation, interaction, community,* as well as about *corporations, knowledge, productivity* and *innovation.*

In the same period, CofPs have become a key analytic tool for sociolinguists, especially scholars working on language and gender. Scholars meticulously parse the differences between *speech community, network analysis, intergroup theory* and *CofPs* (Davies 2005; Meyerhoff 2002), as they consider how to improve social scientific understandings of how communities, interaction and language work. The elaboration of the value CofPs becomes, here too, the elaboration of certain ideologies about *language, discourse, interaction,* and *community* as well as about *objectivity, innovation and change,* and perhaps *scholarly productivity.* CofP (and related concepts, like "best practices) has become a keyword in the new knowledge economy.

The notion of keywords is adapted from Raymond Williams' *Keywords* (1976). The significance of keyword analysis arose for Williams during the writing of what became *Culture and Society,* published in 1958. There, he examined intellectual and historical changes in the use of five keywords: *culture, class, art, democracy* and *industry.* Williams continued to use his approach to analyze issues of contemporary political and economic concern: in a brief paper published in 1985 in the *New Socialist* he analyzed four key words—*management, economic, community* and *law-and-order*—in a coal miners' strike.

Williams was resolutely interested in historicizing the rise of certain formulations, but also in criticizing them. He notes that though, in the main, speakers of the same language use the same words to mean the same things, certain terms—keywords—become sites at which the meaning of social experience is negotiated and contested. Williams wanted to record the variability in meanings available for these words, but he also wanted to consider the often implicit connections that certain meanings had with markedly different ways of understanding culture and society. Literary critic Michael McKeon (1977) argues that keywords are those words which are complex or difficult because (a) they connect areas that we tend to keep separate, (b) they are words whose continuous verbal identity masks radical semantic variation and (c) they often express a contradiction. McKeon argues that

Williams' contribution is to move beyond a chronological approach to historical semantics to a dialectical one (130). In Williams' account semantics becomes not only historical, but also political and critical; lexical analysis becomes a discussion of ideology and hegemony (see Fraser and Gordan 1994). It is precisely here, in this move away from a narrow notion of history, that Williams' work bears some similarity to Foucaultian style genealogy. Lexical labels are one kind of contested representation. Indeed, rather than being dismissed because they are minimal, this minimalism itself requires explanation: how do complex, contextually nuanced discussions get summed up in, entextualized through, a single word? How do words become "compacted doctrines"?

This chapter will (a) analyze the ideologies of language and culture evident in the ways the keyword CofP is used in key articles in the corporate and NGO management literature, and (b) compare the ways CofP is used in feminist and corporate literatures. There are other key social domains where the notion of CofP has also been extensively developed, most notably education, including but not exclusively online education (Gulledge 2007; McLaughlin and Talbert 2006; Ruopp et al. 1992; Palincsar et al. 1998; Palincsar et al. 2004; Schlager et al. 2002). There is, as Gee (2000) notes, a close relationship between the changing forms that work takes, and the ways educational practices are changed, putatively in order to train students for these changing formations; this relationship is an important one to explore further. For the purposes of this chapter, though, I focus on the corporate and feminist literatures; the feminist literature has, as its implicit or explicit aim, critique and transformation of current inequitable social formations. It is thus particularly crucial to consider whether and how our units of social scientific analysis are implicated in ongoing processes of globalization, and the implications of this for the possibility of critique.

STUDYING LINGUISTIC IDEOLOGIES

To study corporate and scholarly frameworks about language is to study ideologies about language. Studies of face-to-face interaction have long been privileged in sociolinguistics and linguistic anthropology, as in anthropological studies more broadly. Gal (1998, 333) argues that one of the salutary effects of recent work in linguistic anthropology is the expansion of empirical foci from face-to-face talk to studies of mass media and the ways they connect disparate communities and textual debates. This does not mean that studies of face-to-face interaction have been displaced, but rather that they have been decentered. Two interrelated arenas in which this transformation has taken place are in studies of languages and publics (Gal and Woolard 2001) and in studies of language ideology (Blommaert 1999; Kroskrity 2000; Schieffelin et al. 1998). Both bodies of work are interested in how "different images of linguistic phenomena gain social credibility and political influence" and "the role of linguistic ideologies and practices in the making of political authority," both within linguistic disciplines and beyond (Gal and Woolard 2001, 2). These methods for analysis also force an attention to history, by asking us to think about when, how and to what ends certain ideas are produced (Inoue 2006; Irvine 2001; Irvine and Gal 2000; McElhinny 2010; Weidman 2006).

Some of the most compelling work on linguistic ideologies comes from studies of colonial era issues (Woolard 1998, 24). Studies of colonial linguistics examine dictionaries, grammars and language guides to show the ways that linguists constructed rather than discovered distinctive linguistic varieties, and the ways their ideas about language were shaped by their own ideas about nation, racialized ethnicity, kinship and gender, as they show how linguistic differences became a resource for naturalizing inequality in colonial settings (Bauman and Briggs 2003; Errington 2008; Fabian 1986; Irvine 2001; McElhinny 2005, 2010; Rafael 1988; Said 1978; Trechter 1999). The ways that our current categories and strategies for analysis might also be inflected by hegemonic political and economic trends has generally received much less analysis—for reasons, perhaps, that are obvious. It is harder to gain perspective on contemporary trends, to escape dominant ideologies and to capture a sense of ongoing, incomplete shifts in paradigms and perspectives. Not all studies of language ideology do this; as Philips (1998, 213) notes, some studies of ideology are merely substituting that concept for the notion of *culture*, in ways that lose the meaning of the word ideology as elaborated within a long Marxist tradition of analysis, and that attend to questions of history and power. Nonetheless, some fine examples of such work include Hill's (2002) analysis of the commodification of endangered languages, and the dangers of certain metaphors about endangered languages, and Heller's (1999) account of why variationist sociolinguistic studies enjoyed particular popularity in Quebec in the 1970s and 1980s as a strategy for legitimizing the local variety of French. (See also the forms of historicization discussed in other chapters in this volume.)

The introduction to this volume flags the emergence in the 1990s of more and more discursive elements that treat language primarily in economic rather than political terms—with an implicit focus on those realms where one would not have seen this emphasis in the past. Also of interest is the changing ways language is understood in corporations, where one might have already expected an economic emphasis. In recent years, new management styles adopted in the context of global competition have intensified awareness of language in corporate circles as something that needs to be managed, in order to enhance productivity or produce corporate brands (see Cameron 2000a, 2000b; Gee, Hull and Lankshear 1996). The interest in CofPs also reflects this new interest in managing interactions in corporate circles (see McElhinny 2010 for further reviews of work on language and neoliberalism). In examining contemporary linguistic ideologies, I turn first to the corporate literature and then to the feminist linguistics literature.

"LINKING COMPETITIVE ADVANTAGE WITH COMMUNITIES OF PRACTICE": CORPORATE DISCOVERIES OF COMMUNITY OF PRACTICE

Not all corporations may be interested in corporate restructuring. As Heller and Duchêne (this volume) note, an emphasis on flexibility in the new economy exists in tension with a focus on increasing taylorization. Arguably, also, a focus on tertiarization has a different kind of weight in national settings that are losing primary and secondary sectors to other global sites than in those sites that are still gaining primary and secondary sectors. Corporations attracted to the competitive advantage associated with CofPs may be those that focus more on the production and circulation of information and symbolic goods, rather than those focused on the production of services or products or services or products or on harvest and extraction. Nonetheless, there are discussions of the utility of CofPs in a wide range of settings, from family medicine to the European defense industry, from IBM to community development work. Corporate proponents of the notion of CofP write about it with the kind of breathless prose associated with the release of a new kind of dishwashing detergent. They are a new tool, a new product, something to be "discovered" and "identified." Hinton argues that "Communities of Practice arose as a tool to facilitate knowledge sharing in a learning environment" (2003, 6), while Brown and Isaacs talk about the "discovery" of CofP (1996–1997, 2). Even Etienne Wenger wrote in a widely cited article in the *Harvard Business Review* (Wenger and Snyder 2000) that "a new organizational form is emerging" and that "communities of practice are the new frontier." Such strategies for framing CofPs take it from concept and keyword to buzzword, from contested tool to promotional discourse.

In the context of changing industrial reorganization, corporations are being advised to reorganize from Fordist models to "learning organizations" that must adapt if they want to survive (Martin 1994, 209). In order to counter precisely such understandings (understandings for which he is not entirely blameless!) and to challenge the idea that CofPs are a "fad," Etienne Wenger has also more recently weighed in with the explanation that "communities of practice are not a recent invention. They are not a business technique. They have been with us since the beginning of humankind" (2005, 1). The point, though, is not whether CofPs are new or old. Invocations of tradition and timelessness themselves are ideological, used to construct the inevitability of a particular notion of social formation (Bauman and Briggs 2003; Inoue 2006). The key question is why CofPs are newly fashionable.

In a useful review article, economic geographer Meric Gertler contextualizes the interest in CofPs within a larger interest in "tacit knowledge" in new economies. In studies of innovation that assume that the production and dissemination of knowledge is a fundamental characteristic of contemporary capitalist dynamics, a key distinction is made between tacit and codified knowledge. The tacit component of knowledge is that "defies codification or articulation—*either* because the performer herself is not fully conscious of all the secrets of successful performance or because the codes of language are not well enough developed to permit clear explication" (2003, 78). In an era when everyone is presumed to have relatively easy access to codified knowledge, tacit knowledge has come to preoccupy management theorists because the creation of unique products/processes is seen to rely upon accumulating and leveraging "intangible" assets. Tacit knowledge is seen as particularly recalcitrant because it defies easy articulation, can only be acquired experientially, may require a shared social context and is difficult to exchange over long distances. The knowledge management literature is thus concerned with how to *produce tacit knowledge*; how to *find, measure and appropriate tacit knowledge*; and how to *share tacit knowledge*, especially amongst organizations with different units that are located far from one another.

Gertler argues that at least three different solutions are conventionally presented to these problems in the industrial management literature, each of which contains its own ideologies of space and scale and, I would argue, communication: *learning regions, knowledge enablers* and *CofPs*. The *learning region* literature principally addresses the dilemma of how tacit knowledge is shared, arguing that tacit knowledge does not travel easily; it argues for (or assumes) the importance and necessity of face-to-face interaction between partners with basic similarities (characterized by Gertler as "the same language, common 'codes' of communication, shared conventions and norms, and personal knowledge of each other based on past histories of collaborations" [2003, 84]), and assumes that industries will look locally first for appropriate forms of tacit knowledge. Certain places, like Silicon Valley in the United States, or the Ottawa region in Canada, are seen as regions where relevant tacit knowledge is produced, and are seen to have perhaps an uncatchable economic advantage, because they are the "first movers" in certain industries.

The literature on a *knowledge enablers'* perspective documents the use of knowledge activists (sometimes, management consultants) who diffuse tacit knowledge, making heavy use of "structured story-telling" (Lesser and Storck 2001, 84) and sharing "war stories" (Hinton 2003, 6). Production of tacit knowledge remains localized, but this perspective is more optimistic about its wider dissemination through certain key individuals than the learning regions perspective.

The *CofPs* perspective is seen as distinct from each of these, in that (in at least some iterations) it de-emphasizes the necessity of face-to-face interaction for the production of tacit knowledge and is more optimistic about the possibilities for ready diffusion of tacit knowledge. CofPs are often seen as groups which self-organize to solve problems; the members' shared background is said to facilitate the sharing of tacit knowledge, again with "story-telling" being seen as key. However, they may do this online, at a distance, and so on. Taken as a group, all of these "learning-through-interacting" models tend to reinforce the local over the global, in ways which purport to explain geographical concentration in the context of expanding markets, weakening borders, and cheaper and more pervasive communication technologies (Gertler 2003, 76; see also Duguid 2008a).

In business circles, CofPs are contrasted with *departments, divisions, teams, taskforces, formal workgroups* and *informal networks* (see Agresti 2003, 27; Por and von Bekkum 2003, 5; Wenger and Snyder 2000, 142). The parsing of these differences varies according to different authors' slightly different agendas; however, the sharpest division is between formal and informal groups, which are often also contrasted in terms of management vs. peer control. *Teams* and *workgroups* are assigned specified tasks—to deliver a product or service—with assignments made by management, and the manager responsible for their operation, and are held together by job requirements, or milestones and goals. *CofPs* are generally seen as voluntary, peer-governed, created by members themselves, and held together by a shared passion in the area of the group's expertise, with a key goal being the development of members' own capacities and exchanges of knowledge. John Seely Brown, former director of Xerox Corporation's Palo Alto Research Center (PARC), describes them not as a team or task force or authorized or identified group, but peers in the execution of the "real work" of the organization, held together by a common sense of purpose and a real need to know what others know (cited in Amidon, 1997, 1). CofPs are generally seen as being composed of people with shared or similar types of work, rather than the different kinds of work that may be brought together by more formal teams. There is an extensive literature assessing the utility of CofPs for organizations. However, CofPs are generally promoted as having at least five valuable functions in corporations and NGOs: (1) socializing novices, (2) developing and managing institutional memory and knowledge, (3) being more flexible than traditional corporate hierarchies, (4) serving as "safe" places to try out innovation and (5) helping to construct virtual communities in a global economy. I treat each of these in turn now.

First, CofPs are seen as good for socializing novices, and thus for codifying and sharing tacit knowledge. In the corporate literature, the dilemma this is framed as addressing is the fact that talented knowledge workers may circulate amongst different sites or between different organizations, or both. This implies significant agency for workers that belies the experience of many workers themselves (a point I discuss further below). A number of articles focus on the need for incorporating new members of an organization into the community (Lesser and Storck 2001, 832), in order to rapidly increase their productivity, particularly in organizations that are dispersed and where supervisors are in different sites (836).

Second, CofPs are seen as good for developing and maintaining long-term organizational memory. Lesser and Storck (2001) studied ten companies with "existing communities of practice" (for sociolinguists, of course, this raises the question of what a company without a CofP might look like) and found that in virtually every case a CofP resulted in the development of a structured repository, where workers deposited "knowledge artifacts" like research papers, presentations and other forms of intellectual capital that could be used by others. In CofPs, people transfer and formalize "tacit knowledge." Though this could again be framed as a way of dealing with the worker who "chooses" to move on (e.g., in an entrepreneurial spin-off that becomes a competitor), it is also notably an effective strategy for capturing the social and intellectual capital of workers who might be laid off at times of corporate downsizing.

Third, CofPs are seen as flexible, as a way of overcoming the problems of slow-moving, traditional corporate hierarchies in a fast-moving virtual economy (Lesser and Storck 2001, 832), as a way of handling unstructured problems and sharing knowledge outside of traditional structural boundaries. Bond (2004) believes CofPs negotiate the duality of structure, that is, the dilemma that structure enables as it constrains, and that overly institutionalized communities seek to conserve existing practices rather than promote innovations. In order to develop new competencies and creative solutions to problems, organizations are supposed to be autonomous, flexible and responsive. Note the flexibility described here is not affixed to individuals but rather to organizations.

Fourth, CofPs are said to act as breeding grounds for innovation because they are "safe" places to share challenges (Lesser and Storck 2001, 839). The focus on peer interaction is seen as constructing a shared set of common goals. Peer interaction here is idealized as nonconflictual, as indeed it has sometimes been in some sociolinguistic accounts (see McElhinny 1997).

Finally, the principal question debated about CofPs in the management literature is whether they are effective for addressing the dispersal of corporate sites (cf. Gertler 2008 for a review; Lesser and Storck 2001). Gertler (2001) notes that for CofP proponents occupational proximity (and often similarity) is seen as more significant than geographical proximity, and so learning is seen as possible at a distance using new technologies and business travel. The "local" is thus not seen as critical for competitive advantage. However, Gertler notes that a focus on occupational similarity does not explain how relational proximity is cultivated, nor does it consider how

> systemic institutional influences might play an important role in helping determine which practices will flow between locations most easily and which will not. The unspoken assertion in the communities of practice literature is that the adoption of new routines . . . is a relatively easy and unproblematic matter, depending solely on the volition of the individuals comprising the community of practice and an enlightened senior management. (2001, 26)

Gertler notes that Brown and Duguid (2000) stand in clear contrast to other proponents of CofPs in arguing that CofPs are usually most productive and creative when they are face-to-face communities that meet regularly and develop their own subculture, style, judgment and slang.

Strikingly, also, the emphases embedded in the notion of CofPs align with an Anglo-American industrial model, which is distinguishable from other models (Japanese, German, etc.). Gertler (2003) (drawing on Christopherson 2002 and Lam 2000, 91–92) argues that under different models of governing capital, labor and corporate governance, the concept of the firm will vary, and so will the kinds of social relationships that form between economic actors. The American-style industrial model is shaped by the drive to maximize short-term investment returns, so that U.S. strengths have emerged in project-oriented industries like electronic media, computer services, advertising, engineering and industrial design. Because U.S. workers have little expectation of continuous employment, there is little loyalty to employers, and trust is invested more in other workers in similar positions rather than employers. The employees themselves act as individual technology-transfer agents, and thus as the route for the sharing of tacit knowledge. Within such a context, the influence of the employer's practices is overstated, while the significance of national institutional features is understated (Gertler 2003, 93). This is also true, I will argue, of the literature in feminist sociolinguistics. In its focus on peer relations and individuals, rather than on larger scales of social interaction, CofP thus could be said to reflect ideologies of social relations framed within Anglo-American industrial structures.

SILICON VALLEY SOCIAL SCIENCE?
COMMUNITY OF PRACTICE IN SOCIOLINGUISTICS

A year after Lave and Wenger (1991) was published, Penny Eckert and Sally McConnell-Ginet (1992) published an influential article on CofPs that disseminated the concept to, and has influenced its use in, sociolinguistics. As Murray's (1998) study of social networks in the development of sociolinguistics argues, we need to use our own tools as social scientists to elaborate sociological histories of how ideas arise and disseminate.

A key site at which CofP was extensively developed was the Institute for Research on Learning (IRL), in Palo Alto, California, where Etienne Wenger (now an independent consultant) and Penny Eckert (now a faculty member at Stanford) both worked, alongside other well-known ethnographers and linguists interested in corporate interaction (e.g., Brigitte Jordan and Charlotte Linde). IRL was situated close to Stanford, and to many key Silicon Valley corporate campuses. An online description describes IRL as a non-profit organization founded in 1986 in Palo Alto, California, committed to understanding what leads to successful learning in the schools, the workplace, and everyday life. A basic premise of IRL research, that people learn best when they are engaged with others, leads IRL's researchers to perceive schools and workplaces as communities of learners and to focus on the design of environments, technology, and activities that support learning as a collaborative activity. IRL pursues its research in collaboration with schools, universities, corporations, and government agencies—in the actual settings in which learning takes place.[3]

IRL was already a rather hybrid sort of research organization, connected in complicated ways with XEROX PARC (where linguistic anthropologists Marjorie Harness Goodwin and Charles Goodwin also spent a year as they continued to develop their approach to language as an *activity*, which has some resonance with notions of *practice*). IRL was a relatively short-lived institution (about ten years), funded initially by XEROX in 1986 with the hope of developing some kind of intelligent tutoring system.

I was associated with IRL as a "legitimate peripheral participant"; I was a graduate student in linguistics at Stanford from 1987 to 1993. I regularly visited Penny Eckert, a member of my dissertation committee, at IRL, participated in a weekly discourse analysis session run by Brigitte Jordan, and was hired as an research assistant for a project directed by IRL employee Charlotte Linde, in which I analyzed and coded videotapes of when and how people in two different settings used new computer technology in their workplaces.

Penny Eckert (Stanford) and Sally McConnell-Ginet (Cornell) both have positions at influential U.S. institutions for the education of graduate students, taught a widely attended course on language and gender in 1991 that introduced the notion of CofP to a wide audience of graduate students and faculty at the University of California Santa Cruz who were participating in one of the biennial summer institutes sponsored by the Linguistic Society of America, and played key roles in the development of the International Gender and Language Association, which grew out of the regular conferences hosted by the Berkeley Women and Language group. It's not at all inappropriate, then, to frame the notion of CofPs as Silicon Valley social science—a notion developed by and within a distinctively hybrid organization, to meet the distinctive challenges of its place and time.

As Meyerhoff (2002) and others have noted, CofP has been widely embraced by researchers working on language and gender, but has not been as extensively used by scholars working on racialization, ethnicity, aging or other axes of social differentiation. CofP participates in a family cluster of notions in studies of language and gender—gender as activity, gender as performance, gender as accomplishment, gender as practice—all of which suggest that gender is something one continually does in order to challenge the idea that gender is something one has (McElhinny 2003). Although these all have slightly different trajectories, histories and uses, they all critique essentializing analytic categories, since gender (like "race") remains stubbornly linked to essentialist biological explanations in both popular and scientific discourse (Cameron 2006). CofP differs from these other concepts in having a more highly developed theory of how learning takes place, and a more developed notion of community. CofP is attractive to gender researchers because it offers strategies for investigating gender as a learned and thus mutable category, it foregrounds the likelihood of and reasons for differences among women and men (including crosscultural variability) and it suggests how gendered practices might vary across the life span, through participation in different practices (Mallinson and Childs 2007; Meyerhoff 2002, 539).

If the corporate literature has as its sharpest distinction the difference between the formality of departments, taskforces and formal workgroups and the relative informality of CofPs, in sociolinguistics CofP is distinguished from *speech communities* and *social networks* (Davies 2005; Meyerhoff 2002). Creese (2005) notes that both speech community and CofP share a resistance to the idea of a normative human subject, either as ideal speaker or a rational learner; as a consequence both share a commitment to ethnography. Miriam Meyerhoff succinctly summarizes the way most sociolinguists understand the notion of community of practice: it is a "recent addition to the sociolinguistic toolbox" (2002, 526) or a "novel perspective" (527), but not a novel social form, and not an analytic meant to replace others. The difference between speech community and CofP is sometimes said to be one of scale: CofP usually picks out a smaller group than that picked out by speech community. More critically, however, and probably more precisely, the use of CofP is meant to complicate some of the abstractions associated with groupings according to ethnicity, gender or shared place of living: it is not meant "to dispense with global categories, but to attach them to personal and community experience in such a way that the structure of variation makes everyday sense" (Eckert 2000, 222). CofPs offer a way of explaining, as Eckert and McConnell-Ginet (2007, 35) note, apparently contradictory aggregated data. A CofP also does not focus exclusively on language, but looks at other semiotic practices by which speakers construct and maintain social categories. Social networks and CofPs are distinguished in part by degrees of agency (membership in a dense network can be by chance, but in a CofP is purposive) (Meyerhoff 2002, 531); Holmes and Meyerhoff (1991) argue that social networks are more role based, vs. practice based, and thus the links are more structurally understood.

There are a variety of ways of writing the intellectual history of the notion of "practice," each of which legitimates different political and analytic practices. Although many commentators start with Bourdieu, Klassen's (2008) particularly helpful and succinct account begins with Karl Marx's notion of praxis as a way of centering critical analyses that consider the relative forms of power maintained by dominant and dominated classes, and strategies for transformation of social structures and practices that collude in oppression. She traces a genealogy forward through Pierre Bourdieu's work on practice, defined as taken for granted, habitual, common sense; Michel de Certeau's distinction between practices (of the powerful) and tactics (of the less powerful); and Henri Lefebvre's notion of inventive praxis (which attended to the habitual like Bourdieu, but also practices of transformation like Marx). Klassen (2008, 148) argues that practice serves to draw scholars away from doctrinal and official discourses of religions, states, and elites, and toward the "everyday" actions, movements and sensations of "ordinary" people in ways that reorient scholars from a focus on large-scale social and economic structures to the agency and action of people living within those structures.

Like other kinds of practice theory, the notion of CofP reacts against structural-determinist social theories (e.g., British-American structural-functionalism, determinist strands of Marxism and French structuralism) that did not incorporate a sufficient sense of how human actions make structure (cf. McElhinny 1998). In a general account of practice theory, Ortner (1996) points out that the practice-based approach moves beyond a view of social behavior as ordered by rules and norms, but that it also grants actors a great deal of agency, thus perhaps reproducing the hegemonic model of personhood (abstract individualism) of Western commodity-based societies. Davies (2005) too critiques what she sees as an implicit focus on choice in the notion of CofP. In the case of sociolinguistic theory, the sense of structure critiqued is that which was elaborated in some of the earliest and best-known large studies of sociolinguistic variation and change, where a tendency to view individual behavior as merely reproducing the structures of the group denied individual agency, collapsed the notion of social structure with the notion of style, and assumed static categories of class, gender and race that were presupposed as relevant, and understood as directly rather than indirectly indexed by speech (Davies 2005, 559). Notions of CofPs react against structural models, but these models, like the corporate models that Martin describes, may be already disappearing.

In critiquing the celebration of flexibility in many different realms, Martin (1994) asks whether the embrace of practice-based theory allows us to resist older systems, but not see emerging systems with new forms of repression. She herself notes that there is some delight in seeing changes in new corporations that eliminate some management–labor hierarchies, try to include women and minorities more, integrate mental and manual labor, and treat workers as whole people, while employing agile and innovative people. She is worried, however, that this ideal (like any other) presents a narrow ideal of the able person that will discriminate against many, underplays the physical and emotional effects of changes on downsized workers, and passes over the loss of jobs with pensions, health insurance and unemployment insurance. Stability, security and stasis are also, she argues, valuable.

CONCLUSIONS: LINGUISTIC IDEOLOGIES OF PERFORMANCE AND FLEXIBILITY

When I first presented this material at a conference, some questioners assumed I was looking at how corporations adopted CofP from social scientists as a new organizational buzzword and then "corrupted" it. A sophisticated version of this argument is that of Lave, who notes the ways the notion of CofP has traveled in ways that were sometimes generative, sometimes worrisome, and flags (using personalistic linguistic ideologies of meaning—Hill 2008) that the term was not intended to be normative or prescriptive but rather descriptive, and those who use it seem ignorant of these original intentions (2008, 283). She also asks why the notion of CofPs "migrated" into business and education—though arguably it was embedded in these from the start (294). The attempt to draw the boundary can itself be seen as trying to clearly separate zones corrupted by capitalist forces from those that are not so troubled. Indeed, studies of neoliberalism (defined here as market fundamentalism associated with globalization) have often focused on "the intrusion" or "penetration" of market forces into spheres where they are construed as having had little impact before, or have no business being. For instance, Gibson-Graham (1996) considers the ways that "globalization scripts" and "rape scripts" share not only a lexicon (the terminology of "penetration" and the opportunities to tap "virgin" markets) but also a narrative about how power works, as an act of nonreciprocal penetration, after which something is lost, never to be regained (see also Freeman 2001). Arguably, these studies sometimes develop their moral and critical edge by assuming a boundary between where market forces *should* reasonably go, and where they should not, in ways that may leave the study of the operation of market forces in certain settings (like corporations) understudied.

With the analytic unit of CofPs, however, we can see the tightening hold of market forces on previously unmonitored interactions, spaces and practices within corporations in ways that ultimately lead to more surveillance of workers. A focus on misuse or corruption assumes that academic and corporate spheres are distinct, unrelated and mutually uninfluential in order to cast the academic sphere as innocent of corporate or capitalist leanings. But we know that the academy is also, and increasingly, a site shaped by financial logics of accountability and productivity (Strathern 2000). Rather than asking if corporations influenced the academy or the academy influenced corporations, a more productive framework is to consider how, in these intertwined settings, we are all elaborating tools for working through seemingly new forms of identity and community, in new economic situations—with potential for progressive and conservative uses in each setting. Thrift notes that most methods are no longer, if they ever were, the domain only of academic researchers, since there are thriving "methods communities in areas like market research and political consultancy" (2008, 106). Scholars, like corporations, are elaborating new ideologies of personhood, community and organizational structure. In this final section, I'd like to compare and contrast ideologies of *flexibility*, *power and scale*, and *community* in the corporate and sociolinguistic literatures because they address precisely these three domains, of personhood, community and organizational structure.

Flexibility

CofPs could be seen as marking the needs of, as they highlight the potential limitations of, the "knowledge economy." The Fordist model of industrial organization has been radically revised. Although the assembly line and machinery for mass production and mass marketing are not gone (their sites have shifted, from First World to Third World settings, from steel mills to call centers), ideologically, now, "the organization is a fleeting, fluid network of alliances, a highly decoupled and dynamic form with great organizational flexibility" (Martin 1994, 209). Corporations and individuals alike are told they need to become more agile and adaptable (18; see also the introduction to this volume). *Flexible specialization* refers both to the ways labor and products are changing: labor markets vary as workers move (or are moved) in and out of work, labor processes change (with workers taking on managerial tasks, and managers assembly tasks), and products change, customized in small batches for specific groups of customers with just-in-time processes (40). Flexible organizations and individuals are supposed to be able to respond quickly to changes in their environments, and initiate changes in innovative ways (144). For individuals, this might mean adapting to new work environments, or being able to take on a wide range of roles in a given organization. Martin (1994) asks how the social and economic formations of late capitalism are leading to transformations in ideas about the body and organizations in a large number of domains (immunology, economics, new age philosophy, government organizations, sports philosophy, psychology) to which the attribute of flexibility, or the ability to adapt to constant change, is now attributed, and the ways in which it is marked as a desirable trait. Progressive thought is not immune from these tendencies, even as it attempts to critique existing power structures. For instance, as Martin notes, feminist, antiracist scholars Sonia Johnson and Chela Sandoval celebrate the flexibility of the oppressed. Johnson imagines that those who are most outside the system are least constrained by it, and therefore may be most likely to challenge the system. Sandoval celebrates the flexibility required in the development of an oppositional consciousness among Third World feminists (Martin 1994, 157–158). Both are elaborating a version of standpoint thought, familiar from Marxist, antiracist and feminist thought, which argues that those who most oppressed by a system can see its flaws most clearly; however, what is new is the elaboration of the possibility of resistance in terms of the idiom of flexibility.

But individuals are not as interchangeable as machines, and indeed some of the articles on CofPs note that people are often reluctant to participate in change or to share their ideas and expertise with others if they feel their own jobs are in jeopardy (Amidon 1997, 2). The question of which forms of intellectual social capital belongs to individuals and to workplaces is thus a contested one. In order to work towards interchangeability, companies must "capture" forms of knowledge previously linked with individuals and make them part of the institution; they thus embrace the contradiction of sponsoring or nurturing, recording and auditing, "informal" social interactions in the workplace. (This is in part what the new discourse of "best practices" also is linked to.) But to sponsor "informal" social interactions is also to monitor and marketize them. There is always, after all, the danger those innovative and informal social networks will spin off into their own start-up company. Paying attention to CofPs is necessitated by flexible specialization (40), but the need to do so also marks the edge of unease with it—too much flexibility takes the workers outside organizational control.

The focus on CofPs in corporations can be seen as a means to elaborate flexibility in organization and in communication. Yet flexibility has its limits, and its problems. As Martin notes, "[I]n their resistance, these people often embrace a vigorously emerging systems thinking that may embody entirely new forms of repression" (1994, 248). The focus on flexibility, as studies of training and retraining have shown (Dunk 1996), places the onus on individuals to deal with loss of jobs, or the inability to get the jobs they want. It obscures the larger political and economic trends that link flextime and the right to work at home with corporate downsizing, the greater use of part-time work (casualization), and the greater use of freelancers/consultants. Gaining flexibility, Martin argues, often means giving up security (1994, 146). The corporate literature on CofP is striking for the ways in which the economic and political forces that require employee mobility are described with agentless passives, nominalizations and independent clauses, when in fact it is companies which are delayering, downsizing, unstaffing—that is, firing—significant portions of the workforce (see Martin 1994, 221).

(a) "As employee mobility continues to increase across organizations. . . ." (Lesser and Storick 2001, 836)

(b) "Given the aging of the workforce population and the increased worker mobility that has been witnessed within the United States over the last several years. . . ." (838)

Corporations are constructed as dealing with, but not initiating, change. The notion of flexibility, as Martin (1994, 145) notes, is Janus-faced, as all keywords are. Who is free to initiate action? It also reflects some ambivalence: how does one run an organization that creates such freedom, and yet keep it under organizational control? This is an example of the tension between flexibilization and taylorism, described in the introduction. And when does the vaunted flexibility in a worker become acquiescence, passivity, compliance, accommodation? In an economy where many corporations have downsized, where key portions of intellectual and even service labor are increasingly also sent off shore, where workers do not experience lifelong employment or lifelong security, where companies are being reformulated for just-in-time production, companies must find a way of creating institutional memory that does not rely on the persistence of individuals in one place. This requires methods for capturing social and intellectual capital in the absence of workers.

If one agrees that feminist scholarship has as its primary goal the identification of inequitable social formations, with an aim to redressing them, one question we need to ask is where and how our current analytic concepts enable such critique. Such critique begins by attending fully to the historical conditions under which forms of analysis, and identity, are changing. Indeed, one of the central theoretical goals of materialist feminism is to understand "why representations of identity are changing. . . . and how these changes in identity are connected to historical shifts in the production of life under late capitalism" (Hennessey and Ingraham, 1997, 9). It is striking to note that a focus on elaborating these discourses of flexibility in feminist sociolinguistics emerges in the late 1980s and early 1990s, in such critical and influential books as *Gender Articulated: Language and the Socially Constructed Self* (Hall and Bucholtz 1995). Many of us—and I decidedly include myself (see McElhinny 1995, 1998)—were imbricated in the elaboration of these ideas. To the extent that we saw such ideas as a scientific advance—a better way of understanding gender—we were not fully attending to the conditions that were leading to changes in the way identity was produced, and therefore not fully attentive to whether the elaboration of these new ways of thinking about gender were describing, or prescribing, the same forms of personhood prescribed in other settings. The focus on the development of a variety of new ways of conceptualizing gender in sociolinguistics and elsewhere—on gender as performance, activity, practice—could be seen as precisely spelling out what ideologies of personhood should be in these new economies (cf. McElhinny 2003). These approaches to gender are often prescribed by social scientists, as much as they are described.

There are differences in intellectual genealogical and methodological approach among feminist sociolinguists who focus on gender as activity, accomplishment, performance or practice, but all these approaches focus on gender as socially constructed. Social construction has increasingly come under critique by progressive scholars as not sufficiently theorizing its own conditions of production. Historical anthropologist Michel-Rolph Trouillot notes that "[c]onstructivism's dilemma is that while it can point to hundreds of stories that illustrate its general claim that narratives are produced, it cannot give a full account of the production of any narrative" (1995, 13). Constructivism is not, Trouillot argues, fully attentive to sociohistorical processes, and "tracking power requires a richer view of historical production than most theorists acknowledge" (1995, 25) (see also Grewal and Kaplan 1994; Hacking 1999; McElhinny 2007). We need to ask when, where and how these social scientific discourses themselves have a constitutive role in the processes of globalism, in the ways they help elaborate ideologies of flexible personhood as desirable, and indeed already achieved, in ways that naturalize dominant ideologies of what people should be and do. In *Materialist Feminism and the Politics of Discourse* Rosemary Hennessey argues, "A decentred, fragmented, porous subject is better equipped for the heightened alienation of late capitalism's refined divisions of labor, more readily disciplined by a pandemic corporate state, and more available to a broad nexus of ideological controls" (1993, 9) The elaboration of discourses of flexibility and fragmentation of subjectivities may therefore in and of themselves not be an adequate challenge to inequitable institutions and relationships, but they may instead be harnessed to them. So, how is power analyzed in institutional settings in the feminist linguistics and corporate literatures we have been examining here? How and where does it help to change our unit of analysis?

Power and Scale

Some of the questions about power and scale raised by Martin (1994) appear in recent articles in sociolinguistics assessing and critiquing at least some of the uses of CofP (see Barton and Tusting 2005 for one review). Numerous commentators argue that the notion of CofPs focuses on what is shared in a community, in a way which obscures questions of power, including such questions as how the community arose, how membership is defined, where and how differentiation occurs within the community, and challenges in moving from nonparticipation, or peripheral participation, to full participation (Creese 2005; Davies 2005; Duguid 2008b; Griffiths n.d.; Keating 2005; Lea 2005; Myers 2005). At stake here is a wider definition of how to understand power. Eckert and Wenger (2005) have argued that the notion of CofP does take into account notions of power, in studying the way definitions of legitimacy and competence (including how and who defines competence) are assessed within a CofP. They argue against a structuralist definition of power (i.e., one that assumes the existence of a structure that confers power according to position, and that assumes one can explain or predict who is seen as powerful by articulating the structure itself). They also, however, argue against notions of power that assume stratification with a well-defined top or bottom (582). Other commentators however argue that the notions of speech community (Creese 2005), activity theory (Keating 2005; Martin 2005) or affinity spaces (Gee 2005) more effectively address questions of ambiguity and negotiation, power and conflict, by examining notions of learning that are focused not just on institutional reproduction but also transformation, and by explicitly attending to the historical formation of and changing shape of CofPs.

There is more consensus on the need to link CofPs to other forms of institutional and systemic analysis. A number of studies have called for studies that link microlevel analysis of CofP with macrolevel analysis (Bergvall 1999; Davies 2005; Eckert and McConnell-Ginet 2007). This is akin to Gertler's (2001) concerns about how the unit of analysis in the corporate CofP literature is assumed as the corporation, rather than linked to larger systems like national educational systems or state industrial policy. In the inaugural issue of *Gender and Language*, which has as its theme "unanswered questions and unquestioned assumptions in the study of language and gender," Eckert and McConnell-Ginet (2007) argue the field of language and gender needs to (a) do more comparison of different but similar communities to explore generalizations about how practice contributes to the elaboration of identity, and (b) relate CofP to social networks, institutions and more global imagined communities. CofP, they emphasize, does not offer a new analytic unit, or replace other units, but offers fresh perspectives on familiar units.

Lave has also recently argued that the notions of legitimate peripheral participation needed to be unpacked more in *Situated Learning* in order to make "clearer that (and how) institutions, capital, and forces of production give people power over legitimacy, peripherality, and participation without dividing one from another" (2008, 285). In some recent articles, scholars have argued that because CofP is crucially tied up with the notion of learned social behavior, it might be better suited to the study of certain groups or certain periods in people's lives than others (see Bergvall 1999). Workplaces (Castellano 1996; Wenger 1998) and adolescent cultures and schools (cf. Bucholtz 1999; Castellano 1996; Eckert 2000; Mendoza-Denton 2008) have received particular scrutiny. Meyerhoff (2002) argues that this is an accident of how the framework has been used, and not an inherent limitation, and it is certain the concept can be applied to a very wide range of groups.

And yet, we might still want to try to explain why workplaces and youth have received particular scrutiny. Davies argues that perhaps it is easier to determine what counts as a common enterprise in a group whose activity arises in relation to an institution (even if opposition to it) rather than to self-constituted groups, and thus the notion retains some of the flavor of its development in the context of professional groups (2005, 562). Likewise, Keating (2005) notes that the notion of CofP suggests a flexible but nonetheless stable community that doesn't capture some of the mobile, ever-changing social formations of e.g. Portuguese migrant women in the UK. Gee (2000) argues that CofPs are a sociotechnical device of the new capitalism. Their elaboration in businesses is shaping their instantiation in schools that, in complex and class-linked ways, are retooling themselves to produce the new kinds of workers required in a knowledge economy. He argues there is class differentiation in the implementation of different organizational forms in schools, with peer-centered CofPs given more prominence in classrooms serving middle-class students, while more highly structured back-to-basics programs with more discipline and less flexibility are aimed at working class and poor youth. That the analytic notion of CofP is being used most commonly to describe precisely the same sites where it is often being prescribed (if not always in the same ways) suggests the ways that our analytic notions arise out of our research sites; it also suggests the need for caution in applying these same concepts without critique. And yet it is also the case that sometimes the contradictions within concepts, practices and institutions can also hold the seeds for their transformation. Does the focus on "community" in CofP challenge more individualized notions of self in neoliberal economics?

Community

Both corporate and sociolinguistic perspectives open up analytic space for thinking about flexible forms of community, not necessarily tied to or defined by place. Notions of speech community, though notably redefined to take into account diversity and difference (McElhinny and Patrick 1993) still often remain tied to a particular locale while the notion of CofP makes it possible to imagine a more dispersed community (Heller and Duchêne, this volume; Sharratt and Usoro 2003; Thomson et al. n.d.). CofP thus participates in what Thrift (2008) calls the explosion of a new set of research methods to think about space and place.

The elaborate focus on community discovery and construction in this corporate literature might indeed seem to challenge the individualization linked with neoliberal regimes of the self in a globalizing economy (Hennessey 1993, 6), especially given the discursive gap that opens between communities and producers/consumers as language is inscribed more in a language of profit rather than pride (see the introduction to this volume). These regimes of individualization have been described in some of the recent work on language, gender and neoliberalism (Inoue 2007, Kingfisher 2006; Yang 2010) which considers how neoliberal (or, market fundamentalist) structures affect, or attempt to affect, notions of personhood. Harvey has noted that neoliberalism is "a theory of political economic practices that proposes that human well-being can best be advanced by liberating individual entrepreneurial freedoms and skills within an institutional framework characterized by strong private property rights, free markets, and free trade" (2005, 2). Rose (1996) elaborates some of the new regimes of self associated with neoliberalism, in which the ideal adult person is self-governing, responsible, autonomous, self-sufficient, independent, and entrepreneurial. This self is not incidentally or accidentally also the idealized Western masculine self (Kingfisher 2002), and thus has attracted significant feminist analysis (see McElhinny 2010 for further details). However, a focus on community does not necessarily challenge neoliberal ideologies of personhood as socially atomized, but may instead obscure, as we will see, some of the ways power works (Amin and Roberts 2008; Duguid 2008b; Harris and Shelswell 2005; Muehlmann 2008). In this it might be like the notion of family, which used to describe workplace settings can obscure the power relations between employers and employees (Bakan and Stasiulis 1997; Goldstein 1995). When, for instance, live-in domestic workers are construed as "one of the family," unpaid overtime is reframed not as exploitative but as part of a kinship obligation, and the families of domestic workers (from whom they may be separated because of the conditions of work) are erased from political and economic consideration.

In similar ways, a focus on community can also lend itself to addressing neoliberal dilemmas. A focus on CofP zeroes in on the governance and self-governance of face-to-face interaction, but it particularly focuses on the interstices of corporate life. It commodifies and captures knowledge previously understood as belonging to individuals because of their lives and histories in a corporation. It alienates social and intellectual capital. It makes previously "informal" spaces and interactions part of the company's business. Amin and Roberts (2008, 23) note this, even if in a way skewed to consider people only as workers or employees:

> Organizations are purposefully seeking to engineer informality, iterative purposefulness, and productive idleness, in order unlock new social energies and improvisations . . . After so many years of close corporate monitoring of employees and elaborate measures to eliminate idleness, autonomy and sociality, this re-evaluation of independent social energy is widely perceived as a progressive development of equal benefit to employees and employers. Yet it also comes with new risks. For example, as the social is nurtured in the workplace, work comes to dominate every aspect of the social, resulting in forms of premature employee burnout. (2008, 23)

What is striking about the use of CofP is the way that it is a form of regimentation of relationships within organizations previously understood as "informal" or even "counterproductive." "Consider," as one article has it,

> that the most widespread and pervasive learning in your organization may not be happening in training rooms, conference rooms, or boardrooms, but in the cafeteria, the hallways and the café across the street. Imagine that through e-mail exchanges, phone visits, and bull sessions

with colleagues, people at all levels of the organization are sharing critical business knowledge. (Brown and Isaacs 1996–1997, 1)

There is an excitement, but also a nervousness, about what precisely the corporation is missing out on.

Gertler (2003, 88) notes that the ideologies of geography evident in discussions of *local* and *face-to-face* interaction conflate ideas about physical separation and cultural differences. Specifically, effective communities are said to rely on fairly high degrees of shared or similar norms, in ways that also however police who is deemed an acceptable participant. Similar ideologies are evident in many ideologies of nationalism. Anderson (2006) suggests that nationalism commands emotional legitimacy by creating bonds of fraternal solidarity; nonetheless recent works query whether Anderson's work conflates the trope of imagined community with the reality (see Bauman and Briggs 2003; Silverstein 2000) in their considerations of previously colonized nations defined by outmigration (Rafael 2000) or in settler colonial nations fractured by racism (Thobani 2007). Lave (2008, 291) notes that most CofP studies remain silent on how race, class, and ethnicity shape corporations and CofP. The application of the notion of CofP in the corporate literature seem unfettered by hierarchy, rather oblivious to difference, indeed, requiring and prescribing similarity. Only the occasional article (e.g., Swan, Scarbrough and Robertson 2002) suggests the need to offer more complicated notions of power.

This rather idealized focus on what is shared and similar may also be part of what makes CofPs attractive to some feminist scholars. In some academic studies of language and gender, a focus on CofPs seems to have replaced an earlier cultural feminist approach to talking about women's interactions as naturally more cooperative and consensual, or markedly different from men, as it makes some of the same arguments. Nonetheless, sociolinguistic studies of CofPs have also had a more critical edge to them, attentive to hierarchies of power within them (see, especially, work by Eckert 2000; Mendoza-Denton 2008).

New knowledge, and new tools for managing knowledge, are never simply about "updating" the academy, or industrial practice (see also Hennessey 1993, 1); they are never simply about "progress." In both contexts, I argue, we are elaborating, and perhaps promoting, ideologies about the desirability of "flexible" people in a "flexible economy" that can have progressive but also conservative political impacts. In both contexts there is an emerging sense of disquiet linked to precisely this duality, as some academic researchers wonder whether the concept of CofPs gives them enough purchase on talking about inequalities of power and participation, while corporate ethnographers worry about whether CofPs might be introducing an unmanageably flexible, informal and egalitarian structure into the workplace. Miyako Inoue points out that "the study of neoliberal governmentality alerts us to the unstable political valence of all techniques and practices of gender empowerment. None of the fundamental critical strategies in feminist theory . . . come with guarantees that they are essentially critical, liberating, or progressive in determinate contexts" (2007, 82). What we need, she argues, is a

> robust critical theory that enables us to discern the disquieting slippage between our key words and the marketed and market-rooted buzz words that mimic and deceptively take our critique and threaten to colonize it, and that have profound effects upon how all of us think and act in the globalized social formation in which we now live and work. (2006b, 89)

To these growing lists of critical strategies we can add the notions of *practice* and of *community*. Foregrounding these concerns may allow us to consider when and how the uses of CofPs contribute to the elaboration of ideologies linked to the new capitalism, and when and how they can serve to critique it.

Williams closed the first edition of *Keywords* with a reflexive, inclusive gesture, noting that the publishers had kindly agreed to include some blank pages at the end of the book, not only for making notes, but also as "a sign that the inquiry remains open and the author will welcome all amendments, corrections and editions towards the revised edition which it is hoped will be necessary" (1983, 23–24). Offering detailed accounts of conflicted and confusing histories and usages is not, according to Williams, meant to result in clarity, but in consciousness.

> I do not share the optimism, or the theories which underlie it, of that popular kind of inter-war and surviving semantics which supposed that clarification of difficult words would help in the resolution of disputes conducted in their terms and often evidently confused by them . . . the variations and confusions of meaning are not just faults in a system, or errors of feedback, or deficiencies of education . . . Indeed they have often, as variations, to be insisted upon, just because they embody different experiences and readings of experience, and this will continue to be true, in active relationships and conflicts, over and above the clarifying exercises of scholars or committees. What can really be contributed is not resolution but perhaps, at times, just that extra edge of consciousness . . . [This] is an exploration of the vocabulary of a crucial area of social and cultural discussion, which has been inherited within precise historical and social conditions and which has to be made at once conscious and critical—subject to change as well as to continuity—if the millions of people in whom it is active are to see it as active; not a tradition to be learned, nor a consensus to be accepted, not a set of meanings which, because it is "our language", has a natural authority; but as a shaping and reshaping, in real circumstances and

from profoundly different and important points of view: a vocabulary to use, to find our own ways in, to change as we find it necessary to change it, as we go on making our language and history. (24–25)

Can we still use the notion of CofP? Like Martin, I want to say that "there is no vantage point from which I can say confidently that the developments that I have described are 'good' or 'bad'" (1994, 249). The challenge as progressive scholars is not to sort the conservative concepts from the progressive ones, the tainted from the pure. Indeed, many scholars note how progressive intellectuals often reproduce structures of inequality and domination (Bauman and Briggs 2003 xi; see also Amit 2000; Inoue 2007; Song 2009; Strathern 2000). We are asked, however, to consider the range of *uses* of concepts that can be harnessed to many ends. We can neither celebrate as liberatory, or condemn as contaminated, CofPs, or any of a range of other methods emerging from, as they study, changing social contexts. Instead, we need to be attentive to the romances linked with any such terms or methods—here, romances of community, flexibility, choice, consensus, local, individual, similarity, innovation—and ask whose interests are served, in given instances, by such terms.

NOTES

1. Earlier versions of this paper were presented at IGALA-4 in Valencia Spain (November 8–10, 2006), in a panel on "Language and Neoliberal Governmentality, co-organized by Miyako Inoue and Bonnie McElhinny, at AAA 2006, San Jose, California (November 15–19, 2006), at a workshop on language and neoliberalism at the University of Toronto (Feb. 16–17, 2007) organized as part of the FAS Year of Languages, as a plenary talk at the Conference on Language and Globalization: Policy, Education and Media sponsored by the Georgetown Linguistic Society, March 30- April 1, 2007, and at Alexandre Duchêne's workshop on language and the new economy in Fribourg, May 2009. Thanks to Eugenia Tsao for her work as a research assistant wading through this vast literature. My thanks to Kori Allan, Charles Briggs, Lisa Davidson, Alexandre Duchêne, Meric Gertler, Monica Heller, and Miyako Inoue for helpful conversations and thoughtful comments.
2. Note, though, that Chrysler, the multinational auto-maker, sometimes lays claim to coining the term—see Haas et al. n.d.
3. http://portal.acm.org/citation.cfm?id=142750.142991. Accessed Nov. 6, 2010.

REFERENCES

Agresti, William. 2003. "Tailoring IT Support to Communities of Practice." *IT Professional* 5–6: 24–28.
Amidon, Debra. 1997. "Emerging Community of Knowledge Practice." *Knowledge Inc.* 2(3): 1.
Amin, Ash, and Joanne Roberts. 2008. "The Resurgence of Community in Economic Thought and Practice." In *Community, Economic Creativity, and*

Organization, edited by Ash Amin and Joanne Roberts, 11–36. Oxford: Oxford University Press.

Amit, Vered. 2000. "The University as Panopticon: Moral Claims and Attacks on Academic Freedom." In *Audit Cultures: Anthropological Studies in Accountability, Ethics and the Academy*, edited by Marilyn Strathern, 215–236. London: Routledge.

Anderson, Benedict. 2006. *Imagined Communities: Reflections on the Origin and Spread of Nationalism*. New York: Verso.

Bakan, Abigail, and Daiva Stasiulis, eds. 1997. *Not One of the Family: Foreign Domestic Workers in Canada*. Toronto: University of Toronto Press.

Barton, David, and Karin Tusting. 2005. "Introduction." In *Beyond Communities of Practice: Language, Power and Social Context*, edited by David Barton and Karin Tusting, 1–13. Cambridge: Cambridge University Press.

Bauman, Richard, and Charles Briggs. 2003. *Voices of Modernity: Language Ideologies and the Politics of Inequality*. Cambridge: Cambridge University Press.

Bergvall, Victoria. 1999. "Towards a Comprehensive Theory of Language and Gender." *Language in Society* 28: 273–293.

Blommaert, Jan, ed. 1999. *Language Ideological Debates*. Berlin: Mouton de Gruyter.

Bond, Peter. 2004. "Communities of Practice and Complexity: Conversation and Culture." *Organisations & People* 11(4). Accessed May 2, 2011. http://www.leader-values.com/resources/AMED2004Nov.asp.

Brown, John Seely, and Paul Duguid. 1991. "Organizational Learning and Communities of Practice: Toward a Unified View of Working, Learning and Innovation." *Organizational Science* 2(1): 40–57.

Brown, John Seely, and Paul Duguid. 2000. *The Social Life of Information*. Boston: Harvard Business Press.

Brown, Juanita, and David Isaacs. 1996–1997. "Conversation as a Core Business Process." *The Systems Thinker*. 7(10): 1–6.

Bucholtz, Mary. 1999. "'Why Be Normal'? Language and Identity Practices in a Community of Nerd Girls." *Language in Society* 28: 203–223.

Cameron, Deborah. 2000a. *Good to Talk? Living and Working in a Communication Culture*. London: Sage.

Cameron, Deborah. 2000b. "Styling the Worker: Gender and the Commodification of Language in the Globalized Service Economy." *Journal of Sociolinguistics* 4(3): 323–347.

Cameron, Deborah. 2006. "Unanswered Questions and Unquestioned Assumptions in the Study of Language and Gender: Female Verbal Superiority." *Gender and Language* 1(1): 15–26.

Castellano, Maria. 1996. "Building Community across Different Belief Systems: An Ethnographically Informed Perspective on the Role of Narrative and Dialogue." In *Gender and Belief Systems: Proceedings of the Third Berkeley Women and Language Conference*, edited by Natasha Warner, Jocelyn Ahlers, Leela Bilmes, Monica Oliver, Suzanne Wertheim and Melinda Chen, 133–143. Berkeley, CA: Berkeley Women and Language Group.

Cox, Andrew. 2005. "What Are Communities of Practice? A Comparative Review of Four Seminal Works." *Journal of Information Science* 31(6): 527–540.

Creese, Angela. 2005. "Mediating Allegations of Racism in a Multiethnic London School: What Speech Communities and Communities of Practice Can Tell Us about Discourse and Power." In *Beyond Communities of Practice: Language, Power and Social Context,* edited by David Barton and Karin Tusting, 55–77. Cambridge: Cambridge University Press.

Davies, Bethan. 2005. "Communities of Practice: Legitimacy Not Choice." *Journal of Sociolinguistics* 9(4): 557–581.

Duguid, Paul. 2008a. "'The Art of Knowing': Social and Tacit Dimensions of Knowledge and the Limits of the Community of Practice." In *Community, Economic Creativity, and Organization*, edited by Ash Amin and Joanne Roberts, 69–85. Oxford: Oxford University Press.

Duguid, Paul. 2008b. "Prologue: Community of Practice Then and Now." In *Community, Economic Creativity, and Organization*, edited by Ash Amin and Joanne Roberts, 1–10. Oxford: Oxford University Press.

Dunk, Thomas. 1996. "Culture, Skill, Masculinity and Whiteness." In *The Training Trap: Ideology, Training and the Labour Market*, edited by Thomas Dunk, Stephen McBride, Randle W Nelsen, 1–12. Winnipeg: Fernwood Publishing

Eckert, Penelope. 2000. *Linguistic Variation as Social Practice*. Oxford: Blackwell.

Eckert, Penelope, and Sally McConnell-Ginet. 1992. "Think Practically and Look Locally: Language and Gender as Community-based Practice." *Annual Review of Anthropology* 21: 461–490.

Eckert, Penelope, and Sally McConnell-Ginet. 2007. "Putting Communities of Practice in Their Place." *Gender and Language* 1(1): 27–38.

Eckert, Penelope, and Etienne Wegner. 2005. "Dialogue: Communities of Practice in Sociolingustics: What Is the Role of Power in Sociolinguistic Variation?" *Journal of Sociolinguistics* 9(4): 582–589.

Endsley, Scott, Margaret Kirkegaard, and Antonio Linares. 2005. "Working Together: Communities of Practice in Family Medicine." *Family Practice Management* 12(1): 28–32.

Errington Joseph. 2008. *Linguistics in a Colonial World*. Oxford: Blackwell.

Fabian, Johannes. 1986. *Language and Colonial Power: The Appropriation of Swahili in the Former Belgian Congo 1880–1938*. Cambridge: Cambridge University Press.

Fraser, Nancy, and Linda Gordan. 1994. "A Genealogy of *Dependency*: Tracing a Keyword of the U.S. Welfare State." *Signs* 19(2): 309–336.

Freeman, Carla. 2001. "Is Local: Global as Feminine: Masculine? Rethinking the Gender of Globalization." *Signs* 26(4): 1007–1037.

Gal, Susan. 1998. "Multiplicity and Contention Among Language Ideologies." In *Language Ideologies*, edited by Bambi Schieffelin, Kathryn Woolard and Paul Kroskrity, 317–331. Oxford: Oxford University Press.

Gal Susan, and Kathryn Woolard, eds. 2001. *Languages and Publics: The Making of Authority*. Manchester: St. Jerome Publishing.

Gee, James. 2000. "Communities of Practice in the New Capitalism." Review of William Greider's *One World, Ready or Not: The Manic Logic of Global Capitalism*, Jeremy Rifkin's *The End of Work: The Decline of the Global Labor Force and the Dawn of the Post-Market Era* and William Julius Wilson's *When Work Disappears: The World of the New Urban Poor*. The *Journal of the Learning Sciences* 9(4): 515–523.

Gee, James. 2005. "Semiotic Social Spaces and Affinity Spaces: From *The Age of Mythology* to Today's Schools." In *Beyond Communities of Practice: Language, Power and Social Context*, edited by David Barton and Karin Tusting, 214–233. Cambridge: Cambridge University Press.

Gee, James, Glynda Hull, and Colin Lankshear. 1996. *The New Work Order: Behind the Language of the New Capitalism*. Sydney: Allen & Unwin.

Gertler, Meric. 2001. "Best Practice? Geography, Learning, and the Institutional Limits to Strong Convergence." *Journal of Economic Geography* 1: 5–26.

Gertler, Meric. 2003. "Tacit Knowledge and the Economic Geography of Context, or The Undefinable Tacitness of Being (There)." *Journal of Economic Geography* 3: 75–99.

Gertler, Meric. 2008. "Buzz Without Being There? Communities of Practice in Context." In *Community, Economic Creativity, and Organization*, edited by Ash Amin and Joanne Roberts, 203–226. Oxford: Oxford University Press.

Gibson-Graham, J. K. 1996. *The End of Capitalism (as We Knew It): A Feminist Critique of Political Economy*. Oxford: Blackwell.

Gongla, P., and Christine R. Rizzuto. 2001. "Evolving Communities of Practice: IBM Global Services Experience." *IBM Systems Journal* 40(5): 842–862.

Goldstein, Tara. 1995. "Nobody Is Talking Bad: Creating Community and Claiming Power on the Production Lines." In *Gender Articulated: Language and the Socially Constructed Self*, edited by Kira Hall and Mary Bucholtz, 375–400. New York: Routledge.

Grewal, Inderpal, and Caren Kaplan. 1994. "Transnational Feminist Practices and Questions of Postmodernity." In *Scattered Hegemonies: Postmodernity and Transnational Feminist Practices*, edited by Inderpal Grewal and Caren Kaplan, 1–36. Minneapolis: University of Minnesota Press.

Griffiths, Morwenna. n.d. *A Feminist Perspective on Communities of Practice*. Accessed May 2, 2011. http:orgs.man.ac.uk/projects/include/experiment/morwenna_Griffiths.pdf.

Gulledge, Elizabeth. 2007. "The 'Community of Practice' Concept: Origins, Outcomes and Implications for Programs in Education." Paper presented at the annual meeting of the American Association of Colleges for Teacher Education, Hilton New York, New York, NY, February, 2007. Accessed February 7, 2011. http://www.allacademic.com/meta/p142372_index.html.

Haas, Roland, Wilfried Aulbur, and Sunil Thakar. n.d. *Enabling Communities of Practice at EADS (European Aerospace, Defence and Space Corporation) Airbus*. Accessed May 2, 2011. http://www.eecs.umich.edu/~ackerm/courses/04–1.si670/haas.pre-press.pdf.

Hacking, Ian. 1999. *The Social Construction of What?* Cambridge, MA: Harvard University Press.

Hall, Kira, and Mary Bucholtz, eds. 1995. *Gender Articulated: Language and the Socially Constructed Self*. New York City: Routledge.

Harris, Steven Robert, and Nicola Shelswell. 2005. "Moving beyond Communities of Practice in Adult Basic Education." In *Beyond Communities of Practice: Language, Power and Social Context*, edited by David Barton and Karin Tusting, 158–179. Cambridge: Cambridge University Press.

Harvey, David. 2005. *A Brief History of Neoliberalism*. Oxford: Oxford University Press

Heller, Monica. 1999. "Heated Language in a Cold Climate." In *Language Ideological Debates*, edited by Jan Blommaert, 143–170. Berlin: Mouton de Gruyter.

Hennessy, Rosemary, and Chrys Ingraham, eds. 1997. *Materialist Feminism: A Reader in Class, Difference, and Women's Lives*. New York: Routledge.

Hennessey, Rosemary. 1993. *Materialist Feminism and the Politics of Discourse*. New York: Routledge.

Hill, Jane. 2002. "'Expert Rhetorics' in Advocacy for Endangered Languages: Who Is Listening, and What Do They Hear?" *Journal of Linguistic Anthropology* 12(2): 119–133.

Hill, Jane. 2008. *The Everyday Life of White Racism*. Malden, MA: Wiley-Blackwell.

Hinton, Brad. 2003. "Knowledge Management and Communities of Practice: An Experience from Rabobank Australia and New Zealand." Paper presented at the IAMA World Food and Agribusiness Symposium, Cancun Mexico. June 2003. Accessed May 2, 2011. http:www.ifama.org/conferences/2003Conference/papers/Lington.pdf.

Holmes, Janet, and Miriam Meyerhoff. 1999. "The Community of Practice: Theories and Methodologies in Language and Gender Research." *Language in Society* 28: 173–183.

Inoue, Miyako. 2006. *Vicarious Language: Gender and Linguistic Modernity in Japan.* Berkeley: University of California Press.

Inoue, Miyako. 2007. "Language and Gender in an Age of Neoliberalism." *Gender and Language* 1(1): 79–92.

Irvine, Judith. 2001. "The Family Romance of Colonial Linguistics: Gender and Family in Nineteenth-Century Representations of African Languages." In *Languages and Publics: The Making of Authority,* edited by Susan Gal and Kathryn Woolard, 13–29. Manchester, UK: St. Jerome Publishing.

Irvine, Judith, and Susan Gal. 2000. "Language Ideology and Linguistic Differentiation." In *Regimes of Language: Ideologies, Polities, and Identities,* edited by Paul Kroskrity, 35–84. Santa Fe, NM: School of American Research.

John, Vaugh. 2006. "Community Development Research: Merging (or Submerging) Communities of Practice? A Response to Van Vlaenderen." *Community Development Journal* 41(1): 50–64.

Keating, Maria Clara. 2005. "The Person in the Doing: Negotiating the Experience of Self." In *Beyond Communities of Practice: Language, Power and Social Context,* edited by David Barton and Karin Tusting, 105–138. Cambridge: Cambridge University Press.

Kimble, Chris, Paul Hildreth and Peter Wright. 2000. "Communities of Practice: Going Virtual." In *Knowledge Management and Business Model Innovation,* edited by Yogesh Malhotra, 220–234. Hershey, PA: Idea Group Publishing.

Kingfisher, Catherine, ed. 2002. *Western Welfare in Decline: Globalization and Women's Poverty.* Philadelphia: University of Pennsylvania Press.

Kingfisher, Catherine. 2006. "What D/discourse Analysis Can Tell Us about Neoliberal Constructions of (Gendered) Personhood: Some Notes on Commonsense and Temporality." *Gender and Language* 1(1): 93–106.

Klassen, Pamela. 2008. "Practice." In *Key Words in Religion, Media and Culture,* edited by David Morgan, 136–147. New York: Routledge.

Kroskrity, Paul, ed. 2000. *Regimes of Language: Ideologies, Polities, Identities.* Santa Fe, NM: School of American Research Press.

Lave, Jean. 2008. "Epilogue: *Situated Learning* and Changing Practice." In *Community, Economic Creativity, and Organization,* edited by Ash Amin and Joanne Roberts, 83–296. Oxford: Oxford University Press.

Lave, Jean, and Etienne Wenger. 1991. *Situated Learning: Legitimate Peripheral Participation.* Cambridge: Cambridge University Press.

Lea, Mary. 2005. "'Communities of Practice' in Higher Education: Useful Heuristic or Educational Model?" In *Beyond Communities of Practice: Language, Power and Social Context,* edited by David Barton and Karin Tusting, 180–197. Cambridge: Cambridge University Press.

Lesser, Eric, and John Storck 2001. "Communities of Practice and Organizational Performance." *IBM Systems Journal* 40(4): 831–841.

Lesser, Eric, and Kathryn Everest. 2001. "Communities of Practice: Making the Most of Intellectual Capital." *Ivey Business Journal* 65(4): 37–41

Liedtka, Jeanne. 1999. "Linking Competitive Advantage with Communities of Practice." *Journal of Management Inquiry* 8(1): 5–16.

Mallinson, Christine, and Becky Childs. 2007. "Communities of Practice in Sociolinguistic Description: Analyzing Language and Identity Practices Among Black Women in Appalachia." *Gender and Language* 1(2): 173–206.

Martin, Emily. 1994. *Flexible Bodies: Tracking Immunity in American Culture From the Days of Polio to the age of Aids.* Boston: Beacon Press.

McDermott, Richard. 1999. "Nurturing Three Dimensional Communities of Practice: How to Get the Most Out of Human Networks." Accessed May 2, 2011. http://www.nickols.us/Dimensions.pdf.

McElhinny, Bonnie. 1995 "Challenging Hegemonic Masculinities: Female and Male Police Officers Handling Domestic Violence." In *Gender Articulated*, edited by Kira Hall and Mary Bucholtz, 217–243. New York: Routledge.

McElhinny, Bonnie. 1997. "Ideologies of Public and Private Language in Sociolinguistics." In *Gender and Discourse*, edited by Ruth Wodak, 106–139. London: Sage Publishers.

McElhinny, Bonnie. 1998. "Genealogies of Gender Theory: Practice Theory and Feminism in Sociocultural and Linguistic Anthropology." *Social Analysis* 42(3): 164–189.

McElhinny, Bonnie. 2003. "Theorizing Gender in Sociolinguistics and Linguistic Anthropology." In *The Language and Gender Handbook*, edited by Janet Holmes and Miriam Meyerhoff, 21–42. Oxford: Basil Blackwell.

McElhinny, Bonnie. 2005. "'Kissing a Baby Is Not at All Good For Him': Infant Mortality, Medicine and Colonial Modernity in the U.S.-Occupied Philippines." *American Anthropologist* 107(2): 183–194.

McElhinny, Bonnie. 2007. "Language, Gender and Economies in Global Transitions: Provocative and Provoking Questions about How Gender is Articulated." In *Words, Worlds, Material Girls: Language and Gender in a Global Economy*, edited by Bonnie McElhinny, 1–38. Berlin: Mouton de Gruyter.

McElhinny, Bonnie. 2010. "The Audacity of Affect: Gender, Race and History in Linguistic Accounts of Legitimacy and Belonging." *Annual Review of Anthropology* 39: 309–328.

McElhinny, Bonnie, and Peter Patrick. 1993. "Speakin and Spokin in Jamaica: Consensus and Conflict in Sociolinguistics." In *Nineteenth Proceedings of the Berkeley Linguistic Society*, edited by Joshua Guenter, Barbara Kaier and Cheryl Zoll, 280–290. Berkeley, CA: Berkeley Linguistics Society.

McKeon, Michael. 1977. "Review of *Keywords*." *Studies in Romanticism* 16: 128–139.

McLaughlin, Milbrey W., and Joan E. Talbert. 2006. "Developing Communities of Practice in Schools." In *Building School-Based Teacher Learning Communities: Professional Strategies to Improve Student Achievement*, edited by Milbrey McLaughlin and Joan Talbert, 38–63. New York: Teachers College Press.

Mendoza Denton, Norma. 2008. *Homegirls: Language and Cultural Practice among Latina Youth Gangs*. Oxford: Blackwell.

Meyerhoff, Miriam. 2002. "Communities of Practice." In *The Handbook of Language, Variation and Change*, edited by J. K. Chambers, Peter Trudgill and Natalie Schilling-Estes, 526–548. Hoboken, NJ: Wiley.

Mitchelle, John, Sarah Wood, and Susan Young. 2001. *Communities of Practice: Reshaping Professional Practice and Improving Organisational Productivity in the Vocational Education and Training (VET) Sector: Resources for Practitioners*. Melbourne: Australian National Training Authority.

Muehlmann, Shaylih. 2008. *Where the River Ends: Environmental Conflict and Contested Identities in the Colorado Delta*. Ph.D. diss., University of Toronto.

Murray, Stephen. 1998. *American Sociolinguistics: Theories and Theory Groups*. Amsterdam: John Benjamins.

Myers, Greg. 2005. Communities of Practice, Risk and Sellafield. In *Beyond Communities of Practice: Language, Power and Social Context*, edited by David Barton and Karin Tusting, 198–213. Cambridge: Cambridge University Press.

Ortner, Sherry. 1996. "Making Gender: Toward a Feminist, Minority, Postcolonial, Subaltern, etc., Theory of Practice." In *Making Gender: The Politics and Erotics of Culture,* edited by Sherry Ortner, 1–20. Boston: Beacon Press.

Palincsar, Annemarie Sullivan, Jane Cutter, and Shirley Magnusson. 2004. "A Community of Practice: Implications for Learning Disabilities." In *Learning about Learning Disabilities* (3rd ed.), edited by Bernice Wong, 485–510. San Diego, CA: Academic Press.

Palincsar, Annemarie Sullivan, Shirley Magnusson, Nancy Maano, Danielle Ford, and Nancy Brown. 1998. "Designing a Community of Practice: Principles and Practices of the GisML Community." *Teaching and Teacher Education* 14(1): 5–19.

Philips, Susan. 1998. Language Ideologies in Institutions of Power: A Commentary." In *Language Ideologies: Practice and Theory*, edited by Bambi Schieffelin, Kathryn Woolard and Paul Kroskrity, 211–228. Oxford: Oxford University Press.

Por, George, and Erik von Bekkum. 2003. "Innovation and Communities of Practice: The Great 'Symphony' Paradox." Excerpted from *Emerging Principles, Practices, and Politics of Knowledge Economics*. Accessed May 2, 2011. http://www.community-intelligence.com/pdf/Communities_of_Innovation.pdf.

Rafael, Vicente. 1988. *Contracting Colonialism: Translation and Christian Conversion in Tagalog Society under Early Spanish Rule*. Ithaca, NY: Cornell University Press.

Rafael, Vicente. 2000. *White Love and Other Events in Filipino History*. Durham, NC: Duke University Press

Rose, Nikolas.1996. *Inventing Our Selves: Psychology, Power and Personhood*. Cambridge: Cambridge University Press

Ruopp, Richard, Shahaf Gal, Brian Drayton, and Meghan Pfister, eds. 1992. *LabNet: Toward a Community of Practice*. Hillsdale, NJ: Lawrence Erlbaum Associates.

Said, Edward. 1978. *Orientalism*. London: Routledge and Kegan Paul.

Schieffelin, Bambi, Kathryn Woolard, and Paul Kroskrity, eds. 1998. *Language Ideologies: Practice and Theory*. Oxford: Oxford University Press.

Schlager, Mark, Judith Fusco, and Patricia Schank. 2002. "Evolution of an Online Education Community of Practice." In *Building Virtual Communities: Learning and Change in Cyberspace*, edited by K. Ann Renninger and Wesley Shumar, 129–158. Cambridge: Cambridge University Press.

Sharratt, Mark, and Abel Usoro. 2003. "Understanding Knowledge-Sharing in On-Line Communities of Practice." *Knowledge Management* 18(2). Accessed May 2, 2011. http://www.ejkm.com/volume-1/volume1-issue-2/issue2-art18.htm.

Silverstein, Michael. 2000. "Whorfianism and the Linguistic Imagination of Nationality." In *Regimes of Language: Ideologies, Polities and Identities*, edited by Paul Kroskrity, 85–139. Santa Fe, NM: School of American Research Press.

Song, Jesook. 2009. *South Koreans in the Debt Crisis: The Creation of a Neoliberal Welfare Society*. Durham, NC: Duke University Press.

Strathern, Marilyn, ed. 2000. *Audit Cultures: Anthropological Studies in Accountability, Ethics and the Academy*. London: Routledge.

Swan, Jacy, Harry Scarbrough, and Maxine Robertson. 2002. "The Construction of 'Communities of Practice' in the Management of Innovation." *Management Learning* 33–34: 477–496.

Thobani Sunera. 2007. *Exalted Subjects: Studies in the Making of Race and Nation in Canada*. Toronto: University of Toronto Press

Thomson, Rosemary, Doris Reeves-Lipscombe, Bronwyn Stuckey, and Mandia Mentis. n.d. "Discourse Analysis and Role Adoption in a Community of Practice." Accessed May 2, 2011. http://www.epsquare.org/stuckey_etal_AERA_Discourse_analysis.pdf.

Thrift, Nigel. 2008. "Re-Animating the Place of Thought: Transformations of Spatial and Temporal? Description in the Twenty-First Century." In *Community,*

Economic Creativity, and Organization, edited by Ash Amin and Joanne Roberts, 90–115. Oxford: Oxford University Press.

Trechter, Sara. 1999. "Contextualizing the Exotic Few: Gender Dichotomies in Lakhota." In *Reinventing Identities: The Gendered Self in Discourse*, edited by Mary Bucholtz, A. C. Liang and Laurel Sutton, 101–122. New York: Oxford University Press,

Trouillot, Michel-Rolph. 1995. *Silencing the Past: Power and the Production of History*. Boston: Beacon Press.

Vlaenderen, Hilde Van. 2004. "Community Development Research: Merging Communities of Practice." *Community Development Journal* 39(2): 135–143.

Weidman, Amanda. 2006. *Singing the Classical, Voicing the Modern: The Postcolonial Politics of Music in South India*. Durham, NC: Duke University Press.

Wenger, Etienne. 1998. *Communities of Practice*. New York: Cambridge University Press.

Wenger, Etienne. 2005. "Communities of Practice in 21st Century Organizations: Foreword to the CEFRIO Guidebook." Accessed May 2, 2011. http://www.calstat.org/learningCenter/pds/05–01–11_CEFRIO_foreword_final.pdf.

Wenger, Etienne, Richard McDermott, and William Snyder. 2002. "Seven Principles for Cultivating Communities of Practice." Excerpted from *Cultivating Communities of Practice: A Guide to Managing Knowledge*. Boston: Harvard Business School Press. Accessed May 2, 2011. http://www.askmecorp.com/pdf/7Principles_CoP.pdf.

Wenger, Etienne, and William Snyder. 2000. "Communities of Practice: The Organizational Frontier." *Harvard Business Review* 78(1): 139–145.

Williams, Raymond. 1983 [1958]. *Culture and Society 1780–1950*. New York: Columbia University Press.

Williams, Raymond. 1983 [1976]. *Keywords: A Vocabulary of Culture and Society*. 2nd ed. Oxford: Oxford University Press.

Williams, Raymond. 1985. "Mining the Meaning: Keywords in the Miners' Strike." *New Socialist* 25(March): 6–9.

Woolard, Kathryn. 1998. "Introduction: Language Ideology as a Field of Inquiry." In *Language Ideologies: Practice and Theory*, edited by Bambi Schieffelin, Kathryn Woolard and Paul Kroskrity, 3–50. Oxford: Oxford University Press.

Yang, Jie. 2010. "The Crisis of Masculinity: Class, Gender and Kindly Power in Post-Mao China." *American Ethnologist* 37(3): 550–562.

Contributors

Lindsay Bell is a PhD candidate in the Department of Sociology and Equity Studies in Education at the University of Toronto. Her research interrogates the social relations engendered by large-scale natural resource extraction. Her current work focuses on labor migration and class inequalities in Canada's diamond basin.

Adrian Blackledge is professor of bilingualism at the University of Birmingham, UK. His research interests include the politics of multilingualism, linguistic ethnography, education of linguistic minority students, negotiation of identities in multilingual contexts, and language testing, citizenship, and immigration. His publications include *Multilingualism: A Critical Perspective* (with Angela Creese; Continuum, 2010), *Discourse and Power in a Multilingual World* (John Benjamins, 2005), *Negotiation of Identities in Multilingual Contexts* (with Aneta Pavlenko; Multilingual Matters, 2004), *Multilingualism, Second Language Learning and Gender* (coedited with Aneta Pavlenko, Ingrid Piller and Marya Teutsch-Dwyer; Mouton de Gruyter, 2001) and *Literacy, Power and Social Justice* (Trentham Books, 2001).

Josiane Boutet is one of the founders of sociolinguistics in France. In 1985 she initiated a new interdisciplinary field in France, "Language and Work," which brought together sociologists, linguists and psychologists. She is now professor at La Sorbonne-Paris, and executive coeditor of the French sociolinguistics journal *Langage et Société*. Her recent publications include *Construire le sens* (Peter Lang, 2000), *Paroles au travail* (L'Harmattan, 2005) and *La vie verbale au travail* (Octarès 2008).

Angela Creese is professor of educational linguistics at the University of Birmingham, UK. She researches multilingualism in urban multilingual classrooms, using linguistic ethnography. Her publications include *Multilingualism: A Critical Perspective* (with Adrian Blackledge; Continuum Books, 2010), *Ecology of Language* (vol. 9 of the *Encyclopedia of Language and Education*, with Peter Martin and Nancy Hornberger;

Springer, 2008) and *Teacher Collaboration and Talk in Multilingual Classrooms* (Multilingual Matters, 2005).

Michelle Daveluy is professor of anthropology at Université Laval (Canada). Her research onboard Canadian Navy ships was funded by the Social Sciences and Humanities Research Council of Canada and the University of Alberta. The initial phase of this project was conducted in Halifax, Nova Scotia, and she remains adjunct professor at Saint Mary's University. She is a founding member of the Forum international des anthropologues and past president of the Canadian Anthropology Society. Also interested in the language dynamics of the circumpolar world, she is a steering committee member of the International PhD School for Studies of Arctic Societies (IPSSAS) and research associate at the Canadian Circumpolar Institute of the University of Alberta.

Alfonso Del Percio is a PhD candidate and research assistant at the Institute of Media and Communication Management (University of St. Gallen, Switzerland) and at the Institute of Multilingualism (University and HEP of Fribourg, Switzerland). He holds a MA in German and French studies. His research interests focus on language and neoliberal economy, language and inequality, nationalist ideologies as well as discourses within institutions of power.

Alexandre Duchêne is professor of sociology of language and director of the Institute of Multilingualism of the University and HEP of Fribourg (Switzerland). He is a member of the executive board of the Réseau francophone de sociolinguistique. His work focuses on the role of language in the globalized new economy (with an emphasis on language at work) and on the reproduction of social inequalities within institutions of power. His recent publications include a monograph *Ideologies Across Nations* (Mouton de Gruyter 2008), and two edited volumes *Langage, Genre et Sexualité* (with Claudine Moïse; Nota Bene, 2011) and *Discourses of Endangerment* (with Monica Heller; Continuum 2007).

Susan Gal is Mae and Sidney G. Metzl Distinguished Service Professor of Anthropology and Linguistics at the University of Chicago. Her research interests center on language and politics in Europe. Her first book was *Language Shift: Social Determinants of Linguistic Change in Bilingual Austria*, and she has since published widely on language ideology, multilingualism and its political economic sources and consequences, and the history of European linguistics. More recently she coauthored a comparative and historical work, *The Politics of Gender After Socialism*, and coedited *Reproducing Gender: Politics, Publics and Everyday Life After Socialism*. In 2001 she coedited, with Kathryn Woolard, *Languages and Publics: The Making of Authority* (St. Jerome's Press, Manchester). In

2002, Gal was the recipient of a Simon Guggenheim Memorial Fellowship; in 2007 she became a member of the American Academy of Arts and Sciences. She is currently engaged in a project on the nature of mass media and communication in the communist and postcommunist periods in the east of Europe, and another book, nearing completion, on the nature of linguistic and social differentiation.

Monica Heller is professor at the Ontario Institute for Studies in Education and the Department of Anthropology, University of Toronto, as well as a Fellow of the Royal Society of Canada. Her work focuses on the role of language in the construction of social difference and social inequality in the globalized new economy, with a focus on francophone Canada. She is an associate editor of the *Journal of Sociolinguistics*. Her most recent books include *Bilingualism: A Social Approach* (ed., Palgrave, 2007) and *Paths to Postnationalism: A Critical Ethnography of Language and Identity* (Oxford University Press, 2011).

Kathryn Jones is director of policy and research at the *Y Ganolfan Cynllunio Iaith* "Welsh Centre of Language Planning" in Wales. She obtained her BA Hons in Modern English Studies at the University of Middlesex and received her MA and PhD at Lancaster University. She was director of the Foreign Language Centre at Beijing University in 1989–1991, has worked as language, education and language planning consultant for various public agencies of the UK, and has taught social history of Welsh and language policy and planning at Bangor University. She has conducted and published research on the use of the Welsh language and its social and political implications in a variety of contexts. Her publications include *Welsh Language Socialization Within the Family* with Delith Morris (2007) and *Multilingual Literacies: Reading and Writing Different Worlds* with Marilyn Martin-Jones (2000).

Beatriz P. Lorente is lecturer in the University Town Writing Program of the Centre for English Language Communication at the National University of Singapore (NUS). She completed her PhD in Language Studies at NUS in 2007. Her dissertation, titled "Mapping English Linguistic Capital: The Case of Filipino Domestic Workers in Singapore," was awarded the inaugural Wang Gungwu Medal and Prize for best PhD thesis in the humanities and social sciences. Her main research interests are in language and globalization, language and migration, and language policy.

Bonnie McElhinny is director of the Women and Gender Studies Institute, and associate professor of anthropology and women and gender studies at the University of Toronto. She is founding coeditor of *Gender and Language*. Recent publications include *Words, Worlds, Material Girls: Language and Gender in a Global Economy* and articles in *American*

Anthropologist, Philippine Studies and the *Annual Review of Anthropology.* Her research focuses on historical and contemporary investigations of North American interventions into Filipino health care and childcare practices, and reactions and resistance to them.

Joan Pujolar is professor in the Department of Arts and Humanities of the Universitat Oberta de Catalunya (Spain). He studied English and Catalan Philology at the Universitat Autònoma de Barcelona and received his MA and PhD at Lancaster University. He researches language use in multilingual contexts, specifically how different linguistic varieties serve to construct social identities in terms of ethnicity, gender, age and class. His publications include *Gender, Heteroglossia and Power: A Sociolinguistic Study of Youth Culture* (2001) and *Bilingualism and the Nationstate in the Postnational Era* (2007).

Jacqueline Urla is professor of anthropology at the University of Massachusetts–Amherst. She specializes in the study of the discourse and practice of minority language politics, and has conducted ethnographic research on Basque language revival. Her forthcoming book, *Reclaiming Basque: Language, Nation, and Cultural Activism* (University of Nevada Press, Basque Book Series) examines the intersecting logics of nationalism and governmentality at work in contemporary Basque language revitalization.

Index

An environmentally friendly book printed and bound in England by www.printondemand-worldwide.com